the
**complete
cookery**
over 3 million copies sold

the
complete
cookery
over 3 million copies sold

revised by
maggie black
with
dorothy midgley

foulsham
LONDON · NEW YORK · TORONTO · SYDNEY

ACKNOWLEDGEMENTS

The publisher would like to thank the following for kindly supplying photographs for this book

Billingtons Sugars page 216
Bovril page 52
British Chicken Information Service page 72
The British Egg Information Service page 141,189
California Raisins page 213
The Fresh Fruit and Vegetable Information
    Bureau pages 97,108
National Dairy Council page 192
Pasta Information Bureau page 124
Quality British Chicken page 77
Rank Hovis MacDougal page 69, 153, 217, 224
Sea Fish Industry Authority page 24
U.S. Rice Council page 120

Photography on pages 17, 28, 29, 32, 49, 53, 61 64, 65, 68, 76, 80, 116, 117, 121, 129, 133, 136, 137, 140, 144, 149, 152, 160, 172, 180, 181, 184, 188 and 212 Dave Jordan

Photography on pages 20, 57, 101, 105, 168, 177, 185, 220 and 221 Tim Rose

Home Economist Mary Gwynn

Stylist July Williams

The publisher and photographers are very grateful to David Mellor, James Street, London WC2 for supplying white china and kitchenware, cutlery and cruets and Habitat for supplying patterned fabrics.

Book design by Stonecastle Graphics Ltd, Maidstone, Kent.

Illustrations Elaine Hill

foulsham

The Publishing House, Bennetts Close, Cippenham, Slough, Berkshire, SL1 5AP

ISBN 0-572-02969-1

Printed in China through Colorcraft Ltd., Hong Kong

FOREWORD

The first NEW WORLD Cookery Book was published in 1927 as a companion for the Regulo New World gas cookers which were making life easier for cooks who were unaccustomed to cooking with such easily controlled heat! The book was regularly reprinted and revised for the next 70 years. Over 3 million copies have been sold and it is regarded as one of the most successful cookery books published.

This edition has been completely revised and rewritten to incorporate recent changes in the cookery field. The recipes have been devised with the latest technology in mind and are suitable for all gas or electric cookers. Microwave cooking, home freezing and preserving are explained. With the adoption of healthier eating habits by the majority of the population and the increasing interest in a vegetarian or demi-vegetarian diet , meat eaters and non-meat eaters alike will find in *The Complete Cookery* up-to-date advice on buying, preparing and cooking food for family meals and entertaining. All the recipes have been tested under home cookery conditions and are interesting, economical and nutritious.

CONTENTS

1
HORS D'OEUVRE AND OTHER STARTERS

Hors d'oeuvre are, strictly speaking, assorted small cold appetisers served at the very beginning of the meal, before the soups, in a full, formal menu. However, since dinner-party menus now seldom consist of more than three courses, a plate of assorted hors d'oeuvre has come to be just one possible starter among many.

Whatever starter one chooses, it must look, smell and taste appealing to stimulate the diner's interest and appetite for the rest of the meal. It must use differently prepared ingredients from the dishes to come, and have a different texture and main colour. It must also be attractively garnished as a promise of delicious foods to follow, and should taste delicious in itself but not spoil the palate for later flavours.

Mixed small hors d'oeuvre always look intriguing. The items may consist of eggs, fish, fruit, meat or vegetables; small portions are arranged on the diners' plates before the meal or are offered in separate small dishes or heaps on a tray or platter at the table. Larger portions of a single item such as a salad, savoury 'cocktails', filled pastry cases or a pâté can also be served as starters, while hot or cold soups (Chapter 2) are still one of the most popular ways to start a meal.

MIXED HORS D'OEUVRE

A choice of the following dishes can be served on a mixed hors d'oeuvre platter or small plates; those suitable for serving in larger portions as single starters are marked with an asterisk. Other popular single starters follow.

Eggs

Use hard-boiled (hard-cooked) eggs in one of these ways:
1. * Halve, quarter or slice, and coat with Mayonnaise (page 134), Chaudfroid Sauce (page 91) or Sour Cream Dressing (page 134) and garnish.
2. * Set halved eggs in aspic jelly or firmly jellied consommé with a vivid vegetable garnish on top (when turned out). (See Oeufs en Gelée, page 10.)
3. * Serve as stuffed eggs (page 147).

Fish

Anchovies are generally sold as fillets canned in oil, and are used in stuffings or salads for a piquant flavour or to garnish small hors d'oeuvre plates.

Caviar: Real caviar is very expensive but black or red lumpfish 'caviar' can be bought in small jars for stuffing small hollows in vegetables, e.g. avocados, celery, or it can be sprinkled as a dramatic garnish on cold eggs or fish.

Herrings*: Serve Soused (pickled) Herrings (page 30), boned and divided into small fillets, then rolled up. Small fillets of smoked herring (bloaters, buckling, kippers) can be served in mixed hors d'oeuvre; whole fish or large fillets are sometimes served as a single starter with lemon wedges and brown bread and butter.

Mussels*: Fresh mussels are usually served as a single hot starter or main course (page 35), but pickled mussels are sold by some fishmongers and smoked mussels are available in cans. A few can be added to a mixed fish hors d'oeuvre platter sprinkled with lemon juice and chopped parsley.

Oysters*: Fresh oysters are generally served alone as a cold single starter (page 10), but canned oysters in brine and smoked oysters can be used in the same way as smoked mussels.

Prawns or Shrimps: Cold cooked, peeled prawns or shrimps can be served in a 'cocktail', as a single starter or in the same way as smoked mussels in a mixed hors d'oeuvre.

Sardines*: Fresh sardines are served as a hot single starter or main course, but small top-quality canned sardines in olive oil are a delicacy served cold. They are served in the oil on a large mixed hors d'oeuvre tray, but are drained for placing on individual plates ahead of the meal. Brisling (canned small sprats) are served in the same way.

Smoked Fish*: Mackerel, sardines, sprats and trout are now popular. Smoked mackerel or trout are served whole as a single cold starter with lemon wedges, or can be made into a pâté. Split hot or cold-smoked fillets can be used in mixed hors d'oeuvre. Small smoked sardines and smoked sprats are used in the same ways.

Smoked Salmon* is generally served as a single cold starter, very thinly sliced, with lemon juice and brown bread, while trimmings are used for mousses, pâtés etc. A little shredded smoked salmon, however, makes an attractive rosy addition to a mixed hors d'oeuvre platter.

*Tuna Fish** is widely available canned in oil or brine. It is rather filling for a mixed hors d'oeuvre plate but a small quantity can be used sprinkled with a piquant dressing.
Canned Mackerel steaks or meat can be used in the same way as tuna.

Fruit*

Most fruits, such as avocados, grapefruit, melons, papaya and pears are served as single starters, or in first-course 'cocktails' or salads. Some, however, may be used in mixed hors d'oeuvre cut into small balls or cubes, in segments or slices, for their tangy flavour and decorative colour. They are usually served with French Dressing (page 132).

Meats*

Cold cooked or smoked meats, ham or bacon, offal, poultry, game and various continental sausages can be sliced and served as a first-course platter of assorted cold meats. Meats may also be made into a pâté and served as a single starter, or may be chopped and used in a salad. A mixed hors d'oeuvre selection may also include sliced continental sausages, shredded smoked raw beef or ham, or small thin fillets of poultry or game in a Chaudfroid Sauce (page 91), or in aspic.

Vegetables

Beans: Mix cooked green beans* or dried, soaked and cooked haricot (navy) beans with thin shreds of raw onion, and toss in French Dressing (page 132) while still hot. Sprinkle haricot beans with chopped parsley when cold.
Beetroot (Beet): Slice cold cooked beetroot thinly and mix with onion and French Dressing (page 132) in the same way as for beans (above).
*Carrot**: Serve grated (shredded) carrot in the same way as celeriac (below), or mixed with it.
*Celeriac (Knob celery)**: Peel, cut into fine strips, sprinkle with salt and leave to stand for 1 hour. Drain and toss in mayonnaise seasoned with a little French mustard.
Celery:
1. Wash and shred the celery, and place on ice or in cold water until the shreds curl. Drain and sprinkle with salt.
2. Cut well-hollowed celery into 5 cm/2 in lengths and stuff hollows with soft cheese or pâté.
Cucumber:
1. Peel and slice, sprinkle with salt and leave on a tilted plate for 30 minutes. Drain and sprinkle with French Dressing (page 132) and chopped parsley.
2. Peel and slice, and mix with thinly sliced raw onion and vinegar. Leave for 30 minutes, then drain off the vinegar before serving.
3. *Cut unpeeled cucumber into 5 cm/2 in chunks. With a teaspoon, remove the seeds from one end to make a hollow cup. Leave the second end intact. Stuff as for celery (above), and pour a little mayonnaise or natural yoghurt over each cucumber cup.

*Leeks or Other Vegetables**, e.g. mushrooms, onions, cooked and cooled in the dressing styled 'à la Grecque' (page 11) can be served in small portions. Drain before use.
Mushrooms: Serve small portions of either fresh button mushrooms marinated in a spicy dressing (page 132) or drained canned mushrooms.
Olives: Drained stuffed green olives or black (ripe) olives in brine can be included in mixed hors d'oeuvre. Choose large smooth olives from Greece or Spain if possible.
Potatoes: Serve as Potato Mayonnaise in either style given on pages 130, 131. Use small new potatoes, halved or quartered, or old potatoes, diced.
*Tomatoes**:
1. Skin, slice thinly and sprinkle with a very little sugar and chopped chives, or with French Dressing (page 132) and chopped fresh mint. Add a little grated raw onion if you wish.
2. Serve very small stuffed tomatoes (page 111) on individual plates.

OTHER STARTERS

'Cocktails'

Fish: Use flaked, cooked or canned fish or chopped shellfish; arrange it in stemmed glasses with layers of shredded lettuce and diced cooked vegetables. Season each layer. Mix together equal quantities of thick Mayonnaise (page 134), tomato ketchup or juice and single (light) cream (if using ketchup), and add a little lemon juice. Pour the sauce over the fish salad. Leave to stand, chilled if possible, for 2 hours before garnishing, with chopped parsley, capers, anchovies or gherkins, and serving.
Note:
Prawn Cocktail (page 34) is a popular fish cocktail. For Fresh Tomato Sauce, see page 91.
Fruit: Mix together neatly prepared pieces or small balls of two or three types of fruit, e.g. skinned grapefruit segments and melon balls. A chopped fresh herb such as mint adds scent and flavour. Pour over the ingredients a fairly sharp syrup mixed with a little lemon juice. Chill well before serving.

Fruit and vegetables can be mixed in a cocktail, for instance Spiced Mushrooms (above) and melon balls, or diced cucumber and orange segments.

Eggs

1. Cook and serve baked eggs (page 139) in greased ramekins or in large halved, hollowed tomatoes, or small cooked globe artichokes. Add a little cream sauce and tomato ketchup, or cheese sauce before cooking. Serve one egg per person as a hot starter.
2. *Oeufs en Gelée*: Set a little firm aspic jelly or jellied consommé in individual moulds. Arrange two or three small watercress leaves on the jelly and cover thinly with more jelly. When set, put a cold poached egg or a spoonful of creamy scrambled egg in each mould. Chill. Cover with cooled liquid jelly, and chill again. Turn out and serve one per person.

Other suitable dishes in which eggs are a main ingredient are small filled pancakes (page 168), hot or cold soufflés (page 142), mousses, Scotch Eggs (page 146) and egg salads.

Fish

Chopped Herring: Soak 3 salted herrings overnight, skin and bone them, then rinse. Mince with 1 small onion, 1 peeled and cored cooking apple, 25 g/1 oz white bread without crusts, and 1 hard-boiled (hard-cooked) egg. Add a little vinegar and sugar to taste. Mash or pound, then shape into a mound and garnish with sieved hard-boiled egg yolk. Serves 6.

Oysters: Make sure all the shells are tightly closed. Scrub them, then open over a bowl, reserving the liquor. Remove beards, then arrange oysters in deep shells on crushed ice or chilled plates. Add reserved liquor. Offer cayenne pepper, lemon wedges and thin rolls of brown bread and butter.

Smoked Whole Fish: Behead fish, and serve one per person on small plates garnished with watercress. (Serve only a fillet of large mackerel.) Offer cayenne pepper etc. as for oysters.

Smoked Salmon: Spread thinly sliced smoked salmon on individual plates. Offer the same accompaniments as for oysters.

Soused Herring: Arrange rolled fillets on individual plates, and garnish with a little salad.

Taramasalata: A smoked cod's roe pâté.

Any fish mayonnaise or mousse, pâté or salad makes a good starter. Fish Mornay (page 26) or Smoked Mackerel Pâté (page 37) are popular starters. So are deep-fried whitebait served with cut lemon.

Fruit

Avocados: Split lengthways, remove stones and sprinkle flesh at once with lemon juice or French Dressing (page 132). Fill hollow left by stone with Vinaigrette Sauce (page 132) (Avocado Vinaigrette) or with any well-flavoured fish mixture, such as lumpfish caviar, prawns in mayonnaise (Avocado Royale), mashed smoked haddock or shredded smoked salmon. Serve half an avocado per person on a small plate, and provide small spoons. Halved avocados with suitable fillings can also be baked at 180°C/350°F/Gas Mark 4 for 20 minutes and served hot.

Grapefruit: If possible, prepare well ahead of time. Cut in half crossways. With a grapefruit knife, cut the flesh free from the skin, without removing it, then cut through the membranes separating the sections. Remove the core. Dust with fine sugar to taste, and add a little ground cinnamon, sherry or maraschino liqueur. Chill. Garnish each half grapefruit with a piece of maraschino cherry or a sprig of mint in the centre. Serve half a grapefruit per person. Halved grapefruit can be baked like avocados; sweeten before baking but add sherry or liqueur afterwards.

Melon: (Cantaloupe, Honeydew):
1. Cut in segments without peeling, and remove seeds. Cut flesh free from skin and cut in sections, but leave in place. Serve one wedge per person, and provide fruit knives and forks. Offer sugar and ground ginger separately.
2. Serve very small melons cut in half, with the seeds scooped out. The hollows can be filled with another fruit, or with cucumber, orange and mint salad. Serve half a melon per person.
3. Cut melon flesh into cubes or balls, and mix with skinned orange or grapefruit segments, sliced banana or other fruit. Serve chilled in small glasses or bowls.
4. Peel, remove seeds, cut in thin slices and serve with slices of Parma ham.

Pears: Peel, halve and core, then cut in thin slices lengthways. Simmer in water or tea, until beginning to soften. Sprinkle with crumbled blue cheese and grill until bubbling. Serve hot.

Watermelon: Peel, slice or cube and chill. When serving, provide small spoons for removing the seeds as well as knives and forks.

Meats

Chaudfroid of Chicken: Serve small fillets of chicken or other poultry coated with a Chaudfroid Sauce (page 91) or Mayonnaise (page 134).

Pâtés: Serve a home-made pâté or terrine, or bought pâté or liver sausage cut in slices. Arrange on individual plates and serve with hot dry toast fingers or crispbreads.

Smoked Beef or Ham: Serve Westphalian smoked beef or ham in thin slices.

Other assorted cold meats, especially pork products, can be offered in the same way or on a large platter garnished with parsley and salad garnishes (see below).

Salads

Make small attractive individual salads, following any of the recipes in Chapter 9.

Vegetables

Globe Artichokes: Break off stems by laying each head on the edge of a table, then bending the stem until it snaps. It will bring furry bits of 'choke' away with it. Trim the tops of the leaves, then boil the artichokes in salted water until tender. Drain upside down, remove centre leaves and take out the furry 'chokes' inside.

Serve one artichoke per person, either hot with melted butter, holding a baked egg, or cold with the hollow filled with vinaigrette sauce, French Dressing (page 132) or mild savoury Mayonnaise (page 134).

Alternatively, serve the artichoke bottoms (fonds) only, hot or cold, with any of the stuffings given for vegetables (page 111).

Asparagus: Scrape stalks of thick asparagus. Tie in bundles, and trim the ends of the stems evenly. Stand upright in a deep narrow pan. Fill the pan with boiling water to cover only the stems. Cover the pan, and cook the asparagus for 15–20 minutes or until the stems are tender. Drain well. Serve hot or cold with melted butter or Hollandaise Sauce (page 87).

Chartreuse of Vegetables: Use cooked or salad vegetables. Line a loaf tin or mould with a decorative pattern of vegetables, e.g. asparagus and carrot, dipped in a little liquid aspic near setting point. Fill the mould with an almost-set vegetable mousse or purée containing aspic. Trickle in enough aspic to fill any gaps. Chill until ready to serve, then turn out. Serve sliced or in wedges.

Crudités: These are raw vegetables, cut in small fingers or pieces and used as 'dunkers' with Mayonnaise (page 134). Suitable items are: carrot 'matchsticks; blanched cauliflower florets; blanched Brussels sprouts; short lengths of celery stalk; courgettes (zucchini) or cucumber, cut in thin 'sticks'; radishes, whole; green or red peppers, cut in rings; spring onions (scallions), trimmed; tomato wedges.

Arrange on individual plates with a small bowl or ramekin of dip in the centre of each plate.

Ratatouille: Serve cold Ratatouille, following the recipe on page 109.

Stuffed Peppers: See page 111.

Tomatoes: Serve skinned and thinly sliced, sprinkled with grated onion or thin onion rings, and with a chopped fresh herb (basil or mint). Sprinkle with French Dressing (page 132).

For stuffed tomatoes, see page 93.

Vegetables à la Grecque

Courgettes (zucchini), celery, fennel bulbs, leeks, aubergines (eggplants), button mushrooms, button onions and peppers can all be served 'à la Grecque', using the following recipe:

	Metric	Imperial	American
Vegetables (see above)	450 g	1 lb	1 lb
Garlic clove, skinned	1	1	1
Tomatoes, skinned and chopped	350 g	12 oz	¾ lb
Coriander seeds, crushed	1.5 ml	¼ tsp	¼ tsp
Lemon juice	30 ml	2 tbls	2 tbls
Olive oil	60 ml	4 tbls	4 tbls
Water	175 ml	6 fl oz	¾ cup
Bay leaf	1	1	1
Bouquet garni	1	1	1
Salt and pepper			

1. Prepare the vegetables, cutting them in pieces small enough to cook in 20 minutes.
2. Crush the garlic over the chopped tomatoes in a bowl.
3. Put all the remaining ingredients in a heavy pan, and bring to the boil.
4. Add the garlicky tomatoes, and cook, uncovered, for 25 minutes, adding the prepared vegetables when appropriate. Cook until tender and serve hot or cold.

Garnishes

Garnishes for plates of mixed hors d'oeuvre can be as small as a single radish 'rose' (see below); such small garnishes are valuable because they provide the light stimulus the appetite needs, while making an individual plate of mixed hors d'oeuvre look like a Victorian posy or picture. They can also, with good effect, be used to garnish larger single dishes.

Salad items are only one among dozens of different types of food used to garnish savoury dishes. A chopped herb such as parsley is one type, a rosette of savoury butter is another, cooked pastry shapes or fried bread triangles are others. Salad garnishes are, however, the most useful for embellishing large or small hors d'oeuvre.

Carrot Curls: Top and tail small raw carrots, and scrape. Cut lengthways into paper-thin slices with a vegetable peeler. Roll up and secure with cocktail sticks. Put in iced water until they stay curled when sticks are removed. Use on open sandwiches, salads, and pale-coloured dishes or hors d'oeuvre such as egg mayonnaise.

Gherkin Fans: Use cocktail gherkins. Slice each one lengthways almost to the end, then spread slices into the shape of a small fan. Use on hot or cold dishes, especially fish.

Lemon Butterflies: Cut thin half slices of a lemon in half again, almost to the centre, and gently draw the segments apart to form two joined 'wings'. Place a tiny piece of parsley in the centre. Use on hors d'oeuvre and fish dishes.

Orange Twists: Cut thin slices of orange through the rind and flesh almost to the centre, then twist cut edges in opposite directions. For a garnish, put a small sprig of parsley into the twist, or for decorating a sweet dish use a washed, halved glacé cherry.

Radish Roses: Top and tail radishes. Cut down through the centre to within 5 mm/¼ in of the bottom. Make a second cut at right angles to the first, then two or four more to cut radishes into eight or 16 'leaves'. Drop into iced water until radishes open out like 'roses'.

Savoury Butters: A pat of chilled savoury butter is sometimes served as a flavoursome garnish on steaks, grilled fish, etc. A smooth savoury butter can also be piped in rosettes or lines on a cold joint, bird, mousse or similar dish to garnish it.

Tomatoes Van Dyke: Using a thin-bladed sharp knife, cut a firm tomato horizontally in half, using tiny zigzag cuts instead of a straight slicing movement. Put a tiny piece of parsley on each half. Use on grilled meat dishes, salads and hors d'oeuvre. (Other fruits and vegetables can be prepared in the same way.)

HERBS, SPICES AND SEASONINGS

While garnishes improve the appearance of a dish, herbs, spices and essences, among other substances, add to its flavour. Seasonings improve flavour without being obvious themselves. Any flavouring or seasoning can be added to food in a number of different ways.

You can use fresh or dried herbs, but fresh herbs have a better, more vital flavour and scent. Even freshly home-dried herbs do not have quite the same aroma and taste, and any dried herbs soon become flavourless or musty if unused. If you buy dried herbs they should be replaced every few months. Since dried herbs are more concentrated, use only about half as much as when using fresh herbs. The quantities suggested in this book are for dried herbs except when a recipe definitely says fresh herbs should be used. Always, however, adapt herb (or spice) quantities to suit your own taste.

Herb butters for garnishing and flavouring are made by beating chopped fresh herbs into softened butter.

Centuries of experience have shown which common herbs suit certain foods best. Here are some of them.

Name	Features	Common Uses
Basil/sweet Basil	Dries well, tastes stronger when cooked.	With tomatoes, green or dried beans, peppers.
Bay	Stronger when dried.	In bouquet garni. In casseroles, marinades, milk puddings and custards and curries.
Capers	May be in oil or brine. Drain before use.	With fish, lamb. In tartare sauce.
Chervil	Delicate. Use plenty.	In sauces, green salads. Mix with other herbs being used as it brings out their flavour.
Chives	Mildly oniony.	Chopped and used instead of parsley on many dishes, popular in salads.
Dill	Leaves and seeds used.	Leaves used mainly with fish, seeds in pickles.
Garlic	Small bulbs called 'cloves' are grouped together in a 'head'. Strong flavour.	In curries, salads, sauces, spicy stews. With lamb.
Horseradish	Grated and used raw, usually sold as a sauce or cream.	With roast beef, cold smoked fish.
Lemon balm	Leaves have lemony scent and taste.	In stuffings, drinks.

Name	Features	Common Uses
Marjoram and oregano	Used a lot as alternative to thyme. Popular herb with many uses. Oregano is called wild marjoram.	In Greek, Italian and (oregano) Mexican dishes. With lamb, pork, pasta, in stuffings, spicy stews.
Mint	Many types, e.g. apple mint, spearmint.	Mint sauce flavouring served with lamb. Chopped leaves used on new potatoes, peas. Whole leaves used in drinks and to make a 'tea'.
Mixed herbs	Dried mixture, usually marjoram, parsley, sage, tarragon and thyme.	In stews, casseroles, stuffings. With vegetables.
Parsley	Green colour makes chopped parsley our favourite garnish. Also has pleasant flavour and contains iron.	Used in bouquet garni, very widely used for garnishing savoury dishes, especially pale-coloured ones.
Rosemary	Strongly flavoured. Use the spiny leaves carefully and sparingly.	With roast and stewed lamb, chicken, veal. In drinks.
Sage	Strongly flavoured. Use with care.	With pork in all forms, in stuffings for duck, goose. With onions.
Savory	Summer and winter savory are two types used the same way.	With eggs, green and dried beans, white meats.
Tarragon	Use French tarragon rather than Russian.	Used in many classic sauces; with chicken, fish.
Thyme	One of the most popular herbs. Many types, many uses.	In bouquet garni. With meat. Especially in stews. In stuffings. In dishes cooked in wine. On fish, chicken.

2
STOCKS AND SOUPS

Soups serve two different purposes. First, there are soups used as a light course before the main dish: a clear soup (consommé) is the type most often served at a formal meal or there may be a choice of clear soup or a light puréed or cream soup. Formal or not, choose a soup which will stimulate the taste-buds and appetite; 180 ml/⅓ pt/¾ cup is usually enough per person as a starter.

Second, there are hearty, main-course soups which, with bread or rolls and followed by salad and cheese or fruit, make a complete meal. Such soups often contain solid bite-sized pieces of meat, fish, vegetables or pasta. In this case, serve 275–575 ml/½–1 pt/1¼–2½ cups per person.

Stock

Stock is the liquid containing some of the soluble nutrients extracted during the (usually long) cooking of meat, fish, bones and/or vegetables and is an essential base for good soups and gravies and for many sauces, casseroles and braised dishes.

General Rules When Making Stock
1. Use only fresh ingredients.
2. If the stock is to be used at once, hot, skim the fat off the surface, first with a skimmer, then with soft kitchen paper to remove the last traces
   OR
   strain and cool completed stock as quickly as possible. Store in cold place, preferably a refrigerator. Do NOT store fish stock except by freezing.
3. Always use unrefrigerated stock within a few hours in warm weather and use refrigerated (chilled) stock within three days; stock is one of the favourite breeding-places for bacteria.
4. Stored stock must be brought quickly to the boil before use.

TYPES OF STOCK

Basic Meat Stock

Used for broths, purées, thickened soups, sauces, stews, etc.

Makes 1 l/1¾ pt/4⅓ cups (approx)

Freeze 1 month

	Metric	Imperial	American
Cooked or raw bones of meat or poultry and/or cooked or raw meat trimmings, bacon rinds	1 kg	2 lb 3 oz	2 lb 3 oz
Salt			
Vegetables (carrot, celery, leek, onion), prepared	500 g	1 lb 2 oz	1 lb 2 oz
Bay leaf	1	1	1
Black peppercorns	3–6	3–6	3–6

1. Break or chop large bones. Wipe to remove dust and splinters. Put with any meat trimmings in a large pan. Cover with cold water and add 2.5 ml/½ tsp salt per 1l/1¾ pt/4⅓ cups. Bring slowly to simmering point.
2. Add the vegetables. Include the onion skin if making brown stock. Add the bay leaf and peppercorns.
3. Simmer slowly, uncovered, for 3 hours, adding extra water if needed.
4. Strain, skim off fat, then use.
5. Alternatively, stand the pan in chilled water to cool quickly, skim off fat and store (see left).
6. If to be frozen, boil down to half quantity before freezing.

Notes:
1. For well-coloured Brown Stock, bake bones before use in a fairly hot oven (220°C/425°F/Gas Mark 7) until browned.
2. For pale stock (sometimes called White Stock),

use veal bones and white peppercorns, and substitute a strip of lemon rind for carrot.

3. For Chicken Stock, use chicken meat bones and trimmings and cook as above.

Stock For Consommé

Used for clear soups (consommés).

Makes 1.5 l/2½ pt/6¼ cups (approx)

Freeze 1 month

	Metric	Imperial	American
Shin of beef			
(leg of beef)			
or half			
meat and half			
bone	*1 kg*	*2 lb 3 oz*	*2 lb 3 oz*
Cold water	*2. 3 l*	*4 pt*	*10 cups*
Salt	*5 ml*	*1 tsp*	*1 tsp*
White peppercorns	*6*	*6*	*6*
Medium onion	*1*	*1*	*1*
Medium carrot	*1*	*1*	*1*
Small celery stalk	*½*	*½*	*½*
Celery seeds	*2.5 ml*	*½ tsp*	*½ tsp*
Bouquet garni	*1*	*1*	*1*

1. Cut the meat into small pieces, chop bones, and remove marrow-fat which will make the stock cloudy.
2. Put the meat, bones and water into a large pan, add the salt and peppercorns, and bring slowly to the boil. Add 15 ml/1 tbls cold water to make the scum rise. Skim well.
3. Simmer very gently for 1 hour.
4. Meanwhile, peel the onion and carrot but leave whole. Add all the vegetables to the pan with the celery seeds and bouquet garni, cover and simmer for another 3 hours.
5. Strain into a chilled bowl standing in cold water.
6. When cold, remove all the fat from the surface. Clarify (page 18), then use or freeze (page 250).

Notes:
1. For fine brown consommé, bake the bones for 30–40 minutes at 220°C/425°F/Gas Mark 7 before use.
2. After making Stock for Consommé, you can use the meat and bones for Basic Meat Stock but add a little extra fresh meat.
3. You can clarify the beef fat for dripping.

Fish Stock

Used for fish soups, chowders, sauces and stews.

Makes 1 l/1¾ pt/4⅓ cups or quantity of water used (see recipe)

Freeze 1 month

	Metric	Imperial	American
Bones, skins and			
heads from			
filleted or other			
fish, and/or			
trimmings of			
white fish	*750 g*	*1 lb 10 oz*	*1 lb 10 oz*
Salt	*5 ml*	*1 tsp*	*1 tsp*
Onion	*50 g*	*2 oz*	*2 oz*
Celery stalk	*1*	*1*	*1*
White peppercorns	*6*	*6*	*6*
Bouquet garni	*1*	*1*	*1*

1. Clean the fish, remove and discard the eyes, and break up the bones. Put in a pan with the other ingredients and cover with 1 l/1¾ pt/4⅓ cups cold water or as needed to cover.
2. Bring gently to simmering point, cover and simmer gently for 40 minutes.
3. Strain through a fine sieve. Use at once, or cool quickly and freeze.

Note: Vegetable Stock is made almost exactly like Fish Stock. Use any mixture of soaked pulses, root vegetables, peas, beans, onions, leeks, celery etc. with salt, peppercorns and a bouquet garni. Chop the vegetables and put in a pan with boiling water to cover (instead of cold). Bring gently back to the boil, reduce heat and simmer for 40 minutes, then strain and use. Not suitable for freezing.

Note: Starchy vegetables e.g. potatoes are not suitable.

Chicken Broth

Serves 8

Freeze 1 month without rice or barley

	Metric	Imperial	American
Small old boiling fowl or carcass and trimmings of cooked chicken	1	1	1
Sets of giblets and feet of chicken	1–2	1–2	1–2
Water	2 l	3½ pt	8⅔ cups
Medium onion, halved	1	1	1
Celery stalk, chopped	1	1	1
White pepper	1.5 ml	¼ tsp	¼ tsp
Blade of mace	1	1	1
Salt	5 ml	1 tsp	1 tsp
Long grain rice or blanched pearl barley - see note (3) below	25 g	1 oz	2 tbls
Chopped parsley	5 ml	1 tsp	1 tsp

1. Joint and wash old fowl, or break up carcass. Wash giblets and feet.
2. Put in a large pan with the water, vegetables and seasonings.
3. Heat gently to simmering point, then cover and simmer for 3 hours if using raw bird, 1½ hours if using carcass.
4. Strain and skim off all fat. Boil down to half quantity and freeze concentrated stock at this point if you wish.
5. Return broth to the pan, and reheat to simmering. Add rice or barley and simmer for 20–40 minutes until cooked.
6. Meanwhile chop a few bits of chicken meat, and add to the broth if you wish.
7. Sprinkle with chopped parsley at serving point.

Notes:
1. This broth makes its own stock. Use the same recipe without rice or barley for basic *Chicken Stock.*
2. Chicken meat not used in the broth can be added to a fricassée (page 79).
3. To blanch barley or rice, wash grain well; put in a pan, cover with cold water, and bring to boiling point, then strain and rinse in cold water.

Scotch Broth

Serves 8

Freeze 1 month without barley (see note below)

	Metric	Imperial	American
Scrag end neck of mutton or lamb (neck slices)	500 g	1 lb 2 oz	1 lb 2 oz
Basic Meat Stock (page 14)	1.7 l	3 pt	7½ cups
Salt and pepper			
Blanched barley (see above)	100 g	4 oz	½ cup
Large carrot	1	1	1
Large onion	1	1	1
Medium turnip	1	1	1
Celery stalks	2–3	2–3	2–3
Chopped parsley	2.5 ml	½ tsp	½ tsp

1. Cut the meat off the bones and cube it, removing fat and marrow.
2. Put the lean meat and bones in a large pan with the stock and bring to simmering point. Skim.
3. Add the seasoning and barley. Cover and simmer for 1 hour.
4. Prepare and dice the vegetables, and add them. Simmer, covered, for a further 1 hour.
5. Remove from the heat, take out the bones and skim off the fat.
6. Return to the heat, add the parsley and simmer for a few minutes. Taste, re-season if needed, and serve.

Note: Cook barley separately if freezing. Freeze it separately without liquid, then combine when re-heating.

Opposite: *Scotch Broth makes a satisfying lunch or supper dish*

Cod Fish Chowder

Serves 4

Not suitable for freezing

	Metric	Imperial	American
Middle cut fresh cod	600 g	1 lb 4 oz	1 lb 4 oz
Rindless bacon rashers (slices)	2	2	2
Butter	15 g	½ oz	1 tbls
Medium onion, sliced	1	1	1
Medium potatoes, sliced	3	3	3
425 g/15 oz can of tomatoes	1	1	1
Fish Stock (page 15)	575 ml	1 pt	2½ cups
Salt and pepper			
Bay leaf	1	1	1
Strip of lemon rind	1	1	1
Chopped parsley			

1. Skin and bone the fish and cut into cubes. Chop the bacon.
2. Melt the fat in a deep pan, and fry the bacon and onion gently for 5 minutes, shaking the pan, until the bacon and onion are soft but not browned.
3. Add the fish and potatoes. Sieve in together the canned tomatoes, their juice, and the fish stock. Add all the remaining ingredients except the parsley.
4. Cover and simmer for 30–40 minutes until the fish is soft but not broken up, and the potato slices are cooked through.
5. Remove bay leaf and lemon rind, and sprinkle with parsley.

CLEAR SOUPS OR CONSOMMÉS

Clear Stock or Consommé

Makes 1 l/1¾ pt/4⅓ cups (approx)

Freeze 2 months

	Metric	Imperial	American
Lean shin of beef (beef leg)	100 g	4 oz	¼ lb
Cold water	125 ml	4 fl oz	½ cup
Stock for Consommé (page 15), cold	1.1 l	2 pt	5 cups
Small onion, quartered	1	1	1
Small carrot, quartered	1	1	1
Small celery stalk, cut in small pieces	1	1	1
White peppercorns	6	6	6
Salt	1.5 ml	¼ tsp	¼ tsp
Crushed egg shell and egg white	1	1	1
Dry sherry (optional)	10 ml	2 tsp	2 tsp

1. Shred the beef, removing fat, and soak in cold water for 15 minutes.
2. Strain the stock to remove fat, and prepare the vegetables.
3. Put all the ingredients, except the sherry, into a deep pan. Heat slowly to simmering point, whisking constantly, until a froth comes to the top
4. Remove the whisk, bring back to the boil, then reduce the heat at once, cover and simmer very gently for 1½ hours. If the stock boils, the froth will break up and cloud the consommé.
5. Strain the stock through a scalded cloth or jelly bag, holding back the froth with a spoon. Slide the froth into the cloth or bag last.
6. Strain the consommé again, through the filter of egg white.
7. Add more salt if needed and dry sherry if you wish.

Notes: The consommé should be clear and sparkling and should 'jelly' when cold. It can be served reheated or cold, and usually has a garnish which will not cloud it, for example, a julienne (matchsticks shreds) of carrot, turnip and leek. Briefly cook the garnish, rinse in hot water and add to the heated consommé just before serving.

Consommé Brunoise

Serves 4–6

Freeze 2 months (raw garnish)

	Metric	Imperial	American
Consommé	1.1 l	2 pt	5 cups
Carrot, diced	15 ml	1 tbls	1 tbls
Turnip, diced	15 ml	1 tbls	1 tbls
Celery, diced	15 ml	1 tbls	1 tbls
Leek, cut in fine rings	15 ml	1 tbls	1 tbls

1. Heat the consommé to boiling in a clean, fat-free pan.
2. Cook the vegetables in salted water until tender.
3. Rinse in hot water, and add to the consommé just before serving.

Note: You can use a 113 g/4 oz/¼ lb packet frozen mixed vegetables instead of the diced vegetables if you wish.

PURÉES AND THICKENED SOUPS

Solid vegetables and pulses make the best purées for serving as soups. Meat, fish and watery vegetables usually need a good deal of thickening material and/or cream when puréed to give a creamy consistency.

One type of vegetable can be used or a mixture, but any type is improved by including an onion, fresh herbs (page 12) and a few bacon rinds (removed before puréeing).

Vegetable purée is excellent as a side dish vegetable or as a 'bed' for other foods such as eggs; use the same basic recipe as for soups but with less liquid.

Fresh Tomato Purée

Scald and skin the tomatoes, then chop, removing the hard cores. To each 1 kg/2¼ lb of prepared tomatoes, add 2.5 ml/½ tsp sugar and 5 ml/1 tsp salt. Simmer the tomatoes with very little water until soft, then rub through a stainless sieve.

To use as a cocktail, or as the base for tomato aspic, etc., season with salt and pepper, and with Worcestershire sauce, lemon juice or dry sherry to taste. Serve chilled.

Add to tomato or meat soups for a fresh flavour, or dilute with cream, add a little mayonnaise and seasoning, and use as a dip.

Use instead of milk with a butter and flour roux for tomato sauce, or add to mayonnaise for 'red' mayonnaise.

Tomato Soup

Serves 4–6

Freeze 1 month (before adding milk)

	Metric	Imperial	American
Medium carrot	1	1	1
Medium onion	1	1	1
Celery stalks	2–3	2–3	2–3
Bacon scraps	50 g	2 oz	2 oz
Butter or margarine	25 g	1 oz	2 tbls
Tomatoes, quartered	700 g	1½ lb	1½ lb
Bouquet garni (fresh herbs)	1	1	1
Chicken Stock, White Stock or vegetable stock	575 ml	1 pt	2½ cups
Salt			
Milk	275 ml	½ pt	1¼ cups
Cornflour (cornstarch)	10 ml	2 tsp	2 tsp
Pepper			
Pinch of sugar			

1. Prepare and slice the carrot and onion. Chop the celery and bacon.

2. Melt the fat in a saucepan and toss the vegetables and bacon in it for 2–3 minutes to coat.
3. Add the tomatoes, bouquet garni, stock and a pinch of salt. Cover and simmer for 45 minutes or until tender.
4. Remove the bouquet garni and rub the remaining ingredients through a nylon sieve.
5. Return the purée to the saucepan. Heat and add the milk.
6. Blend the cornflour smoothly with a little cold milk, and stir in. Stir, over a low heat until soup thickens. Simmer for a few minutes, and season with salt, pepper and sugar.

Split Lentil Purée

Serves 4–6

Freeze 2 months (before adding milk)

	Metric	Imperial	American
Split red lentils	175 g	6 oz	6 oz
Basic Meat or Vegetable Stock (page 15)	1 l	1¾ pt	4⅓ cups
Medium onion, sliced	1	1	1
Carrot	50 g	2 oz	2 oz
Celery stalks, sliced	2	2	2
Potato, peeled and sliced	1	1	1
Bacon fat or margarine	15 ml	1 tbls	1 tbls
Bacon or ham bone (optional)	1	1	1
Bay leaf	1	1	1
Blade of mace	1	1	1
Parsley stalks	4	4	4
Milk (for soup)	275 ml	½ pt	1¼ cups
Salt and pepper			

1. Wash the lentils. Bring the stock to the boil, and pour over the lentils in a bowl.
2. In a large, deep pan, fry the vegetables gently in the fat for about 10 minutes until well gilded and slightly softened. Stir and turn them over frequently. Take off the heat.
3. Add the bacon or ham bone, if used, then the lentils and hot liquid, to the fried vegetables. Tie the herbs in a piece of muslin, and add to the pan.
4. Replace the pan on the heat, cover and simmer for 45 minutes–1 hour until the lentils and vegetables are soft.
5. Remove the bone and herb bundle. Process the soup in a blender or food processor. Rinse out the pan.
6. If making soup, return the purée to the pan and add the milk. Season to taste. Reheat, and serve hot.

Vegetable Soup

Serves 4–6

Freeze 1 month (without milk)

	Metric	Imperial	American
Vegetables, *including onion*	600 g	1 lb 4 oz	1 lb 4 oz
Bacon rind	25 g	1 oz	1 oz
Butter, margarine *or other fat*	15 g	½ oz	1 tbls
Stock–see note (2) *below*	1.1 l	2 pt	5 cups
Bouquet garni *(optional)*	1	1	1
Salt and pepper			
Milk	150 ml	¼ pt	⅔ cup
Cornflour *(cornstarch) to thicken–see method and note (3) below*			
Extra stock or milk *depending on flavour of vegetables*			

1. Prepare and chop the vegetables.
2. Fry the vegetables and bacon rind gently in the fat for about 6 minutes without browning; toss occasionally.
3. Add the stock, bouquet garni if using, and seasoning. Heat, and simmer until the vegetables are soft.
4. Purée the vegetables with some of the cooking stock by sieving or processing in a blender or food processor.
5. Add the remaining stock and milk, and measure the soup. Return to the pan and add 30 ml/2 tbls cornflour (cornstarch) per 575 ml/1 pt/2½ cups puréed soup, blended smoothly first with a little stock or milk.
6. Stir over heat until the soup boils, then cook for 5 minutes.

Notes:
1. Choose vegetables which will cook in the same time. Strongly-flavoured green vegetables, e.g. cabbage or kale, are better kept for broths. Watery vegetables, e.g. marrow (summer squash) are not suitable. Freeze-dried vegetables and pulses must be fully soaked before use.
2. Basic Meat Stock (page 14) or White Stock (page 15) can be used, depending on the flavour and colour of the vegetables and desired purée.
3. Pulses need no starch thickening. For most other vegetables, use the proportion of cornflour (cornstarch) suggested in the recipe.

Vegetable Soup in the tureen with from left, Lentil Soup (page 19), Tomato Soup (page 19) and Watercress Soup (opposite).

CREAM SOUPS

(Purées and thickened soups with cream)

Mushroom Soup

Serves 4–6

Freeze 1 month (before thickening)

	Metric	Imperial	American
White button mushrooms	175 g	6 oz	2 cups
Shallot	1	1	1
Butter or margarine	15 g	½ oz	1 tbls
Chicken Stock or White Stock	575 ml	1 pt	2½ cups
Salt and pepper			
Plain (all-purpose) flour	25 g	1 oz	¼ cup
Milk	50 ml	2 fl oz	¼ cup
Egg yolks	2	2	2
Single (light) cream	150 ml	¼ pt	⅔ cup
Chopped parsley (optional)			

Mushroom Soup served with crusty wholemeal bread.

1. Slice the mushrooms and shallot. Chop 3 or 4 mushrooms and keep aside for garnishing. Put the rest with the shallot in a saucepan and simmer in the fat until tender.
2. Add the stock and seasoning, cover and simmer for about 10 minutes until the vegetables are very soft.
3. Purée by sieving or in a blender or food processor.
4. While the soup is simmering, cook the chopped garnishing mushrooms in a little water.
5. Blend the flour and milk smoothly and add to the soup.
6. Return the soup to the pan and simmer, stirring, until thickened.
7. Blend the egg yolks into the cream and add to the soup. DO NOT BOIL.
8. Strain, garnish with mushrooms and sprinkle with parsley if wished.

Variations: For Watercress or Cucumber Soup substitute 2 bunches watercress or 1 cucumber for mushrooms and proceed as above.

Oxtail Soup

Serves 6

Freeze 2 months (unthickened)

	Metric	Imperial	American
Oxtail, washed and jointed	1	1	1
Dripping	50 g	2 oz	¼ cup
Large carrot, sliced	1	1	1
Medium onion, sliced	1	1	1
Celery stalk, sliced	1	1	1
Bouquet garni	1	1	1
Black peppercorns	6	6	6
Lean ham or bacon	100 g	4 oz	4 oz
Basic Meat Stock (page 14)	2.3 l	4 pt	10 cups
Salt and pepper			
Plain (all-purpose) flour or cornflour (cornstarch)	50 g	2 oz	½ cup
Extra stock, cold			
Juice of 1 lemon			
Red wine or port (optional)	15 ml	1 tbls	1 tbls

1. Put the joints into cold water, and bring to boiling point. Drain and dry.
2. Melt the dripping in a heavy pan, and fry the smaller joints until well browned all over; turn as required.
3. Remove the joints and fry the sliced vegetables until golden-brown.
4. Put all the joints and vegetables in a large deep pan with the bouquet garni, peppercorns, ham or bacon, stock and seasoning. Reserve the fat in the smaller pan. Bring the stock gently to the boil. Cover and simmer for 5 hours.
5. Meanwhile, brown the flour or cornflour in the reserved fat.
6. Strain the soup into a clean pan. Reserve a little meat and a few slices of carrot for garnishing. (Use the rest for oxtail stew with a little of the soup.)
7. Skim all fat off the soup.
8. Blend the browned flour or cornflour to a smooth cream with cold stock, and stir half into the soup. Bring to the boil, stirring, and cook for 5 minutes.
9. Season with lemon juice, salt and pepper.
10. Blend in the remaining thickening if needed, and cook for a few minutes longer, stirring.
11. Add the meat and vegetable garnish, and the wine or port if you wish.

ACCOMPANIMENTS FOR SOUPS

1. *Croûtons of Fried Bread*: Small dice of dry bread, fried until golden-brown. Bread slices can also be buttered and cut into dice, then bake-fried. Served with consommés, purées and thickened soups.
2. *Sippets*: Small triangles or dice of toast. Serve as croûtons.
3. *Fairy Toast*: Very thin slices of bread baked in a cool oven.
4. *Melba Toast*: Bread slices, toasted, then split through the centre. Grill or bake, untoasted sides up, until crisp. Serve with any hot soup.
5. *Cheese Croûtons*: Small bread rounds toasted on one side, then buttered and sprinkled with grated cheese on the other, and toasted. Serve with thickened soups and hearty broths.
6. *Grated Cheese*: Serve with hearty meat or vegetable soups such as minestrone.
7. *Quenelles*: Very light, tiny forcemeat balls, served with or in some fish soups, in Mock Turtle Soup and similar soups.
8. *Small Dumplings, Forcemeat Balls or Cocktail Frankfurters*: Added to pulse purées and other substantial meat and vegetable soups, or served with them.
9. *Sliced or Shredded Vegetables*: Usually added to the appropriate soup, but can also be served separately.

3
FISH AND SHELLFISH

Buying Fish

When buying fresh fish, remember the following points:
1. Choose fish in its best season as it then has better flavour and is cheaper.
2. Medium-sized fish have a better flavour than small fish of their type and are less coarse than larger fish.
3. Any fish must be really fresh. Check that:
   (a) fish do not smell stale or unpleasant;
   (b) the eyes are bright and full, not sunken;
   (c) the skin is slightly glossy but not slimy. A fresh herring has bright silver scales and fins, and red-rimmed eyes. A fresh mackerel is glossy with mother-of-pearl colouring. Both look dull when stale. Flat fish look stale first on the dark side. The bright spots on plaice turn brown when it stales.
   (d) the flesh is firm, not flabby;
   (e) steaks or fillets have solid, not fibrous or limp flesh.

How Much Fish to Buy

Whole fish: 1 small (225–350 g/½–¾ lb) fish per person or 350 g/¾ lb of a large fish if bought with its head on.
Fillets: 175–225 g/6–8 oz whole small fillets, e.g. plaice, or 175 g/6 oz of a large fillet, e.g. cod, per person.
Pieces, steaks, cutlets, slices: 175 g/6 oz of a large piece, e.g. middle cut salmon, per person. One (175–225 g/6–8 oz) steak, cutlet or slice per person.

TO PREPARE FISH BEFORE COOKING

A fishmonger will normally prepare bought fish by gutting, removing fins and head, skinning and filleting as required. Ask for any heads, bones, skins and trimmings for stock-making (page 15).

TO COOK FISH

Fish can be easier and cheaper to cook than meat since its delicate flesh only needs brief cooking. It has excellent food value, having as much protein as meat, and unlike meat, containing vitamin D.
Some types of smoked fish are eaten raw but others, and all fresh fish, must be cooked.

To Test When Fish is Cooked

1. The flesh looks opaque, and on white fish a milky curd may show. The flakes separate easily when tested with a thin skewer.
2. The flesh separates easily from the bone, and there is no red blood round the bone.

To Poach Fish

Poaching is one of the best ways to cook fish, especially delicate or smoked fish. Cook in flavoured liquid or Fish Stock (page 15) either in the oven or in a frying pan (skillet).
Put the fish into cool liquid, and time the cooking from when the liquid begins to shiver. If the fish will be eaten cold, heat the liquid gently, and keep it shivering for 5–12 minutes according to size of fillet, then turn off the heat and let the fish cool in the liquid in the closed pan.
To cook in the oven, place steaks or small fillets in a shallow baking dish and sprinkle with lemon juice. Pour in almost enough liquid to cover. Lay greased foil or baking paper on top. Place in the oven heated to 180°C/350°F/Gas Mark 4 and simmer for the times below. If serving the fish without the liquid or if using it for a sauce, remove fish pieces with a slice, and drain over the dish. Strain the liquid into a pan for a sauce, and return the pieces to the dish.

Poaching Times

Small thin fillets:	4–7 minutes
Medium and thick fillets:	6–9 minutes
Steaks, and whole fish or	
a cut up to 900 g/2 lb:	8–15 minutes
Larger fish:	5–12 minutes

Alternatively, poach for 9 minutes per 2.5 cm/1 in thickness or for 6–8 minutes per 450 g/1 lb. Allow 5–8 minutes extra for frozen or stuffed fish or rolled fillets. Allow 6–9 minutes extra when steaming fish (see page 26).

Poaching Liquid

1. White fish fillets, smoked fish: Use equal quantities milk and water, 5–10 ml/1–2 tsp butter, a sprinkling of white pepper, a few parsley stalks and a strip of lemon rind. Salt fish after cooking if needed.
2. Steaks, whole fish: Use half as much dry white wine as water, 15 ml/1 tbls white vinegar per 1 l/3/4 pt/4 1/3 cups liquid, 1 sliced onion, 1 sliced carrot, 2 sliced celery stalks and a bouquet garni (parsley stalks, sprig of thyme, bay leaf and a few black peppercorns tied in a muslin square). Simmer for 30 minutes, strain, cool and use. Add salt after cooking if needed.

Poached Smoked Haddock

Serves 4

Freeze 1 month

	Metric	Imperial	American
Smoked haddock fillets or golden cutlets	450–500 g	1 lb– 1 lb 2 oz	1 lb– 1 lb 2 oz
Poaching liquid 1			
Melted butter			
Chopped parsley			

1. Cut off any fins, and cut the fish in serving portions if needed. Place in one layer in a large frying pan (skillet).
2. Pour in enough poaching liquid to cover all but the top. Cover and simmer for 10–15 minutes until tender.
3. Lift each piece on a fish slice (slotted spatula), drain, and place on a warmed plate or dish.
4. Brush with butter and sprinkle with parsley. Strain a little poaching liquid around each portion.
5. Serve for breakfast, as a supper dish or use in kedgeree, omelets, a soufflé etc.

Cod's Roe (fresh, raw)

Serves 4

Freeze 2 months (without sauce)

	Metric	Imperial	American
Uncooked cod's roe	450 g (approx)	1 lb (approx)	1 lb (approx)
White vinegar	15 ml	1 tbls	1 tbls
Salt			
Parsley or Shrimp Sauce (page 88)	450 ml	3/4 pt	2 cups
Squares of hot buttered toast	4	4	4

1. If possible, poach a whole roe without any splits in the covering membrane.
2. Wash the roe, tie in muslin, and place in a pan of hot water with the vinegar and salt added and poach for 20 minutes.
3. Drain and leave to stand for 10 minutes to firm up. Meanwhile, heat the sauce.
4. Slice the roe, and pour the sauce over. Serve on toast.

Plaice Fillets with Grapes

Serves 4

Oven temp 180°C/350°F/Gas Mark 4

Not suitable for freezing

	Metric	Imperial	American
Fresh plaice fillets	8	8	8
Salt and pepper			
White grapes	225 g	8 oz	1/2 lb
Milk or white wine	60 ml	4 tbls	4 tbls
Butter, flaked	50 g	2 oz	1/4 cup
Extra butter	15 g	1/2 oz	1 tbls
Flour	15 g	1/2 oz	1 tbls
Extra milk	225 ml (approx)	8 fl oz (approx)	1 cup (approx)
Egg yolks, beaten	2	2	2

1. Lay the fillets flat and season lightly.
2. Halve and pip the grapes. Arrange a few on each fillet, and reserve the remainder for garnishing.
3. Fold the fillets in half. Arrange in one layer in a shallow baking dish or tin (pan). Add the milk or wine and flaked butter.
4. Cover loosely with greased foil and poach in the oven for 12–15 minutes or until cooked.
5. Meanwhile, blend the extra butter and flour and heat gently in a small pan, stirring constantly, for 2 minutes. Remove from the heat.
6. Lift the fish fillets onto a serving dish and keep warm. Strain the cooking liquid into a measuring jug and add enough milk to make 275 ml/1/2 pt/1 1/4 cups.
7. Replace the butter-flour mixture over heat, and pour in the liquid gradually, stirring constantly until the sauce thickens. When cooked, beat in the egg yolks and pour the sauce over the fish. Garnish with reserved grapes.

Fresh fish is nutritious, easy-to-cook and provides variety in the diet.

Fish Mornay

Serves 4–6

Not suitable for freezing

	Metric	Imperial	American
Thick white fish			
fillets or	900 g	2 lb	2 lb
cutlets	(approx)	(approx)	(approx)
Fish Stock (page 15)	125 ml	4 fl oz	½ cup
Dry white wine	125 ml	4 fl oz	½ cup
Butter for greasing			
Thick Cheese Sauce			
(page 88)	450 ml	¾ pt	2 cups
Grated hard cheese	40 g	1½	3 tbls
Fresh white			
breadcrumbs	30 ml	2 tbls	2 tbls
Melted butter			

1. Prepare the fish. Cut large fillets into serving portions.
2. Poach gently in the stock and wine for 12–20 minutes.
3. Drain, reserving the cooking liquid, and arrange the fish in one layer in a greased ovenproof baking dish.
4. Simmer down the cooking liquid to half its volume, and stir into the cheese sauce.
5. Pour over the fish. Sprinkle thickly with the grated cheese and breadcrumbs then with melted butter. Brown lightly under the grill (broiler).

Note: This recipe can be used with other sauces, e.g. parsley or shrimp sauce, with or without the cheese topping. It is then suitable for salmon or coarser fish steaks, e.g. conger. Poach thick steaks for 20 minutes.

To Steam Fish

1. Wash, clean and prepare the fish according to kind. Sprinkle with salt, pepper and lemon juice and wrap in greased greaseproof (waxed) paper.
2. Place over boiling water in a steamer.
3. Fillets of fish will require 12–20 minutes according to thickness. For thicker cuts allow twice the time recommended for poached fish (page 23).

To Stew or Casserole Fish

1. Wash, clean and prepare fish according to kind. Cut into small pieces suitable for serving.
2. Put the fish into a casserole with milk, poaching liquid or a sauce, cover and cook until tender.

Classic Fish Stew

Serves 4

Freeze 1 month (before adding flour)

	Metric	Imperial	American
Fresh white fish			
fillet or			
steaks (coley			
cod, hake etc.)	900 g	2 lb	2 lb
Medium onions,			
chopped	4	4	4
Garlic cloves,			
chopped (minced)	2	2	2
Chopped parsley	10 ml	2 tsp	2 tsp
White vinegar	15 ml	1 tbls	1 tbls
Olive oil	75 ml	3 fl oz	⅓ cup
Salt and pepper			
Water	1.5 l	2½ pt	6¼ cups
Flour	50 g	2 oz	½ cup
Slices of French			
bread, toasted	8	8	8

1. Remove skin and bones from fish and cut into 8 cm/3¼ in pieces. Put it in a deep bowl.
2. Add the onions, garlic, parsley, vinegar and oil and season well. Leave in a cool place overnight.
3. Put the water in a saucepan and bring to the boil. Add the fish, lower the heat and simmer for 1 minute.
4. Add the other ingredients from the bowl. Bring back to the boil, lower the heat and simmer for 15 minutes.
5. Mix the flour to a smooth cream with cold water, and stir in. Simmer for 5 minutes longer.
6. Put two toasted bread slices in each of 4 warmed soup plates and strain the fish cooking liquid over them. Serve the fish and onion mixture separately, with the bowls of soup.

Mackerel Casserole

Serves 4

Oven temp 200°C/400°F/Gas Mark 6

Freeze 1 month

	Metric	Imperial	American
Large skinned fresh			
mackerel fillets	4	4	4
Margarine	15 ml	1 tbls	1 tbls
Thinly sliced leeks,			
white parts only	2	2	2
226 g/7¼ oz can of			
tomatoes	1	1	1

Dried dill leaves	15 ml	1 tbls	1 tbls
Mild paprika	2.5 ml	½ tsp	½ tsp
Juice of ½ lemon			
Salt			
Sour cream	150 ml	¼ pt	⅔ cup

1. Grease the inside of a shallow bake-and-serve casserole or baking dish with a lid.
2. Put in the prepared fillets, overlapping if required. Cover with the leeks and tomatoes. Sprinkle with dill leaves, paprika, lemon juice and a little salt.
3. Pour sour cream over, cover and cook in the oven at the temperature above for 30 minutes.

To Bake Fish

Baking is the best and easiest way to cook most medium-sized whole fish, steaks and cutlets. They keep all their own flavour and full food value, and do not flake. They can be stuffed but do not need rich sauces.

General Method

Either put the fish in a well-greased ovenproof dish; or lay each piece separately on greased non-stick baking parchment or foil. Sprinkle with flaked butter, chopped parsley and lemon juice or wine, then enclose completely. Bake at 190°C/375°F/Gas Mark 5 for 15–25 minutes, depending on size and thickness.

Baked Cod or Hake Steaks

Serves 4

Oven temp 190°C/375°F/Gas Mark 5

Freeze 2 months (without sauce)

	Metric	Imperial	American
Cod or hake steaks, 225 g/ 8 oz/½ lb each	4	4	4
Salt and pepper			
Margarine for greasing			
Shallot, finely chopped (minced)	1	1	1
Small mushrooms, finely chopped (minced)	2	2	2
Velouté Sauce (hot) (page 85)	275 ml	½ pt	1¼ cups
Prepared mustard	5 ml	1 tsp	1 tsp
Grated cheese	25 g	1 oz	2 tbls
Lemon butterflies (page 12)	4	4	4

1. Wash the steaks, pat dry and season. Place each on a piece of greased foil and sprinkle with shallot and mushroom. Wrap.
2. Place in a greased baking tin (pan), and bake at the temperature above for 30 minutes.
3. Meanwhile, make the sauce, adding the mustard and cheese.
4. Unwrap the fish parcels, and tip any liquid into the sauce.
5. Arrange the steaks on a warmed serving dish, and top each with a lemon butterfly. Serve the sauce separately.

Cod with Savoury Stuffing

Serves 4

Oven temp 190°C/375°F/Gas Mark 5

Freeze 1 month

	Metric	Imperial	American
Cod cutlets	4	4	4
Tomatoes, skinned	100 g	4 oz	¼ lb
Small onion, chopped	1	1	1
Butter	15 g	½ oz	1 tbls
Salt and pepper			
Cayenne pepper			
Butter, melted	25 g	1 oz	2 tbls

1. Trim the cutlets and remove the bones.
2. Cut the tomatoes in small pieces and simmer until soft.
3. Fry the onion in the butter until golden, season well and mix with the tomato.
4. Spoon the stuffing into the gaps between the cutlet flaps. Make the cutlets into neat rounds and secure with string.
5. Place in a greased shallow baking dish and brush with melted butter.
6. Cover loosely with greased foil and bake at the temperature above for 15 minutes. Remove the foil and bake for another 5–10 minutes. Remove the string before serving.

Smoked Haddock Soufflé

Serves 4

Oven temp 190°C/375°F/Gas Mark 5

Not suitable for freezing

	Metric	Imperial	American
Unsalted butter for greasing			
Raw smoked haddock	225 g	8 oz	½ lb
Milk	275 ml	½ pt	1¼ cups
Extra milk or single (light) cream			
Butter or margarine	50 g	2 oz	¼ cup
Flour	75 ml	5 tbls	5 tbls
Pepper			
Grated Gruyère cheese	50 g	2 oz	¼ cup
Pinch of grated nutmeg			
Salt (optional)			
Eggs, separated	4	4	4
Egg white	1	1	1

1. Prepare an 850 ml/1½ pt/3¾ cup soufflé dish by tying a paper collar around it rising well above the rim. Grease the inside of the dish and collar with unsalted butter.

2. Rinse the fish, pat dry, and put in a frying pan (skillet) with the milk. Simmer until tender. Remove from heat.
3. Take out the fish, skin and flake, removing any bones. Add enough extra milk or cream to the cooking liquid to make it up to the original quantity.
4. Melt the fat in a saucepan, stir in flour and cook for 2 minutes, stirring. Add the milk gradually, stirring constantly until the sauce thickens. Remove from heat and beat hard until the sauce leaves the sides of the pan cleanly.
5. Place in a bowl and beat in the flaked fish, a little pepper, the cheese and nutmeg. Taste and add a little salt if you wish.
6. Beat the egg yolks, one by one, into the haddock mixture. Whisk all the egg whites until stiff. Using a metal spoon, stir 1 tbls egg white into the haddock mixture, then carefully fold in the rest.
7. Turn gently into the prepared dish. Bake at the temperature above for 35 minutes. Serve immediately.

Note: If you wish, bake in four 225 ml/8 fl oz/1 cup moulds for 20 minutes.

Opposite: *Baked Plaice Fillets served with Tomato Sauce (page 90).*

Below: *Smoked Haddock Soufflé cooked in individual dishes makes a delicious starter.*

Baked Sole or Plaice Fillets

Serve 1 or 2 fillets per person, depending on size

Oven temp 190°C/375°F/Gas Mark 5

Freeze 1 month

Sole or plaice fillets, fresh or frozen
  and thawed
Seasoned flour
Lemon juice
Stuffing (rice, pasta, roe or shrimp -
  see pages 93–94)
Butter for greasing
Fish Stock (page 15) or milk

1. Rinse the fillets and pat dry. Toss in
    seasoned flour and sprinkle with lemon
    juice.
2. Put a little stuffing on the skin side of each
    fillet, then roll up the fillet or fold it over.
3. Place in one layer in a greased ovenproof
    dish or baking tin (pan), pour a little stock or
    milk around the fish and bake at the
    temperature above for 20 minutes.
4. Serve with White, Tomato or Fish Sauce
    (pages 88–90).

Baked Mackerel

Serves 4

Oven temp 190°C/375°F/Gas Mark 5

Freeze 1 month

	Metric	Imperial	American
Whole fresh			
mackerel	4	4	4
Oil for greasing			
Prepared mustard	10 ml	2 tsp	2 tsp
Salt	5 ml	1 tsp	1 tsp
Pepper	1.5 ml	¼ tsp	¼ tsp
Vinegar	30 ml	2 tbls	2 tbls
Water	30 ml	2 tbls	2 tbls

1. Clean the mackerel and cut 3 diagonal
    slashes in the skin on each side. Place the
    fish in one layer in an oiled ovenproof dish.
2. Mix together the remaining ingredients and
    pour over the fish. Cover with foil and bake
    at the temperature above for 30 minutes.

Note: Any recipe for baking mackerel can be used
for herring. Bake for 15–20 minutes.

Soused Herrings

Serves 4

Oven temp 160°C/325°F/Gas Mark 3

Freeze 1 month

	Metric	Imperial	American
Fresh herrings	*4*	*4*	*4*
Salt and pepper			
Bay leaf	*1*	*1*	*1*
Black peppercorns	*10*	*10*	*10*
Blade of mace	*1*	*1*	*1*
Whole cloves	*2*	*2*	*2*
Vinegar or			
vinegar and			
water			

1. Clean, rinse and split the herrings, reserving the roes. Bone the fish. Season the flesh sides, and place a piece of roe on each.
2. Roll up the herrings towards the tail with the skin side out, and pack into a casserole. Add the bay leaf, peppercorns, mace and cloves and enough vinegar, or vinegar and water, to cover the fish. Cover tightly, and bake at the temperature above for 1 hour. Serve hot or cold.

Note: For Herrings and Tomatoes, use 700 g/1½ lb tomatoes boiled in 150 ml/¼ pt/⅔ cup vinegar and water, sieved and cooled for the sauce. Use tomato instead of roe, add a quartered onion to the casserole and use parsley instead of bay leaf. Use only 6 peppercorns. Tie all the spices in muslin. Serve hot.

Sole au Gratin

Serves 2 persons per medium sole

Oven temp 190°C/375°F/Gas Mark 5

Freeze 2 months (without sauce)

	Metric	Imperial	American
Dover or lemon	*700 g*	*1½ lb*	*1½ lb*
sole	*(approx)*	*(approx)*	*(approx)*
Butter for			
greasing			
Sherry or milk	*150 ml*	*¼ pt*	*⅔ cup*
Cheese Sauce			
(coating			
consistency-			
page 88)	*275 ml*	*½ pt*	*1¼ cups*
Browned			
breadcrumbs			

1. Skin and wipe the prepared fish. Lay it in a greased, shallow baking dish with the liquid. Cover and bake at the temperature above for 25 minutes.
2. Meanwhile, make enough Cheese Sauce to cover the fish. Pour it over the fish, and sprinkle with browned crumbs.

Notes:
1. The quantity of sherry or milk given should be enough for most fish. Increase it for a big flat fish or more than one fish, in a large pan.
2. The cooking time given should be long enough for all flat fish and for whole round fish or a cut up to 700 g/1½ lb. Firm-fleshed coarse fish or larger round whole fish may take up to 50 minutes to bake.
3. 'Au gratin' means a dish topped with crumbs. Although cheese sauce is used for most dishes 'au gratin', plain white sauce, parsley sauce, egg sauce or a similar sauce can be used. In this case, season the fish after baking with a little salt and pepper.
4. Use this recipe to cook other types of fish *au gratin*.

Trout in White Wine

Serves 4

Oven temp 180°C/350°F/Gas Mark 4

Freeze 2 months

	Metric	Imperial	American
Fresh trout	*4*	*4*	*4*
Butter	*40 g*	*1½ oz*	*3 tbls*
White wine	*150 ml*	*¼ pt*	*⅔ cup*
Button mushrooms,			
sliced	*125 g*	*4 oz*	*4 oz*
Salt and pepper			
Lemon wedges			

1. Clean, rinse and dry the trout. Remove the eyes if leaving the head on, and trim tail. Grease a shallow baking dish with 15 g/½ oz 1 tbls of the butter.
2. Lay the trout in the dish, and dot with the remaining butter. Pour in the wine.
3. Cover the trout with the sliced mushrooms, and season. Cover and bake at the temperature above for 20–25 minutes. Serve with lemon wedges.

To Grill (Broil) Fish

This method is excellent for both fillets and cutlets and for small whole fish. When whole fish are cooked, cut 2 or 3 deep gashes through the skin and flesh on each side to let heat penetrate. The prepared fish should be brushed with a little oil or melted fat. The grill (broiler) should be preheated and the grill pan grid lightly greased. Cook fish slowly on both sides taking care not to break the fish when turning it. The grill may be turned up for the final few minutes to brown the fish, which will take 2–5 minutes in the case of fillets and 3–6 minutes for cutlets and larger fish.

Grilled Haddock with Spinach

Serves 4

Freeze 2 months

	Metric	Imperial	American
Fresh haddock			
fillets	700 g	1½ lb	1½ lb
Butter	50 g	2 oz	¼ cup
Garlic clove	1	1	1
Salt			
Thin slices day old			
bread	4	4	4
Oil	60 ml	4 tbls	4 tbls
Fresh spinach	900 g –1.4 kg	2–3 lb	2–3 lb

1. Cut the fish into four pieces. Melt the butter. Crush the garlic with a little salt, and add to the butter.
2. Place the fish, skin side down, on the greased grid of the grill (broiler) pan. Pour over the butter and garlic. Grill (broil) the fish until browned and cooked through.
3. Meanwhile, cut the crusts off the bread, cut into 4 triangles and fry in the oil until golden-brown. Drain on soft kitchen paper and keep warm.
4. Cook the spinach and drain well to extract as much water as possible. Pile the spinach in a heated dish, lay fish on top and garnish with the fried bread triangles.

Grilled Trout with Almonds

Serves 4

Freeze 2 months (without parsley)

	Metric	Imperial	American
Medium trout,	4	4	4
of even size			
Butter	50 g	2 oz	¼ cup
Flaked (slivered)			
almonds	50 g	2 oz	½ cup
Extra butter as			
needed			
Lemon juice	60 ml	4 tbls	4 tbls
Black pepper			
Chopped parsley			

1. Prepare the trout, making 3 slits in the skin on each side. Place them on the greased grid of the grill pan. Dot with butter. Grill (broil) gently for 8–15 minutes, turning after 5 minutes. Remove to a warmed serving dish, and keep warm.
2. Pour off the butter in the grill (broiler) pan into a frying pan (skillet). Add the almonds, and a little extra butter if needed. Fry gently, stirring and tossing until they begin to brown.
3. Immediately add the lemon juice and pepper, and pour over the fish. Serve sprinkled with parsley.

Halibut Steaks with Barbecue Sauce

Serves 3

Freeze sauce only 1 month

	Metric	Imperial	American
Small onion,			
chopped	1	1	1
Butter, melted	25 g	1 oz	2 tbls
Button			
mushrooms	100 g	4 oz	¼ lb
226 g/7¼ oz can of			
tomatoes	1	1	1
Chilli sauce,			
to taste			
Soft brown			
sugar	10 ml	2 tsp	2 tsp
Salt and pepper			
Lemon juice	5 ml	1 tsp	1 tsp
Halibut steaks	3	3	3

1. Cook the onion in some of the melted butter until soft. Quarter the mushrooms and add to the onion.
2. Roughly chop the tomatoes and add to the pan with the chilli sauce, sugar, salt and pepper, and lemon juice. Cook gently for about 15 minutes.
3. Meanwhile, lay the fish steaks on the greased grid of the grill (broiler) pan, season and brush with melted butter. Grill (broil) for 5–6 minutes each side until well cooked.
4. Serve with the sauce poured round the fish.

Grilled Plaice with Sour Cream Sauce

Serves 4

Not suitable for freezing

	Metric	Imperial	American
Plaice fillets	4	4	4
Butter, melted	25 g	1 oz	2 tbls
Salt and pepper			
Sour cream	150 ml	1/4 pt	2/3 cup
Chopped capers	10 ml	2 tsp	2 tsp

1. Wash and trim the fillets. Place them on the grid of the grill (broiler), brush with melted butter and season.
2. Grill (broil) under moderate heat for 5–6 minutes, or until tender. Place the fillets on a warmed serving dish and keep warm.
3. Heat the sour cream and add the capers. Pour this mixture over the fillets and serve.

Grilled Plaice with Sour Cream Sauce is a tasty and economical main course.

To Fry Fish

The two main methods of frying are deep frying (in deep oil or pure fat) and shallow frying (in shallow fat).

For Deep Frying, you need a deep, heavy, flat-based pan and a wire frying basket to fit it. Use a refined oil which reaches a high temperature safely, such as corn or sunflower oil, or good quality lard or white fat. All other fats must be clarified.

1. Cut the fish into small serving portions. Coat with seasoned flour, beaten egg and crumbs or a coating batter (page 170).
2. Fill the pan not more than 1/3 full of oil or fat. Heat it slowly. To see if the oil or fat is hot enough, drop in a 2.5 cm/1 in cube of dry bread. If the fat is hot enough, the bread cube will sink, then rise at once with bubbles round it, and turn golden within 2–3 seconds. Lift out the basket, put in a few fish portions and lower into the pan again.
3. Small thin raw fillets will cook in 3–5 minutes, thicker portions in 5–6 minutes. When cooked, they will rise to the surface. Lift the pan, drain, then transfer the portions to soft kitchen paper and keep warm while cooking any remaining portions.

For Shallow Frying, use a heavy frying pan (skillet). Use oil or fat as for deep frying, or clarified margarine, if a flavoured coating is wanted. Clarified butter and oil mixed together make a better frying

medium than butter alone. Coat the fish in seasoned flour or egg and crumbs, not in batter. Heat 5 mm ¼ in depth of oil or fat in the pan, or enough to come half-way up the fish. Put in the fish portions one by one, waiting a moment between adding each one. Fry gently until golden-brown underneath, turn without piercing the coating, and fry the second sides. Fillets will take 5–8 minutes in all, thicker pieces 6–10 minutes. Drain on soft kitchen paper and keep warm while completing frying.

Note: Fried fish does not freeze well. Prepare fish, then fry after thawing.

Pan-Fried Whiting

Serves 6

	Metric	Imperial	American
Whiting, of even size	6	6	6
Butter	50 g	2 oz	¼ cup
Oil	60 ml	4 tbls	4 tbls
Garnish			
Maître d'Hôtel Butter (page 143)			
Lemon juice			

1. Remove the heads and clean the insides of the fish. Rinse and dry well.
2. Heat the butter and oil together in a large shallow pan and fry the whiting gently for 4 minutes on each side. Remove the fish and drain on soft kitchen paper.
3. Serve garnished with pats of Maître d'Hôtel Butter and a little lemon juice.

Fried Cod's Roe

Serves 1

	Metric	Imperial	American
Cod's roe	100 g	4 oz	¼ lb
Vinegar	5 ml	1 tsp	1 tsp
Salt			
Coating Batter (page 170)			
Oil for deep frying			
Parsley			
Lemon butterflies (page 12)			

1. Wash the roe, tie in muslin and poach in just simmering water with the vinegar and salt for 20 minutes. Drain and leave to cool completely.
2. Cut into fairly thick slices, dip in coating batter, and fry in deep hot oil for 3 minutes until golden-brown.
3. Drain on soft kitchen paper, and serve with parsley and lemon butterflies.

Crispy Plaice Fillets

Serves 4

	Metric	Imperial	American
Plaice fillets	4	4	4
Seasoned flour			
Butter	75 g	3 oz	6 tbls
Oil	30 ml	2 tbls	2 tbls
Lemon juice	15 ml	1 tbls	1 tbls
Garnish			
Chopped parsley	15 ml	1 tbls	1 tbls
Lemon wedges			

1. Coat the fillets in seasoned flour. Heat 50 g/2 oz/¼ cup butter and the oil together in a frying pan (skillet) until hot.
2. Fry the fillets for 6–8 minutes, turning once, until golden-brown and well cooked. Arrange on a warmed serving dish.
3. Add the lemon juice and remaining butter to the frying pan and heat until golden-brown, with a 'nutty' scent. Pour over the fish and sprinkle with chopped parsley. Serve with lemon wedges.

Deep-Fried Sprats or Whitebait

Sprats or whitebait
Flour for coating
Oil for deep frying
Salt and cayenne pepper

Garnish
Parsley
Lemon wedges

1. Whitebait must only be cooked when very fresh, and should be kept on ice until required. Rinse and dry the fish thoroughly.
2. Put plenty of flour onto a piece of paper or into a polythene bag with seasonings and toss the fish in it a few at a time. Shake off any surplus flour.
3. Place the fish in batches in a frying basket, separating them from each other. Fry in very hot oil for 2 minutes, then turn onto soft kitchen paper.
4. When all the fish have been fried, replace them in the basket and re-fry for a minute to reheat them. Drain on kitchen paper and sprinkle with salt and cayenne pepper.
5. Serve at once with parsley, lemon and brown bread and butter.

SHELLFISH

To Choose Fresh Shellfish

Lobsters and crabs should feel heavy for their size. Shellfish with 2 shells must be tightly closed. An open raw oyster, mussel or scallop is dead and probably poisonous.

Only buy shellfish from a reputable supplier or harvest them from a known pure water supply.

To Dress a Crab

Turn it on its back. Twist off the legs and claws. With tail towards you, press it up with your thumbs firmly until it breaks free. Tap sharply all round the shell just inside the dark line and lift off the inner piece of shell. Discard the small transparent stomach bag in the main shell just under the head, and the fawn, feathery 'dead men's fingers'. Pick out the meat from the main shell, putting the white and brown meat in separate bowls. Crack the claws and legs with nutcrackers and pick out the meat.

To dress and serve cold: Scrub and dry the main shell. Flake the white meat, and mix with a little French Dressing (page 132). Cream the brown meat and any coral with 15–30 ml/1–2 tbls fresh brown breadcrumbs, then mix with salt, pepper and a little lemon juice. Fill both ends of the shell with the brown meat mixture and place the white meat in a broad strip in the centre. Garnish with finely chopped hard-boiled (hard-cooked) egg and chopped parsley. Serve on a bed of lettuce.

Lobster

Place a cooked lobster on a chopping board with the tail spread out behind. Insert the point of a large kitchen knife in the middle of the head, and split the body lengthways through the shell into two equal halves. Pull out the intestinal tract which runs from head to tail and discard the contents of the head and the sponge-like gills. Reserve any dark mustard-coloured meat for flavouring a sauce and any bright pink coral for making lobster butter, a rare luxury.

To dress and serve cold: Place the half lobster, cut side up, on a suitable plate. Crack the claws and arrange round the shell. Fill the head cavity with a little Russian salad (page 131). Serve with mayonnaise and cucumber salad and provide thin forks or lobster picks.

Prawns and Shrimps

Nearly all prawns, shell-on or peeled, are imported ready-cooked, and are sold fresh or in frozen packs. Prawns from cold-water seas, which are a delicate pink when boiled, are better eaten in cold dishes or used, before peeling, as a handsome garnish than the tightly-curled darker warm-water types. Warm-water prawns are best in cooked dishes.

Cooked shrimps are also widely available frozen or canned for use in mixed seafood dishes, for fillings, in sauces and for garnishing.

To boil uncooked prawns or shrimps for use, treat like lobster, but boil prawns for 10 minutes only, shrimp for 7 minutes, drain and cool, then peel if required. To peel, remove the tail, then the head, using your thumbnails, crack open the body shell on the belly side and peel it off. Remove the dark vein.

Prawn Cocktail

Serves 6

Not suitable for freezing

	Metric	Imperial	American
Boiled, peeled			
prawns (shrimp)	*350 g*	*12 oz*	*¾ lb*
Lemon juice			
Crisp lettuce			
leaves	*6*	*6*	*6*
Mild paprika			
Shell-on cooked			
whole prawns			
(shrimp)	*6*	*6*	*6*
Sauce			
Mayonnaise			
(page 134)	*45 ml*	*3 tbls*	*3 tbls*
Tomato ketchup	*45 ml*	*3 tbls*	*3 tbls*
Single (light)			
cream	*45 ml*	*3 tbls*	*3 tbls*
Lemon juice			

1. Sprinkle the prawns with a little lemon juice. Shred the lettuce and arrange in 6 individual glasses. Pile an equal quantity of prawns in each glass.
2. Mix together all the sauce ingredients, blending well. Pour over the prawns and sprinkle with a little paprika.
3. Perch a whole shell-on prawn on the edge of each glass.

Oysters

Large oysters are among the world's finest shellfish. They are wasted in cooked dishes, for which smaller oysters or frozen or canned oysters can be used.

To Prepare and Serve Oysters

Oysters, like mussels, must be tightly closed when bought. They are difficult to open. Use a special oyster knife or a very sharp kitchen knife. Work the knife-blade between the shells, and cut the ligament hinge which keeps the shells shut. Hold the oyster with the bowl-shaped deep shell underneath and the flat shell on top. Open the oyster and free it from the shell. Serve 6–12 oysters per person, each on its deep half-shell in its own liquor. Place the shells on crushed ice on individual plates. Offer cayenne pepper, vinegar, lemon wedges and rolls of brown bread and butter separately.

Mussels

If you harvest your own, make sure that it is in a pure water area. Most mussels sold commercially are farmed in carefully-chosen places, and are normally only in season when there is an R in the month. Like oysters, they are normally sold alive in the shell, although frozen, canned and pickled mussels can be bought for cooking, or as snacks.

To Prepare Mussels

Wash in several changes of clean water. Scrub well. Scrape off the 'beards' near the hinges of the shells with a sharp knife. Examine all the shells. As you do so, discard any open ones. Leave the rest under a running cold tap for 10 minutes.

Put the mussels into a large pan. Peel and slice 1 onion, and add to the pan, with a bay leaf and a parsley sprig. Pour equal quantities of white wine and water over the mussels. Use 150 ml/$\frac{1}{4}$ pt/$\frac{2}{3}$ cup liquid to 2.3 l/4 pt/5 pt mussels. Cover. Place over medium heat for 5 minutes. Shake the pan several times. The shells should now be open. Discard any which are not. Strain off the liquor into a measuring jug for use in sauces etc. Discard the empty half-shells, onion and flavourings. Leave the mussels on the half-shell for dishes such as the Seafood Corals below, or remove and discard the shells, reserving only the mussels.

Seafood Corals

Serves 6 (as first course)

Freeze 1 month (mussels and liquor separately without sauce)

	Metric	Imperial	American
Fresh mussels	2.3 l	4 pt	10 cups
White wine	150 ml	¼ pt	⅔ cup
Onion, sliced	1	1	1
Bay leaf	1	1	1
Parsley sprig	1	1	1
Butter	25 g	1 oz	2 tbls
Sauce			
Single (light) cream	150 ml	¼ pt	⅔ cup
Chopped parsley	15 ml	1 tbls	1 tbls
Tomato paste	30 ml	2 tbls	2 tbls
Black pepper			

1. Put the prepared mussels into a large pan with the wine, onion, bay leaf, parsley and butter.

2. Bring to the boil over medium heat, and cook for 5 minutes, covered, shaking the pan occasionally.
3. Discard any mussels which have not opened in the pan. Strain off the liquid from the pan, and discard the empty half shells. Place the full ones in a warmed serving dish. Keep warm.
4. Strain 275 ml/½ pt/1¼ cups of the liquid into a saucepan. Add the sauce ingredients and heat, stirring well. Pour over the mussels.

Note: The dish may be served as a first course or a main course. Allow about 575 ml/1 pt/2½ cups mussels per person as a main course.

COOKED, FROZEN AND CANNED FISH DISHES

Kedgeree

Serves 2–3

Freeze 2 months

	Metric	Imperial	American
Long grain rice	100 g	4 oz	¼ lb
Smoked haddock fillet, skinned	225–370 g	8–12 oz	½–¾ lb
Butter or margarine	50 g	2 oz	¼ cup
Egg, beaten	1	1	1
Salt and cayenne pepper			
Hard-boiled (hard-cooked) egg	1	1	1
Milk			
Chopped parsley	5 ml	1 tsp	1 tsp

1. Cook the rice in fast-boiling salted water for 11–12 minutes. Drain.
2. While cooking, pour boiling water on the fish, and leave for 5 minutes.
3. Drain and flake the fish, and stir into the rice with the fat, beaten egg, salt and cayenne. Chop the hard-boiled egg white and stir in.
4. Add a little milk if the mixture is too dry. Heat gently, stirring, until thoroughly heated through.
5. Pile on a warmed plate and sieve the hard-boiled egg yolk on top. Sprinkle with parsley.

Note: Frozen haddock can be used.

Tuna and Mushrooms

Serves 4

Not suitable for freezing

	Metric	Imperial	American
Button mushrooms	50 g	2 oz	½ cup
Green pepper	1	1	1
Butter	25 g	1 oz	2 tbls
198 g/7 oz can of tuna fish in brine	1	1	1
297 g/10½ oz can of condensed mushroom soup	1	1	1
Single (light) cream	125 ml	4 fl oz	½ cup
Salt and pepper			
Cooked long grain rice	350 g	12 oz	¾ lb
Chopped parsley			

1. Rinse the mushrooms, dry and slice thinly. De-seed and dice the green pepper. Sauté the mushrooms and pepper gently in the butter for 3 minutes.
2. Drain and flake the fish and add it to the pan. Toss well. Add the canned soup, cream and seasoning and heat through well.
3. Serve on a warmed serving plate in a ring of rice, sprinkled with parsley.

Fish and Tomato Scallops

Serves 4

Freeze 1 month

	Metric	Imperial	American
Cooked white fish, flaked	225 g	8 oz	½ lb
Well-seasoned White Sauce (page 84)	275 ml	½ pt	1¼ cups
Butter	25 g	1 oz	2 tbls
Fresh breadcrumbs	50 g	2 oz	½ cup
Capers	5 ml	1 tsp	1 tsp
Whole tomato, skinned and cut in slices	1	1	1
Mashed potatoes	225 g	8 oz	½ lb

1. Mix the fish with the sauce. Divide the mixture between four well-greased deep scallop shells.
2. Melt the butter and stir in the breadcrumbs and capers. Sprinkle this over the fish mixture.
3. Put one slice of tomato on each shell and pipe mashed potatoes round the edge. Brown under a hot grill (broiler).

Sardine Rolls

Makes 6 large or 12 small snacks

Freeze 1 month (before reheating)

	Metric	Imperial	American
127 g/4½ oz can of sardines in oil	1	1	1
Streaky bacon rashers (slices)	6	6	6
Prepared mustard	5 ml	1 tsp	1 tsp
A few drops of Worcestershire sauce			

1. Drain the sardines. Remove the rind from the bacon and grill (broil) until the fat is 'milky'.
2. Spread each rasher (slice) with a little mustard and sprinkle with 1–2 drops of sauce. Roll each rasher (slice) round a sardine.
3. Return to the grill (broiler), and cook, turning, until the bacon is crisp. Serve very hot, cut in half if desired, and speared on cocktail sticks.

Fish Pie

Serves 3

Oven temp 220°C/425°F/Gas Mark 7

Freeze 1 month

	Metric	Imperial	American
275–350 g/10–12 oz cod fillet	1	1	1
White, Egg or Parsley Sauce (page 88)	275 ml	½ pt	1¼ cups
Grated rind of ½ lemon			
Salt and pepper			
Mashed potato (can be from pkt)	450 g	1 lb	1 lb
Butter	25 g	1 oz	2 tbls
Browned breadcrumbs			

1. Poach the fish (page 23), then drain, skin and flake. Mix with the sauce, lemon rind and seasoning.
2. Place in a greased 700 ml/1¼ pt/3 cup deep pie dish. Cover with mashed potato, dot with butter and sprinkle with crumbs. Bake at the temperature above for 20–25 minutes.

Note: A puff or flaky pastry lid can be used instead of potato.

Italian Baked Cod

Serves 3

Oven temp 190°C/375°F/Gas Mark 5

Freeze 1 month

	Metric	Imperial	American
Frozen pieces of			
cod fillet	450 g	1 lb	1 lb
(approx 150 g/	(approx)	(approx)	(approx)
5 oz each)	(3 pieces)	(3 pieces)	(3 pieces)
Butter for greasing			
Oil for frying	15 ml	1 tbls	1 tbls
Medium onion,			
chopped	1	1	1
226 g/7¼ oz can			
of tomatoes	1	1	1
Salt and pepper			
Dried mixed herbs	5 ml	1 tsp	1 tsp
Chopped celery	30 ml	2 tbls	2 tbls

1. Thaw the fillets, wash and dry and lay them in a buttered ovenproof dish.
2. In a saucepan, heat the oil and sauté the onion gently until soft. Add the tomatoes, a little seasoning and the herbs. Bring gently to the boil, reduce the heat and simmer, stirring, for 5 minutes, or until reduced to a purée. Stir in the celery.
3. Spoon the mixture over the cod. Cover with greased foil. Bake at the temperature above for 25–30 minutes.

Note: If you wish, sprinkle with grated Parmesan cheese 7–8 minutes before the end of the cooking time.

Smoked Mackerel Pâté

Serves 8

Freeze 1 month

	Metric	Imperial	American
700 g/1½ lb			
smoked mackerel	2	2	2
Salt and pepper			
Butter, softened	125 g	4 oz	½ cup
Single (light)			
cream	30 ml	2 tbls	2 tbls
Dry white wine	30 ml	2 tbls	2 tbls
Good pinch of			
ground allspice			
Black (ripe) olives,			
stoned (pitted),			
skinned and			
chopped	4–6	4–6	4–6

1. Remove head, skin and bones from the fish and flake with a fork.
2. Put the fish in a food processor or blender and start processing. With the motor running, add all the remaining ingredients in order, except the olives. Process only until just smooth.
3. Turn the pâté into a dish, knocking out the air-holes. Cover with foil or clingfilm and refrigerate until needed. Use within 24 hours if not frozen.
4. Just before serving, garnish with the olives.

Simmered Trout

Serves 2

Freeze 1 month (freeze sauce separately)

	Metric	Imperial	American
Frozen rainbow			
trout	2	2	2
Butter or			
margarine	75 g	3 oz	⅓ cup
Flour	15 ml	1 tbls	1 tbls
Good pinch of			
ground mace			
Good pinch of			
grated nutmeg			
Few grains of			
cayenne			
Chicken stock	450 ml	¾ pt	2 cups
Parsley sprigs	2	2	2
Bay leaf	1	1	1
Strip of lemon			
rind			
Dry white			
vermouth			
(optional)	15 ml	1 tbls	1 tbls
Salt and pepper			

1. Thaw, clean and behead trout. Trim the fins and tail, rinse and dry.
2. Melt the fat in a large deep heavy frying pan (skillet). Stir in the flour, spices and cayenne. Add the fish and brown them on each side.
3. Add the remaining ingredients. Bring to simmering point. Cover and cook gently for 15 minutes until the fish is tender but not soft.
4. Remove the fish to a warmed serving dish. Raise the heat and boil down the liquid a little to the thickness you want. Pour over the fish and serve hot.

Fishburgers

Serves 3–4

	Metric	Imperial	American
Cooked fish (see note)	225 g	8 oz	½ lb
Butter or margarine	25 g	1 oz	2 tbls
Mashed potato	225 g	8 oz	½ lb
Beaten egg to bind			
Seasoned flour or beaten egg and breadcrumbs			
Finely chopped parsley	15 ml	1 tbls	1 tbls
Salt and pepper			
Fat or oil for shallow frying			

1. Make sure that the fish is free of skin and bone. Flake it.
2. Melt the fat in a frying pan. Off the heat, mix in the fish, potato, parsley and seasoning, and enough beaten egg to bind. Mix thoroughly.
3. Turn the mixture onto a floured surface, and form into small flat cakes. Coat with seasoned flour, or with egg and breadcrumbs.
4. Fry gently in shallow fat, turning as required, until heated through and golden-brown on both sides.

Note: The type of fish, herb flavouring and coating can all be varied. Canned salmon, smoked haddock or smoked mackerel make excellent fish burgers. You could add a little tomato sauce or ketchup to canned salmon for a rosier colour and good flavour, or use chopped chives instead of parsley. Fine oatmeal or cracker crumbs flavoured with paprika make a good alternative to flour or breadcrumbs.

Fish Cakes

Serves 3–4

Cooking time 6–8 minutes

	Metric	Imperial	American
Cooked fish	225 g	8 oz	½ lb
Butter or margarine	25 g	1 oz	2 tbls
Mashed potatoes	225 g	8 oz	½ lb
Finely chopped parsley	15 ml	1 tbls	1 tbls
Salt and pepper			
Beaten egg to bind			
Seasoned flour or beaten egg and breadcrumbs			
Fat or oil for shallow frying			

1. Remove any bone or skin, and flake the fish. Melt the fat. Add the fish, potatoes, parsley and seasonings and mix in enough beaten egg to bind.
2. Turn the mixture onto a floured board and form into small flat cakes. Coat with flour or egg and breadcrumbs and shallow fry in fat or oil until golden-brown on both sides.

4
MEAT AND OFFAL

Quality of Meat

The best quality meat cuts used for roasting, grilling and frying come from the parts of the animal which are least exercised. The tougher or fattier, cheaper cuts are generally braised, stewed or boiled. Do not choose any cut, however, which has excessive fat on it or which has any discoloured fat. The fat on beef should be creamy-coloured, the fat on lamb or pork white and firm. Although young veal may have 'foamy' bubbles around the tender bones, the lean meat of an adult animal should be resilient and finely grained with a 'marbling' of fat between the fibres. Reject any meat with discoloured or mottled patches. Lean beef flesh should be bright red when first cut; lamb is dull red; pork and veal from very young animals are pale pink and darker pink from older animals.

Offal (Variety Meats)

Offal comprises the parts cut off the carcass before it is hung and jointed. The main offal meats are the brains, feet, head, heart, kidneys, liver, lungs sweetbreads, tail, tongue and tripe. Sausages and dripping are often classed as offal, and some people use the caul, lights and melts. Most offal meats are as nutritious as muscle meat or more so, and most are also much cheaper. The many traditional dishes using them provide tasty, nutritious, economical family meals.

Storing Meat

Meat which is neither frozen nor chilled when purchased must not be stored long. It should be unwrapped, wiped (not washed), then wrapped in plastic or foil without excluding air. Place on a plate in case the meat drips. Most meats can then be stored for 2–3 days in the coldest part of the refrigerator, although mince, sausages and offal should be used within a day of purchase.

COOKING MEAT

Since meat is expensive, consider carefully how you will cook each piece. By using the best method, you can make a cheap, tough cut as tender and as tasty as a prime one.

Top quality meats are suitable for cooking in dry heat, that is for roasting or baking, grilling and frying. Cheaper cuts generally need cooking in moist heat, i.e. pot-roasting, braising, boiling or stewing. In some methods, both dry and moist heat are used. For instance, braised or casseroled meat is usually sealed by frying before liquid is added to the pot.

MEAT CUTS AND THEIR COOKING METHODS

Meat Cuts (UK)	Cooking Method
BEEF	
Sirloin with or without fillet	High or low temp. roasting
Wing rib fillet	
Flat rib	
Forerib (on bone or boned and rolled)	
Top rib ⎫	Low temp. roasting,
Back rib ⎬ leg of mutton	pot-roasting or
cut	braising
(may be partly boned, and rolled)	
Thick flank (top rump)	
Topside	
Brisket, fresh (on bone or boned and rolled)	Pot-roasting, braising
Aitchbone	
Flank	Pot-roasting, braising,
Hindquarter flank	or boiling
Silverside (fresh)	(flank can be stewed
Salted brisket	or cubed and used in
Salted silverside	puddings and pies)
Salted flank (for pressed beef)	
Shin	Boiling
Chuck ⎫ shoulder	Casseroling and
Bladebone ⎭ (Scotland)	stewing
Clod	(Blade can be cubed
Sticking (neck)	and used in
Leg	puddings and pies)
Skirt	

Steaks

Fillet, Chateaubriand, tournedos, rump, porterhouse, sirloin, entrecôte, minute, T-bone	Grilling and frying

LAMB

Leg (fillet end) = gigot (Scotland) Shoulder (on bone or boned, stuffed and rolled) Saddle Loin (on bone, or boned, stuffed and rolled)	High or low temp. roasting
Best end of neck (on bone or boned, stuffed and rolled)	Low temp. roasting
Fillet Loin cutlets Chump chops Cutlets from Best end of neck (also used for hot-pots) Noisettes (boned Best end cutlets)	Grilling and frying
Half shoulder Breast	Low temp. roasting, pot-roasting, braising
Middle neck Leg (shank end)	Braising, stewing
Scrag end of neck Shank end of leg	Stewing, boiling

PORK

Tenderloin (pork fillet)	Grilling, frying or braising, also cubed or sliced for dishes using simmered meat, e.g. fricassées, vols-au-vent
Leg Fillet end Knuckle end (on bone or boned and stuffed)	High or low temp. roasting
Loin (on bone or boned, stuffed and rolled) Bladebone (on bone or boned and stuffed)	High or low temp. roasting (Bladebone can also be boiled, either fresh or pickled)
Hand and Spring (Hand and shank together)	Low temp. roasting, stewing or boiling
Hand (on bone or boned) Spare rib Chinese-style spare ribs (from rib case)	High or low temp. roasting or braising (Hand of pork can also be boiled)
American-style spare ribs (from belly)	Barbecuing
Belly (draft or flank pork), fresh or pickled	Braising, stewing or boiling (thick end of belly can also be roasted with or without stuffing)
Head Chap (lower jaw and cheek) fresh or salted Trotters	Boiling
Any lean cut	Cubed for pies, etc

Steaks (slices), chops and cutlets

Slices of fillet end of leg, spare rib chops, chump chops, middle or foreloin chops or cutlets	Grilling, frying, baking, braising or stewing

Note: In Scotland, the hand and spring with blade and ribs is called a shoulder; it is usually cut in half, boned, rolled and cut to order.

BACON AND GAMMON

Bacon forehock Butt (lean end of forehock) Fore slipper (also part of forehock) Prime collar End collar Gammon slipper Middle gammon Corner gammon Gammon hock	Boiling as joints (Bacon forehock can also be baked as a single piece. End collar is baked or boiled for pressing. Middle or corner gammon can be sliced and grilled as well as boiled. Gammon hocks can be parboiled, then baked.)
Streaky bacon (top streaky, prime streaky and thin streaky) Back bacon (flank, long back and oyster, short back, back and ribs, top back)	Cut into rashers (slices) for grilling and frying (Top and prime streaky bacon, back and ribs, or top back bacon, can be boiled in one piece. Top back bacon can also be braised in one piece or cut into chops.)

Note: A ham is either boiled or is parboiled, then baked.

VEAL

Leg	High or low temp. roasting in the piece; grilling or frying (slices). See also escalopes below.
Loin (on bone or boned, stuffed and rolled)	
Fillet	
Shoulder (oyster)	High or low temp. roasting, pot-roasting, braising, stewing. Can also be used cubed, in dishes such as fricassées, pies.
Breast (can be boned, stuffed and rolled)	Low temp. roasting, pot-roasting, braising and stewing
Best end of neck	Low temp. roasting, braising; also as cutlets, baking, grilling and frying
Middle neck	As cutlets, baking, braising and stewing; boned and cubed, as pie veal
Scrag	Stewing and boiling (Knuckle is used for Osso Bucco, page 63)
Hock	
Knuckle	

Chops, cutlets, escalopes, steaks

slices of fillet (steaks)	
loin chops, best end cutlets, thin slices from fleshy part of leg (English escalope) or from topside cut across grain (Continental escalopes)	Grilling and frying, baking, braising

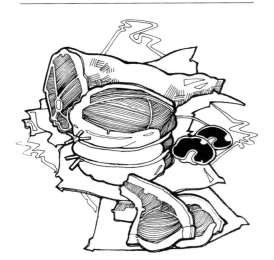

USUAL COOKING METHODS FOR OFFAL

Calves' and lambs' liver and kidneys	Grilling and frying
Lambs' fry (liver, lights, heart, melts, sweetbreads)	Frying
Ox liver	Frying, braising, in faggots etc.
Ox kidney	In puddings, pies
Calves' and lambs' brains, sweetbreads	Frying and braising
Ox-tail	Stewing
Cow heel, calf's foot, veal knuckle, pig's trotters	Stewing or boiling for stock, aspic. (Pig's trotters can be boned, crumbed and fried or fricasséed after boiling)
Ox tongue, fresh or pickled	Boiling, braising
Sheep's and pigs' tongues	Boiling, braising; also used in sauces dishes, e.g. fricassées
Ox heart, sheep's hearts, pigs' hearts	Stewing, braising, baking (Ox heart and sheep's hearts can be stuffed)
Calf's, pig's or sheep's head	Boiling, for use in brawn, etc
Tripe	Stewing
Marrow-bones	Boiling, baking

GENERAL DIRECTIONS FOR COOKING MEAT

1. Make sure that any frozen meat is completely thawed.
2. Wipe the meat with damp, soft kitchen paper. Do not wash it.
3. Take out any bone if required. (A craft butcher will generally bone out a joint of meat when you buy it. He will also score the rind on pork.)
4. Trim any surplus fat off the meat if the butcher has not already done so and put aside beef or pork fat for rendering down.
5. Marinate the meat if required. Coarser meat cuts in particular are often more tender and flavoursome if marinated before cooking, and can sometimes be treated like prime cuts, e.g. grilled or fried. Marinades are on page 92.
6. Wash salted meat well, or soak in fresh water if very salty.
7. Stuff or tie a joint into a neat shape if required, or trim small pieces neatly.

ROASTING

Roasting once meant cooking on a revolving spit before an open fire, but today oven-roasting (which is, in fact, baking) is the method normally used.

Roasting Times

Overcooked roast meat may be dry, stringy and flavourless. The shape, size and weight of a meat joint determine how long it should be cooked for. Obviously a thin, flat piece of meat cooks more quickly than a square piece of the same weight because the heat reaches its centre faster. Likewise, a joint with a bone cooks faster than a boned and rolled joint because the bone conducts heat faster than solid muscle does. It is therefore wise to allow a few minutes more cooking time than is given in the Table below if you are cooking a squarish or boned and rolled joint. It is also wise to give a stuffed joint a little extra time to make sure the stuffing is very thoroughly cooked.

Other factors which affect the cooking time are:

(a) a large joint takes less time for its weight than a small one;
(b) a joint roasted in a covered pan, wrapped in foil or in a roasting bag may take a little longer than one roasted in an open pan. See below.

A foolproof way to ensure that meat is fully cooked but not overcooked is to use a meat thermometer. Insert it in the thickest part of a joint, without touching bone, just before you put the meat in the oven. When the thermometer registers the right internal temperature (see the Table of Cooking Times), the meat is done. This takes any uncertainty out of using roasting as a cooking technique although you will still need to work out how long it will take by weight, to know when to start cooking.

TABLE OF TIMES FOR OVEN-ROASTING MEAT

Meat	High temp. roasting	Low temp. roasting	Meat thermometer temp.
	210°C/420°F/Gas Mark 6 or 7	160°C/325°F/Gas Mark 3	
Beef with bone	15/20 min per 450 g/1 lb + 15 min extra	25 min per 450 g/1 lb + 25 min extra	60°C/140°F (Very rare; good cold)
Beef without bone, rolled	20/25 min per 450 g/1 lb + 20/25 min extra	30/35 min per 450 g/1 lb + 30/35 min extra	70°C/158°F (Medium rare; pinkish inside when cold)
Lamb with bone	20/25 min per 450 g/1 lb + 20/25 min extra	30/35 min per 450 g/1 lb + 30/35 min extra	77°C/170°F (Well done; dryish cold)
Lamb without bone, rolled	25 min per 450 g/1 lb + 25 min extra	30/35 min per 450 g/1 lb + 30/35 min extra	82°C/180°F
Pork with bone	30 min per 450 g/1 lb + 30 min extra	40/45 min per 450 g/1 lb + 40/45 min extra	88°C/190°F
Pork without bone, rolled	35 min per 450 g/1 lb + 35 min extra	not recommended unless you ensure that the internal temperature of the meat reaches at least 88°C/190°F	
Veal with bone	25 min per 450 g/1 lb + 25 min extra	30/35 min per 450 g/1 lb + 30/35 min extra	82°C/180°F
Veal without bone, rolled	30 min per 450 g/1 lb + 30 min extra	40 min per 450 g/1 lb + 30 min extra	

Covered Roasting

Season well and add a little well-flavoured stock or wine to the pan or foil wrapping. Uncover or open the foil wrapping for the last 30 minutes of the cooking time.

Roasting bags and wraps, designed to keep the oven clean, can be used. Sprinkle a little flour into the bag before cooking and use to make pan-juice gravy at the end of cooking. Follow the supplier's instructions for cooking and open the bag for the last 30 minutes of the cooking time.

Pot-roasting is a form of covered roasting especially suited to coarse joints. The meat is seared all over in hot fat in a deep pan or casserole. It is then oven-cooked in the pan or casserole on a wire rack, or with root vegetables and a little liquid as in braising. The pan or casserole is tightly covered, and the meat is roasted slowly at 150–160°C/300–325°F/Gas Mark 2–3 for about 45 minutes per 450 g/1 lb.

General Instructions for Roasting

1. Choose a roasting pan which will just hold the meat and any potatoes you roast with it. (For cooking roast potatoes, see page 99.) Alternatively, place the meat on a trivet or rack in the pan, with its fattiest side uppermost and its largest cut surfaces exposed. Insert a meat thermometer if using one.
2. Brush the meat with fat or oil, or put 2 or 3 knobs of dripping on top. Do not salt the flesh, but after brushing with oil, salt the scored rind of pork for crisp crackling.
3. Place the meat in the oven, and cook for the time calculated. If you need to turn it during cooking, use tongs or two spoons, not a fork. Piercing the meat will let the juices run out.
4. During cooking, baste often with the fat and juices in the pan. If you wish, froth the meat by sprinkling with flour and salt 20 minutes before the end of the cooking time to crisp the surface.
5. Let the meat 'rest' on a warmed carving dish at room temperature while you make gravy and dish up vegetables. It will be easier to carve.

Standard Accompaniments for Roast Meats

Beef: Roast potatoes (page 99), Yorkshire pudding (page 167), horseradish cream (page 91), gravy;

Mutton: Roast potatoes, redcurrant jelly, onion sauce (page 88), gravy;

Lamb: New potatoes (page 99), garden peas (page 102), mint sauce (page 91), redcurrant jelly, gravy;

Pork: Roast potatoes, sage and onion forcemeat balls or stuffing, apple sauce (page 86), gravy;

Veal: Roast or creamed potatoes, basic herb forcemeat balls or stuffing (page 93), bacon rolls (page 75), gravy.

Beef Pot-Roast

Oven temp 150°C/300°F/Gas Mark 2

Freeze 2 months

	Metric	Imperial	American
Brisket of beef, boned and rolled	1.8 kg	4 lb	4 lb
Salt and pepper			
Dripping or lard	25 g	1 oz	2 tbls
Onion stuck with 2 cloves	1	1	1
Water	275 ml	½ pt	1¼ cups
Optional vegetables			
Carrots, halved lengthways	4	4	4
Small onions, halved	4	4	4
Brown Stock, page 14 (optional)	175 ml	6 fl oz	¾ cup

1. Tie the meat if necessary wipe it and pat dry. Season it lightly.
2. Heat the fat in a large flameproof casserole (Dutch oven). Fry the meat in the fat until browned on all sides.
3. Add the onion and the water. Cover the casserole tightly. Put in the oven at the temperature above for 3 hours. Baste 2 or 3 times while cooking.
4. If adding vegetables, take the meat out of the casserole 1 hour before the end of the cooking time. Put in the vegetables and replace the meat on top of them. Cover and return to the oven.
5. Remove the meat and vegetables to a serving dish and keep warm. Skim excess fat off the juices in the casserole. Swill round and scrape up any crusted juices. Season. If more gravy is wanted than the liquid supplies, add the brown stock. Reheat to boiling point, and strain into a warmed gravy boat. Serve with the meat and vegetables.

GRILLING

Grilled (broiled) foods are cooked by radiant heat. This method is only suited to small prime cuts of meat, i.e. tender chops and cutlets, top quality steaks, calves' or lambs' liver and kidneys, gammon steaks (slices), sausages and gammon or back bacon rashers (slices); any coarser meat stays tough. Beef steaks can be up to 4.5 cm/1¾ in thick, but other meats should be 1.5 cm/½ in thick or less. Most meat is improved by marinating in Basic Marinade (page 92) for at least 2 hours before cooking.

General Directions for Grilling Meat

1. Prepare the meat. Trim excess fat off steaks or chops, and snip the edges of escalopes, sliced gammon or bacon to prevent curling. Marinate beef, lamb, pork or veal if wished.
2. Preheat the grill (broiler), if necessary. (Please refer to the users' handbook supplied with your cooker.) Grease the grid.
3. Season the meat with pepper, and brush lightly all over with fat or oil.
4. Place the meat on the grid, and grill (broil) under high heat until lightly browned. Turn over with tongs or a spatula; do not pierce with a fork. Brown the second side quickly. Reduce the heat to cook the meat through if required, turning once or twice. Serve very hot.

Grilling Times

Grill (broil) medium-thick steaks (2 cm/¾ in thick) for 5–6 minutes for rare, 7–8 minutes for medium-rare or 8–10 minutes for well done. A 4 cm/1¾ in fillet steak will need 6–8 minutes for rare, 8–10 minutes for medium, 10–12 minutes for well done. Thicker steaks will take a few moments longer. Very thin steaks may be ready by the time they are browned.

Chops will take 12–18 minutes to cook through. Seal both sides under high heat, then reduce the heat and cook gently. Cutlets will cook through in 8–10 minutes, crumbed escalopes in 5–6, thin slices, e.g. bacon, in 4 minutes.

Standard Accompaniments for Grilled Meats

Mashed potatoes (page 99), potato straws (page 99) or crisps; Maître d'Hôtel Butter (page 143); grilled tomatoes (page 106); grilled mushrooms (page 104); fresh watercress sprigs.

SAUSAGES

Pork or beef sausages (with or without skins) can be grilled, 'dry' fried or baked with hardly any fat. Some sausages, such as black puddings and horseshoe-shaped continental boiling rings, are boiled. Other continental sausages, such as frank-furters, can be steamed while Spanish chorizo and similar spicy sausages are usually cut up and sim-mered in casseroles.

There are also many types of sausage such as liver sausage, mortadella and salami which are sold ready for eating. Your supplier will tell you which kinds he stocks, and which contain garlic.

To prepare British sausages for cooking, separate them into links. Moisten them well with tepid water to soften the skins; do not prick them.

To grill, heat the grill if necessary, until mod-erately hot, and grease the grid. Place the sausages on the grid, and cook, turning frequently, until brown and glossy on all sides; 50 g/2 oz sausages will take 15–20 minutes to cook through, 25 g/1 oz sausages (chipolatas) 10–12 minutes, 15 g/½ oz cocktail sausages 6–7 minutes.

To fry, film a frying pan (skillet) with fat by rubbing with pork rind or lard. Put in the sau-sages, and turn often over low heat until cooked through and browned; they take about the same time as when grilled.

To bake, film a baking tin (pan) with fat. Heat the oven to 200°C/400°F/Gas Mark 6. Put the pan con-taining the sausages in the oven, and cook, turn-ing 3 or 4 times, until browned on all sides. 50 g/2 oz sausages will take 30 minutes, chipolatas 20 minutes, cocktail sausages 12 minutes.

Notes:
1. Cumberland Sausage is a local type of pork sausage without links. Coil up the whole long sausage like a Catherine Wheel on a greased baking sheet. Bake in the oven at 160°C/325°F/Gas Mark 3 for 30–45 minutes, depending on thickness.
2. Mutton or venison sausages are made by a few craft butchers. Cook as for pork or beef saus-ages, but give venison sausages a few minutes longer to ensure they are cooked through.

Grilled or Barbecued Piquant Chops

Serves 8

Freeze 2 months (chops and butter separately)

	Metric	Imperial	American
Piquant Butter			
Softened butter	*225 g*	*8 oz*	*1 cup*
Capers, drained			
and chopped	*45 ml*	*3 tbls*	*3 tbls*
Soft brown sugar	*10 ml*	*2 tsp*	*2 tsp*
Chops			
Best end or loin			
lamb chops (see			
note)	*8*	*8*	*8*
Pepper			
Butter	*225 g*	*8 oz*	*1 cup*
Clear honey	*30 ml*	*2 tbls*	*2 tbls*
White wine			
vinegar	*30 ml*	*2 tbls*	*2 tbls*
Salt			
Rosemary sprigs	*8*	*8*	*8*

1. Make the Piquant Butter by mixing all the ingredients thoroughly. Shape into 16 flat round pats, and chill.
2. Trim 2.5 cm/1 in of the bone ends of the chops, scraping off the meat. Rub the meat with pepper on both sides.
3. Heat the butter, honey and vinegar in a saucepan until the butter melts. Mix well. Brush both sides of the chops with the mixture.

4. Cook the chops under moderate grill (broiler) heat, or on a barbecue grill, for 8–10 minutes on each side. Baste often with the butter mixture while cooking. Season lightly. Make small slit in one side of each chop and insert a rosemary sprig.
5. Wrap the bared bone ends of the chops in foil, then offer as portable or barbecued food.

Note: To vary, use chump chops.

Grilled Lamb Cutlets or Chops

Serves 6

Not suitable for freezing

	Metric	Imperial	American
Lamb cutlets or chops, 2–2.5 cm/¾ – 1 in thick	6	6	6
Salt and pepper			
Oil for brushing			
Medium tomatoes	3	3	3
Mashed potato (page 99)	450 g	1 lb	1 lb
Pats of Maître d'Hôtel Butter (page 143)	6	6	6
Watercress sprigs			

1. Trim any excess fat or skin off the meat. Scrape the ends of the bones clean of meat. Wipe with dampened soft kitchen paper.
2. Season the meat and brush with oil. Heat the grill (broiler), if necessary, and grease the grid.
3. Cut the tomatoes in half across. Brush with oil, and season with salt and pepper.
4. Arrange the cutlets or chops on the grid. Cook under the grill until lightly browned.
5. Turn the cutlets or chops with tongs. Add the tomatoes, cut side up.
6. Brown the second side of the meat. Reduce the heat and cook slowly until cooked through. The outside fat should be crisp and the flesh slightly pink inside when cut. Remove the tomatoes as soon as they are tender; they will be ready before the chops. Place them in the centre of a warmed serving platter.
7. Pipe the mashed potato in a border around the platter.
8. As soon as the cutlets or chops are done, place them on the platter with the bone ends resting on the potato border. Place a pat of Maître d'Hôtel butter on each piece of meat. Garnish the platter with watercress sprigs.

Variation
275 ml/½ pt/1¼ cups Fresh Tomato Sauce (page 90) can be served with the meat instead of grilled tomatoes.

Grilled Kidneys and Bacon

Serves 4

Not suitable for freezing

	Metric	Imperial	American
Sheep's kidneys	8	8	8
Back bacon rashers (slices) without rind	4	4	4
Melted butter or oil	30 ml	2 tbls	2 tbls
Salt and pepper			
Square slices of fried bread without crusts	4	4	4
Chopped parsley			

1. Skin the kidneys and cut them through from the core side, almost to the back. Nick out the split core. Wipe with dampened soft kitchen paper. Cut the bacon rashers (slices) in half.
2. Thread a small poultry skewer through each open kidney, to keep it flat. Brush the kidneys with melted butter or oil. Heat the grill (broiler), if necessary, and grease the grid.
3. Place the kidneys on the grid, cut side up. Add the bacon. Grill (broil) for 5–7 minutes, turning as required and basting the kidneys with fat if needed.
4. When cooked, remove the skewers. Season the kidneys well, and place 2 on each piece of fried bread. Arrange on 4 warmed plates, and garnish each plate with 2 slices of bacon. Sprinkle the kidneys with chopped parsley.

Variation
For *Liver and Bacon*, use 8 slices of calves' or lambs' liver instead of kidneys. Dredge with seasoned flour before brushing with oil. Serve with mashed potato (page 99) instead of fried bread.

Lamb Kebabs

Serves 4

Not suitable for freezing

	Metric	Imperial	American
Lean boned lamb from leg or shoulder	450 g	1 lb	1 lb
Basic Uncooked Marinade, (page 92)			
Lambs' kidneys, skinned	4	4	4
Medium tomatoes	4	4	4
Green pepper, de-seeded	1	1	1
Button mushrooms	8–12	8–12	8–12
Fresh bay leaves			
Salt and pepper			
Oil for brushing			
Yellow Rice (page 119)			

1. Cut the lamb into 2.5 cm/1 in cubes. Marinate overnight in Basic Marinade.
2. Cut the kidneys in half and core them. Quarter the tomatoes. Cut the pepper into pieces and blanch in boiling water for 3 minutes.
3. Remove the lamb from the marinade, together with a few larger pieces of onion. Pat dry.
4. Thread the lamb cubes, kidney, tomatoes, pepper, mushrooms, bay leaves and onion onto 4 long skewers. Season well and brush with oil. Heat the grill (broiler), if necessary, and grease the grid.
5. Grill (broil) the kebabs, turning them often, until the meat is cooked. For pink lamb, allow about 10 minutes, for well-done lamb, 15 minutes.
6. Serve on Yellow Rice.

FRYING

Frying is used for the same high-quality cuts as grilling (broiling), the only difference being that some pieces of lamb, veal and offal may be egged and crumbed instead of being marinated before frying. Steaks, bacon and sausages are most often 'dry-fried' in a pan just filmed with fat or oil. Other solid pieces of meat, e.g. cutlets or floured sliced calves' liver, are usually shallow-fried in 3–5 mm/ 1/8–1/4 in fat or oil. Made-up meat items such as rissoles may be deep-fried.

The fat used may be clarified dripping (for beef), lard (for pork) or a mixture of butter and oil, which is generally thought the best for frying safety and flavour. 'Dry' and shallow frying times are the same as for grilling.

General Directions for Frying Meat

1. Prepare the meat as for grilling (broiling), page 43.
2. If the recipe requires, dip foods in seasoned flour, then in egg and breadcrumbs. Food to be deep-fried can be dipped in coating batter or thin batter and crumbs (page 170) instead.
3. To 'dry' fry, grease a frying pan (skillet) with just enough fat or oil to film the bottom; bacon generally needs no fat. Sear the food until browned on both sides, turning with tongs. Reduce the heat and cook gently until done. To shallow fry, put 3–5 mm/1/8–1/4 in depth of fat or oil in the pan, and make it very hot. Fry the food on both sides until golden-brown, turning with tongs. Reduce the heat, and cook gently until done. To deep fry, use a fairly large, heavy-based saucepan with a frying basket which just fits it. Fill the pan a third full of oil and put in the basket. Heat the oil, and test for correct temperature by using a thermometer or the bread cube test (page 32). Cook the items until golden-brown.
4. Drain shallow-fried and deep-fried items well on soft kitchen paper before serving.

Notes on Other Types of Frying

Sautéing Small pieces of meat or offal are sometimes sautéed, that is shaken and tossed in a shallow pan containing a little hot fat. This method is used to keep items moist, to bring out flavour or to give a golden surface finish. It is used, for instance, to cook kidneys or small thin strips of meat or poultry, to flavour braising vegetables before use, or to give sliced cooked potatoes a golden crust. A mixture of butter and oil should be used. The pan should be covered and shaken when cooking raw food to keep in moisture, but should be left open and the food turned with a spatula to crisp cooked food.

Stir-frying In this oriental method, very small pieces of raw food are sautéed quickly and briefly in an open pan. Assorted foods are prepared ahead and grouped according to how long they take to cook. Oil is heated in the pan, and the foods are put in at intervals and stirred in the fat until cooked through but still crisp. They are then seasoned and served at once.

Peppered Steaks

Serves 4

Freeze 1 month prepared raw steaks

	Metric	Imperial	American
Fillet, entrecôte or sirloin steaks, about 200 g/7 oz each	4	4	4

	Metric	Imperial	American
Whole black peppercorns	15 ml	1 tbls	1 tbls
Whole white peppercorns	10 ml	2 tsp	2 tsp
Garlic clove, skinned	1	1	1
Oil	60 ml	4 tbls	4 tbls
Unsalted butter	50 g	2 oz	1/4 cup
Pats of Maître d'Hôtel Butter (page 143)	4	4	4

1. Trim the steaks neatly. Wipe with dampened soft kitchen paper.
2. Grind the black and white peppercorns coarsely in a food processor or mill.
3. Cut the garlic clove in half and rub it over both sides of each steak. Brush the steaks with oil, then press the peppercorns into the surface of each steak on both sides.
4. Heat the butter in a frying pan (skillet). When very hot, put in the steaks and sear for one minute on each side, turning with tongs. Reduce the heat to low, and fry for 5 minutes for rare steak, about 7 minutes for medium-rare steak and about 9 minutes for well-done steak. Turn with tongs 2 or 3 times while frying.
5. Remove the steaks with the tongs to a warmed serving dish. Place a pat of Maître d'Hôtel Butter on each and serve at once.

Tournedos Steaks with Pâté

Serves 4

Not suitable for freezing

	Metric	Imperial	American
Tournedos steaks	4	4	4
Unsalted butter and oil for shallow frying			
Rounds of crisp fried bread slightly bigger than bases of steaks	4	4	4
Medium sweet sherry	50 ml	2 fl oz	1/4 cup
Brown Stock (page 14)	100 ml	4 fl oz	1/2 cup
Espagnole Sauce (page 86)	100 ml	4 fl oz	1/2 cup
Salt and petter			
Unsalted butter	25 g	1 oz	2 tbls
Round slices of good quality liver pâté	4	4	4
Small watercress sprigs			

1. Trim and wipe the tournedos. Tie into a neat shape. Pat dry.
2. Heat enough butter and oil in a deep frying pan to give 5 mm/1/4 in depth. When very hot, put in the tournedos and fry quickly until seared all over but still rare in the centre. Remove the pan from the heat and take out the steaks. Place the rounds of fried bread on a warmed serving platter and stand one steak on each. Keep warm.
3. Return the pan to low heat, and stir in the sherry and stock. Swill round, then scrape up any drippings with a spoon. Add the Espagnole Sauce and simmer down to the strength and flavour you want.
4. Heat the 25 g/1 oz/2 tbls unsalted butter in a small pan. When very hot, put in the liver pâté slices. Sear quickly on each side, to brown them lightly without melting them. Remove and place one on each tournedos. Place a tiny sprig of watercress on each steak, and garnish the platter with the remainder. Serve at once with the sauce.

Beef Stroganoff

Serves 4

Not suitable for freezing

	Metric	Imperial	American
Fillet steak	700 g	1 1/2 lb	1 1/2 lb
Seasoned flour			
Onions, thinly sliced	275 g	10 oz	10 oz
Mushrooms, thinly sliced	225 g	8 oz	1/2 lb
Sour cream	225 ml	8 fl oz	1 cup
Butter	50 g	2 oz	1/4 cup
Salt and pepper			
Hot cooked rice	700 g	1 1/2 lb	1 1/2 lb

1. Trim any fat off the steak and beat it flat. Slice it if needed, and cut into thin strips. Dust very lightly with seasoned flour.
2. Heat half the butter in the pan over fairly high heat and sauté the onions for about 4 minutes until soft and golden. Add the mushrooms, and sauté for a further 2 minutes. Remove the onions and mushrooms, shake them gently over the pan to drain, then put aside to keep warm.
3. Add the remaining butter to the pan, and allow to get very hot. Put in half the steak, and sauté rapidly for 2–3 minutes. Remove and add to the cooked onions and mushrooms. Repeat the process, using the remaining steak.
4. Return the meat and vegetables on the plate to the pan, and heat together for 1 minute, shaking the pan. Lower the heat, pour in the sour cream, and allow to heat but not boil. Season, and serve at once over the rice.

Veal Escalopes (Wiener Schnitzel)

Serves 4

Freeze 1 month (prepared raw escalopes)

	Metric	Imperial	American
Thin veal escalopes (12.5 x 7 cm/5 x 3 in)	4	4	4
Egg	1	1	1
A few drops of oil			
Dried white breadcrumbs for coating			
Salt and pepper			
Butter and oil for shallow frying			
Anchovy fillets, drained	8	8	8
Lemon slices	4	4	4
Chopped parsley			
Stock and butter (see recipe) or Browned Butter (page 86)			

1. Beat out the escalopes until very thin. Leave to 'rest' for 30 minutes. Wipe with dampened soft kitchen paper.
2. Beat the egg with the oil in a shallow dish. Season the crumbs with salt and pepper. Dip the escalopes in the egg, then coat with crumbs, pressing them on firmly.
3. Heat about 3 mm/⅛ in depth of butter and oil in a frying pan (skillet). Fry 2 escalopes only at a time for 4–6 minutes on each side, turning once only with tongs. Keep the first 2 warm while frying the remaining escalopes. Add more butter and oil if needed.
4. When fried, put 2 crossed anchovy fillets on each escalope, top with a lemon slice, and arrange on a flat serving plate. Keep warm.
5. Stir a little stock and a teaspoon of butter into the juices and fat in the frying pan, swirl round, and heat through. Serve as a sauce with the escalopes. Alternatively, serve Browned Butter.

Note: There are a great many different garnishes and sauces for these simply fried escalopes. Almost every part of Europe has its own version.

Variations
1. Serve each escalope with a poached or fried egg. Garnish with little clumps of chopped beetroot, chopped gherkin, whole green olives and capers.
2. Fry the escalopes for 4 minutes only on each side. Top each with a thin slice of cooked ham and 15 ml/1 tbls grated Parmesan cheese. Spoon some of the frying butter over the cheese, cover the pan and cook gently for 3 minutes or until the cheese is half melted.

Sautéed Kidneys

Serves 4

Freeze 1 month (kidney mixture and rice ring separately)

	Metric	Imperial	American
Ring of boiled rice, made with 225 g/8 oz/½ lb raw long grain rice (page 119)			
Lambs' kidneys	4	4	4
Butter	25 g	1 oz	2 tbls
Small onion, finely chopped	½	½	½
Chopped parsley	15 ml	1 tbls	1 tbls
Salt and pepper			
Coating Brown Sauce (page 85)	150 ml	¼ pt	⅔ cup
Sherry	15 ml	1 tbls	1 tbls

1. Prepare the ring of boiled rice (page 119) on a flat serving dish and keep it warm.
2. Skin and core the kidneys, and slice thinly.
3. Heat the butter in a frying pan (skillet), add the onion, and sauté until soft and golden. Add the kidney and 10 ml/2 tsp chopped parsley, and stir, turning over in the fat and shaking the pan, until the kidney slices change colour.
4. Season and add the Brown Sauce and sherry. Stir round once and bring to the boil.
5. Pour the mixture into the rice ring and garnish with the remaining parsley.

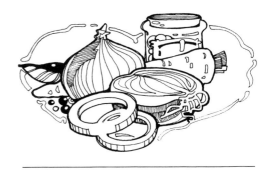

Opposite: *Veal Escalopes may be served with a variety of garnishes, capers, olives and gherkins go particularly well with them.*

Hamburgers

Serves 6

Freeze 1 month

	Metric	Imperial	American
Lean beef mince	550 g	1¼ lb	1¼ lb
Grated onion	15 ml	1 tbls	1 tbls
Pepper			
Worcestershire sauce			
Coarse salt			
Tomato slices	6	6	6
Fried onion rings (page 98)	12	12	12
Chopped parsley			

1. Use finely minced meat; pre-packaged mince is often coarse and fatty.
2. Mix together the mince, onion and a good grinding of pepper. Add 1–3 drops Worcestershire sauce.
3. Form the mixture into 6 round flat patties about 1 cm/½ in thick.
4. Sprinkle a thin layer of salt in a frying pan (skillet). Put in the patties. Place over fairly high heat, and 'dry' fry for 4 minutes or until the patties are evenly browned underneath. Turn them over, and fry for 30–60 seconds, then continue cooking over reduced heat for 1–2 minutes. Rare hamburgers may not need any cooking at the reduced heat.
5. Sprinkle each hamburger with a little more Worcestershire sauce. Top with a tomato slice and 2 onion rings. Sprinkle with parsley.

BAKING

Baked meats are small cuts of meat or offal cooked in the oven in moderate heat, usually with a savoury sauce or vegetables, and generally in a fairly shallow dish, covered with a lid, foil or paper. Small items such as cutlets may be completely wrapped in foil or paper and placed on a baking sheet; they are then said to be baked 'en papillote' (pronounced 'on pap-ee-ot'). Small whole fish or fish steaks are also often cooked like this.

Instead of a lid, the meat or other food may be covered with a pastry crust or batter. Pies and savoury or sweet batter puddings are among the most popular baked foods.

Baked main dishes are convenient because they need almost no attention while cooking, their vegetables and sauce can often be cooked with them, and many can be prepared ahead of time.

Baked Pork Chops

Serves 4

Oven temp 160°C/325°F/Gas Mark 3

Freeze 1 month

	Metric	Imperial	American
Spare-rib pork chops	4	4	4
Oil for frying	30 ml	2 tbls	2 tbls
Small onions, chopped	2	2	2
Small green pepper, de-seeded and thinly sliced	1	1	1
Mushrooms, sliced	100 g	4 oz	1 cup
Beef stock cube	1	1	1
Boiling water	150 ml	¼ pt	⅔ cup
Concentrated tomato paste	30 ml	2 tbls	2 tbls
Lemon juice	30 ml	2 tbls	2 tbls
Salt and pepper			

1. Trim and wipe the chops. Heat the oil in a deep frying pan (skillet) or shallow flameproof casserole (Dutch oven). Fry the chops until browned on both sides.
2. If using a frying pan, warm a shallow baking dish with a lid in the oven.
3. Add the onion, pepper and mushrooms to the meat.
4. Dissolve the stock cube in the water, then stir in the tomato paste and lemon juice. Season well, and pour over the meat and vegetables. Bring to simmering point.
5. If using a frying pan, transfer the contents to the warmed baking dish, and return it to the oven. If using a flameproof casserole, put it in the oven.
6. Bake, covered, at the temperature above for 1–1¼ hours.

Lamb Steaks in Foil

Serves 4

Oven temp 190°C/375°F/Gas Mark 5
220°C/425°F/Gas Mark 7

Freeze 1 month

	Metric	Imperial	American
Lamb shoulder steaks	4	4	4
Salt and pepper			
Butter, softened	25 g	1 oz	2 tbls
French mustard	30 ml	2 tbls	2 tbls
Chopped fresh parsley	30 ml	2 tbls	2 tbls
Capers, drained	15 ml	1 tbls	1 tbls

	Metric	Imperial	American
Good pinch of cayenne pepper			
Squeeze of lemon juice			
Garlic clove, skinned and crushed	1	1	1
Small onion, cut into rings	1	1	1

1. Trim the steaks neatly, and wipe them. Season each with pepper.
2. Mix together the butter, mustard, parsley, capers, cayenne, lemon juice and salt to taste. Mix in the garlic clove.
3. Place each steak on a large square of foil. Spread each with 'devilled' butter and top with a few onion rings. Fold up the foil to enclose the steaks and seal well. Place the parcels on a baking sheet.
4. Bake at the first temperature above for 45 minutes. Open the foil, raise the heat, and cook at the second temperature for 15 minutes to crisp the fat.

Baked Liver

Serves 4–6

Oven temp 180°C/350°F/Gas Mark 4

Freeze 1 month

	Metric	Imperial	American
Calves' liver	450 g	1 lb	1 lb
Butter or margarine for greasing			
Fresh white breadcrumbs	75 g	3 oz	1½ cups
Chopped parsley	5 ml	1 tsp	1 tsp
Dried mixed herbs	1.5 ml	¼ tsp	¼ tsp
Small onion, grated	1	1	1
Salt and pepper			
Tomato ketchup	30 ml	2 tbls	2 tbls
Back bacon rashers (slices) without rind	4–6	4–6	4–6
Beef stock (from cube)	150 ml	¼ pt	⅔ cup

1. Slice the liver thinly, wipe and pat dry. Overlap the slices in a greased shallow 22–23 cm/8½–9 in baking dish or pie plate.
2. Mix together the breadcrumbs, parsley, herbs, onion and seasoning, and moisten with the ketchup.
3. Spread this stuffing mixture over the liver. Arrange the bacon in an overlapping layer on top.

4. Pour in the stock down the side of the dish. Cover with a lid or foil. Cook at the temperature above for 1 hour. Uncover for the last 15 minutes to crisp the bacon. Serve with a green vegetable.

Moussaka

Serves 4

Oven temp 180°C/350°F/Gas Mark 4

Freeze 1 month

	Metric	Imperial	American
230 g/8 oz can of tomatoes	1	1	1
Small potatoes, peeled	450 g	1 lb	1 lb
Butter or margarine	50 g	2 oz	¼ cup
Minced (ground) raw beef or lamb	450 g	1 lb	1 lb
Onion, chopped	1	1	1
Mushrooms, sliced	100 g	4 oz	1 cup
Worcestershire sauce	5 ml	1 tsp	1 tsp
Salt and pepper			
Well-seasoned coating White Sauce (page 84)	275 ml	½ pt	1¼ cups
Grated Cheddar cheese	45 ml	3 tbls	3 tbls
Fresh white breadcrumbs	45 ml	3 tbls	3 tbls

1. Drain and roughly chop the tomatoes.
2. Slice the potatoes thinly. Sauté them in the fat, in a deep pan, until lightly browned. Remove the potatoes from the pan.
3. Put the meat, onion and mushrooms in the pan, and sauté until the meat is browned all over. Add the tomatoes, Worcestershire sauce and seasoning.
4. Place a third of the potatoes in an even layer in the bottom of a greased 1.2 l/2¼ pt/4½ cup casserole. Cover with half the meat mixture, make a centre layer of potatoes, then put in the remaining meat in an even layer and cover with potatoes.
5. Cover with the White Sauce, then sprinkle with the cheese and breadcrumbs. Bake at the temperature above for 45–50 minutes.

Note: 2 or 3 aubergines (eggplants) may be used in place of the potatoes. Peel and slice them onto a plate, sprinkle generously with salt and leave to stand for 30 minutes to draw out the bitter juices. Rinse and dry before cooking in the butter or margarine as for potatoes.

Parslied Hearts

Serves 4

Oven temp 180°C/350°F/Gas Mark 4

Freeze 2 months

	Metric	Imperial	American
Large lambs' hearts	4	4	4
Salt and pepper			
Chopped parsley	30–45 ml	2–3 tbls	2–3 tbls
Butter	50 g	2 oz	¼ cup
Small new potatoes or canned potatoes	8	8	8
Beef stock (from cube) or tomato juice	150 ml	¼ pt	⅔ cup
Worcestershire sauce	5 ml	1 tsp	1 tsp

1. Cut excess fat off the hearts. With scissors, snip out any tubes and the membranes which divide the hearts inside. Wipe well.
2. Season the hearts inside with salt and pepper. Half-fill each with parsley and add about 2.5 ml/½ tsp of the butter. Close the tops of the hearts with very small poultry skewers.

3. Sauté the hearts and potatoes in the remaining butter in a frying pan (skillet), until the hearts are lightly browned on all sides. Add the stock or juice and Worcestershire sauce, and bring to the boil.
4. Transfer the whole contents of the pan to a baking dish or shallow casserole with a lid, scraping out any solid crusty bits in the pan. Cover the dish or casserole tightly.
5. Cook in the oven at the temperature above for 45 minutes–1 hour. Serve from the dish with the liquid as gravy.

Notes:
1. Other stuffings, e.g. Basic Herb Stuffing (page 93), can be used. 15 g/½ oz stuffing is enough for 1 heart.
2. Calves' hearts can be baked in the same way.
3. One or two lambs' hearts make a good meal for a person eating alone.

Cornish Pasties

Makes 6

Oven temp 190°C/375°F/Gas Mark 5

Freeze 2 months

	Metric	Imperial	American
Braising or stewing steak	350 g	12 oz	¾ lb
Large potato	1	1	1

Cornish Pasties.

Toad-in-the-Hole.

Small onion, chopped	1	1	1
Salt and pepper			
Beef stock or water to moisten if needed			
Recipe quantity Shortcrust Pastry/basic pie dough (page 150)			

1. Prepare the meat as for Steak and Kidney Pie (page 54) but cut into tiny dice. Peel and dice the potato.
2. Mix the meat, potato and onion, and season. Moisten if needed.
3. Roll out the pastry and cut into 6 rounds with a 12.5 cm/5 in cutter, saucer or saucepan lid.
4. Divide the filling between the pastry rounds, placing on one half only. Fold the uncovered half over the filling and press the edges to seal. Turn the pasties so that the joined edges are on top. Pinch the sealed edges to make a frill.
5. Place on a baking sheet, and bake at the temperature above for 50 minutes. Serve hot or cold.

Variation
For extra meaty pastries, add 2 tsp. beef stock granules to pastry mix before adding water.

Toad-in-the-Hole

Serves 4

Oven temp 220°C/425°F/Gas Mark 7

Not suitable for freezing

	Metric	Imperial	American
Plain flour	100 g	4 oz	1 cup
Pinch of salt			
Large egg	1	1	1
Milk and water mixed, or light beer	275 ml	½ pt	1¼ cups
Dripping	25 g	1 oz	2 tbls
Sausages	350–450 g	¾–1 lb	¾–1 lb

1. Make a batter with the flour, salt, egg and liquid as for Yorkshire Pudding (page 167).
2. Put the dripping in a baking tin (pan) big enough to contain the sausages with spaces between them. Stand the tin (pan) on a baking sheet. Heat in the oven at the temperature above for 5–7 minutes, until very hot.
3. While heating the fat, skin the sausages if cased. Cut large or long sausages in half. Shape into uniform small rolls.
4. Pour the batter into the piping hot tin (pan). Quickly put in the sausages.
5. Bake for 35 minutes at the temperature above.

Note: Small thin pieces of steak or lamb, split cored kidneys or slices of liver can be used instead of sausages.

Steak and Kidney Pie

Serves 3–4

Oven temp 200°C/400°F/Gas Mark 6

Freeze 2 months (raw or cooked)

	Metric	Imperial	American
Lean stewing steak	*550 g*	*1¼ lb*	*1¼ lb*
Lamb's kidney	*1*	*1*	*1*
Seasoned flour	*30 ml*	*2 tbls*	*2 tbls*
Medium onion, sliced	*1*	*1*	*1*
Brown Stock (page 14)	*275 ml*	*½ pt*	*1¼ cups*
Shortcrust Pastry/basic pie dough, page 150 (weight when made)	*175 g*	*6 oz*	*6 oz*
Beaten egg for glazing			

1. Cut excess fat and any gristle or sinew off the meat. Wipe and cut into 2.5 cm/1½ in cubes. Skin the kidney if needed, core, and cut in small pieces. Coat both with seasoned flour.
2. Put a funnel in the centre of a 575 ml/1 pt/2½ cup deep pie dish. Pack in the meat, kidney and onion loosely. Pour in enough stock to half-fill the dish.
3. Roll out the pastry and cover the dish as on page 157. Make a small hole in the centre. Make a pastry rose and leaves, if liked. Arrange the leaves on the pastry. Brush the surface of the pastry with beaten egg.
4. Cover the dish with foil, not touching the pastry, and stand on a baking sheet. Bake at the temperature above for 1¾ hours. Place the rose beside it for the last 30 minutes. Test that the meat is tender by running a thin skewer into it through the hole.
5. Insert the rose in the hole just before serving.

Note: The pastry will probably brown enough under the foil. If necessary, remove for the last 10 minutes.

Veal and Ham Pie

Serves 6

Oven temp 230°C/450°F/Gas Mark 8
200°C/400°F/Gas Mark 6

Freeze 1 month

	Metric	Imperial	American
Pie veal, cubed	*900 g*	*2 lb*	*2 lb*
Veal shin bone sawn in pieces	*1*	*1*	*1*
Boiling White Stock (page 14)	*850 ml*	*1½ pt*	*3¾ cups*
Salt and pepper			
Chopped parsley	*15 ml*	*1 tbls*	*1 tbls*
Grated lemon rind	*7.5 ml*	*1½ tsp*	*1½ tsp*
Cooked ham or gammon in one piece	*225 g*	*8 oz*	*½ lb*
Hard-boiled (hard-cooked) eggs	*3*	*3*	*3*
½ recipe quantity Rough Puff Pastry (page 150)			
Beaten egg for glazing			

1. Put the veal and bones in a large saucepan with the stock. Season, and add the parsley. Cover and simmer for 2 hours. Cool for 15 minutes.
2. Scoop out the meat and cut into bite-sized cubes if in large pieces. Dice and mix in the ham or gammon. Put a layer of meats in the bottom of a 1.1 l/2 pt/5 cup deep oval pie dish. Shell the eggs and lay them on top. Pack the remaining meat around and over them. Sprinkle with the lemon rind. Add enough stock just to cover the meat. Reserve the rest.
3. Roll out the pastry and cover the pie with it as described on page 148, making a small centre hole. Decorate with trimmings and brush with beaten egg.
4. Bake at the first temperature above for 10 minutes. Reduce the heat and bake at the second temperature for another 20 minutes or until the pastry is risen and golden.
5. Fill up the pie with more hot stock if needed through the centre hole, using a funnel.
6. Serve hot or cold (refrigerated for several hours).

Raised Pork Pie

Serves 6–8

Oven temp 180°C/350°F/Gas Mark 4

Freeze 1 month

	Metric	Imperial	American
Lean pork	*550–700 g*	*1¼–1½ lb*	*1¼–1½ lb*
Salt and pepper			
Dried sage or mixed herbs	*1.5 ml*	*¼ tsp*	*¼ tsp*
Pork bones (use any from the meat, see recipe)	*350 g*	*12 oz*	*¾ lb*
Recipe quantity Hot Water Crust Pastry (page 151)			
Gelatine if needed	*7 g*	*¼ oz*	*¼ oz*

1. Remove any bones and gristle from the meat, and put them in a large pan. Cut the meat into small cubes, and mix it with 2.5 ml/½ tsp salt, a little pepper and the herbs. Refrigerate.
2. Add extra pork bones to those in the pan. Cover with water, add a pinch of salt and simmer gently for 2 hours. Drop a little of the stock on a chilled plate to see if it jells firmly.
3. Make the pastry. Roll out and use to line an 18 cm/7 in hinged pie mould or cake tin as described on page 151.
4. Fill the pastry case with the prepared meat and 30 ml/2 tbls of the stock. Cover the pie as described on page 151, make a small hole in the centre top and decorate as described. Place on a greased baking sheet, and bake at the temperature above for 2¼ hours.
5. While the pie cools, soften the gelatine in 275 ml/½ pt/1¼ cups cooled stock if needed. Dissolve the gelatine in the stock over gentle heat, then bring to the boil. Pour the stock while boiling into the pie through the centre hole, using a funnel. This helps the pie to keep well.

Note: If you wish you can glaze the pie with beaten egg 15 minutes before the end of the cooking time.

STEWING AND CASSEROLING

Stewing is long, slow cooking in flavoured liquid below boiling point (96°C/205°F). It is an excellent way to cook the coarser, cheaper cuts of meat because the gentle cooking makes them moist and tender, and the nutrients which seep into the liquid are not lost since it is served with the meat. The meat is cut up into small pieces which makes it easy to serve.

General Directions for Making Stews

1. Use a cheap, coarse cut if you wish, with or without bone. Wipe it well. Cut off any gristle and excess fat. Keep the fat for rendering down for dripping, if liked..
2. Cut the meat into serving pieces or smaller cubes.

BROWN STEWS

1. Melt some fat in a heavy stewpan, and fry the meat until browned on all sides. Remove.
2. Fry sliced onion and any other vegetables in the same fat until lightly browned and place with the meat.
3. Stir some flour into the fat, blend well and cook slowly until browned.
4. Gradually add the recipe liquid (stock, water, wine, beer, vinegar, etc.). Add salt, bring to the boil and skim. Then add any other flavourings.

5. Return the meat and vegetables to the pan. Cover and simmer until the meat is tender (see below).
6. Remove the meat and vegetables to a warmed serving dish, and pour the sauce over them.

Alternatively:
1. Fry the meat in a large saucepan or deep frying pan (skillet) which will hold all the liquid. Transfer the meat to a heavy casserole with a tight-fitting lid.
   Complete stages 2, 3 and 4 as above.
5. Pour the flavoured liquid over the meat and vegetables in the casserole. Cover and place in the oven at the given temperature until the meat is tender. Serve from the casserole.

Note: *To simmer*
Keep liquid just below the boil at 96°C/205°F. It should bubble with slow plopping sounds at one or two places in the pan.

Ragôuts

Make like other brown stews, but only brown the meat and vegetables lightly, so that the colour is not too dark. Garnish with bacon rolls or as the recipe suggests.

Curries

The basis of curries is the curry sauce given on page 90. Any meat, poultry, etc, cooked or un-cooked, may be used. When using uncooked meat, cut it into small pieces and fry in dripping or oil before adding the onion, apple, curry powder and flour. For cooked meat, slice it and heat in the curry sauce for the last 20–30 minutes of cooking. Servce with boiled rice (page 119).

Beef Olives

Serves 4

Oven temp 160°C/325°F/Gas Mark 3

Freeze 2 months (olives and sauce separately)

	Metric	Imperial	American
Rump or chuck			
steak	*500 g*	*1¼ lb*	*1¼ lb*
Bacon or Ham			
Stuffing			
(page 93)	*100 g*	*4 oz*	*¼ lb*
Seasoned flour	*60 ml*	*4 tbls*	*4 tbls*
Dripping	*45 ml*	*3 tbls*	*3 tbls*
Onion, sliced	*225 g*	*8 oz*	*8 oz*
Brown Stock			
(page 14)	*700 ml*	*1¼ pt*	*3 cups*
Tomato ketchup	*15 ml*	*1 tbls*	*1 tbls*
Carrot, sliced	*1*	*1*	*1*
Salt and pepper			
Mashed potato			

1. Wipe the meat and cut into 4 thin slices. Beat with a cutlet bat to flatten. Leave to 'rest' for 30 minutes.
2. Place an equal portion of stuffing in a small roll in the centre of each slice. Roll up the slices round the stuffing and tie securely with string. Dust the rolls with a little of the seasoned flour.
3. Heat the dripping in a flameproof casserole (Dutch oven) or stewpan. Fry the 'olives', turning them over until browned on all sides. Remove from pan and keep them warm.
4. Fry the onion until light gold in the remaining fat. Add to the 'olives'. Stir the remaining flour into the fat, and cook until browned.
5. Gradually, stir in the stock and bring to the boil, still stirring. Add the ketchup. Return the 'olives' and onion to the casserole or pan, and add the carrot. Season.
6. Cover the casserole or pan tightly. Cook in the oven at the temperature above for 1½–2 hours, or simmer in a stewpan for 1½–2 hours.
7. Cut the strings from the 'olives' and arrange on a bed of mashed potato. Strain the sauce over them.

Carbonnade of Beef

Serves 3

Oven temp 160°C/325°F/Gas Mark 3
200°C/400°F/Gas Mark 6

Freeze 1 month

	Metric	Imperial	American
Stewing steak			
(chuck, blade,			
skirt or flank)	*450–500 g*	*1–1¼ lb*	*1–1¼ lb*
Dripping	*25 g*	*1 oz*	*2 tbls*
Large onion, sliced	*1*	*1*	*1*
Garlic clove,			
crushed			
(optional)	*1*	*1*	*1*
Flour	*15 ml*	*1 tbls*	*1 tbls*
Brown ale	*150 ml*	*¼ pt*	*⅔ cup*
Beef stock (from			
cube)	*450 ml*	*¾ pt*	*2 cups*
Bouquet garni	*1*	*1*	*1*
Salt and pepper			
Pinch each of soft			
brown sugar and			
grated nutmeg			
Red wine vinegar	*5 ml*	*1 tsp*	*1 tsp*
French bread slices,			
5 mm/¼ in thick	*6*	*6*	*6*
Dark French			
mustard			
Soft brown sugar			
(for bread)			

1. Trim excess fat off meat, wipe it and cut it into 4 cm/1½ in cubes.
2. Heat the fat in a flameproof casserole (Dutch oven). Brown the meat in the fat quickly on all sides. Remove it, and fry the onion until golden with the garlic if used.
3. Stir in the flour, reduce the heat, and stir until the flour is light brown. Gradually, stir in the ale and stock. Add the bouquet garni, seasonings and vinegar. Stir round and bring to the boil.
4. Cover the casserole and cook in the oven at the first temperature above for 2 hours.
5. Remove the bouquet garni. Spread the bread slices with mustard, and arrange the bread slices on the casserole. Push them down into the liquid to moisten them; they will rise again.
6. Sprinkle the bread with sugar. Return the uncovered casserole to the oven for about 15 minutes at the second temperature above, so that the bread forms a crust.

Opposite: *Beef Olives served with parslied mashed potato make a delicious main course.*

Classic Brown Stew

Serves 6

Oven temp 160°C/325°F/Gas Mark 3

Freeze 2 months

	Metric	Imperial	American
Stewing steak (chuck or blade)	700 g	1½ lb	1½ lb
Dripping (beef fat)	25 g	1 oz	¼ cup
Onion, sliced	225 g	8 oz	½ lb
Flour	45 ml	3 tbls	3 tbls
Brown Stock (page 14) or water	850 ml	1½ pt	3¾ cups
Salt and pepper			
Bouquet garni	1	1	1
Carrots, sliced	225 g	8 oz	½ lb
Turnip, cubed	100 g	4 oz	¼ lb

1. Trim excess fat off the meat and wipe it well. Cut into slices 2 cm/¾ in thick.
2. Heat the dripping in a flameproof casserole (Dutch oven) or large stewpan. Fry the meat until browned all over. Remove it and fry the onion in the fat until lightly browned. Stir in the flour and stir until well browned.
3. Gradually add the stock or water and bring slowly to boiling point. Season, and add the bouquet garni.
4. Return the meat to the pan. Cover tightly with a lid. Cook in the oven at the temperature above for 2 hours, adding the carrot and turnip after 1 hour. If prepared in a stewpan, simmer on top of the cooker for 1 hour. Skim off any fat, then add the carrot and turnip and simmer for another hour.
5. Re-season and remove the bouquet garni before serving.

Goulash

Serves 4

Oven temp 160°C/325°F/Gas Mark 3

Freeze 1 month (without cream)

	Metric	Imperial	American
Stewing steak (chuck or blade)	700 g	1½ lb	1½ lb
Dripping	50 g	2 oz	¼ cup
Onions, chopped	2	2	2
Green pepper, de-seeded and chopped	1	1	1
Flour	40 g	1½ oz	⅓ cup
Paprika	10 ml	2 tsp	2 tsp
Pinch of grated nutmeg			

	Metric	Imperial	American
Concentrated tomato paste	30 ml	2 tbls	2 tbls
Brown Stock (page 14)	125 ml	4 fl oz	½ cup
Red wine	175 ml	6 fl oz	¾ cup
Tomatoes, skinned and quartered	3	3	3
Salt and pepper			
Sour cream or yoghurt (optional)			
Dumplings (page 67) to serve			

1. Trim excess fat off the meat, wipe it and cut into 3 cm/1¼ in cubes.
2. In a flameproof casserole (Dutch oven), fry the meat in the dripping until browned all over.
3. Remove the meat, add the onion and pepper to the casserole and fry until soft. Stir in the flour, paprika and nutmeg, and fry, stirring, for 1 minute. Remove from the heat.
4. Stir the tomato paste into the casserole with a little stock. Gradually add the remaining stock and the wine, stirring constantly. Return to the heat and stir until the liquid boils. Replace the meat in the casserole. Add the tomatoes. Season.
5. Cover the casserole tightly and cook in the oven at the temperature above for 2 hours, or until the meat is tender.
6. Stir in a little sour cream or yoghurt if you wish just before serving. Serve with dumplings (page 67).

Ragoût of Veal

Serves 4–6

Oven temp 160°C/325°F/Gas Mark 3

Freeze 2 months

	Metric	Imperial	American
Shoulder or breast of veal, boned	900 g	2 lb	2 lb
Dripping	40 g	1½ oz	3 tbls
Onion, sliced	1	1	1
Flour	15 g	½ oz	1 tbls
White Stock (page 14) or chicken stock (from cube)	850 ml	1½ pt	3¾ cups
Salt and pepper			
Carrots	2	2	2
Small turnips	2	2	2
Bouquet garni	1	1	1
Bacon rolls (page 75)			

58

1. Wipe the veal, cut off excess fat, and cut into 3 cm/1¼ in cubes.
2. Heat the dripping in a flameproof casserole (Dutch oven), and fry the veal until browned all over. Remove it and keep it warm.
3. Fry the onion until soft, take out with a slotted spoon and add to the meat.
4. Add the flour to the remaining fat, and stir until light brown. Add the stock gradually to make a smooth sauce. Season well. Return the meat and onions. Remove the casserole from the heat.
5. Top and tail and scrape the carrots and turnips. Add the trimmings to the casserole with the bouquet garni. Cut the prepared vegetables into small strips. Keep aside.
6. Cover the casserole and cook in the oven at the temperature above for 2–2½ hours.
7. Cook the carrots and turnips in boiling, salted water for 15–20 minutes. Drain.
8. When the meat is tender, remove it with a slotted spoon to a hot serving dish. Discard the bouquet garni. Boil up the sauce, skim well and strain it onto the meat. Garnish the dish with the vegetables and bacon rolls.

Haricot of Lamb

Serves 4–6

Oven temp 160°C/325°F/Gas Mark 3

Freeze 2 months

	Metric	Imperial	American
Haricot (navy) beans	100 g	4 oz	¼ lb
Middle neck or breast of lamb	1 kg	2¼ lb	2¼ lb
Dripping	30 ml	2 tbls	2 tbls
Onions, skinned and sliced	2	2	2
Boiling Brown Stock (page 14) or chicken stock (cube)	850 ml	1½ pt	3¾ cups
Bouquet garni	1	1	1
Salt and pepper			

1. Soak the beans in cold water overnight. Drain.
2. Wipe the meat and trim off skin and excess fat. Cut into serving pieces.
3. Melt the fat in a stewpan or flameproof casserole (Dutch oven), and fry the meat until lightly browned. Add the onions and fry until soft.
4. Add the boiling stock, drained beans, bouquet garni and seasoning. Cover, and simmer or cook in the oven at the temperature above for about 3 hours, or until the meat and beans are tender.

5. Drain off the stock into a smaller pan, and boil it down to strengthen the flavour if you wish. Pour it back over the meat and beans. Serve in a warmed serving dish or from the casserole.

Note: Diced cooked carrots and turnips can be added to the dish for the last 4–5 minutes of the cooking time.

Stewed Oxtail

Serves 4–6

Oven temp 160°C/325°F/Gas Mark 3

Freeze 2 months

	Metric	Imperial	American
Oxtail	1	1	1
Seasoned flour	50 g	2 oz	½ cup
Dripping	50 g	2 oz	¼ cup
Onion, sliced	1	1	1
Brown Stock (page 14)	575 ml	1 pt	2½ cups
Salt and pepper			
Bouquet garni	1	1	1
Carrot, sliced	1	1	1
Celery stalk, sliced	1	1	1

1. Rinse the oxtail, and joint it. Cut off any excess fat.
2. Blanch the oxtail by putting it in a large pan, covering it with cold water and bringing it to the boil. Drain off the water, and cover the meat with fresh cold water. (This cleans the tail.) Drain again.
3. Coat the oxtail joints with some of the seasoned flour.
4. Melt the dripping in a flameproof casserole (Dutch oven) and fry the onion until lightly browned. Lift it out with a slotted spoon, put in the oxtail and turn it in the fat to brown all over. Put the meat with the onion.
5. Stir the remaining seasoned flour into the fat. Fry until well browned, stirring constantly. Gradually stir in the stock to make a smooth sauce. Season.
6. Return the onion and oxtail to the sauce. Add the bouquet garni. Cover and cook in the oven at the temperature above for 2½ hours, or until the meat is tender. Add the carrot and celery half-way through the cooking time.
7. Before serving, remove the bouquet garni and skim any excess fat off the stew. Serve the vegetables with the meat.

Minced Beef

Serves 4

Freeze 1 month (without garlic)

	Metric	Imperial	American
Large onion	*1*	*1*	*1*
Garlic clove			
(optional)	*1*	*1*	*1*
Dripping	*15 g*	*½ oz*	*1 tbls*
Raw minced			
(ground) beef	*450 g*	*1 lb*	*1 lb*
Salt and pepper			
Flour	*10 ml*	*2 tsp*	*2 tsp*
Beef stock (from			
cube)	*150 ml*	*¼ pt*	*⅔ cup*
Finely chopped			
parsley	*15 ml*	*1 tbls*	*1 tbls*
Bay leaf	*1*	*1*	*1*
Triangles of fried			
bread	*8*	*8*	*8*

1. Finely chop the onion and squeeze the garlic over it.
2. Heat the dripping in a stewpan. Fry the onion and garlic until soft. Stir in the mince and fry, breaking up any lumps with a fork, until the mixture is evenly browned. Season well.
3. Sprinkle the flour over the mince and stir well.
4. Stir in the stock. Add the parsley and bay leaf. Bring to the boil, reduce the heat and simmer gently for 30 minutes.
5. Remove the bay leaf and garnish with fried bread triangles before serving.

Note: The mince can be served as a main dish by itself or can be used as a filling for stuffed peppers, tomatoes, etc.

WHITE STEWS

Place the prepared cubed meat, vegetables and seasonings in a large stewpan or casserole, pour on hot light-coloured liquid or water, and simmer on the stove or in the oven until the meat is tender. The liquid can then be strained off and thickened with beurre manié (page 84). Serve like a brown stew.

Alternatively, put all the prepared ingredients and cold liquid in a large heavy stewpan or casserole, bring to simmering point and cook as above. Time the dish from when it reaches simmering point.

Fricassées

Use white meat, e.g. veal, young lamb or rabbit. Cook as a white stew. When the meat is tender, drain off the liquid (usually White Stock, page 14).

Use it to make a coating sauce (page 84), using 50 g/2 oz/¼ cup butter or margarine and 50 g/2 oz/½ cup flour to each 575 ml/1 pt/2½ cups liquid. Place the meat and vegetables in a warmed dish, coat with sauce and garnish with bacon rolls (page 75).

Blanquettes

Make as for fricassées but whisk beaten egg yolk and/or cream into the thickened sauce. Reheat WITHOUT boiling.

Beef Hot Pot

Serves 4

Oven temp 160°C/325°F/Gas Mark 3

Freeze 1 month

	Metric	Imperial	American
Shin of beef without			
bone	*450 g*	*1 lb*	*1 lb*
Vinegar	*30 ml*	*2 tbls*	*2 tbls*
Pork sausages			
(50 g/2 oz each)	*225 g*	*8 oz*	*½ lb*
Seasoned flour	*30 ml*	*2 tbls*	*2 tbls*
Potatoes	*450 g*	*1 lb*	*1 lb*
Crisp apple	*1*	*1*	*1*
Tomatoes	*225 g*	*8 oz*	*½ lb*
Onion	*1*	*1*	*1*
Salt and pepper			
Boiling water or			
White Stock			
(page 14) as			
needed			

1. Trim any excess fat off the meat, wipe it and remove from bones before weighing. Weigh it, and cut into small pieces about 2.5 cm/1 in thick. Put them in a bowl, sprinkle with the vinegar and leave for 1 hour, turning the meat over several times. Pat it dry.
2. Cut each sausage into 3 short pieces. Shake the meat and sausage in a plastic bag with the seasoned flour.
3. Peel the potatoes and peel and core the apple. Skin the tomatoes and onion. Slice them all.
4. Place a layer of sliced vegetables and fruit in an ovenproof pot or casserole, and season lightly. Cover with a layer of meat. Repeat the layers until all the ingredients are used, ending with a vegetable and fruit layer.
5. Add enough boiling water or stock to fill the pot or casserole a third full. Cover it tightly.
6. Cook at the temperature above for 2½–3 hours, or until the meat is tender.

Opposite: *Minced Beef used as a filling for peppers and Beef Hot Pot.*

Lancashire Hot Pot

Serves 4–6

Oven temp 180°C/350°F/Gas Mark 4
220°C/425°F/Gas Mark 7

Freeze 2 months

	Metric	Imperial	American
Potatoes, peeled and thickly sliced	900 g	2 lb	2 lb
Dripping or margarine for greasing and brushing			
Middle neck of lamb	700 g	1½ lb	1½ lb
Sheep's kidneys (optional)	2	2	2
Onions, sliced	2	2	2
Salt and pepper			
Boiling water or White Stock (page 14)	275 ml	½ pt	1¼ cups

1. Put a thick layer of potato slices in the bottom of a well-greased casserole or ovenproof pot.
2. Cut the meat into neat pieces. Skin, core and slice the kidneys if used. Put the meat, kidney and onion on top of the potatoes in the casserole or pot. Season well. Pour in the boiling water or stock.
3. Cover the meat and onion with the remaining potato slices in an overlapping layer. Brush well with fat.
4. Cover the casserole or pot tightly. Cook in the oven at the first temperature above for 2 hours, or until the meat and potatoes are tender.
5. Uncover the casserole or pot, raise the heat and cook at the second temperature for 20 minutes or until the potatoes on top are lightly browned. Serve from the casserole.

Irish Stew

Serves 4–6

Oven temp 160°C/325°F/Gas Mark 3

Freeze 2 months

	Metric	Imperial	American
Scrag of lamb or mutton	900 g	2 lb	2 lb
Potatoes, peeled and sliced	900 g–1.4 kg	2–3 lb	2–3 lb
Onions, sliced	2	2	2
Salt and pepper			
Boiling water	450 ml	¾ pt	2 cups

1. Cut the meat into neat pieces.
2. Put alternate layers of meat, potatoes and onions in a casserole, seasoning each layer.
3. Pour in the boiling water, cover the casserole and cook in the oven at the temperature above for 3–3½ hours.

Note: If the casserole is flameproof you can bring it to the boil on top of the cooker before oven-cooking, to shorten the time a little.

Tripe and Onions

Serves 4

Oven temp 160°C/325°F/Gas Mark 3

Freeze 2 months (before making sauce)

	Metric	Imperial	American
Dressed tripe	450 g	1 lb	1 lb
Onions, chopped	225 g	8 oz	½ lb
Salt			
Peppercorns	4	4	4
Parsley stalks	4–6	4–6	4–6
Boiling milk	450 ml	¾ pt	2 cups
Butter or margarine	20 g	¾ oz	1½ tbls
Flour	20 g	¾ oz	3 tbls

1. Cut the tripe into strips or 5 cm/2 in squares. Put in a casserole.
2. Add the onions to the tripe with salt to taste. Tie the peppercorns and parsley stalks in muslin and add to the casserole. Pour in the milk.
3. Cover the casserole. Place over low heat, and simmer for the time the butcher suggests, (see note), or put in the oven at the temperature above for the same time. The tripe should be really tender but do not overcook.
4. Strain off the cooking liquid, and use it to make a white sauce (page 84) with the fat and flour.
5. Remove the muslin bag from the casserole and strain the sauce over the tripe and onions.

Note: Butchers parboil tripe before sale for a variable time.

Variation
This traditional dish is really a fricassée. For a Blanquette of Tripe, add 1–2 beaten egg yolks to the sauce and cook it without boiling for a few minutes before straining it over the tripe.

Fricassée of Veal

Serves 4

Oven temp 160°C/325°F/Gas Mark 3

Freeze 2 months (without sauce)

	Metric	Imperial	American
Fillet or other good quality veal without bone	450 g	1 lb	1 lb
Onion, finely sliced	1	1	1
Parsley sprig, 6 peppercorns and a strip of lemon rind tied in muslin			
Salt			
Boiling water	275 ml	½ pt	1¼ cups
Milk	150 ml	¼ pt	⅔ cup
Butter or margarine	25 g	1 oz	2 tbls
Flour	25 g	1 oz	¼ cup
Bacon rolls (page 75)			
Lemon wedges			

1. Wipe the veal and cut into bite-sized pieces. Put in a casserole with the onion, flavourings tied in muslin, salt and boiling water.
2. Cover the casserole tightly and cook in the oven at the temperature above for 2 hours.
3. Strain off the liquid, and mix 150 ml/¼ pt/⅔ cup with the milk. Make a thick coating white sauce with it, using the fat and flour (page 84).
4. Put the meat in a warmed shallow dish. Remove the muslin bag.
5. Pour the sauce over the meat, and serve it garnished with bacon rolls and lemon wedges.

Variation

For a Blanquette of Veal, add 1–2 beaten egg yolks to the sauce and cook for a few minutes without boiling before straining the sauce over the veal.

BRAISING

This cooking method is very like pot-roasting with liquid. The meat is seared all over in hot fat, then placed on a bed of fried vegetables called a mire-poix in a deep casserole. Enough stock and sometimes wine are added to moisten the vegetables. The liquid tenderises the meat with steam, and provides a sauce. The meat may be cooked in a single piece or cubed as in most stews.

Although it needs more attention than when oven-cooked, it can, if you wish, be cooked in a stewpan over heat.

Braising is a good way to flavour and tenderise a second-quality joint. If braised in one piece, remove the lid of the casserole for the last 30 minutes of cooking to brown it, and make it look and taste like a roast. If braised in a stewpan, it can be roasted at 220°C/425°F/Gas Mark 7 for the last 30 minutes of its cooking time.

Braised Veal Knuckles in Wine (Osso Bucco)

Serves 4

Oven temp 180°C/350°F/Gas Mark 4

Freeze 2 months

	Metric	Imperial	American
Veal knuckles or shanks, sawn in large pieces	4	4	4
Seasoned flour			
Corn or olive oil	60 ml	4 tbls	4 tbls
Medium carrots, thinly sliced	2	2	2
Celery stalk, thinly sliced	1	1	1
Medium onion, finely chopped	1	1	1
Garlic clove	1	1	1
Dry white wine	175 ml	6 fl oz	¾ cup
Flour	15 ml	1 tbls	1 tbls
Beef stock (from cube)	275 ml	½ pt	1¼ cups
Tomatoes, skinned and chopped	225 g	8 oz	½ lb
Chopped fresh herbs, e.g. parsley, basil, mint, chives, thyme	30 ml	2 tbls	2 tbls
Grated rind of ½ lemon			

1. Toss the veal in seasoned flour.
2. Heat the oil in a deep stewpan or flameproof casserole. Fry the veal until browned all over. Remove to a plate.
3. Add the vegetables to the pan or casserole, and squeeze the garlic over them. Sauté the vegetables until golden.
4. Reduce the heat. Return the meat to the pan or casserole and add the wine. Cover and simmer gently for 10 minutes.
5. Blend the flour to a cream with a little of the stock, stir in the rest of the stock and add to the knuckles. Add the tomatoes.
6. Bring back to simmering point. Continue simmering, covered, for 1 hour 40 minutes (or until the meat is tender) or put a casserole in the oven for 1½–2 hours.
7. Sprinkle with herbs and lemon rind before serving. Serve with Yellow Rice (page 119) or Risotto (page 119).

Braising Vegetables or Mirepoix

Freeze 2 months (see note)

	Metric	Imperial	American
Streaky bacon			
without rind	25 g	1 oz	1 oz
Butter or margarine	15 ml	1 tbls	1 tbls
Carrots, thickly			
sliced	100 g	4 oz	¼ lb
Onions, thickly			
sliced	225 g	8 oz	½ lb
Small turnip,			
quartered	1	1	1
Celery stalks, cut			
into 1 cm/½ in			
pieces	2	2	2
Bouquet garni	1	1	1

1. Cut the bacon into small squares.
2. Melt the fat in a suitable braising container, and fry the bacon until the fat runs. Add the vegetables and stir them in the fat until coated and golden.
3. Spread the mirepoix over the base of the container, add the bouquet garni, the meat you are braising and the liquid the recipe requires.

Notes:
1. You can prepare the mirepoix for several dishes at once. Cool and freeze them without the frying fat, in separate portions. To use, thaw one portion. Fry the meat as usual, then turn the thawed vegetables in the fat from frying the meat. Spread, add the bouquet garni, put the meat on the vegetables and braise as directed in the recipe.
2. Braising is a standard cooking method for duck and other birds, and for some vegetables.

Opposite: *Lamb Chops arranged on a bed of vegetables, ready to go in the oven for braising.*

Below: *Duckling braised on a mirepoix of vegetables.*

Braised Lamb Chops

Serves 6

Oven Temp 220°C/425°F/Gas Mark 7

Freeze 1 month (before high temp. oven cooking)

	Metric	Imperial	American
Frozen lamb chops, thawed	6	6	6
Oil for frying			
Rindless back bacon rashers (slices), cut in half	3	3	3
Mirepoix vegetables without bacon (page 64)			
Butter or margarine	30 ml	2 tbls	2 tbls
Bouquet garni	1	1	1
Salt and pepper			
Beef stock (from cube)	275 ml	½ pt	1¼ cups
Basic Brown Sauce, page 85 (see recipe) or Fresh Tomato Sauce (page 90)			

1. Trim the chops, wipe them and fry lightly in oil on each side. Remove from the pan and cover each with a piece of bacon.

2. Prepare the mirepoix vegetables. Melt the fat in a stewpan, and fry the vegetables, stirring well, for 4 minutes, or until golden. Add the bouquet garni and season well. Add enough stock to cover all but the top vegetables. Reserve any left over.

3. Lay the chops on the vegetables, bacon side up. Cover with greased greaseproof paper, greased side down. Put a tight-fitting lid on the pan.

4. Heat to simmering point, and cook for 40 minutes or until the chops are tender.

5. Take out the chops and bacon. Place them in a greased baking tin (pan) and cook in the oven at the temperature above until the bacon is crisp. Reduce the heat and keep warm.

6. Drain the cooking liquid from the vegetables. Keep them warm. Add any remaining stock to the cooking liquid, make up to 275 ml/½ pt/1¼ cups with water if needed, and use to make the brown sauce if used.

7. Serve the meat and vegetables on a warmed serving dish, and the sauce in a warmed gravy boat.

Variation
A small leg or shoulder of lamb, on the bone or stuffed, can be cooked in the same way, without bacon. Simmer for 2–2¼ hours, then oven-cook for about 15 minutes, basting with a little hot fat or stock.

Braised Beef

Oven temp 160°C/325°F/Gas Mark 3

Freeze 2 months

	Metric	Imperial	American
Topside or fresh			
silverside	*1.5 kg*	*3¼ lb*	*3¼ lb*
Dripping or lard	*25 g*	*1 oz*	*2 tbls*
Raw mirepoix bacon			
and vegetables			
(page 64)			
Bouquet garni	*1*	*1*	*1*
Salt and pepper			
Brown Stock			
(page 14)	*175 ml*	*6 fl oz*	*¾ cup*

1. Trim and tie the meat into a neat shape. Heat the fat in a flameproof casserole (Dutch oven), and fry the meat until browned all over. Remove it.
2. Put the mirepoix bacon in the casserole and fry for 2 minutes. Add the vegetables and turn them over in the fat until lightly browned. Spread them over the base of the casserole. Add the bouquet garni and season well.
3. Place the meat on the vegetables. Pour in the stock. Cover the casserole and cook in the oven for 2–2½ hours, or until the meat is tender.
4. Remove the meat to a warmed carving dish. Skim any fat off the cooking liquid. Strain it and use it to make a brown sauce (page 85) or gravy (page 71) to serve with the meat.

BOILING

Although boiling strictly means cooking in boiling liquid, meat (like other animal protein foods) is seldom cooked in liquid at boiling point. Most meats are simmered like a stew, only in one solid piece instead of small cubes or strips. The cheapest and coarsest cuts (except for hams and tongues) are the ones most often 'boiled'.

General Directions for Boiling Meat

1. Choose a heavy-based pan which will hold enough water to cover the meat and any root vegetables and dumplings cooked with it. The pan should be large if cooking dumplings as they swell a good deal. It should also be deep enough to have 10 cm/4 in headspace between its rim and the water.
2. Weigh the meat. The cooking time will vary with the shape and size of the joint. The average time for most salt or pickled meat is 25 minutes per 450 g/1 lb. For hams, see right.

Note: Calculate the cooking time from when the water reaches boiling point. Allow too long rather than too short a cooking time. If the meat is cooking gently, an extra 15 minutes will do it no harm.

3. *Fresh meat*: Prepare the meat as described on page 41. Put it in the empty pan. Pour in enough boiling water to cover it. Add 10 ml/2 tsp salt for each 2.3 l/4 pt/10 cups water. Bring back to the boil. Boil for 5 minutes, skim, then reduce the heat and simmer for the rest of the cooking time.
   Salted or pickled meat: Prepare the meat. Cover it with cold water. Bring to the boil, then continue as for fresh meat. Do not add salt.
4. Root vegetables can be added after skimming to flavour the meat and cooking liquid. Do not add green vegetables.
5. Dumplings can also be added towards the end of the cooking time. Add standard sized dumplings for the last 15–20 minutes (see the recipe on page 67).
6. Use the cooking liquid as stock for making sauces or soup if not too salty.

Boiled Ham

A whole ham is the hind leg of a pig cut off the carcass and cured (salted and flavoured) separately. Most types of cured ham must be boiled before being eaten. Heavily salted fat hams must be soaked for 12–24 hours before being boiled, but a modern mild-cured ham needs only 6–8 hours soaking. It can then be fully boiled, or can be partly boiled and then baked. It can be served hot or cold.

A whole ham is much too large to boil in the average home kitchen. A half ham or smaller piece is more practical. Small bacon and gammon joints are often treated and eaten as ham. Smoked bacon has a more distinctive flavour.

A craft butcher or supplier should be able to advise on how long to soak the ham, gammon or bacon joint you buy from him.

Boil a gammon joint in the same way as ham. The method of handling bacon joints is described on page 67.

To boil a large joint of ham:

1. Soak the joint, changing the water once or twice (see above).
2. Scrape or trim off any 'rusty' bits. Weigh the joint. Put it into a large pan.
3. Cover the joint with cold water, and add 15 ml/1 tbls brown sugar, 12 black peppercorns, 2 whole cloves and 1 bay leaf.
4. Bring the water to boiling point, skim and reduce the heat to simmering point. Simmer for these times:
   Ham joints up to 2.7 kg/6 lb, cook for 20 minutes per 450 g/1 lb. Reduce the time for larger hams, e.g. give a 6.3 kg/14 lb joint only 15 minutes per 450 g/1 lb. Top up the water from time to time if needed.

5. At the end of the cooking time, remove the ham from the pan, and carefully strip off the rind. *If serving hot*, cover the fat side with dry or browned breadcrumbs and brown sugar mixed. *If serving cold*, return to the cooking liquid until quite cold before covering with crumbs and sugar, or with Glaze (page 71).

Variations

1. Remove the ham from the pan one hour before the end of the cooking time. Take off the rind. Cover with browned breadcrumbs and sugar as above. Bake in the oven for 1 hour at 200°C/400°F/Gas Mark 6.
2. Bake as above, but instead of covering with browned breadcrumbs, score the fat with a knife-point into 3.5 cm/1½ in diamond shapes. Stick a whole clove into the centre of each diamond, and spread the fat thickly with brown sugar 'creamed' with malt vinegar before you bake it. Baste twice while baking.

Boiled Bacon

A bacon joint is boiled like ham with the following differences:

Soaking times
Smoked joints from a speciality supplier, 1–12 hours; unsmoked joints from a speciality suppliers, up to 2 hours. Pre-packed, e.g. supermarket, small joints do not need soaking. Put in a pan, cover with boiling water, then drain.

Cooking time
20 minutes per 450 g/1 lb + 20 minutes. The meat can be cooked in water, stock or cider as you prefer. A large joint can also be parboiled and baked like ham (variations 1 and 2).

Serve hot boiled bacon with Pease Pudding (page 117) and Parsley Sauce (page 88). Cold boiled bacon can be used as a cold meat salad. It can also be used for any dish which calls for ham as an ingredient, e.g. Veal and Ham Pie (page 54), Shepherd's Pie (page 70), Stuffed Peppers (page 113).

Note: A small bacon joint, e.g. forehock, can also be cooked like Boiled Salt Beef.

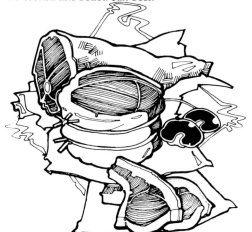

Boiled Salt Beef with Vegetables and Dumplings

Cooking time 3 hours

Freeze 2 months

	Metric	Imperial	American
Salt beef (brisket or silverside)	1.4 kg	3 lb	3 lb
Onions, skinned	900 g	2 lb	2lb
Carrots, prepared and halved lengthways	900 g	2 lb	2 lb
Bouquet garni	1	1	1
Garlic cloves	2	2	2
Suet Dumplings			
Self-raising flour	100g	4 oz	1 cup
Shredded suet	50 g	2 oz	⅓ cup
Small onion, finely chopped	½	½	½
Chopped fresh parsley	1 tbls	1 tbls	1 tbls
Salt and pepper			
Water			

1. Rinse the meat with cold water. Tie it in a neat shape and put it in a large pan. Cover with cold water, and bring to the boil.
2. Boil for 5 minutes to seal the meat. Skim thoroughly. Reduce the heat, cover the pan and simmer for about 3 hours. Add the vegetables after 1 hour and the dumplings (made as below) after 1 hour 20 minutes total cooking time (55 minutes and 1 hour 15 minutes simmering time).
3. To make the dumplings, mix all the ingredients, adding enough cold water to form a fairly stiff dough. Roll into 16 small balls, coat them with flour, and drop them into the liquid around the meat.
4. To serve, lift out the meat, dumplings and vegetables onto a suitable dish for carving. Remove any strings from the meat. Serve some of the cooking liquid in a warmed gravy boat. Use the rest for soup or as a stock.

Notes:
1. If very salty, dilute the cooking liquid with stock or milk and reheat before serving.
2. The dumplings can also be made with well-flavoured dripping. For soup dumplings make 24–28 smaller balls and simmer for 10 minutes only.

Above: *Long slow cooking is the secret of a really delicious Steak and Kidney Pudding.*

Opposite: *Boiled Salt Beef with Vegetables and Dumplings (page 67) is another traditional British dish.*

Steak and Kidney Pudding

Serves 6

Freeze 2 months

	Metric	Imperial	American
Suet Crust Pastry using 225 g/8 oz/ 2 cups flour (page 152)			
Stewing steak (chuck or blade)	450 g	1 lb	1 lb
Ox kidney, cored	150 g	5 oz	5 oz
Seasoned flour	30 ml	2 tbls	2 tbls
Onion (optional)	1	1	1
Beef stock (from cube)	45 ml	3 tbls	3 tbls

1. Make the pastry. Reserve a quarter of it to cover the pudding. Roll out the rest on a floured surface into a circle to fit a greased 1 l/1¾ pt/4⅓ cup heatproof pudding basin (mixing bowl).
2. Line the basin (bowl) with the pastry.
3. Wipe the meat. Wipe, skin and core the kidney. Cut both into medium-sized cubes. Toss in seasoned flour.
4. Put half the meat and kidney into the lined basin, add the onion if used, and pour in the stock. Put in the remaining meat.
5. Roll out the reserved pastry into a round to fit the top of the basin. Dampen the edges of the lining pastry. Put on the round and seal the edges.
6. Cover the basin (bowl) with a floured pudding cloth, pleated in the centre, or greased foil, leaving room for the pudding to swell. Secure with string.
7. Put the basin on a trivet in a large stewpan, and pour in enough boiling water to come half-way up its sides. The water must not touch the cloth if used. Cover the pan. Boil for 3–3½ hours, topping up the boiled water occasionally if needed.
8. Serve from the basin (bowl) wrapped in a folded white napkin.

Shepherds' Pie

Serves 4

Oven temp 220°C/425°F/Gas Mark 7

Freeze 2 months (prepared or cooked before
baking)

	Metric	Imperial	American
Potatoes	700 g	1½ lb	1½ lb
Salt and pepper			
Cold cooked meat			
without bone	600 g	1¼ lb	1¼ lb
Cold cooked bacon			
or ham	50 g	2 oz	2 oz
Dripping	15 g	½ oz	1 tbls
Onion, chopped	1	1	1
Flour	15 g	½ oz	1 tbls
Beef stock (from			
cube)	175 ml	6 fl oz	¾ cup
Tomato ketchup or			
chutney to taste			
Good pinch of			
grated nutmeg			
Butter or margarine	25–50 g	1–2 oz	2–4 tbls
Milk			

1. Peel the potatoes and boil them in salted
   water until tender.
2. Meanwhile, remove any skin, rind and
   gristle from the meat and bacon or ham.
   Mince them finely.
3. Heat the dripping and fry the onion until
   soft. Add the flour and fry for a moment or
   two, stirring, then slowly add the stock.
   Bring to the boil, reduce the heat and
   simmer for 2–3 minutes, stirring. Season
   with salt, black pepper and the ketchup or
   chutney. Stir in.
4. Add the mince, cover the pan and simmer
   for 5 minutes, stirring occasionally.
5. While cooking, drain and mash the potatoes.
   Season with salt, pepper and nutmeg, and
   soften with butter or margarine and a little
   milk.
6. Turn the meat and sauce into a greased deep
   pie dish or oven-to-table baking dish, filling
   it three-quarters full. Cover with the potato
   in an even layer and score a pattern on the
   surface with a fork. Cook in the oven at the
   temperature above for 15–20 minutes until
   the mince is thoroughly heated and the
   potato layer is flecked with brown.

Croquettes

Serves 4

Freeze 1 month (before frying)

	Metric	Imperial	American
Cold cooked meat	225 g	8 oz	½ lb
Dripping	25 g	1 oz	2 tbls
Onion, finely			
chopped	25 g	1 oz	1 oz
Flour	25 g	1 oz	¼ cup
Beef stock (from			
cube)	175 ml	6 fl oz	¾ cup
Salt and pepper			
Chopped parsley	10 ml	2 tsp	2 tsp
Bottled savoury			
sauce, any			
kind (with beef,			
lamb or pork)	5 ml	1 tsp	1 tsp
Flour for dusting			
Beaten egg for			
glazing			
Browned			
breadcrumbs			
Oil for deep frying			

1. Remove skin, gristle and surplus fat from the
   meat. Mince the meat finely.
2. Heat the fat in a saucepan and fry the onion
   until soft and golden. Stir in the flour, and
   cook for 1–2 minutes. Gradually stir in the
   stock.
3. Bring to the boil, stirring constantly, and
   simmer until the sauce is very thick. Mix in
   the meat, seasoning, parsley and bottled
   sauce.
4. Turn the mixture into a soup plate, spread it
   out and cool it as quickly as possible.
5. Form the cooled mixture into 8 cork shapes
   (or 16 for cocktail croquettes). Dust with
   flour. Coat with egg and breadcrumbs twice,
   and fry in deep hot oil until the surface is
   crisp. Drain on soft kitchen paper and serve
   at once.

Note: For rissoles, roll out recipe quantity Shortcrust Pastry (page 150) thinly, and cut into 16
rounds, using a 10 cm/4 in cutter; re-roll and cut
trimmings if needed. Place about 15 ml/1 tbls mixture on each round. Dampen the pastry edges,
fold over and seal. Coat with egg and crumbs, then
fry as above.

MISCELLANEOUS RECIPES

Aspic Jelly

(Savoury Jelly for setting and garnishing cold savoury foods)

Makes 1 l/1¾ pt/4⅓ cups (approx)

Not suitable for freezing

	Metric	Imperial	American
Cold White or Brown Stock (page 14)	1 l	1¾ pt	4⅓ cups
White wine or half white wine and half sherry (for red meat dishes)	150 ml	¼ pt	⅔ cup
White wine vinegar	30 ml	2 tbls	2 tbls
Gelatine (unflavored gelatin)	50 g	2 oz	2 oz
Bouquets garni	2	2	2
Egg whites	2	2	2
Crushed egg shells	2	2	2

1. Strain the stock through a cloth into a large saucepan, to make sure it is fat-free.
2. Add all the other ingredients. Whisk, using a scalded whisk, until the gelatine softens.
3. Bring almost to the boil, whisking constantly. Remove the whisk, and let the liquid rise to the top of the pan. Remove from the heat. The egg whites and shells will form a crust.
4. Turn the liquid and crust very gently into a scalded jelly bag, without breaking the crust; let the liquid drip through into a basin.
5. If the liquid is at all cloudy, strain it through the crust in the bag again. It should be sparklingly clear.

To Clarify Butter, Margarine and Other Fats

Among other uses, clarified butter or margarine is used for frying white meats and poultry to make them a light clear golden colour. Heat the fat gently in a saucepan, without letting it change colour, until it stops bubbling. Remove it from the heat and skim off any scum on the top. Leave to stand until any sediment has sunk to the bottom, then pour off the clear golden fat leaving the sediment behind. (Cheap concentrated butter is a good substitute for clarified butter.)

Glazes for Meat

Proper meat glaze is used to add rich flavour to gravy, sauces and sometimes vegetables, or it is brushed over cold meat or poultry to improve its appearance.

The glaze is made by boiling any fat-free strong dark meat stock made with bones until it is syrupy.

It must be freed of fat by straining before being boiled. When it cools, it should be like a rich, clear brown jelly. After cooling, it can be stored for a short time in a heatproof jar in the refrigerator, provided no green or starchy vegetables were used to make the stock. Stored glaze can be brought to brushing consistency by standing its container in hot water.

No set boiling time or storage time can be given for glaze because these depend on how the stock was made in the first place, and on its flavour.

A substitute glaze can be made by dissolving 60 ml/4 tbls gelatine (unflavored gelatin) in 150 ml/¼ pt/⅔ cup water with 5 ml/1 tsp meat or yeast extract. It must be used while still hot; keep it in a warm container while brushing it over cold meat, a pâté or galantine.

Other products are sometimes used to give a shiny surface to meat or poultry. Examples of their use are:

a. Hot meat or poultry can be brushed with butter or oil just before serving;
b. The crackling on roast pork can be brushed with smooth apricot jam, redcurrant jelly, sieved jelly marmalade or honey mixed with mustard. Jam or jelly should be warmed to liquify it before use. The glaze is brushed over the crackling 6–8 minutes before the end of the cooking time, and the joint is returned to the oven to set the glaze.
    Crackling can also be brushed with butter or oil and salt, and put back in the oven at a fairly high temperature for a few minutes.

Gravy

Properly, thin or pan-juice gravy should be served with unstuffed roast meat, poultry or game, thick gravy should be served only with a stuffed meat, poultry or game dish. However, clearing the fat from the meat juices to make thin gravy takes time and care, so thickened gravy is more often served by many cooks.

Thin or clear gravy: After removing a roast from the tin (pan), pour off as much clear fat as possible, keeping back all the juices and sediment. Sprinkle with salt and pepper. Add stock, wine or water, or a mixture. Place the tin over low heat, and stir, scraping up any solid sediment, until the mixture boils. Off the heat, skim off carefully every scrap of fat. Strain the gravy into a warmed gravy boat.

Thick gravy: Pour off the fat as above, keeping back the juices and sediment. Sprinkle a little flour over the surface, and stir in. Season, place the tin over low heat, and stir until the flour browns. Add liquid as above (about 275 ml/½ pt/1¼ cups to each 25 ml/5 tsp flour). Stir constantly until the gravy boils. Strain into a warmed gravy boat.

5
POULTRY AND GAME

ROASTING

All poultry and all young game birds, rabbits, hares and suitable cuts of venison can be roasted. Older or badly shot birds, rabbits or hares are best jointed, then braised, casseroled or stewed. An older chicken or duck can be roasted if steamed first.

Preparation

Make sure that a frozen bird is properly thawed. Prick the skin of a fat duck all over with a fine skewer to let fat run out. Stuff if you wish; small and some young birds are not usually stuffed. Traditional stuffings are given on page 74 under *Accompaniments*. If not stuffed, season the cavity of any poultry or game with salt and pepper; put a knob of butter and/or an onion in the cavity before trussing.

Game birds, hares and rabbits and venison have dry meat and should be larded or barded.

Larding: Thread strips of fat bacon into a larding needle and thread into the meat.

Barding: Snip rindless fat bacon to prevent curling, and tie it over the breasts of birds or the backs of rabbit or hares.

Foil-roasting: Tender meat such as chicken breasts can be covered or wrapped in greased foil to prevent them drying out before the rest is cooked. An older or dry bird can be wholly wrapped in foil for roasting if you wish, and roasted for a little longer than usual, uncovering for the last 20–30 minutes to brown.

General Method

Put the prepared bird, animal or venison joint on a trivet, and brush with melted butter, dripping or oil. Put in a shallow roasting tin (pan). A chicken can be roasted for a third of the cooking time on its side, for a further third of the time on the second side, and for the remaining time breast up. Roast for the times given opposite. Keep the cooked meat warm on a carving or serving dish while making gravy if used and while dressing vegetables and any last-minute accompaniments.

A large or elderly bird or a coarse piece of venison can be pot-roasted.

Roasting Times

The following times are only a guide. Completely accurate times for roasting cannot be given because much depends on the size and age of a bird, rabbit or hare, whether it has been hung and for how long. The roasting time for a stuffed item is always calculated on the total weight including the stuffing. A stuffed bird or other meat must always be cooked at a high temperature, at least 200°–220°C/400°–425°F/Gas Mark 6–7 for 20 minutes to heat the centre of the stuffing. Today, it is also thought wise to cook unstuffed poultry at the same high temperature for 20 minutes, but it can then finish cooking at a lower temperature. (See low Temp. Cooking Times below.) The low Temp. Cooking Time is the total time the meat will take to cook including 20 minutes at a high temperature to start with, if used.

Test whether a bird or game animal is cooked by running a skewer into the thickest part of the thigh. The meat should be tender and any juices which run out should be colourless.

Opposite: *Roast Chicken served with roast potatoes, bacon, sausages and seasonal vegetables makes an economical Sunday lunch.*

TABLE OF ROASTING TIMES FOR POULTRY/GAME

Poultry	High Roasting Temp. 200°–220°C/400°–425°F/ Gas Mark 6–7 throughout	Low Roasting Temp. 20 minutes at 200°–220°C/ 400°–425°F/Gas Mark 6–7. The remaining time at 160°C/325°F/Gas Mark 3
Chicken	20 minutes per 450 g/1 lb + 20 minutes	25–30 minutes per 450 g/1 lb + 25 minutes
Turkey up to 4.5 kg/ 10 lb	20 minutes per 450 g/1 lb + 20 minutes	25 minutes per 450 g/1 lb + 25 minutes

For turkeys over 4.5 kg/10 lb (oven-ready stuffed weight), calculate the total cooking time and deduct 1 hour.

Duck	20 minutes per 450 g/1 lb	25–30 minutes per 450 g/1 lb
Goose	15 minutes per 450 g/1 lb + 15 minutes	25–30 minutes per 450 g/1 lb
Guinea fowl (Cornish hen)	45–60 minutes according to size	
Quail	15–25 minutes according to size.	

Game	High Roasting Temp. 220°C/425°F/Gas Mark 7 throughout or reduce to 200°C/400°F/ Gas Mark 6 after 10 minutes (average)	Moderate Roasting Temp. 190°C/375°F/Gas Mark 5 throughout.

Note: Temperatures and times vary with size, weight and age. Unstuffed older dry birds can be cooked at the moderate temperature throughout. Cooking suggestions are given below.

Grouse	30 minutes (average) – young birds	30–45 minutes – old birds
Pheasant	40–45 minutes	45 minutes–1 hour
Pigeon	15–20 minutes	20–30 minutes
Partridge	25–30 minutes (baste well with butter)	30–40 minutes (baste well with butter or sour cream)
Wild duck, widgeon, teal	20–25 minutes (teal 18–20 minutes)	25–30 minutes (not teal).
Rabbit and hare	Roast rabbit and hare is inclined to be dry and should be stuffed with a good forcemeat and basted well during cooking. Both meats are really better cooked in other ways, such as casseroles, sautés or fricassées.	

Accompaniments for Roast Poultry and Game

Roast Chicken and Guineafowl

Basic Stuffing or Parsley and Thyme Stuffing (page 93)
Bread Sauce (page 87)
Cocktail Sausages (15 g/½ oz each)
Bacon Rolls (page 75)
Pan-Juice Gravy (page 71)
Watercress as garnish

Roast Turkey

Sausagemeat Stuffing (page 94) and Chestnut Stuffing (page 93) OR Basic Stuffing in crop (page 93)
Bread Sauce (page 87) OR Cranberry Sauce (page 91)
Chipolata Sausages (25 g/1 oz each)
Bacon Rolls (page 75)
Thick Gravy (page 71)

Roast Duck and Goose

Sage and Onion Stuffing (page 93)
Apple Sauce (page 86) OR Cranberry Sauce
    (page 87) OR Cumberland Sauce (page 90)
Thick Gravy (page 71)
Watercress as garnish (duck)

Roast Game Birds

Croûtes of Fried Bread as 'carrier' (small birds)
    OR fried breadcrumbs (larger birds)
Bread Sauce (page 87) for grouse, partridge,
    pheasant and pigeon; Cumberland Sauce
    (page 90) for wild duck
Bacon Rolls (below)
Redcurrant Jelly
Game chips or Potato Straws (page 99)
Gravy made from giblets or Pan-Juice Gravy
    (page 71)
Watercress as garnish

Roast Hare and Venison

Basic Stuffing (page 93) OR Forcemeat Balls
    (page 93)
Bacon Rolls (below)
Redcurrant Jelly OR Cranberry Sauce (page 91)
Potato Straws (page 99) for hare; Roast Potatoes
    (page 99) for venison
Thick Gravy (page 71) or Cumberland Sauce
    (page 90)

Roast Rabbit

Basic Stuffing (page 93) OR Forcemeat Balls
    (page 93)
Bacon Rolls (below)
Redcurrant Jelly OR Cranberry Sauce (page 91)
Potato Straws (page 99) OR Sautéed Potatoes
    (page 107)
Thick Gravy (page 71)

Bacon Rolls for Poultry and Game

Use thinly cut rashers (slices) of bacon. Cut off the
rind and trim the opposite edge. Lay the slices flat.
Hold the flat of a knife-blade on each slice in
turn and stretch the slice by pulling it from under
the blade. Cut in half. Roll up and thread on a
metal skewer. Bake for 10–12 minutes in a small tin
(pan) under the roast, turning once, or fry, turning
as needed, until crisp.

Fried Breadcrumbs

Put 25 g/1 oz/2 tbls butter or margarine in a frying-
pan (skillet) and melt it. Season 50 g/2 oz/½ cup
fine white breadcrumbs lightly with salt and pepper, and add to the pan. Stir constantly over medium heat, turning the crumbs over until they are
evenly golden and crisp. Drain at once on soft
kitchen paper. Serve warm or at room temperature.

FRYING AND GRILLING

Small whole birds can be spatchcocked for frying
or grilling (broiling). Tender, fleshy poultry and
rabbit portions or joints can be cooked in the same
ways, and so can cutlets and chops from roasting
cuts of venison. Any of these can be grilled on a
barbecue. The thin fillets or strips of meat called
aiguillettes can be fried but are not suitable for
grilling.

Preparation

Birds, joints or cuts to be fried can be rolled in
seasoned flour, or in beaten egg with a top coating
of flour or crumbs. For grilling (broiling), they can
be coated likewise and dotted with fat, or they can
just be seasoned, then brushed with melted fat or
oil. They can also be dipped in batter and fried.

Method

Deep fry or shallow fry in oil or fat, depending on
the recipe. Grill (broil) under medium heat, turning pieces as required; baste often during grilling.
Drain either fried or grilled meat on soft kitchen
paper, and serve while still really hot.

Spatchcocked Chicken or Pigeon

Serves 4

Freeze 2 months (prepared raw birds)

	Metric	Imperial	American

Poussins or spring
    chickens or
    large pigeons
	2	2	2

Butter, melted	60 ml	4 tbls	4 tbls
Salt and pepper			
Bacon rolls (left)			
Watercress			

1. Split the birds in half, cutting through the
    back only. Flatten, skin side down, taking
    out the breast-bone if you wish. Break the
    joints and remove the wing pinion joints.
    Skewer to keep flat.
2. Brush both sides of each bird with melted
    butter. Season lightly. Grill (broil) under
    medium heat, basting well and turning once
    or twice to cook both sides. Cook for about
    20 minutes in all.
3. Serve half a bird to each person, garnished
    with bacon rolls and watercress.

Chicken Maryland

Serves 4

Freeze 1 month (prepared raw chicken and bacon
    only)

	Metric	Imperial	American
Oven-ready chicken	1 kg	2¼ lb	2¼ lb
Seasoned flour	45 ml	3 tbls	3 tbls
Egg and bread-crumbs for coating			
Butter or margarine	50 g	2 oz	¼ cup
Oil (or use oil for deep frying, omitting fat)	30 ml	2 tbls	2 tbls
Bacon rolls (page 75)	8	8	8
Bananas	4	4	4
Sweetcorn Fritters (page 171)			

1. Cut the chicken into small joints or portions.
   Coat with seasoned flour. Egg and crumb
   twice.
2. Heat the butter and oil in a large frying-pan
   (skillet), and fry the chicken pieces until
   lightly browned all over. Reduce the heat
   and continue frying gently for 20 minutes or
   until tender. Alternatively, deep fry in hot oil
   for about 10 minutes.
3. Drain on soft kitchen paper, and keep hot.
4. Slice the bananas lengthways and fry in hot
   butter for 3 minutes, turning once.
5. Serve the chicken and bananas with hot
   bacon rolls and sweetcorn fritters.

Below: *Chicken Maryland with accompaniments of
fried bananas, bacon rolls and sweetcorn fritters.*

Opposite: *Stir-Fried Chicken can be varied to include
any seasonal vegetables.*

Stir-Fried Chicken

Serves 4

Not suitable for freezing

	Metric	Imperial	American
Chicken breast meat without bone	350 g	12 oz	¾ lb
Green pepper, cored and de-seeded	1	1	1
Carrots, sliced very thinly	100 g	4 oz	¼ lb
Cabbage, finely shredded	175 g	6 oz	6 oz
227 g/8 oz can of pineapple rings in natural juice	1	1	1
Soy sauce	10 ml	2 tsp	2 tsp
Mild vinegar	15 ml	1 tbls	1 tbls
Corn oil	45 ml	3 tbls	3 tbls

1. Cut the chicken meat and pepper separately into small strips. Drain the pineapple rings, reserve the juice and cut the rings into small segments.
2. Heat 30 ml/2 tbls of the oil in a large frying pan (skillet). Toss the chicken meat in the hot oil until white all over. Remove the chicken, leaving the oil in the pan.
3. Put the remaining oil, pepper strips and carrot in the pan and stir for about 2 minutes. Add the shredded cabbage and stir 1 minute longer.
4. Replace the chicken, and sprinkle the soy sauce over it. Stir until thoroughly mixed.
5. Add the pineapple pieces, juice and vinegar. Stir round and simmer gently for 3 minutes. Taste and stir in a little water if you prefer a milder flavour.
6. Serve very hot with wholewheat noodles.

Variation
Other vegetables can be added or substituted for those above, e.g. sliced mushrooms, bean sprouts, cucumber or chopped celery.

BOILING AND STEWING

As in cooking fish and meat, 'boiling' poultry or game really means simmering it gently in plenty of liquid. The method is used for cooking a large, elderly boiling fowl or chicken to be served hot coated with a sauce. It is also used for cooking a fowl or other poultry or game meat which will be used for a dish such as a fricassée (page 79), chaud-froid (page 82) or Vol-au-vent filling (page 83) for which the meat must be cooked separately from its sauce.

Stewed poultry and game is usually cut into bite-sized pieces or serving portions and simmered in a well-flavoured stock or sauce. Traditionally, a stew is cooked in a sealed pot over an open fire or on top of the stove, but today it can equally well be simmered in a decorative bake-and-serve casserole in the oven where it needs less attention. The only difference in cooking method, therefore, between a modern stew and a casseroled dish is the quantity of liquid used. A casseroled dish is also more likely to have foreign or unusual ingredients or flavourings, and richer ones.

General Method (boiling)

Remove the skin. Squeeze a little lemon juice over a poultry or game bird, or a jointed blanched rabbit. Truss firmly. Cover the base of a stewpan with a cloth which has long enough ends to fold over the bird or meat. Put the bird or meat on it. Cover with boiling salted water or stock and add an onion stuck with cloves and a bouquet garni if you wish. Bring back to the boil, cover, reduce the heat and simmer until tender. A large boiling fowl may take 2–3 hours, a rabbit 1–1¼ hours. Remove from the stewpan by lifting the ends of the cloth, drain thoroughly and keep warm under a hot damped cloth or greased paper. Make a coating white sauce (page 84) using the stock as part of the liquid. Parsley Sauce (page 88) or Egg Sauce (page 88) are suitable for chicken; Onion (page 89) or Mustard Sauce (page 88) for rabbit.

General Method (stewing)

Joint a bird or rabbit or cut the meat into small pieces. Cut up any vegetables to be cooked with it. Put them in a heavy stewpan or flameproof casserole. If you wish, fry them gently in a little fat, to flavour and brown them. Add enough hot liquid to cover all the ingredients. Bring slowly to the boil, cover, reduce the heat and simmer very gently on the stove or in the oven until tender. The time will depend on the size of the meat pieces, their type and whether they are fried beforehand. Serve with mashed potatoes, noodles, dumplings or fried bread.

Note: Some poultry and game stews are nowadays called casseroles. Others have traditional names such as Jugged Hare or Civet of Venison. Strictly, such dishes are only stews if the raw ingredients are cooked in the liquid which makes their sauce.

Cooked poultry or game meat reheated in a sauce which has been made separately is not a stew. See Salmi of Game (page 83).

Chicken Casserole

Serves 6–8

Oven temp 180°C/350°F Gas Mark 4

2 months, cooked (1 month if using tomatoes)

	Metric	Imperial	American
Chicken quarters	4	4	4
Seasoned flour	25 g	1 oz	¼ cup
Streaky bacon rashes (slices), without rinds	3	3	3
Butter or margarine	75 g	3 oz	⅓ cup
Oil	30 ml	2 tbls	2 tbls
Mushrooms, sliced	100 g	4 oz	1 cup
Medium onions, chopped	2	2	2
Hot chicken stock	450 ml	¾ pt	2 cups
Tomatoes, skinned and halved (optional)	225 g	8 oz	½ lb
Salt and pepper			

1. Cut the chicken quarters in half. Skin them, and dust with half the seasoned flour. Cut the bacon into small pieces.
2. Heat half the fat and oil in a flameproof casserole (Dutch oven). Add the bacon, mushrooms and onion and fry gently until the mushrooms soften. Remove with a slotted spoon.
3. Add the remaining fat and oil to the casserole and put in the chicken pieces. Fry them until golden all over. Put with the vegetables.
4. Stir the remaining flour into the casserole and cook for 2 minutes. Gradually add the stock, and the tomatoes if used. Stir until simmering then return the chicken and vegetables.
5. Cook in the oven at the temperature above for 45 minutes–1 hour. Season if required. Serve from the casserole.

Variations
1. *Chicken Marengo*: Add 1 carrot and 1 celery stalk, sliced, to the vegetables. Use 275 ml/½ pt/1¼ cups chicken stock only, with 150 ml/ ¼ pt/⅔ cup tomato juice and 30 ml/2 tbls sherry added to it.
2. *Coq au Vin*: Use 12 button onions instead of onions. 'Flame' the chicken with 60 ml/4 tbls warm brandy after frying it, before removing it from the casserole. Use 150 ml/¼ pt/⅔ cup chicken stock only, with 450 ml/¾ pt/2 cups red wine and a pinch each of sugar and grated nutmeg. Omit the tomatoes.

3. *Chicken Chasseur*: Use only 15 g/½ oz/2 tbls seasoned flour, and coat the chicken pieces with all of it. Use only 1 onion and 50 g/ 2 oz/½ cup mushrooms and only half the fat and oil. Use 150 ml/¼ pt/⅔ cup Espagnole Sauce (page 86) and 30 ml/2 tbls white wine instead of the stock; add only 2 skinned and chopped tomatoes.

Stewed Pigeons or Rabbit

Serves 6

Freeze 2 months (raw or cooked)

	Metric	Imperial	American
Woodpigeons or large wild rabbit joints	3	3	3
Seasoned flour	20 ml	1½ tbls	1½ tbls
Butter or margarine	50 g	2 oz	¼ cup
Basic Brown Sauce (page 85)	575 ml	1 pt	2½ cups
Red wine (optional)	175 ml	6 fl oz	¾ cup
Salt and pepper			
Large onion, sliced	1	1	1

1. Halve the pigeons lengthways or cut rabbit joints in half. Toss in seasoned flour.
2. Melt the fat in a frying pan (skillet), and brown the meat all over.
3. Meanwhile, heat the sauce to simmering point in a stewpan. Transfer the meat to the pan, and add the wine if used. Season.
4. Fry the onion in the remaining fat until browned and add to the pan. Half-cover and simmer for 35–45 minutes, or until tender. (Rabbit may cook in less time than pigeon, depending on size and toughness.)
5. Transfer the meat and onions to a heated serving dish to keep warm. Simmer the sauce, uncovered, to the strength you prefer and pour over the meat. Serve with noodles, dumplings or boiled rice.

Note:
This is a good recipe for elderly or badly shot birds or other game meat. Other game birds or hare joints can be used in the same way. Adjust the cooking time as required.

Chicken or Rabbit Fricassée

Serves 4

Freeze 2 months (before making sauce)
Do not freeze completed dish.

	Metric	Imperial	American
Chicken or rabbit leg joints	4	4	4
Onion	1	1	1
Whole cloves	3	3	3
Carrot	1	1	1
Salt and pepper			
A few drops of lemon juice			
Parsley stalks	4	4	4
Bay leaf	1	1	1
Blade of mace	1	1	1
Egg yolk	1	1	1
Single (light) cream	30 ml	2 tbls	2 tbls
Butter	40 g	1½ oz	3 tbls
Flour	40 g	1½ oz	3 tbls
Chopped parsley			
Bacon rolls (page 75)	4	4	4
Fried bread triangles			

1. Put the chicken or rabbit leg joints in a stewpan. Add the onion stuck with the cloves, and the carrot, season and sprinkle with lemon juice.
2. Tie the parsley stalks, bay leaf and mace in a small piece of muslin (cheesecloth), and add to the pan.
3. Cover with water. Season lightly and add a few drops of lemon juice.
4. Bring slowly to the boil, skim well and reduce the heat to simmering. Simmer gently for 45 minutes or until the joints are tender.
5. Blend the egg yolk and cream in a small bowl, and keep aside. Melt the butter in a fairly large pan, add the flour and stir over low heat for 2–3 minutes. Do not let the flour colour. Remove from the heat.
6. Strain off 575 ml/1 pt/2½ cups of the cooking liquid into a jug. Drain off the rest into a separate bowl (reserve it for stock) and remove the muslin bag. Gradually stir the liquid in the jug into the butter-flour roux. Return to the heat and stir until the sauce thickens.
7. Add the joints and vegetables, and simmer very gently for 3 minutes. Add a little of the sauce to the blended egg and cream, and blend in.
8. Return the mixture to the sauce in the pan, stir in to mix, and reheat gently without boiling. Taste and add a little lemon juice if you wish.
9. Turn into a serving dish and sprinkle with parsley. Garnish with the fried bread triangles and bacon rolls.

Jugged Hare

Serves 6

Oven temp 160°C/325°F/Gas Mark 3

Freeze 2 months (before thickening sauce)

	Metric	Imperial	American
Hare, jointed	1	1	1
Seasoned flour	45 ml	3 tbls	3 tbls
Dripping	50 g	2 oz	¼ cup
Whole cloves	3	3	3
Onion, skinned	1	1	1
Sprig of parsley	1	1	1
Bay leaf	1	1	1
Blade of mace	1	1	1
Dried mixed herbs	2.5 ml	½ tsp	½ tsp
Peppercorns	8	8	8
Pinch of grated nutmeg			
Lemon juice	15 ml	1 tbls	1 tbls
Sugar	2.5 ml	½ tsp	½ tsp
Tawny port	150 ml	¼ pt	⅔ cup
Redcurrant jelly	50 g	2 oz	2 oz
Beef stock	1 l	1¾ pt	4⅓ cups
Butter	25 g	1 oz	2 tbls
Flour	45 ml	3 tbls	3 tbls
Forcemeat Balls (page 93)			
Redcurrant jelly, to serve			

1. Wipe the hare joints. Dredge the joints all over with seasoned flour.
2. Heat the fat in a frying pan (skillet) and fry the hare joints until well browned. Put them into a large casserole.
3. Stick the cloves into the onion; tie the parsley, bay, mace, herbs and peppercorns in a piece of muslin (cheesecloth) and add to the hare with the nutmeg, lemon juice, sugar, half the port and half the jelly.
4. Bring the stock to the boil and pour it into the casserole. Cover tightly with a lid or foil, and cook in the oven at the temperature above for 3¾ hours.
5. Pour off all the liquid into a saucepan, cover the hare and keep warm. Add the remaining wine and jelly to the hot liquid, and bring slowly to the boil, stirring until the jelly dissolves. Remove from the heat.
6. Mix the butter and flour to a smooth paste (beurre manié), and drop little by little into the hot liquid. When dissolved, return the pan to the heat, and stir until the sauce thickens slightly. Pour over the hare.
7. Add forcemeat balls, and serve from the casserole, handing redcurrant jelly separately.

Note: If you have the hare's blood, add it to the thickened sauce and reheat WITHOUT boiling before pouring the sauce over the hare.

Jugged Hare with the traditional accompaniments of red currant jelly and forcement balls.

Civet of Venison

Serves 4–6

Freeze 2 months (before thickening sauce)

	Metric	Imperial	American
Stewing venison, or venison trimmings, cubed	800 g	1¾ lb	1¾ lb
Cooked Red Wine Marinade (page 92)			
Oil	45 ml	3 tbls	3 tbls
Bacon scraps or rindless rashers (slices) cut in small pieces	100 g	4 oz	¼ lb
Button mushrooms	175 g	6 oz	1½ cups
Concentrated tomato paste	15 ml	1 tbls	1 tbls
Butter or margarine	25 g	1 oz	2 tbls
Flour	25 g	1 oz	¼ cup
Salt and pepper			
Sugar	5 ml	1 tsp	1 tsp
Fried bread triangles			

1. Soak the venison in the marinade for 24 hours, then drain the marinade into a jug and reserve it. Dry the meat well with soft kitchen paper.
2. Heat 30 ml/2 tbls of the oil in a stewpan or flameproof casserole (Dutch oven) which will hold all the meat. Fry the bacon and mushrooms until the mushrooms soften. Remove with a slotted spoon.
3. Add the venison and remaining oil to the pan or casserole, and sauté over a fairly high heat to brown the meat all over. Replace the bacon and mushrooms.
4. Mix the tomato paste into the marinade and add the mixture to the venison. Cover the pan or casserole and simmer very gently over a low heat for about 2 hours until the meat is tender.
5. Blend the fat and flour together to make a smooth paste (beurre manié). Take the stew off the heat, and stir in the beurre manié in small spoonfuls. When dissolved, return the pan or casserole to the heat and stir gently until the sauce thickens. Season and add the sugar.
6. Serve in a deep warmed dish, with the fried bread triangles round the edge. Serve with creamed potatoes or buttered noodles.

Note: This stew can also be cooked in the oven at 160°C/325°F/Gas Mark 3.

Chicken Paprika

Serves 4

Freeze 1 month

	Metric	Imperial	American
Chicken portions	4	4	4
Oil	30 ml	2 tbls	2 tbls
Medium onions, sliced	2	2	2
Mushrooms, sliced	50 g	2 oz	½ cup
Tomatoes, skinned and sliced	4	4	4
Garlic clove, peeled and crushed	1	1	1
Paprika	15 ml	1 tbls	1 tbls
Chicken stock	450 ml	¾ pt	2 cups
Salt and pepper			
Cornflour (optional)	15 ml	1 tbls	1 tbls
Chopped parsley	15 ml	1 tbls	1 tbls

1. Trim chicken joints. Heat the oil in a medium-sized saucepan, add chicken joints and fry until lightly browned on all sides. Remove from saucepan.
2. Add onions to oil in saucepan and fry until golden, add mushrooms and tomatoes and cook for 2 minutes.
3. Stir in garlic and paprika. Return chicken joints to the saucepan, pour over stock and season with salt and pepper. Simmer the chicken until tender, about 3/4 hour.
4. Lift chicken joints out of saucepan and arrange on a warmed serving dish. If wished, blend cornflour with a little water and stir into saucepan to thicken sauce. Bring to the boil, stirring, cook 1 minute. Pour sauce over chicken joints and sprinkle with chopped parsley. Serve with mashed potatoes and a green vegetable.

BRAISING

An elderly fowl or duck, or a piece of stewing venison can be braised instead of stewed. Follow the general directions for braising and for making the Mirepoix on page 64, and the recipe for Braised Beef on page 66. Use Chicken Stock (page 15) for braising a fowl (or turkey meat). Use Brown Stock (page 14) for duck, and Meat Stock (page 14) with red wine for a piece of shoulder of venison or a similar cut.

Turkey legs, which take longer to roast than the breast meat, can be cut off before cooking and braised as a separate dish.

Chaudfroid of Chicken or Turkey

Serves 6

Not suitable for freezing

	Metric	Imperial	American
Chicken portions, cooked as for a fricassée (page 79) OR slices of roast turkey breast	6	6	6
Chaudfroid Sauce (page 91), cooled but not yet set	275 ml	½ pt	1¼ cups
Tiny shapes cut from black (ripe) olives and red pepper, to garnish			
Lettuce leaves, to serve			

1. Remove any skin from the chicken or turkey and wipe dry. Trim neatly and arrange on a wire cooling rack standing on a sheet of greaseproof (waxed) paper.
2. Just before the Chaudfroid Sauce reaches setting point, spoon it over the poultry meat, coating the pieces evenly. Using clean tweezers, garnish with the olive and pepper shapes and leave to set.
3. Chill on a tray, keeping the pieces of meat separate. When the Chaudfroid Sauce is quite firm, arrange the pieces of meat carefully on a bed of lettuce leaves for serving.

Note: Six boned chicken breasts poached as above can be used instead of chicken portions. Sieved hard-boiled egg yolk can be sprinkled on the Chaudfroid instead of using the olive and pepper shapes.

Chicken Liver Risotto

Serves 4

Freeze 2 months (without extra butter and cheese)

	Metric	Imperial	American
Butter or margarine	75 g	3 oz	6 tbls
Medium onion, finely chopped	1	1	1
Chicken or turkey livers, halved	225 g	8 oz	½ lb
Celery stalk, chopped	1	1	1
Green or red pepper, blanched, deseeded and chopped	1	1	1
Mushrooms, sliced	100 g	4 oz	1 cup
Ham, diced	50 g	2 oz	¼ cup
White wine	150 ml	¼ pt	⅔ cup
Long grain rice	225 g	8 oz	½ lb
Chopped herbs, e.g. marjoram, thyme, basil, parsley	15 ml	1 tbls	1 tbls
Salt and pepper			
Chicken stock	450 ml	¾ pt	2 cups
Extra butter	25 g	1 oz	2 tbls
Parmesan cheese			

1. Melt 50 g/2 oz/¼ cup of the fat in a heavy saucepan and fry the onion until soft and golden. Add the livers and turn in the fat until just stiffened.
2. Add the remaining fat and the remaining vegetables and ham, and fry, stirring, for 3 minutes. Add the wine and let it bubble for 2 minutes.
3. Stir in the rice, herbs and a little seasoning, and cover with the stock. Bring to simmering point, cover and cook for 15–20 minutes until the stock has almost been absorbed and the rice is tender but not soggy.
4. Stir towards the end of cooking to prevent sticking, and add a very little boiling water if needed. The rice should still be moist when ready. Stir in the extra butter and Parmesan cheese to taste just before serving.

Variations
Diced cooked chicken or turkey meat can also be used, and some cooked shelled prawns (shrimp) can then be added towards the end of the cooking time if you wish.

Salmi of Game

Serves 4–5

Freeze 1 month (garnished meat and sauce separately, complete dish after thawing)

	Metric	Imperial	American
Underdone roast duck, goose, or game bird(s), see recipe			
Salt and pepper			
Mushrooms	12	12	12
Shallots	2	2	2
Carrot	½	½	½
Turnip	½	½	½
Celery stalk	1	1	1
Butter or margarine	65 g	2½ oz	5 tbls
Flour	25 g	1 oz	¼ cup
Herbs, e.g. bay leaf, peppercorns, clove, blade of mace, sprig of thyme, tied in muslin (cheesecloth)			
Red wine or Madeira	150 ml	¼ pt	⅔ cup
Mashed potato (optional)			
Triangles of fried bread from 2 square slices of bread	8	8	8

1. Use one duck or the remains of a goose, 2 pheasants or 3 partridges or pigeons. Guineafowl, woodcock, wild duck, etc., can also be used.
2. Cut the meat off the bones into small pieces without skin. Place the broken-up carcass(es) or bones in a large saucepan. Cover with water, season lightly and simmer for about 1–1 ½ hours to make game stock.
3. Remove the mushroom stalks and cut up the other vegetables.
4. Melt the fat in a saucepan and fry the mushroom caps lightly. Add to the meat. Fry the shallots, mushroom stalks, carrot, turnip and celery until browned. Remove from the pan.
5. Sift in the flour. Stir until it browns, then gradually add 450 ml/¾ pt/2 cups game stock, stirring continuously. Simmer until the sauce thickens. Season, return the fried vegetables to the pan and add the herbs and wine. Continue simmering, uncovered, for 20 minutes.
6. Arrange the meat in a flameproof casserole (Dutch oven) with a lid. Put the mushrooms on top. Strain the hot sauce over them, pressing to squeeze out all the vegetable juices.
7. Cover the casserole and simmer for about 20 minutes to heat the meat through. Turn into a warmed dish. Pipe a border of mashed potato around it if you wish and garnish with the fried bread triangles.

Chicken Vol-au-Vent

Serves 4–6

Oven temp 220–230°C/425–450°F/Gas Mark 7–8

Freeze 2 months (unfilled case) Do not freeze filling

	Metric	Imperial	American
½ recipe quantity Puff Pastry (page 151)			
Beaten egg for glazing			
Chicken meat, poached as for Chicken Fricassée (page 79)	100 g	4 oz	¼ lb
Coating White Sauce (page 84)	150 ml	¼ pt	⅔ cup
Single (light) cream	30 ml	2 tbls	2 tbls
Lemon juice or chopped parsley to flavour			
Sprinkling of paprika			

1. Make a vol-au-vent case with the pastry (page 154). Brush the top with beaten egg, avoiding the edges and the centre cut for the lid.
2. Bake on a dampened baking sheet at the temperature above for 20 minutes. Remove any uncooked pastry inside. Cool if serving cold.
3. Remove any skin from the chicken. Dice or chop the meat.
4. Mix together the White Sauce, cream and lemon juice or parsley. Fold in the chicken. Heat gently if serving hot.
5. Spoon the mixture into the vol-au-vent case. Warm in a very low oven if required.

Variation
For cocktail or buffet vols-au-vent, make 12–16 cases as described on page 153. Keep hot. Heat the chicken mixture and spoon into the cases, piling it up above the pastry. Serve warm.

6
SAUCES, MARINADES AND STUFFINGS

A sauce or dressing is an essential binding and moistening ingredient of many dishes. In others, a well-flavoured sauce, dressing or stuffing adds a valuable flavouring and texture contrast.

SAUCES

The biggest group of sauces consist of those thickened with flour, cornflour or other starch. They may be white or brown, depending on how the starch is cooked, and may be used hot or cold. Other sauces are thickened with breadcrumbs, ground nuts or puréed vegetables or fruit, or by boiling down the basic liquid to reduce it to a syrupy consistency, e.g. meat glaze (page 71). Some rich sauces are thickened by having egg yolk and cream whisked into the liquid. Another group consists of sauces, or more often salad dressings, based on an emulsion of eggs and oil or fat; mayonnaise is the best known example. There are also thin sauces, based on stock, e.g. pan-juice gravy (page 71), sometimes mixed with fruit juice or red or white wine.

The first two recipes below describe the method of making the basic white and brown sauces used as the foundation of many other sauces including the cold sauces stiffened with aspic jelly or gelatine (unflavored gelatin) called chaudfroid sauces (page 91). The French equivalents, Béchamel (white) Sauce, Espagnole (brown) Sauce and Velouté (fawn) Sauce are included among the variously thickened sauces which follow the two basic sauces and their variants.

These two basic sauces are made of:
1. Equal quantities (as a rule) of fat (butter or margarine) and flour cooked together until the starch grains in the flour burst; this mixture is called a roux. When making a white sauce, the flour is not allowed to colour, but for a brown sauce it is cooked until nut-brown, taking care that it does not burn.
2. Liquid (which is stirred into the roux). This may be milk, milk and water or cream, stock, stock and wine, or the cooking liquid of boiled meat, fish or vegetables.
3. Seasonings and flavourings, added to taste, enough to give the sauce the characteristic flavour and sometimes texture of the added ingredient.

The consistency of a roux-based sauce can vary:
1. *Pouring Sauce*: Use 15 g/½ oz/ 1 tbls fat and 15 g/½ oz/2 tbls flour to 275 ml/½ pt/1¼ cups liquid;
2. *Coating Sauce*: Use 25 g/1 oz/2 tbls fat and 25 g/1 oz/¼ cup flour to 275 ml/½ pt/1¼ cups liquid;
3. *Binding Sauce or panada*: Use 25 g/1 oz/2 tbls fat and 25 g/1 oz/¼ cup flour to 150 ml/¼ pt/⅔ cup liquid. This is used to hold together other ingredients when making rissoles, croquettes, fish cakes, egg cutlets, etc., and as a base for soufflé mixtures.

Note: There are two methods of thickening a sauce besides making a roux.
(a) you can make the raw fat and flour into a paste called beurre manié, and add it by small spoonfuls to hot liquid, OFF the boil. The liquid is brought to the boil when the paste has dissolved;
(b) you can put all the basic ingredients in a saucepan, and heat them together; this is called the 'all-in-one' method.

In both cases, you must take special care to see that the flour is cooked for long enough to burst the starch grains.

Basic White Sauce

Using the proportions of the basic ingredients for the sauce consistency you require, melt the fat in a heavy-based saucepan. Add the flour, and cook together for 2–4 minutes, stirring constantly without letting the flour colour. Add the liquid gradually (preferably hot), stirring well to prevent lumps forming. Bring to the boil, and boil gently for 5–10 minutes to cook the flour completely. Season, and flavour as you wish.

Basic Brown Sauce

Makes 575 ml/1 pt/2½ cups

Cooking time 25 minutes

Freeze 4 months

	Metric	Imperial	American
Onion	1	1	1
Piece of carrot, swede (rutabaga) or turnip			
Small celery stalk	1	1	1
Small tomato	1	1	1
Dripping	25 g	1 oz	2 tbls
Plain (all-purpose) flour	25 g	1 oz	¼ cup
Brown Stock (page 14) or water	575 ml	1 pt	2½ cups
Salt and pepper			
Sprig of parsley			

1. Prepare the vegetables and cut into 5 mm/¼ in pieces.
2. Melt the dripping in a saucepan. Add the vegetables, and cover.
3. Fry very gently for 10 minutes, shaking the pan and turning the vegetables over from time to time.
4. Add the flour, and fry gently over low heat, stirring often, until evenly coloured nut brown.
5. Add the liquid gradually, stirring to prevent lumps forming. Season and add the parsley sprig. Bring to the boil, and skim if required.
6. Replace the lid, and let the sauce simmer for 30 minutes. Strain before use.

Béchamel Sauce

Makes 275 ml/½ pt/1¼ cups (approx)

Freeze 2 months

	Metric	Imperial	American
Milk or half milk and half white stock	275 ml	½ pt	1¼ cups
Small onion	½	½	½
White peppercorns	6	6	6
Bay leaf	½	½	½
Dried mixed herbs or a few sprigs of fresh herbs	2.5 ml	½ tsp	½ tsp
Blade of mace	½	½	½
Butter or margarine	15 g	½ oz	1 tbls
Plain flour	15 g	½ oz	2 tbls
Salt			
Single (light) cream (optional)	15–30 ml	1–2 tbls	1–2 tbls

1. Heat the milk or milk and water, to simmering point, add the onion, peppercorns, bay leaf, herbs and mace. Cover and remove from the heat.
2. Infuse the onions, peppercorns, bay leaf, herbs and mace for 15 minutes in the hot milk.
3. Make a white roux with the fat and flour. Gradually strain in the flavoured milk, stirring constantly, to make the sauce.
4. Bring to the boil and cook gently for 3 minutes, beating constantly to make the sauce glossy.
5. Strain through a fine strainer or scalded piece of muslin (cheesecloth) spread over a bowl (see note). Season with salt and add the cream if you wish. Reheat but do not re-boil.

Note: Pour the sauce into the centre of a cloth. Gather up the corners of the muslin in one hand, and hold it up over the bowl. Twist it with the other hand to squeeze the sauce through.

Velouté Sauce

Makes 150 ml/¼ pt/⅔ cup (without cream)

Freeze 2 months

	Metric	Imperial	American
Button mushrooms	3	3	3
Butter or margarine	40 g	1½ oz	3 tbls
Peppercorns	6	6	6
Dried mixed herbs	1.5 ml	¼ tsp	¼ tsp
Flour	25 g	1 oz	¼ cup
White Stock (page 14)	450 ml	¾ pt	2 cups
Salt and pepper			
A few drops of lemon juice			
Single (light) cream (optional)	150–275 ml	¼–½ pt	⅔–1¼ cups

1. In a medium-sized saucepan, fry the mushrooms in the fat until soft but not coloured. Add the peppercorns and herbs.
2. Stir in the flour, then add the stock gradually, stirring constantly. Continue stirring until the sauce boils.
3. Reduce the heat and simmer very gently for about 10 minutes, stirring occasionally.
4. Strain through a fine strainer or scalded piece of muslin (cheesecloth). Mix in the other ingredients and reheat without boiling.

Espagnole Sauce (Basic French Brown Sauce)

Makes 225 ml/8 fl oz/1 cup

Oven temp 160°C/325°F/Mark 3

Freeze 2 months

	Metric	Imperial	American
Bacon rasher (slice) *without rind*	1	1	1
Shallot	1	1	1
Mushroom stalks *(stems)*	60 ml	4 tbls	4 tbls
Small carrot	1	1	1
Butter	25 g	1 oz	2 tbls
Flour	30 ml	2 tbls	2 tbls
Hot beef stock	450 ml	¾ pt	2 cups
Black peppercorns	6	6	6
Parsley stalks	4	4	4
Concentrated tomato paste	30 ml	2 tbls	2 tbls
Salt			

1. Chop the bacon rasher and vegetables, keeping the bacon separate.
2. In a small flameproof casserole (Dutch oven), fry the chopped bacon in the butter for 2 minutes. Add the vegetables, and fry for another 3 minutes, stirring constantly. Scatter in the flour, and continue stirring until it browns.
3. Remove the casserole from the heat, and gradually stir in the stock. Return the casserole to the heat, and stir until the sauce boils.
4. Tie the peppercorns and parsley stalks in a twist of muslin (cheesecloth), and add this bouquet garni to the casserole with the tomato paste and a little salt.
5. Cover and cook at the temperature above for 1½ hours, stirring occasionally.
6. Strain the sauce, and skim off any fat. Season again if required. Store and reheat when required.

OTHER HOT SAUCES FOR SAVOURY DISHES

Apple Sauce

Makes 450 ml/¾ pt/2 cups (approx)

Freeze 9 months

	Metric	Imperial	American
Cooking (tart) apples, peeled, cored and sliced	450 g	1 lb	1 lb
Sugar	50 g	2 oz	¼ cup
Grated rind and juice of ½ lemon			
Water	45 ml	3 tbls	3 tbls
Butter or margarine	25 g	1 oz	2 tbls

1. Place the apples in a saucepan with the sugar, lemon rind and water and simmer until very soft. Purée by sieving or process in a blender or food processor.
2. Reheat with the fat and with lemon juice to taste until hot. Serve with pork, duck or goose.

Barbecue Sauce

Makes 450 ml/¾ pt/2 cups (approx)

Freeze 9 months

	Metric	Imperial	American
Medium onion, finely chopped	1	1	1
Butter or margarine	50 g	2 oz	¼ cup
Tomato juice	225 ml	8 fl oz	1 cup
Water	100 ml	4 fl oz	½ cup
Tomato ketchup	50 ml	2 fl oz	¼ cup
Worcestershire sauce	15 ml	1 tbls	1 tbls
Red wine vinegar	15 ml	1 tbls	1 tbls
Soft brown sugar	30 ml	2 tbls	2 tbls
Dry mustard	5 ml	1 tsp	1 tsp
Pinch of salt			
Pinch of chilli powder (optional)			
Cornflour (cornstarch) (optional)	15 ml	1 tbls	1 tbls

1. Fry the onion in the fat in a heavy saucepan until soft.
2. Add all the remaining ingredients except the cornflour. Simmer gently for 10 minutes.
3. If you wish to thicken the sauce, blend the cornflour with a little water and blend it in gradually. Bring to the boil, and simmer until thickened.

Brown Butter (Noisette) Sauce

Heat butter gently in a saucepan until light brown. Take off the heat and stir in lemon juice to taste. Serve over brains, white fish, roes or vegetables. For eggs, substitute white vinegar for the lemon juice.

Bread Sauce

Makes 275 ml/½ pt/1¼ cups

Freeze 1 month

	Metric	Imperial	American
Whole cloves	2	2	2
Small onion	1	1	1
Peppercorns	6	6	6
Milk	275 ml	½ pt	1¼ cups
White breadcrumbs	50 g	2 oz	1 cup
Salt	2.5 ml	½ tsp	½ tsp
Pepper			
Single (light) cream			
(optional)	15 ml	1 tbls	1 tbls

1. Stick the cloves in the onion. Put in a saucepan with the peppercorns. Add the milk.
2. Bring to simmering point, cover, and simmer very gently for 15 minutes.
3. Strain the milk over the breadcrumbs. Season. Put in a clean pan. Bring back to just below simmering point, and hold at this temperature for 5–7 minutes. Stir in the cream if used. Allow to reheat but do not boil.

Note: Slightly dry breadcrumbs give the characteristic porridgy type of sauce. Use soft breadcrumbs for a very smooth sauce.

Black Butter Sauce

Makes 100 ml/4 fl oz/½ cup (approx)

Freeze 2 months

	Metric	Imperial	American
Butter	100 g	4 oz	½ cup
Finely chopped			
parsley leaves	15 ml	1 tbls	1 tbls
Vinegar	5 ml	1 tsp	1 tsp
Drained chopped			
capers (optional)	5–10 ml	1–2 tsp	1–2 tsp

1. Heat the butter until nut-brown; take care it does not burn. Lift it off the heat immediately.
2. Add all the other ingredients. Reheat if needed, without boiling. Serve at once, in a very hot sauce boat, with fish, brains or certain vegetables.

EGG-BASED SAUCES

The main ingredients of these sauces are egg yolks and butter. Care must be taken when making or they may curdle. Hollandaise Sauce is usually served with vegetables and egg dishes. Bearnaise Sauce goes well with grilled meats or fish.

Hollandaise Sauce

Makes 275 ml/½ pt/1¼ cups

Not suitable for freezing

	Metric	Imperial	American
Lemon juice	10 ml	2 tsp	2 tsp
Wine vinegar	10 ml	2 tsp	2 tsp
Water	15 ml	1 tbls	1 tbls
Peppercorns	5	5	5
Bay leaf	1	1	1
Egg yolks	3	3	3
Butter, softened	175 g	6 oz	¾ cup
Salt and pepper			

1. Put the lemon juice, vinegar, water, peppercorns and bay leaf into a small saucepan. Boil gently until liquor is reduced by half. Leave to cool, then strain.
2. Put egg yolks and strained vinegar liquor into a double saucepan or basin standing over a pan of simmering water.
3. Whisk until thick and foamy.
4. Whisk in butter a tiny piece at a time, whisking well between each addition.
5. The finished sauce should be thick and shiny and the consistency of mayonnaise. Season with salt and pepper. Serve at once.

Bernaise Sauce

Makes 275 ml/½ pt/1¼ cups

Not suitable for freezing

	Metric	Imperial	American
Tarragon vinegar	30 ml	2 tbls	2 tbls
Wine vinegar	45 ml	3 tbls	3 tbls
Onion, finely			
chopped	15 ml	1 tbls	1 tbls
Egg yolks	2	2	2
Butter, softened	100 g	4 oz	½ cup
Salt and pepper			

1. Put both vinegars and the onion into a small saucepan. Boil gently until the liquid has reduced by one-third. Leave to cool, strain.
2. Put egg yolks and strained liquid into a double saucepan or basin standing over a pan of simmering water. Whisk until thick and foamy.
3. Gradually whisk in the butter a tiny piece at a time, whisking well between each addition.
4. The sauce should be thick and glossy. Season with salt and pepper.

Hot Savoury Sauces Made with 275 ml/½ pt/1¼ cups Basic White Sauce

Name	Extra Ingredients	Notes
Anchovy Sauce	5–10 ml/1–2 tsp anchovy essence A few drops of lemon juice 1–2 drops of red food colouring	Use fish stock if possible, alone or with milk.
Caper Sauce	15 ml/1 tbls capers, chopped 15 ml/1 tbls vinegar from caper jar	Served with fish or boiled lamb. Can also be made with Basic Brown Sauce.
Cheese Sauce	50 g/2 oz grated hard cheese (Cheddar, Cheshire, etc.) or more to taste. A little prepared mustard	If for an 'au gratin' dish, reserve some of the cheese for the topping.
Dutch Sauce	1 egg yolk A few drops of lemon juice, and white wine or vinegar	Reheat but do not boil after adding egg. Add flavourings to taste.
Egg Sauce	1 chopped hard-boiled egg	
Hollandaise Sauce (mock)	1–2 egg yolks A little milk or white stock Lemon juice Cayenne pepper and salt	Called Mock Hollandaise because real Hollandaise (page 87) is a butter-egg emulsion sauce. If using 2 egg yolks, add them separately, stirring over low heat until blended and thick before adding flavourings.
Maître d' Hôtel Sauce	15 g/½ oz butter 10 ml/2 tsp chopped parsley 5 ml/1 tsp lemon juice Cayenne pepper and salt	Add parsley to sauce, and bring to the boil. Take off heat and whisk in butter and lemon juice a little at a time, then season. Serve with chicken, fish or vegetables. For fish make sauce with half fish stock and half milk.
Mushroom Sauce (white)	50–100 g/2–4 oz/½–1 cup button mushrooms	Simmer the mushrooms in the milk before making a coating sauce. Strain and chop mushrooms, then make the sauce with the flavoured milk. Add the chopped mushrooms.
Mustard Sauce	15 ml/1 tbls French mustard 5 ml/1 tsp white vinegar 5 ml/1 tsp sugar (optional) 15 g/½ oz/1 tbls butter	Mix mustard, vinegar and sugar, and whisk into hot sauce. Reheat to just below the boil and whisk in butter in small pats. Do not boil.
Onion Sauce (white)	2 large onions, chopped	Boil onions in salted water until soft, add to sauce.
Parsley Sauce	15 ml/1 tbls finely chopped parsley 25 g/1 oz/2 tbls butter	Rinse chopped parsley, add to hot sauce. Bring to the boil, take off the heat and whisk in the butter.
Prawn or Shrimp Sauce	50 g/2 oz prepared fresh, frozen or canned prawns or shrimps 5 ml/1 tsp lemon juice Cayenne pepper	Make sauce with half fish stock, half milk or all milk if fish stock is not available. Thaw frozen shellfish, rinse and drain all shellfish well, then pat dry and chop. Add to sauce with lemon juice and seasoning.

Name	Extra Ingredients	Notes
Tartare Sauce (hot) (can also be made with Béchamel Sauce)	1 egg yolk 15 ml/1 tbls single (light) cream 5 ml/1 tsp chopped parsley 5 ml/1 tsp chopped gherkin 5 ml/1 tsp drained chopped capers Lemon juice Salt and cayene pepper	Mix egg yolk and cream and stir into cooled sauce. Add parsley and heat below the boil until sauce thickens. Add remaining ingredients, using enough lemon juice to sharpen.

Hot Savoury Sauces Made with 275 ml/½ pt/1¼ cups Basic Brown Sauce

Name	Extra Ingredients	Notes
Mushroom Sauce (brown)	100 g/4 oz button mushrooms	Chop mushroom stalks and fry with other vegetables for the sauce. Add mushroom caps to the sauce 10 minutes before the end of the simmering time. Strain with other vegetables, remove from strainer, then chop and return to the sauce.
Onion Sauce (brown)	Use 1 extra onion instead of carrot, celery and tomato when making the sauce. Add 5 ml/1 tsp red wine vinegar and 2.5 ml/½ tsp French mustard to the sauce.	
Italian Sauce	1 small onion, chopped 6 mushrooms, chopped 25 g/1 oz/2 tbls butter or margarine 45 ml/3 tbls sherry or wine (optional) Sprig of thyme 1 bay leaf Salt and cayenne pepper	Fry the onion and mushrooms in the fat, add to the sauce with the sherry or wine and herbs before simmering it. Simmer, then season, skim if needed, and strain before use.
Pepper Sauce (Poivrade Sauce)	2 shallots, finely chopped 8 black peppercorns Sprig of thyme 1 bay leaf 45 ml/3 tbls red wine 20 ml/4 tsp red wine vinegar Freshly ground black pepper	Simmer all the ingredients except the ground pepper until the liquid is reduced by a third. Strain it into the hot sauce and season with pepper.
Salmi Sauce	2 shallots, finely chopped 25 g/1 oz/¼ cup button mushrooms, finely chopped 15 ml/1 tbls oil 150 ml/¼ pt/⅔ cup game stock Sprig of thyme 1 bay leaf 10 ml/2 tsp redcurrant jelly	Fry the vegetables in the oil until golden, add the stock and herbs and cook gently until the liquid is reduced by half. Strain into the sauce, add the jelly and simmer until it melts.

Cumberland Sauce

Makes 275 ml/½ pt/1¼ cups

Freeze 6 months

	Metric	Imperial	American
Grated rind and juice of 1 orange and 1 lemon			
Water	75 ml	3 fl oz	⅓ cup
Port or cream sherry	75 ml	3 fl oz	⅓ cup
Red wine vinegar	30 ml	2 tbls	2 tbls
Redcurrant jelly	100 g	4 oz	¼ lb
Prepared mustard	1.5 ml	¼ tsp	¼ tsp
Salt and cayenne pepper			

1. Simmer the grated rind in the water for 5 minutes.
2. Add the port or sherry, vinegar, jelly and mustard, and stir over gentle heat until the jelly melts.
3. Add the fruit juice and season to taste. Simmer until well heated.
4. Serve hot or cold with pork, ham or any roast game bird or venison.

Curry Sauce

Makes 275 ml/½ pt/1¼ cups (approx)

Freeze 2 months

	Metric	Imperial	American
Dripping or oil	30 ml	2 tbls	2 tbls
Small onion, chopped	1	1	1
Small apple, peeled, cored and chopped	½	½	½
Curry powder to taste	15 ml (approx)	1 tbls (approx)	1 tbls (approx)
Flour	15 g	½ oz	2 tbls
Stock or cooking water from vegetables	450 ml	¾ pt	2 cups
Sultanas (golden raisins)	25 g	1 oz	3 tbls
Tomato, skinned, quartered and de-seeded	1	1	1
Soft brown sugar	2.5 ml	½ tsp	½ tsp
Salt			
Chutney or plum jam	10 ml	2 tsp	2 tsp
Lemon juice			

1. Heat the fat or oil in a saucepan. Add the onion and fry until soft. Add the apple and fry for another 2 minutes.
2. Sprinkle in the curry powder and flour. Fry, stirring, until well browned.
3. Add the stock or water gradually, stirring constantly. Bring slowly to the boil.
4. Add the remaining ingredients and cover the pan. Reduce the heat and simmer gently for 1 hour, stirring occasionally.

Fresh Tomato Sauce

Makes 275 ml/½ pt/1¼ cups (approx)

Freeze 9 months

	Metric	Imperial	American
Fresh tomatoes	600 g	1¼ lb	1¼ lb
Garlic clove	½	½	½
Small onion	1	1	1
Carrot	75 g	3 oz	3 oz
Celery stalk	1	1	1
Water	50 ml	2 fl oz	¼ cup
Salt and pepper			
Sugar or clear honey (optional)	5 ml	1 tsp	1 tsp
Chopped parsley (optional)			

1. Chop the tomatoes roughly and put in a large saucepan. Finely chop the garlic and add to the tomatoes.
2. Quarter the onion, grate (shred) the carrot and chop the celery stalk. Add to the pan with the water and a little seasoning.
3. Heat the pan gently to boiling point. Reduce the heat until it simmers. Cover, and simmer for 45 minutes–1 hour.
4. Sieve the vegetables and juice into a clean pan. Add the sugar or honey if desired and re-season. Reheat before use, and sprinkle with chopped parsley if poured over pasta or vegetables.

Note: The sauce can be refrigerated for 2 days before reheating.

COLD SAVOURY SAUCES

Chaudfroid Sauce

Makes 575 ml/1 pt/2½ cups

Not suitable for freezing

	Metric	Imperial	American
Aspic jelly (page 71)	150 ml	¼ pt	⅔ cup
Basic White Coating Sauce (page 84) or Béchamel Sauce (page 85)	275 ml	¼ pt	1¼ cups
Double (heavy) cream	150 ml	¼ pt	⅔ cup

1. Melt the aspic jelly if required, and cool to barely tepid.
2. Cool the white or Béchamel sauce to the same temperature if hot, or warm very slightly.
3. Stir the jelly and cream into the sauce. Use when quite cold but not yet set to coat chicken, fish, eggs, etc. (See Chaudfroid of Chicken or Turkey, page 82).

Mint Sauce

Makes 150 ml/¼ pt/⅔ cup (approx)

Freeze 9 months

	Metric	Imperial	American
Chopped fresh mint	60 ml	4 tbls	4 tbls
Sugar	10 ml	2 tsp	2 tsp
Boiling water	15 ml	1 tbls	1 tbls
Vinegar to taste	30 ml (approx)	2 tbls (approx)	2 tbls (approx)

1. Put the mint in a sauce boat. Add the sugar and water; stir until the sugar melts.
2. Stir in vinegar to taste. Leave for 2 hours before serving with lamb.

Tartare Sauce

Makes 175 ml/6 fl oz/¾ cup (approx)

Not suitable for freezing

	Metric	Imperial	American
Mayonnaise	150 ml	¼ pt	⅔ cup
Chopped parsley	5 ml	1 tsp	1 tsp
Chopped gherkin	5 ml	1 tsp	1 tsp
Chopped drained capers	5 ml	1 tsp	1 tsp
Chopped fresh chives, chervil or tarragon	5 ml	1 tsp	1 tsp
Tarragon vinegar or lemon juice	10 ml	2 tsp	2 tsp

1. Mix all the ingredients well.
2. Leave to stand for at least 1 hour before serving with grilled or fried fish, meat, rissoles, etc.

Cranberry Sauce

Makes 700 ml/1¼ pt/3 cups (approx)

Freeze 9 months

	Metric	Imperial	American
Fresh or frozen raw cranberries	450 g	1 lb	1 lb
White sugar	350 g	12 oz	1½ cups
Water	275 ml	½ pt	1¼ cups

1. Pick over fresh cranberries. Thaw and drain frozen fruit.
2. Put the sugar and water in a heavy saucepan, and heat slowly to the boil. Simmer the syrup for 4 minutes.
3. Add the cranberries, cover, and boil gently for 4–8 minutes until all the cranberries have popped. Cool and serve chilled.

Note: If you wish, pack the hot sauce into warmed dry jars, cover and refrigerate. The sauce will keep without being frozen for up to 2 weeks.

Horseradish Cream

Makes 225 ml/8 fl oz/1 cup (approx)

Not suitable for freezing

	Metric	Imperial	American
Grated fresh horseradish	30 ml	2 tbls	2 tbls
White vinegar or lemon juice	10 ml	2 tsp	2 tsp
White sugar	10 ml	2 tsp	2 tsp
Prepared English mustard	1.5 ml	¼ tsp	¼ tsp
Double (heavy) cream	150 ml	¼ pt	⅔ cup

1. Mix together the horseradish, vinegar or lemon juice, sugar and mustard.
2. Whip the cream until it just makes a visible trail when drips from the beater fall on it. Fold in the other ingredients.
3. Chill. Serve with beef or smoked mackerel.

MARINADES

A marinade is a liquid or mixture of liquids in which food is soaked before or instead of being cooked, primarily to tenderise it but also, as a rule, to improve its flavour. The liquid usually consists of an acid such as wine, vinegar or lemon juice mixed with oil and flavourings such as herbs and spices.

Meats and fish are the foods most often marinated, especially meat which is likely to be tough when cooked. If the meat is casseroled or grilled afterwards, the marinade is sometimes included in the cooking liquid or is used to baste the meat during cooking.

The marinade may be cooked or uncooked. An uncooked marinade works more slowly but more subtly on the food. Cooked, i.e. boiled, marinades have the merit, however, that they can be re-boiled and re-used 2 or 3 times. Either type can be strained for use as a sauce with the food.

Fish and small pieces of meat usually only need a few hours in a marinade, but large tough joints of meat may need 2–3 days, or longer in cold weather. The food must be turned in the marinade and basted with it while soaking, to moisten and impregnate it all over. An easy way to do this is to put the marinade and food in a large polythene bag, and place it in a bowl; then simply turn the bag over from time to time. Do not put the marinade directly into a metal bowl.

Many recipes recommend a specific marinade. The following ones are for general use.

Basic Uncooked Wine Marinade

Makes 275 ml/½ pt/1¼ cups (approx)

Freeze 1 month

	Metric	Imperial	American
Onion, sliced	½	½	½
Sprig of dried thyme or marjoram			
Bay leaf	½	½	½
Parsley stalks, chopped	4–6	4–6	4–6
Strip of lemon peel	1	1	1
Salt and pepper			
Red or white wine (see method)	225 ml	8 fl oz	1 cup
White wine vinegar	15 ml	1 tbls	1 tbls
Corn oil	30–45 ml	2–3 tbls	2–3 tbls

1. Tie the onion, herbs and lemon peel loosely in a piece of cloth, and place in a glass, earthenware or plastic dish which will hold the food.
2. Season the food well all over and add it to the dish.

3. Mix the liquids together and pour them over the food. Use white wine for fish, white meat or poultry, red wine for red meat or game.
4. Marinate fish for at least 30 minutes, white meat or poultry for 2–4 hours, red meat or game for 6–8 hours or overnight. Turn the food over from time to time, to make sure every part is soaked.
5. Strain the marinade if you want to use it as a braising liquid or in a casserole, or for basting.

Note: Give foods longer soaking in very cold weather.

Variations
1. Add a few fennel or dill seeds to the herbs if used for fish. Substitute lemon juice for vinegar.
2. Add a few juniper berries and 2 allspice berries if used for game.

Basic Cooked Red Wine Marinade

(for red meat or game)

Makes 1.5 l/2½ pt/6¼ cups (approx)

Freeze 1 month

	Metric	Imperial	American
Carrot, sliced	1	1	1
Onion, sliced	1	1	1
Bay leaves	2	2	2
Black peppercorns	10	10	10
Water	1 l	1¾ pt	4⅓ cups
Salt	15 ml	1 tbls	1 tbls
Red wine	275 ml	½ pt	1¼ cups
Juice of 1 lemon			
White sugar	5 ml	1 tsp	1 tsp
Juniper berries (for game)	4	4	4

1. Put the carrot, onion, bay leaves and peppercorns in a stewpan and cover with the water. Add the salt.
2. Cover the pan, and simmer until the vegetables are tender.
3. Add the wine, lemon juice, sugar and berries if used. Stir to dissolve the sugar. Allow to cool, then pour over red meat or game in a glass, earthenware or plastic bowl.
4. Marinate as required.

Note: If left for longer than 36 hours, strain off the marinade on the second day, re-boil it, allow to cool and pour it over the meat again. Repeat after another 2 days if you wish, or if the marinade has been stored. Do not re-boil more than twice.

Basic Herb Stuffing (Forcemeat)

Makes 175 g/6 oz (approx)

Freeze 1 month

	Metric	Imperial	American
Margarine, melted	50 g	2 oz	¼ cup
Fresh white or brown breadcrumbs	100 g	4 oz	2 cups
Pinch of grated nutmeg			
Finely chopped parsley	30 ml	2 tbls	2 tbls
Dried mixed herbs	2.5 ml	½ tsp	½ tsp
Grated lemon rind	1.5 ml	¼ tsp	¼ tsp
Salt and pepper			
Beaten egg	1	1	1

1. Mix the ingredients together in the order given. Season well, and use enough egg to bind.
2. Use to stuff boned meat, a chicken, fish or hollowed vegetables.

Note: For forcemeat balls, form the stuffing into small balls. Sauté until lightly browned all over, deep fry or bake in a greased pan in a moderate oven for about 20 minutes, turning once or twice.

Variations
1. *For Bacon or Ham Stuffing*, use shredded suet or vegetable shortening instead of margarine, and add 50 g/2 oz/¼ cup chopped cooked bacon or ham. Omit the nutmeg.
2. For *Sage and Onion Stuffing*, add 1 medium onion, blanched and finely chopped, and use 2.5–5 ml/½–1 tsp dried sage instead of parsley and mixed herbs.
3. For *Parsley and Thyme Stuffing*, use dried thyme instead of dried mixed herbs.

Chestnut Stuffing

Makes stuffing for neck end of a 6.3 kg/14 lb turkey

Freeze 1 month

	Metric	Imperial	American
Sweet chestnuts	900 g	2 lb	2 lb
Stock or milk	275 ml	½ pt	1¼ cups
Butter or margarine	50 g	2 oz	¼ cup
Salt and pepper			
Pinch of ground allspice			
White sugar	2.5 ml	½ tsp	½ tsp

1. Slit the rounded sides of the chestnuts, then bake or boil them in water for 20 minutes. While still hot, strip off the shells and inner skins.
2. Simmer the chestnuts in the stock or milk for 20 minutes or until tender. Drain, reserving the stock.
3. Sieve the chestnuts or purée in a food processor. Stir in the fat, seasoning, spice, sugar and any stock needed to make a fairly soft stuffing. Use for stuffing turkey, duck or guinea fowl.

Tomato Stuffing

Makes 350 g/12 oz/¾ lb (approx)

Freeze 2 weeks

	Metric	Imperial	American
Tomatoes, skinned and chopped	225 g	8 oz	½ lb
Fresh white or brown breadcrumbs	75 g	3 oz	1½ cups
Small onion, chopped	1	1	1
Salt and pepper			
A few grains of cayenne pepper			
Dripping or margarine, melted	25 g	1 oz	2 tbls

1. Simmer the tomatoes in a small saucepan until soft.
2. Mix thoroughly with all the remaining ingredients.

Note: A squeeze of garlic and a little chopped fresh basil can be added to the stuffing, for extra flavour.

Rice Stuffing

Makes 225 g/8 oz/½ lb (approx)

Freeze 1 month

	Metric	Imperial	American
Long grain rice	50–75 g	2–3 oz	4–6 tbls
Water	450 ml	¾ pt	2 cups
Strip of lemon rind			
Small onion, finely chopped	1	1	1
Seedless raisins (optional)	50 g	2 oz	½ cup
Butter or margarine	25 g	1 oz	2 tbls
Chopped parsley	30 ml	2 tbls	2 tbls
Pinch of dried thyme			
Salt and pepper			
Egg, beaten (optional)	1	1	1

1. Boil the rice in the water with the lemon rind for 12–15 minutes until just tender. Drain. Discard the rind.
2. Mix the rice with the onion, raisins if used, fat, parsley, thyme and seasoning. If you wish, bind with some of the beaten egg.

Variations
1. For stuffing *fish*, flavour with 2.5 ml/½ tsp curry powder instead of thyme, and add one skinned, de-seeded small tomato, finely chopped.
2. For stuffing *chicken*, add the chicken's liver, finely chopped, and 25 g/1 oz/¼ cup flaked (slivered) almonds if using raisins.

Sausagemeat Stuffing

Makes 600 g/1¼ lb (approx)

Freeze 2 weeks

	Metric	Imperial	American
Sausagemeat	450 g	1 lb	1 lb
Dried mixed herbs	5 ml	1 tsp	1 tsp
Fresh white breadcrumbs	50 g	2 oz	1 cup
Grated lemon rind	1.5 ml	¼ tsp	¼ tsp
Stock or beaten egg			

1. Mash the sausagemeat, breaking up any lumps.
2. Mix in all the other ingredients, using a little stock or egg to moisten.
3. Use to stuff a 1.4 kg/3 lb chicken.

Note: To stuff a 5 kg/11 lb turkey, make the stuffing with 1.4 kg/3 lb sausagemeat, 15 ml/1 tbls herbs, 175 g/6 oz/3 cups breadcrumbs, and 2.5 ml/½ tsp lemon rind.

Fruit Stuffing

Makes 350–400 g/12–14 oz (approx)

Freeze 2 weeks

	Metric	Imperial	American
Prunes or dried apricots	100 g	4 oz	¼ lb
Cooked long grain rice or fresh white breadcrumbs	150 g	5 oz	1 cup (2½ cups)
Butter, melted	40 g	1½ oz	1½ oz
Pinch of dried mixed herbs			
Grated rind and juice of ½ lemon			
Salt and pepper			
Egg, beaten	1	1	1

1. Soak the fruit overnight in water to cover. Drain.
2. Stone prunes and chop. Chop apricots. Mix with the rice or breadcrumbs, butter, herbs, lemon and seasoning. Add extra ingredients if you wish. Bind with beaten egg.
3. Use for stuffing pork, or a duck or goose.

Duxelles (Classic Mushroom Stuffing)

Makes 100 g/4 oz/¼ lb

Freeze 6 months

	Metric	Imperial	American
Tattered mushrooms or stems	225 g	8 oz	½ lb
Butter or margarine	10 ml	2 tsp	2 tsp
Oil	10 ml	2 tsp	2 tsp
Chopped parsley	2.5 ml	½ tsp	½ tsp
Shallot, chopped	30 ml	2 tbls	2 tbls
Onion, chopped	15 ml	1 tbls	1 tbls
Salt and pepper			

1. Twist the mushrooms or stems in a dry cloth, to remove as much moisture as possible. Chop.
2. Heat the fat and oil in a frying pan (skillet). Add the mushrooms, parsley, shallot and onion. Fry gently for 8–10 minutes until mushrooms are dried, separate and brown. Season and cool.
3. Use when required as a stuffing or for flavouring soups, sauces or stews and casseroles. A good way to use up unwanted field mushrooms or stems. Store for 2 weeks in the refrigerator or freeze.

7
VEGETABLES AND VEGETABLE DISHES

FOOD VALUE OF VEGETABLES

Vegetables supply important vitamins, minerals, carbohydrate and dietary fibre as well as protein. To get the best value from them, however, they must be carefully chosen, and properly prepared and cooked if necessary.

CHOOSING VEGETABLES

Pick garden vegetables in peak condition, and use them as soon as possible after gathering (except for stored winter root vegetables). When buying vegetables choose those which look freshest and are well-shaped.

a. Roots, tubers and bulbs should be firm and unblemished. Avoid coarse hairy carrots, potatoes or onions which have begun to sprout, and any misshapen vegetables.
b. Green leaf vegetables should be crisp and springy without any yellowed edges on the leaves. Dark green leaves have most vitamin value.
c. Pea or bean pods should be bright green, well-filled (except mangetouts) and should snap easily. Choose dried pulses which look clean from a shop with a good turnover of produce.
d. Cauliflower heads should be white and compact. Avoid limp broccoli, oversized pumpkin or marrow (squash), celery with any slimy patches, fennel or asparagus with coarse bulbs or stems, wrinkled aubergines (eggplants) or peppers.

PREPARING VEGETABLES

All vegetables begin to lose vitamin value when gathered, lose it faster when the vegetables are peeled or cut up, and faster still when they are put in water or heated.
To minimise this loss:
1. Prepare and use all vegetables as soon as possible after gathering or buying them. Do not leave them lying about.
2. Serve vegetables raw or only lightly cooked as often as possible (see below and Chapter 9).
3. Peel vegetables only if coarse-skinned or blemished. Cook and serve unpeeled whenever possible as valuable vitamins lie just under the skin.
4. If vegetables must be cut up, avoid chopping them finely or grating them if you can. Cut roots into chunks, shred leaves with a sharp knife or tear them.
5. Most mineral salts and vitamins B and C are water-soluble, so do not soak any vegetables unless you have to, and then only briefly. Steaming, either in a steamer or with only very little water in the pan, minimises vitamin loss. Keep the cooking liquid for making gravy, sauces or soups.
6. When boiling, put most vegetables into boiling water. When cooking a lot of green vegetables, bring the water to the boil, then add the vegetables a little at a time so that the water does not go off the boil; keep it boiling to cook the vegetables as quickly as possible. Cook the vegetables only until just tender, never until soft and mushy.
7. The worst vitamin loss occurs when cooked vegetables are kept hot, waiting to be served. Serve them as soon as they are cooked.

Roots, Tubers and Bulbs

Scrub in cold water if earthy. Top and tail, cut out blemishes, scrape, peel or skin if necessary. Rinse in cold water. If vegetables must wait before cooking, keep them in cold unsalted water.

Green Leaf Vegetables

Cut off any discoloured leaves. Cut off thick stalks and any coarse ribs or separated leaves. Rinse in cold water and drain in a colander. If green vegetables must wait before cooking, wrap in a damp cloth or soft kitchen paper.

Legumes and Pulses

Top and tail young green beans; string and slice if older. Remove fresh peas or broad (lima) beans from pods, discarding any yellowed ones, and wash. Pick over dried pulses, rinse in a sieve to check for stones and soak before use (page 114).

Other Vegetables

Follow directions below, or particular recipes for special treatment.

COOKING VEGETABLES

Cooking Times

The times given below are only approximate. Vegetables from the garden, cooked immediately after harvesting, take less time than vegetables which have been stored. The age and size of the vegetables also affect their cooking time. Small young vegetables cut into small pieces cook more quickly than large or whole older ones.

Boiling

Today, experts recommend that most vegetables should be put into boiling salted water or stock using the minimum quantity of liquid which is practical. Green leaf vegetables need about 150 ml/ ¼ pt/⅔ cup liquid per 1 kg/2¼ lb vegetables. Very watery vegetables, e.g. marrow (squash), should be steamed, rather than boiled. Pulses need long cooking (page 114).

Parboiling

This simply means boiling until the vegetables (or other foods) are partly cooked before cooking is completed by another method.

Steaming

Use a pan with a steamer on top which has a perforated base, or a colander or metal sieve balanced on a pan and covered by a lid. Bring the water to the boil in the lower pan before putting the lightly salted vegetables in the upper container. Cover and cook for about twice as long as when boiling. Serve sprinkled with fresh herbs or a sauce if the vegetables have lost some colour.

Oven-Cooking

A few vegetables, e.g. globe artichokes, cannot be cooked in the oven. Otherwise, most vegetables can be boiled (or rather simmered), braised, baked or roasted in the oven. It is not practical to cook vegetables for a side dish by themselves in the oven but they can usually be cooked over or under another dish or dishes. Allow slightly longer for simmering in the oven than when boiling on the hob.

To simmer: Put the vegetables in a casserole, cover with boiling water and with a lid; cook until tender.

To braise: Prepare the vegetables as in directions below. Melt a little butter or margarine in a flameproof casserole or frying pan (skillet), and brown the vegetables lightly all over. Transfer to a casserole if needed, add a little stock or sauce and seasoning, and cover with a lid; cook until tender. As a rule, serve from the casserole.

To bake: Generally, scrub and rinse roots, scrape or peel and split lengthways if large. Scrub potatoes without peeling, prick skins and rub with oil. Make a small cross-cut in the tops of tomatoes or large onions, rub with oil. Place on the greased oven shelves or on a lightly greased baking sheet. Cut marrow (squash), aubergine (eggplant), avocado, etc., in half lengthways without peeling, prick the skins, and remove seeds or stones; place cut side down in a well-greased baking tin (pan). Place whole or sliced mushrooms or stuffed vegetables side by side in a greased baking dish, put a dab of fat or a little sauce on each (stuffed vegetables should stand stuffing side up). For other vegetables follow directions below or individual recipes.

To roast: Scrape or peel suitable vegetables. Melt 50–100 g/2–4 oz/¼–½ cup dripping or other fat in a shallow tin (pan) in a hot oven (about 220°C/425°F/ Gas Mark 7), add raw or parboiled vegetables and baste well. Season. Baste and turn while cooking, to colour. (Alternatively, roast round a joint or under it if on a trivet.)

To cook 'au gratin': Slice boiled or steamed vegetables; divide cauliflower into sprigs or leave whole. Place in a lightly greased ovenproof dish. Sprinkle with browned breadcrumbs and dot with fat, or cover with Cheese Sauce (page 88), sprinkle with grated cheese and breadcrumbs. Bake in a fairly hot oven until cheese topping has melted and browned lightly. (Small quantities of hot sliced vegetables can be browned under the grill/broiler).

Other Cooking Methods for Vegetables

To curry: Simmer freshly-cooked vegetables cut in small pieces in Curry Sauce (page 90). Leftover vegetables can be reheated in the sauce but they lack food value and flavour.

To cook vegetable fritters: Sliced parboiled vegetables can be dipped in a Coating Batter (page 170), and shallow or deep fried (page 171). Small vegetables such as peas or mixed diced vegetables should be bound with thick batter or panada (page 170) and dropped by spoonfuls into deep hot fat (page 171).

To purée: Boiled or steamed vegetables can be rubbed through a sieve or puréed in a food processor or blender. The purée can be thickened and made smoother by adding mashed potato or thick white sauce, or it can be made richer by adding egg yolks and/or cream, and reheating gently without boiling. Vegetable marrows (squash), cucumbers, peppers and French (green) beans are not suitable for purées.

Opposite: *Fresh vegetables make a colorful display at all times of the year.*

COOKING DIRECTIONS FOR
SPECIFIC VEGETABLES

The following list describes the most usual (but not the only) ways of preparing and cooking many common vegetables, and the average time they take. Note that all vegetables need seasoning, and most vegetables cooked in liquid are improved if a few fresh herbs are added to the water or chopped and used as a garnish. Use margarine instead of butter for dressing vegetables if you prefer.

Roots, Tubers and Bulbs

Artichokes (Jerusalem):
Scrub well under water, and put at once into cold water with 15 ml/1 tbls vinegar.

To boil: Cut in chunks or slices, put at once into boiling salted water with a little lemon juice. Cook about 20 minutes. Drain, serve with butter and chopped herbs or in white sauce.

To steam: Leave whole, season with salt, cook as in general steaming method on page 96 for 40 minutes. Slice and serve as for boiled artichokes.

To purée: Mash, sieve or process cooked artichokes in a blender or food processor. For each 450 g/l lb raw artichokes used, add to purée 15 ml/1 tbls milk and 20 g/¾ oz/1½ tbls butter. Season well.

Beetroot:
Rinse without breaking skin or tap root. Trim off leaves, leaving 2.5 cm/1 in stalk.

To boil: Cook in boiling salted water until skin rubs off easily – 1–1½ hours for small young beetroot, up to 2½ hours for large ones (usually served cold). Rub off skins. Serve baby beetroot hot in white sauce. Slice large beetroot and serve as salad in vinegar or lemon juice. Keep separate from other salads to avoid staining.

To bake: Seal any broken skin with a little flour and water paste. Wrap in greased foil, or place in shallow baking tin (pan). Bake at about 180°C/350°F/Gas Mark 4 or on a low shelf under a joint cooking at a higher temperature. Time 1–2 hours depending on size. Serve as for boiled beetroot.

Carrots:
Top and tail. Wash and scrub young carrots. Scrape old ones.

To boil: Quarter or slice large old carrots. Put in just enough boiling salted water to cover. Cook young carrots 10–30 minutes; old ones 15–40 minutes. Serve in parsley sauce.

Alternatively, simmer for about 10 minutes in 20 g/¾ oz/1½ tbls butter per 450 g/l lb roots, then add about 90 ml/6 tbls boiling salted water and boil until tender. Serve in the cooking liquid.

To purée: Mash, sieve or purée boiled carrots in a blender or food processor. Mix with mashed potato, add butter and a little cream. Season well.

To braise: Melt 15–25 g/½–1 oz/1–2 tbls fat in a casserole in the oven at 160°C/325°F/Gas Mark 3. Toss carrots in the fat with a little sugar, salt and pepper. Add 30–60 ml/2–4 tbls cold water or to half-cover roots. Cover and cook in oven for 40–80 minutes until tender, depending on size. Serve with cooking liquid.

Celeriac:
Top and tail, scrape or peel. Keep in cold water if roots must wait.

To boil: Cut in chunks or slices, cook in just enough boiling salted water to cover for 20–40 minutes. Serve with seasoning, butter and chopped parsley or in a white sauce.

To purée: Cut in small pieces, then treat as carrots.

To braise: Cut in chunks, then cook as carrots, without sugar, for 45–60 minutes.

Kohlrabi:
Use small-medium kohlrabi; prepare like turnips.

To boil: Cook in boiling salted water for 30–60 minutes. Peel if cooked with skin. Season and sprinkle with melted butter or serve in a white sauce.

To purée: Treat as celeriac.

Onions:
Peel off outer brown skin under water. Leave whole or quarter, as required.

To boil: Put into boiling salted water, cook 35 minutes–1½ hours, depending on size.

To braise: Leave whole if small, quarter or slice if large. Braise as for carrots without sugar, at about 180°C/350°F/Gas Mark 4.

To roast: Leave whole; cook in baking tin (pan) in hot fat at 200–225°C/400–425°F/Gas Mark 6–7 for 1–1½ hours, or cook around a joint.

To bake: Use medium-large onions. Leave skins on. Top and tail, and cut small cross in top. Season. Fill cut cross with butter. Bake at 200°C/400°F/Gas Mark 6 for about 1½ hours. Skin, dot with butter and season with salt, pepper and nutmeg.

Alternatively, parboil large onions. Treat as above but wrap in greased foil, leaving it open at the top. Bake in a shallow tin (pan) at 180°C/350°F/Gas Mark 4 for 1–1¼ hours. Serve as above.

To deep fry: Skin and slice into thin rings. Dip in milk, then toss in seasoned flour. Fry until golden and crisp.

To shallow fry: Skin, slice into thin rings, pat dry. Use about 45 ml/3 tbls fat or oil for 450 g/l lb prepared onions. Heat in frying pan (skillet), add onions and fry until soft and browned, turning often.

Parsnips:
Wash well, peel, and if old split and remove hard centre core. Cut into serving pieces.

To boil: Cook in boiling salted water until tender. Serve in White, Parsley or Béchamel sauce (pages 84, 85, 88). Alternatively, mash with a little butter or margarine, seasoning and nutmeg.

To braise: Cut in small wedge-shaped pieces. Braise like onions for about 45 minutes.

To roast: Roast as onions for 45 minutes–1 hour.

Potatoes (new):
Wash and scrub. Leave skin on or scrape. Cut out any blemishes.

To boil: Put into boiling salted water with sprig of mint. Boil for 15–20 minutes. Serve tossed in melted butter and sprinkled with chopped fresh parsley.

To steam: Cook as in general steaming method (page 96) for about 20 minutes. Serve like boiled potatoes.

Potatoes (old):
Wash and scrub. Only peel if skins are scarred or tough. (You can remove them after cooking).

To boil: Boil gently in minimum of boiling salted water for about 30 minutes until tender. Drain well. Toss in dry pan over low heat to dry off. Peel if you wish. Serve sprinkled with chopped fresh parsley or chopped onion and parsley.

To mash: Boil, dry and peel potatoes. Beat until smooth with potato masher, fork or electric beater. Add knob of butter or margarine, milk or cream and seasonings including nutmeg. Sprinkle with chopped parsley.

To bake: Wash, dry and prick skins with fork. Rub with oil for crisp skins. Place on oven shelf or baking sheet and bake at 200–220°C/400–425°F/ Gas Mark 6–7 for 1–2 hours until soft. Serve slit open with butter or margarine in slit. (For stuffed baked potatoes, see page 113).

To roast: Peel, and halve or quarter if large. Parboil in salted water for 5–10 minutes if you wish, for crisper potatoes and shorter roasting time. Drain and dry as boiled potatoes. Heat dripping or lard in a roasting tin (pan) at 200–220°C/400–425°F/Gas Mark 6–7. Put in potatoes, baste to coat with fat, roast for 1–2 hours, basting often. (45 minutes–1 hour if parboiled).

Alternatively, roast around a joint being cooked by high temperature roasting.

To fry chips: Peel potatoes. Cut into sticks about 1 cm/½ in thick and 7–8 cm/3 in long. Soak in cold water for 10 minutes to remove surface starch. Drain and dry with a cloth or soft paper. Put into a frying basket and lower into hot oil or fat. Cook until tender but barely golden. Lift out the basket, letting the fat drain back into the pan. Drain chips on soft kitchen paper. Shortly before serving, reheat oil or fat and fry chips again until crisp. Drain on soft paper. Serve sprinkled with salt. (If frying a lot of chips, fry them in batches the first time then fry all together the second time.)

To fry French fries or potato straws: Cut French fries into sticks 5 mm/¼ in thick and 5 cm/2 in long. Cut potato straws into 'matchsticks'. Fry as above.

To fry crisps (game chips): Peel potatoes, and cut into paper-thin slices. Soak in cold water as above, then drain and dry well. Fry in hot oil or fat until crisp and brown. Sprinkle with salt before serving, or store in an airtight tin.

Note: Oil is good for frying although clarified dripping (page 71) can be used. Take care not to let oil or fat overheat. As it heats, test for readiness by dropping a 2 cm/¾ in cube of bread into the pan. If it browns in 45 seconds the oil or fat is ready for first frying of chips, etc. If it browns in 30 seconds it is ready for second frying of chips, etc. (and for frying crisps.)

Swedes (rutabaga) and turnips:
Top and tail. Wash and peel swedes thickly. Peel old turnips. (New baby turnips may not need peeling.) Cut old large roots into slices. Discard any roots which look fibrous or woolly.

To boil: Cook until tender in just enough boiling salted water to cover. Small turnips need about 30 minutes. Large turnips or swedes (rutabaga) may need longer. Drain well and serve in White or Parsley Sauce.

To mash or purée: Drain boiled roots well. Mash like potatoes, draining off any liquid which forms. Reheat with butter or margarine, cream and seasonings including nutmeg. They are good mixed with mashed carrots.

To roast: Cook round a joint like potatoes.

Note: When cooking root vegetables, the smaller you cut the pieces the shorter the cooking time.

Green Vegetables

Broccoli (white, purple or green):
Cut off wilted or discoloured leaves, trim stalks to within 10 cm/4 in of head. Divide large heads into florets. Wash in salted water and rinse well.

To boil: Cook for 10–15 minutes in boiling salted water until tender. Serve seasoned with freshly ground black pepper and with melted butter or Hollandaise sauce (page 87).

To steam: Season with salt and cook as in general steaming method for 20–25 minutes. Serve like boiled broccoli.

Brussels sprouts:
Remove any yellowed or wilted leaves and cut stalk level with sprout. Cut a cross in the stalk end. Wash well.

To boil: Put into boiling salted water a few at a time to keep the water on the boil. Allow about 150 ml/¼ pt/⅔ cup water per 900 g/2 lb sprouts. Cover and cook for 8–12 minutes until tender, shaking the pan from time to time. Drain, season and serve with melted butter sprinkled over.

Cabbage (hard white, Savoy):
Discard wilted and badly discoloured leaves. Trim off stem. Quarter cabbage and take out hard core. Wash well in salted water, rinse in fresh water and drain. Shred, cutting from outside to stalk.

To boil: Cook as for Brussels sprouts adding to pan little by little. Cabbage should be tender but not soggy. Season well.

To braise: Cut into wedges instead of shredding. Parboil 5 minutes. Drain well. Fry a chopped onion in oil or dripping, in a heavy pan, then add the cabbage. Just cover with well-flavoured stock, add a bay leaf and parsley sprig, and put a lid on the pan. Cook gently for 1 hour. Drain before serving.

Cabbage (Spring and Summer):
Leave quartered, or tie loose leaves in bundles. Cook like hard white cabbage.

Cabbage (red):
Prepare and shred like hard white cabbage. For cooking methods, see recipes.

Cabbage (Chinese): See lettuce (Cos/Romaine).

Cauliflower:
Cut off any wilted or discoloured leaves (or all the leaves if you will divide head into florets). Cut off stalk so that cauliflower will stand level on it if head will be cooked whole. Wash well in salted water. Rinse. Divide head into florets if you wish.

To boil: Place whole head, stalk down in a pan containing 5–6 cm/2–2½ in boiling salted water. Season, cover the pan and cook gently for about 20 minutes. Drain. Season well. Sprinkle with melted butter, or coat with White Sauce or Cheese Sauce (pages 84 and 88).

Alternatively, cook florets like Brussels sprouts, for about 10 minutes.

Note: Young cauliflower leaves can be cooked and served like cabbage, with the cauliflower or separately.

Opposite: *Vegetables can be cooked in a variety of ways.*

Below: *Cauliflower steamed and coated with cheese sauce makes a light lunch dish or is delicious served as a vegetable with cold meat.*

Curly kale:
Discard any discoloured leaves. Unless they are young and tender, strip leaves from stems. Wash in salted water, rinse well.

To boil: Cook like cabbage, for 10–20 minutes.

Lettuce (round soft-leaved/Boston):
Usually served as green salad mainstay, or as a 'bed' for cold dishes, but if plentiful or slightly overgrown, can be cooked as a vegetable. Separate leaves, discard stalk. Wash leaves in several changes of cold water.

To cook: Put in a pan with plenty of moisture still on the leaves. Season. Cover the pan and cook over gentle heat for 5–6 minutes until the lettuce is tender, shaking the pan from time to time. (Lettuce leaves are often cooked with young garden peas. They also make a good alternative to spinach.)

Lettuce (iceberg, Webb's):
These lettuces are also usually used for salads, but being firm-hearted with crisp leaves make a good cooked vegetable. If you wish, cook outer leaves as above and keep hearts for salads. Alternatively cook as follows. First remove any torn or wilted outside leaves, trim off root and stalk, and wash well. Halve or quarter if large.

To stew: Melt about 25 g/1 oz/2 tbls butter or margarine per lettuce in a deep frying pan (skillet), season and add lettuce hearts, halved or whole lettuces in one layer. Cover the pan and simmer until lettuces are tender.

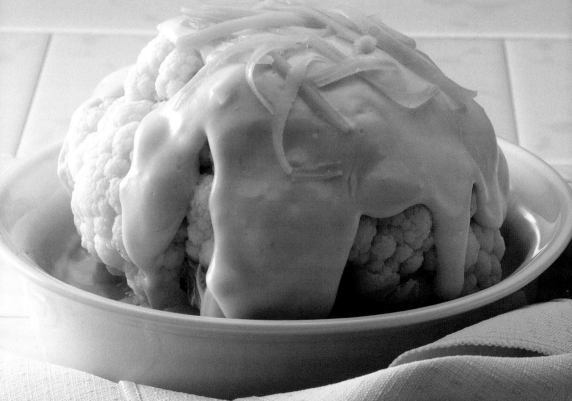

Lettuce (Cos/Romaine):
Prepare like iceberg or Webb's lettuce. Tie leaf tops together, making neat bundles.

To braise: Blanch for 5 minutes in boiling salted water, then cook like Braised Celery (right).

(Chinese cabbage can be treated like Cos/Romaine lettuce.)

Spinach:
Remove stems and any coarse ribs. Wash in several changes of cold water.

To boil: Melt enough butter or margarine in a saucepan to film the bottom. Season the wet spinach leaves and add to the pan. Cover and cook gently for 10–15 minutes until the spinach is tender, shaking the pan from time to time. Drain well, pressing out water. Season with salt, pepper and nutmeg and sprinkle with melted butter.

If you prefer, put 1 cm/½ in salted water in the pan and bring to the boil instead of using fat.

To purée: Boil the spinach, drain and press out excess moisture. Chop finely, sieve or purée in a food processor or blender. Add 15–30 ml/1–2 tbls melted butter, for each 700 g/1½ lb spinach, and about 30 ml/2 tbls cream, season with salt, pepper and nutmeg, and reheat until very hot. Alternatively, mix with 150 ml/¼ pt/⅔ cup coating White Sauce (page 84), season and reheat.

Note: Swiss chard leaves can be cooked like boiled spinach. The stalks are cooked like celery.

Legumes (fresh)

Broad (lima) beans:
Very young beans can be cooked and eaten in the pods. Top and tail, and string as for runner beans (below). Usually, however, broad (lima) beans are allowed to fill out, and are removed from pods and washed before cooking. Old beans with tough skins should be covered with boiling water and left to soak for 5 minutes. Drain well and remove outer skins.

To boil: Put beans into a little boiling salted water, cover the pan and cook gently for 20–40 minutes (depending on age) until beans are tender. Drain. Season. Serve plain or sprinkled with chopped fresh parsley. Alternatively, serve in parsley sauce, using some of the bean cooking liquid to replace some of the milk. For extra flavour, add some diced fried or grilled bacon, or serve in fresh Tomato Sauce or Curry Sauce (page 90).

Beans (bobby, French/green, runner):
These beans are all prepared and cooked in the same way, the cooking time depending on size. Discard any very limp or discoloured beans. Top and tail, and remove any strings from the edges of older beans. Slice runner beans diagonally into 3 cm/1½ in lengths.

To boil: Add beans a few at a time to about 2.5 cm/1 in boiling salted water. Cover and cook for 7–15 minutes until tender. Drain well, toss in butter and serve sprinkled with fresh herbs (tarragon, savory, basil or parsley).

Peas (garden):
Discard discoloured and overfilled bulbous pods. Shell peas. If they must wait, put in colander and cover with washed pods. Pods can be used for soup.

To boil: Put peas a few at a time into a little boiling salted water. Add a sprig of mint and 5 ml/1 tsp sugar for each 450 g/1 lb peas. Cover and cook gently for 10–12 minutes until tender. Do not boil fast as this breaks the skins, and do not overcook because the peas toughen. Drain well, removing the mint. Toss in melted butter or margarine before serving. (If you wish, a little grated onion or a shredded lettuce leaf can be boiled with the peas for flavour.)

To oven-cook: Soak peas in boiling water for 2–3 minutes. Drain, and put peas in a casserole with a little melted butter or margarine, salt and sugar. Turn the peas in the fat, to coat. Add a little water, cover and cook in the oven at 160°C/325°F/Gas Mark 3 for about 1 hour.

Peas (mangetout/snow peas):
Prepare and cook like young French (green) beans. Cook for 2–3 minutes only in as little boiling salted water as possible. Drain and season with ground black pepper, then toss in plenty of melted butter.

Preparation and cooking methods for dried legumes and other pulses are on pages 114–115.

Other Vegetables

Artichokes, globe
Remove coarse outside leaves. Snap off stalk sharply over table edge because this brings the lower part of the hairy 'choke' away with the stalk. Trim pointed ends of leaves square. Soak heads briefly in cold salted water sharpened with lemon juice or vinegar to get rid of any insects. Rinse in clean water.

To boil: Place stem side down in enough boiling salted water just to cover. Cover and cook for 30–40 minutes, depending on size. Artichokes are done when a leaf pulls out easily. Drain artichokes upside down. Remove centre leaves and take out hairy 'choke'. Replace leaves or fill hollow with melted butter or Hollandaise Sauce (page 87). Serve hot or cold. The leaves are picked off and the soft ends are nibbled one by one, dipped in butter or sauce. When all are eaten the fond or base is eaten with a knife and fork.

Asparagus:
Home-grown asparagus should be used as soon as cut and graded according to the thickness of the stalks like asparagus sold ready bundled. Trim woody ends of stalks, and scrape any coarse thick ones. Tie into bundles, and put into cold salted water.

To boil: Asparagus must be cooked standing upright so that the stems are in the water but the buds cook in the steam only. A special asparagus pan can be bought for cooking it, or the bundle can be placed, buds uppermost, in a jar standing in a pan of boiling salted water. The water should cover most of the stem end. Cover the pan, and boil for 14–20 minutes depending on the thickness of the stems. When the green tops are tender, the asparagus is ready. Drain and dry off in a warm place for a moment or two. Serve with a sauce boat of plain melted butter of Hollandaise Sauce (page 87).

Notes:
1. Special asparagus plates are sold with a hollow for the butter or sauce. The hot asparagus is lifted in one's fingers by the stalk end, the bud is dipped in the butter and the tender bud and end of the stalk are eaten. Thin asparagus which can almost all be eaten has a better flavour than coarse thick asparagus.
2. Asparagus can be served cold with vinaigrette sauce instead of butter.

Asparagus (sprue):
Thin asparagus stalks called sprue or grass asparagus are sold loose. Cut the points and tender green stems into short lengths. Cook in gently boiling salted water for 5–8 minutes, then drain and use in omelets, salads, soufflés etc.

Aubergine (eggplant):
Purple aubergines are the commonest in Britain, but other coloured varieties are sometimes available. All are cooked in the same ways, the method depending on the dish being made. Wash and dry the aubergines. Remove any stem. If cooking whole, slit the skin in several places, and sprinkle with salt. If the flesh only is wanted, place the fruit (whole or halved lengthways) under the grill, and toast for a few minutes until the skin scorches and peels off easily. To remove any bitterness, the aubergine can be cut in slices 1 cm/½ in thick, sprinkled with salt and left on a tilted plate for 30 minutes to drain. Rinse with cold water and drain again.

For serving on their own, aubergines are best baked, although they can also be grilled or fried as fritters. They are often stuffed like potatoes, peppers, tomatoes, etc. Aubergine slices are also included in many dishes from southern Europe such as Moussaka and Ratatouille.

To bake: Nick aubergine skins in several places. Cut in half lengthways and brush with oil. Place cut side down in a greased baking tin (pan). Bake at 180°C/350°F/Gas Mark 4 for 20–30 minutes or until aubergines are tender. Serve cut side up, topped with finely-chopped sautéed vegetables, or a well-flavoured cheese or meat sauce, or use for stuffing (see recipe, page 111). (If you prefer, grill (broil) the halved aubergines cut side up for about 20 minutes under a low heat, taking care that they do not char.)

To fry: Cut aubergines into slices 7 mm/⅓ in thick. Sprinkle with salt, and leave on a tilted dish for 30 minutes. Rinse and dry. Coat with egg and breadcrumbs or a thick coating batter, and deep fry.

Celery:
Cut off outer celery leaves for flavouring and garnishing. Cut off and discard root end and coarse outer stalks. Treat stalks according to the dish

being made. Leave head whole or split in half lengthways, or for some dishes, separate the stalks (the inside 'heart' is usually left whole). Scrape any thick stalks thoroughly. Rinse and dry.

To boil: Cut separated stalks into 2 cm/¾ in lengths. Put into the minimum of boiling salted water a few at a time. Boil for 15–20 minutes. Drain, season and serve sprinkled with melted butter or in a White, Cheese or Parsley sauce, made with the celery's cooking liquid.

To braise: Remove coarse outer stalks from 4 small or 2 halved large heads of celery. Tie thread round tops or stalks, making bundles. Skin and chop 1 onion and 1 slice fat bacon, and fry in a heavy pan in dripping or bacon fat. Add enough stock to half-cover the celery. Bring to the boil. Add celery. Baste the celery with the stock, cover the pan and cook gently for 1–1½ hours until tender. Baste from time to time. When celery is tender, remove, and boil down stock until syrupy. Pour over the celery to serve.

Chicory (endive):
Wash and dry. Remove root end and any torn outer leaves. With a pointed knife, take out bitter centre core. Boil as celery.

Courgettes (zucchini):
Trim off ends of small courgettes, and wash. Cut larger ones into 1 cm/½ in diagonal slices.

To boil: Put whole or sliced courgettes into the minimum of boiling salted water sharpened with lemon juice. Boil for 6–10 minutes until tender. Drain. Serve sprinkled with melted butter and chopped fresh herbs or in a white or parsley sauce.

To bake: Parboil whole courgettes for 4 minutes. Drain well. Heat about 50 g/2 oz/¼ cup butter per 450 g/1 lb courgettes in a shallow baking tin (pan) in the oven heated to 190°C/375°F/Gas Mark 5. Add courgettes, coat with the fat and bake for about 25 minutes.

Alternatively (if stuffing courgettes), halve them lengthways after parboiling, and cook as aubergines but for a shorter time.

To sauté: Fry a little chopped onion in butter and oil in a frying pan (skillet), add sliced courgettes and toss in the fat until soft and golden.

To deep fry: Parboil sliced courgettes for 4 minutes, drain and dry well on soft kitchen paper, then coat with batter and fry as aubergines.

Cucumber:
Only peel rough-skinned outdoor cucumbers. Trim ends. Slice like courgettes if large, or cut into 10 cm/4 in lengths, then quarter these lengthways. Leave seeds in unless large and tough. Do not boil cucumber.

To steam: Season pieces or slices, put in a steamer or colander over boiling water, cover and cook for about 10 minutes. Serve with melted butter and chopped fresh herbs or in parsley sauce.

To bake: Cut in thick slices or halve lengthways. Put in a baking tin (pan), dot with butter and chopped fresh herbs. Bake as courgettes.

To fry: Steam slices for 5 minutes, then dry. Dredge with seasoned flour and sauté as courgettes.

Fennel:
Cut off root end. Cut off and keep feathery leaves for garnishing. Trim off top stems, and remove coarse outer sheaths. Leave whole if small, quarter lengthways if large.

To boil: Put into the minimum of boiling salted water sharpened with lemon juice. Boil for 10–15 minutes, or until soft. Drain thoroughly. Serve with lemon-flavoured parsley butter sprinkled over. Good in salads, with fish, or served 'à la Grecque' (page 11).

Leeks:
Take off root. Trim off tops of leaves and remove any coarse outer leaves down to the root end. If serving whole, lay each leek flat so that the fan-shaped leaf head lies on its edge, and make a deep vertical cut through all the leaves. Turn the leek so that the fan-shaped part lies flat, and repeat the cut so that the top green leaves are like a tassel. Wash thoroughly between the leaves to remove dirt and stones. Small leeks can then be boiled or braised.

Alternatively, cut off most of the green leaf part, wash leaves and boil like cabbage for a purée or soup; slice the white part thickly or thinly as usage requires.

To boil: Leave whole or cut into 10–15 cm/4–6 in lengths. Put into the minimum of boiling salted water sharpened with lemon juice, boil for 20–30 minutes depending on size. Drain thoroughly, and serve sprinkled with melted butter or a well-flavoured white sauce.

To braise: Remove green leaves for soup; leave white parts whole. Parboil for 5 minutes then cook as braised celery.

Mushrooms:
Peel large, old field mushrooms and trim ragged edges. Rinse any mushrooms in cold water and drain. Cut off end of stalk then remove if only caps are required. Use stalks and peelings for Duxelles (page 94) or for flavouring soups, etc. Slice or chop mushrooms if recipe requires it.

To bake: Place mushroom caps, gill side up, in a greased shallow baking dish. Squeeze a little lemon juice over and season with salt and black pepper; add a pinch of ground mace if you wish. Dot with butter. Cover loosely with greased foil, and bake at 190°C/375°F/Gas Mark 5 for 10–20 minutes, depending on size. Serve with the juices. A little milk or wine and water can be added to the dish, or the mushrooms can be sprinkled with grated cheese instead of spice.

To grill (broil): Prepare as for baking, or brush with oil instead of dotting with butter. Grill under moderate heat until tender, turning once if the mushrooms are large and solid.

To fry: Quarter or slice mushrooms if large or if recipe requires. Sauté gently in butter and oil, or margarine, until tender. Season well and sprinkle with lemon juice.

Peppers (large)
Large bell peppers may be red, yellow or green, the red ones being sweetest. (Small red or green chilli peppers are of the same family but very hot and only used sparingly for flavouring.) Before use, bell peppers must be cleaned of inside membrane and the seeds attached to them and to the central core. Depending on how the pepper will be used, either cut out the stem end and core and scrape out membranes and loose seeds; or halve peppers and do the same. For some recipes, the peppers should also be skinned: they can be toasted over an open flame until the skin scorches and can be peeled off, or they can be scorched under the grill (broiler) as aubergines (eggplants). They can also be blanched, if required, by being plunged into boiling water for 2–3 minutes. Drain well.

Whole or halved peppers can be stuffed after cleaning, then baked without any other preparation, the baking time depending on the type of stuffing. Alternatively, chopped or sliced peppers can be shallow fried gently for 10–20 minutes in a little olive oil.

Sweetcorn:
Sweetcorn cobs begin to toughen as soon as harvested, so must not be stored. Use only plump, pale-coloured, home-grown cobs (bright yellow ones are elderly) or use frozen whole cobs, thawed, or canned kernels. Peel the green outer husks off whole cobs, and keep them if the cobs will be boiled. Discard the 'silk', and trim off the stem ends. To strip corncobs, cut off the kernels in long strips with a sharp knife.

To boil whole corn: Place a few husks in a pan, lay cobs on top and cover with boiling unsalted water. Boil for 8–10 minutes or until a kernel is easily detached from the cob. Drain well. Serve with freshly ground black pepper, salt and melted butter. (Special small forks are sold for eating corn on the cob; one is stuck in each end of the cob, to hold it by while nibbling the kernels.)

To boil kernels: Put into the minimum of boiling unsalted water and boil for about 5 minutes. Drain, season and sprinkle with melted butter.

To bake whole corn: Put cobs in a baking tin (pan) with a little butter and enough milk to cover. Bake at about 190°C/375°F/Gas Mark 5 for 30–40 minutes until a kernel comes off the cob easily. Drain, baste with melted butter and return for 4–5 minutes. Alternatively, wrap each cob in greased foil and bake under a joint or other dish for 45–60 minutes.

To barbecue: Wrap in foil as for baking, place on barbecue grill and cook for 45–60 minutes, turning from time to time.

To roast: Coat with melted butter, put in a roasting tin (pan) with a little more butter and cook, turning often, at 190°C/375°F/Gas Mark 5 for 20–35 minutes until a kernel lifts off the cob easily. Serve with the cooking butter from the tin.

Opposite: *Sweetcorn with melted butter.*

Tomatoes:

Remove stalk, then prepare according to proposed use. To halve or slice, cut across, not through, stem end. To skin, dip in boiling water for 1 minute, then into cold water before stripping off skin. If flesh only is wanted, cut off caps at stem end or halve tomatoes, then scrape out seeds, pulp and any membrane with a teaspoon.

To bake: Cut a small cross in the top of each tomato and leave whole or halve. Place whole or halved tomatoes cut side up in a greased shallow baking tin (pan). Season cut sides of halved tomatoes well. Dot either with butter or margarine, filling the cross cut in whole tomatoes. Sprinkle with chopped fresh basil, savory or tarragon if you wish. Bake at 180°C/350°F/Gas Mark 4 for 15–20 minutes depending on size.

To grill (broil): Halve tomatoes, season cut sides well and dot with butter or margarine. Place cut side up on greased grill rack, and grill under medium heat until tender. Turn large tomatoes once; small ones cook through without turning.

To fry: Halve or slice tomatoes. Season well. Fry for a few minutes on each side in hot bacon fat, butter or margarine. Remove from pan with a fish slice (slotted spatula) or turner.

Vegetable marrow (squash):

Small marrows have a much better flavour than large ones and can be cooked whole. Large marrows can be halved and baked in the skin for stuffing, but are otherwise peeled, and cut into rings or chunks, the seeds and fibrous centre being removed. Marrow should not be boiled; it is too watery. It is better to steam or bake it.

To steam: Peel the marrow, halve it lengthways, and remove seeds and fibre. Cut into serving pieces. Season well. Place in the perforated upper pan of a steamer or in a colander over boiling water, cover and steam for 15–20 minutes depending on size of pieces.

To bake (1): Cut peeled marrow into 2.5 cm/1 in rings; remove seeds and fibre. Place in a greased ovenproof dish in one layer, season well, and dot with butter or margarine. Cover loosely with greased foil and bake at 190°C/375°F/Gas Mark 5 for about 35 minutes until tender. Serve with the cooking juices from the marrow. (Marrow rings can be filled with stuffing before baking if you wish.)

To bake (2): Cut the unpeeled marrow in half lengthways, scoop out seeds and fibre. Season cut side. Place cut side up in a well-greased baking or roasting tin (pan). Fill the hollows with a suitable stuffing. Bake, stuffed side up, at 180°C/350°F/Gas Mark 4 for 1–1½ hours, depending on size of marrow and type of stuffing (see recipe, page 111).

Vegetables au Gratin

Serves 4

Oven temp 220°C/425°F/Gas Mark 7

Not suitable for freezing

	Metric	Imperial	American
Vegetables, boiled as above (for types and quantities see below)			
Ingredients for Cheese Sauce (coating consistency), page 88			
Grated Cheddar cheese	25 g	1 oz	¼ cup
Fine dry white breadcrumbs or browned breadcrumbs	25 g	1 oz	¼ cup

1. Arrange the vegetables in a greased shallow ovenproof or flameproof dish.
2. Make the Cheese Sauce using some of the vegetable cooking liquid in place of some of the milk.
3. Pour the sauce over the vegetables, making sure they are all coated.
4. Mix together the grated cheese and breadcrumbs. Scatter over the dish.
5. Bake at the temperature above for 10 minutes or until the cheese has melted and browned slightly, or place under a hot grill (broiler) until the topping is golden-brown.

Note: Suitable vegetables are:
600 g/1¼ lb Jerusalem artichokes
700 g/1½ lb broccoli
1 medium whole head cauliflower
1 large head of celery, sliced
700 g/½ lb leeks
600 g/1¼ lb onions
600 g/1¼ lb sliced and diced mixed vegetables

Potatoes Lyonnaise

Serves 6

Freeze 1 month

	Metric	Imperial	American
Potatoes	900 g	2 lb	2 lb
Onions, sliced	275 g	10 oz	10 oz
Butter or margarine	50 g	2 oz	¼ cup
Salt and pepper			
Chopped parsley			

1. Scrub the potatoes. Boil them in their skins. Drain, then peel and cut into slices 5 mm/¼ in thick.
2. Fry the sliced onions in the fat until golden-brown. Remove from the pan with a slotted spoon. Put in the potato slices, and sauté until golden on both sides.
3. Layer the potatoes and onions in a serving dish. Sprinkle with chopped parsley.

Sautéed Potatoes

1. Cut parboiled or boiled potatoes into small slices 5 mm–1 cm/¼–½ in thick.
2. Heat butter and oil or margarine in a frying pan (skillet). Add the potato slices, and turn in the fat until the potatoes are patched with rusty brown on both sides.
3. Drain on soft kitchen paper. Serve sprinkled with chopped parsley.

Duchesse Potatoes

Makes 450 g/1 lb

Oven temp 200°C/400°F/Gas Mark 6

Freeze 3 months

	Metric	Imperial	American
Potatoes	500 g	1 lb 2 oz	1 lb 2 oz
Egg	1	1	1
Single (light) cream	15 ml	1 tbls	1 tbls
Butter or margarine	15 g	½ oz	1 tbls
Salt and pepper			
Pinch of grated nutmeg			
Beaten egg for brushing			

1. Boil the potatoes, drain thoroughly and peel, if necessary. Sieve into a bowl.
2. Beat in the egg and cream together, then the fat and seasonings.
3. Put the mixture into a forcing (pastry) bag fitted with a large rose nozzle. Pipe into rosettes on a greased baking sheet. Brush with beaten egg.
4. Bake at the temperature above for 15 minutes or until potato rosettes are golden-brown. Use as a side dish or garnish.

'French-Style' Parsnips

Serves 4

Freeze 1 month (before frying)

	Metric	Imperial	American
Parsnips	3–4	3–4	3–4
Salt	10 ml	2 tsp	2 tsp
Lemon juice	10 ml	2 tsp	2 tsp
Egg, beaten	1	1	1
Fine dry breadcrumbs	100 g	4 oz	1 cup
Butter and lard mixed, or margarine	50 g	2 oz	¼ cup
Chopped parsley	10 ml	2 tsp	2 tsp

1. Wash and peel the parsnips. If large, cut in half lengthways.
2. Bring a pan of water to the boil, add the salt and lemon juice, then the parsnips. Boil for 40 minutes or until the parsnips are tender.
3. Drain the parsnips well, and pat dry.
4. Brush the parsnips with beaten egg, and roll in breadcrumbs. Shallow fry in the fat, turning as required, until golden-brown on all sides.
5. Arrange in a pyramid in a warmed serving dish and sprinkle with parsley.

Creamed Mushrooms

Serves 4

Not suitable for freezing

	Metric	Imperial	American
Mushrooms	225 g	8 oz	½ lb
Milk	450 ml	¾ pt	2 cups
Salt and pepper			
Pinch of grated nutmeg			
Butter or margarine	25 g	1 oz	2 tbls
Flour	25 ml	1½ tbls	1½ tbls
Single (light) cream	30 ml	2 tbls	2 tbls
Squeeze of lemon juice			

1. Rinse the mushrooms. Remove the stalks and chop or slice depending on size.
2. Put the mushrooms and stalks in a pan with half the milk and the seasonings. Cover and simmer for about 10 minutes until just soft.
3. In a second pan, make White Sauce (page 84) with the butter, flour, remaining milk and the strained milk in which the mushrooms have been cooked.
4. Add the mushrooms to the thickened sauce, and reheat gently. Stir in the cream and lemon juice. Serve with fried bread.

Red Cabbage Casserole

Serves 4–6

Oven temp 180°C/350°F/Gas Mark 4

Freeze 3 months

	Metric	Imperial	American
Red cabbage	1 kg	2¼ lb	2¼ lb
Bacon fat or dripping	25 g	1 oz	2 tbls
Onion, chopped	1	1	1
Sharp eating apples, peeled, cored and sliced	3	3	3
Golden syrup or brown sugar	15–30 ml	1–2 tbls	1–2 tbls
Cold water	30 ml	2 tbls	2 tbls
Red wine vinegar	30 ml	2 tbls	2 tbls
Juice of ½ lemon			

1. Shred the red cabbage finely, discarding any discoloured leaves and coarse ribs.
2. Melt the fat in a frying pan (skillet) and fry the onion until soft and golden.
3. Layer or mix the cabbage, onion (with the fat), apples and syrup or sugar in a casserole, seasoning each layer well.
4. Pour the water, vinegar and lemon juice over the cabbage.

Red Cabbage Casserole with frankfurters.

5. Cover the casserole tightly. Cook at the temperature above for 1½ hours, stirring occasionally to moisten the cabbage.

Notes: Red cabbage must be cooked with an acid or it turns dull purple. It is particularly good with fatty meats such as pork, or frankfurters can be added for last 30 minutes.

Cauliflower with Tomatoes

Serves 4

Freeze 1 month

	Metric	Imperial	American
Medium cauliflower	1	1	1
Salt			
Firm tomatoes	225 g	8 oz	½ lb
Margarine	25 g	1 oz	2 tbls
Garlic clove	1	1	1
Onion, thinly sliced	1	1	1
Black pepper			
Chopped parsley			

1. Separate the cauliflower head into florets. Boil for about 10 minutes in salted water until almost tender.
2. Meanwhile, skin the tomatoes, quarter them and remove the seeds. Cut the flesh into small pieces.
3. Melt the fat in a large frying pan (skillet). Squeeze the garlic over the sliced onion, and fry the slices until soft and golden. Stir in the tomato and heat. Season with pepper.
4. Drain the cauliflower and turn into a warmed serving dish. Spoon over the contents of the frying pan. Sprinkle with parsley.

Ratatouille

Serves 4–6

Freeze 3 months

	Metric	Imperial	American
Aubergines (eggplants)	3	3	3
Salt			
Large onions	2	2	2
Garlic clove	1	1	1
Green pepper	1	1	1
Courgettes (zucchini)	2–3	2–3	2–3
Tomatoes	4–6	4–6	4–6
Margarine	75 g	3 oz	⅓ cup
Pepper			
Bay leaves	2	2	2
Chopped parsley			

Ratatouille is a colourful dish.

1. Slice the aubergines (eggplants) and sprinkle with salt. Leave in a colander for 30 minutes, then rinse with cold water and dry on soft kitchen paper.
2. Halve and slice the onions. Crush the garlic. De-seed and slice the pepper. Slice the courgettes (zucchini). Skin the tomatoes and quarter them.
3. Melt the fat in a saucepan. Add the onions, garlic and pepper, cover the pan and simmer 5 minutes without browning. Drain and add the aubergines, and all the other ingredients except the parsley.
4. Cover the pan, and cook gently for 30 minutes.
5. Remove the bay leaves. Turn the ratatouille into a warmed dish, if serving hot, and sprinkle with parsley. Cool in the pan, then turn into a chilled serving dish and garnish, if serving cold.

Macedoine of Vegetables

Makes 500 g/18 oz (approx)

Freeze 3 months

	Metric	Imperial	American
Turnip	1	1	1
Carrots	100 g	4 oz	1/4 lb
Potatoes	225 g	8 oz	1/2 lb
A few each of			
runner beans and			
cauliflower florets			
Shelled peas	225 g	8 oz	1/2 lb
Water	850 ml	1½ pt	3¾ cups
Salt	5 ml	1 tsp	1 tsp
Butter	50 g	2 oz	4 tbls
Pepper			

1. Prepare all the vegetables, keeping them separate. Then cut the turnip, carrots and potatoes into 1 cm/½ in dice. Cut the beans diagonally into 1 cm/½ in slices.
2. Bring the water to the boil and add the salt. Add the turnip and carrots and boil for 3 minutes. Add the beans and boil for another 3 minutes.
3. Add the remaining vegetables. Boil for 5–10 minutes until all are tender but not mushy.
4. Drain (reserve the cooking liquid for soup). Toss the vegetables lightly in the butter, and season to taste.
5. Use as a side dish, or as a border round a meat dish.

Stir-Fried Vegetables

Serves 4

Freeze 1 month (without syrup)

	Metric	Imperial	American
Carrots	2	2	2
Garlic clove	1	1	1
Small piece of stem			
ginger in syrup,			
drained			
Small green or red			
pepper	1	1	1
Onion	1	1	1
Celery stalks	2	2	2
Sharp eating apple	1	1	1
White wine vinegar	15 ml	1 tbls	1 tbls
Light soft			
brown sugar	50 g	2 oz	1/3 cup
Sherry	15 ml	1 tbls	1 tbls
Water	15 ml	1 tbls	1 tbls
Oil for frying	30 ml	2 tbls	2 tbls
Salt and pepper			

1. Scrape the carrots and cut into thin 'matchsticks'. Blanch in boiling water for 2 minutes. Drain. Finely chop the garlic and ginger. Sprinkle both on the carrot, on a small plate.
2. De-seed the pepper and slice it thinly. Cut the onion into thin strips from stem to root end. Slice the celery finely. Peel, core and shred the apple.
3. Heat the vinegar and sugar in a saucepan until the sugar melts. Stir in the sherry and water. Take off the heat.
4. Heat the oil in a large deep frying pan (skillet). Add the carrot, garlic and ginger and stir over moderate heat for 2 minutes.
5. Add the remaining vegetables and apple, and stir for another 2 minutes.
6. Pour in the vinegar-sherry syrup, and simmer for 2 minutes. Season to taste.
7. Turn into a warmed dish, and serve at once.

Note: Bean sprouts can be added to this dish with the onion, celery and apple.

STUFFED VEGETABLES

The vegetables most often stuffed are aubergines (eggplants), whole cabbage or cabbage leaves, courgettes (zucchini), mushrooms, onions, peppers, potatoes, tomatoes and vegetable marrow (squash). Recipes for stuffed cabbage leaves, braised stuffed onions, baked stuffed potatoes and a whole vegetable marrow are given later.

To prepare other vegetables:
a. bake aubergines (page 103) and remove pulp. Add it to stuffing; fill skins;
b. halve raw courgettes or marrow lengthways, scoop out seeds, cover cut sides with stuffing; or cut large marrow into rings as for baking (page 106);
c. pile stuffing on large flat blanched mushrooms;
d. cut stem end off peppers or halve them across or lengthways, remove membranes and seeds, fill with stuffing. Replace stem ends if stuffing whole peppers;
e. prepare tomatoes like peppers.

After stuffing, dot the vegetables with fat or sprinkle with oil. Cover with browned breadcrumbs or grated cheese and breadcrumbs if you wish. Place stuffing side up in a greased baking tin (pan). Cover loosely with greased foil. Bake until the stuffing is cooked if necessary and the vegetable is tender if stuffed while raw, or is thoroughly hot. Top with a little well flavoured sauce or garnish if not covered with crumbs or cheese before baking.

The usual average baking time for cooked or tender vegetables with a quick-cooking stuffing is 25–30 minutes at 180°C/350°F/Gas Mark 4 but they can be baked at a lower temperature under a joint or other dish for 1–1¼ hours.

Here are some typical stuffings, giving the approximate quantities needed for each type of vegetable. For other stuffings, see Chapter 6, pages 93–94.

For 2 large baked, halved aubergines (eggplants):

	Metric	Imperial	American
Chopped mushrooms	100 g	4 oz	¼ lb
Chopped onion (sautéed together in oil)	1	1	1
Chopped ham	50 g	2 oz	¼ cup
Soft wholemeal breadcrumbs	50 g	2 oz	1 cup
Tomato ketchup	15 ml	1 tbls	1 tbls
Aubergine pulp			
Salt and pepper			

For 2 large halved courgettes (zucchini):

	Metric	Imperial	American
Small eggs, beaten	2	2	2
Soft wholemeal breadcrumbs	40 g	1½ oz	¾ cup
Grated Cheddar cheese	25 g	1 oz	¼ cup
Small onion, chopped	1	1	1
Chopped fresh parsley	15 ml	1 tbls	1 tbls
Pinch of dried thyme			
Salt and pepper			
Courgette pulp			
Oil	25–50 ml	1–2 fl oz	

For 2 halved red peppers, 4 large blanched flat mushrooms, or 8 de-seeded whole tomatoes:

	Metric	Imperial	American
Green pepper, skinned, seeded and chopped	½	½	½
Soft wholemeal breadcrumbs	40 g	1½ oz	¾ cup
Grated Cheddar cheese	50 g	2 oz	½ cup
Chopped ham	75 g	3 oz	⅓ cup
Chopped spring onion (scallion) bulb	15 ml	1 tbls	1 tbls
Small egg, beaten	1	1	1

Note: Add chopped mushroom stalks to stuffing for mushrooms.

Stuffed Vegetable Marrow

Serves 4–6

Oven temp 180°C/350°F/Gas Mark 4

Not suitable for freezing

	Metric	Imperial	American
Medium marrow (squash)	1	1	1
Salt and pepper			
Small onion, finely chopped	1	1	1
Butter or margarine			
Beef mince	350 g	12 oz	¾ lb
Soft white or wholemeal breadcrumbs	25 g	1 oz	½ cup
Chopped parsley	15 ml	1 tbls	1 tbls
Chopped fresh mixed herbs	15 ml	1 tbls	1 tbls
Tomato ketchup or sauce	5–10 ml	1–2 tsp	1–2 tsp
Egg, beaten	1	1	1
Cheese Sauce (coating consistency), page 88	275 ml	½	1¼ cups

1. Wash the marrow (squash), remove any stalk, and cut in half lengthways. Scoop out seeds and fibre.
2. Lay the marrow halves, cut side up, in a well-greased baking tin (pan). Sprinkle with salt and pepper.
3. Fry the onion in a little butter or margarine until soft.
4. Mix the fried onion with all the remaining ingredients except the cheese sauce, adding the egg last to bind the mixture.
5. Pile the mixture on the cut marrow halves.
6. Cover with greased foil, and bake at the temperature above for about 1 hour.
7. Pour off any liquid given out by the marrow during baking. Cover both halves with cheese sauce. Return to the oven for 20–30 minutes, until the marrow is tender and the sauce well glazed.

Over page: Stuffed Cabbage Leaves cooked in tomato sauce make a satisfying supper dish.

Stuffed Cabbage Leaves

Serves 6

Oven temp 180°C/350°F/Gas Mark 4

Freeze 2 months

	Metric	Imperial	American
Large green cabbage leaves	12	12	12
Beef mince, browned in oil, drained	450 g	1 lb	1 lb
Cooked brown rice	30 ml	2 tbls	2 tbls
Grated onion	45 ml	3 tbls	3 tbls
Egg, beaten	1	1	1
Cold water	30 ml	2 tbls	2 tbls
Salt and pepper			
Fresh Tomato Sauce (page 90)	450 ml	¾ pt	2 cups
Corn oil	10 ml	2 tsp	2 tsp
Skinned chopped tomatoes or canned tomatoes, drained	225 g	8 oz	½ lb
Clear honey	15 ml	1 tbls	1 tbls
Lemon juice	15 ml	1 tbls	1 tbls

1. Cut any tough ribs out of the cabbage leaves. Drop them into boiling water for 3 minutes. Drain.
2. Mix in a bowl the mince, rice, onion, egg, water and seasoning. Put about 20 ml/4 tsp mixture on each cabbage leaf. Fold the sides of each leaf over the stuffing, then roll up from top end, making small parcels.
3. Place the stuffed rolls in a greased casserole. Add the tomato sauce, oil, and chopped or canned tomatoes. Cover with a lid or foil. Bake at the temperature above for 1½ hours.
4. Add the honey and lemon juice, and bake for another 30 minutes. Serve from the casserole as a supper dish.

Braised Stuffed Onions

Serves 6

Oven temp 220°C/425°F/Gas Mark 7

Freeze 1 month

	Metric	Imperial	American
Large Spanish onions	6	6	6
Salt and pepper			
Basic herb forcemeat (page 93) OR sausagemeat	175–225 g	6–8 oz	6–8 oz
Brown Stock (page 14)	150 ml	¼ pt	⅔ cup
Bacon rashers (slices) without rind, cut in half across	3	3	3
Meat extract			

1. Skin the onions and boil for 20 minutes. Drain well. Take out the centres, and season the cavities.
2. Chop the centre flesh and mix well with forcemeat or sausagemeat. Spoon the mixture back into the cavities, piling any extra on top.
3. Place the onions, stuffing side up, in a baking tin (pan). Pour the stock round them. Put a piece of bacon on top of each.
4. Bake at the temperature above for 1 hour until onions are tender.
5. Transfer the onions to a serving dish and keep warm. Dissolve a little meat extract in the stock, and serve in a sauce boat with the onions.

Baked Stuffed Potatoes

Serves 4

Oven temp 220°C/425°F/Gas Mark 7

Freeze 2 months

	Metric	Imperial	American
Large freshly-baked potatoes	4	4	4
Stuffing (see below)			
Browned breadcrumbs (optional)			
Butter or margarine			

1. Holding the hot potatoes in a cloth, cut each in half, and scoop most of the potato out into a bowl.
2. Mash the potato with a fork, and beat in the stuffing ingredient(s).
3. Pile the mixture into the potato skins. Sprinkle with browned breadcrumbs if you wish. Dot with fat.
4. Return to the oven, stuffing side up, at the temperature above for 10–15 minutes.

Stuffings
a. 75 g/3 oz chopped cooked meat;
b. 100 g/4 oz/1 cup grated Cheddar cheese and 25 g/1 oz/2 tbls butter or margarine, with salt, pepper and nutmeg to taste;
c. 125 g/4 oz/⅔ cup diced cooked vegetables and sprinkling of grated cheese;
d. 75 g/3 oz/½ cup cooked white fish, lemon juice, seasoning;
e. 75 g/3 oz/½ cup flaked cooked smoked fish, 1 chopped hard-boiled egg yolk, chopped fresh parsley, seasoning.

8
PULSES, GRAINS AND PASTA

Pulses, pasta such as macaroni or spaghetti, and grains (cereals), such as rice, can be served instead of potatoes, or can be served with a sauce or small amounts of meat and vegetables to make good, economical main dishes. Basically, they are all cooked by boiling although many dishes are completed in the oven:

PULSES

Soaking and Cooking Pulses

Pulses vary in size and hardness a great deal. All the larger and harder pulses need soaking before being cooked; soya beans, chickpeas and whole green or yellow peas in particular need long soaking. The longer any pulse is soaked for, the quicker it will cook.

Before being soaked, any pulse should be well rinsed and picked over to remove any discoloured seeds or small stones.

There are two soaking methods:
1. The pulses are put in a large bowl, covered with twice their depth of cold water, and are left to stand for several hours or overnight;
2. The pulses are put in a large bowl, covered with boiling water and are left to stand for 1–2 hours.

The pulses can be boiled in the soaking water, or can be drained, rinsed well, and drained again before being boiled in fresh water. A general guide to boiling times is given in the chart on the right; remember, however, that pulses can differ in quality and hardness from package to package, according to where they come from, and need longer cooking the longer they stay on the shelf.

Note: Since pulses take a long time to cook, and freeze and reheat perfectly, it is wise to cook enough for two or three meals at one time.

PLEASE NOTE: Dried red kidney beans must be boiled for a minimum of 10 minutes after soaking before inclusion in any dish.

Pressure Cooking Pulses

1. Wash the vegetables. Place in a bowl, pour over sufficient boiling water to cover and leave to soak for about 1 hour (covered with a lid).
2. Remove trivet from pressure cooker and pour in 1 l/1¾ pt/4⅓ cups for every 225 g/8 oz vegetables to be cooked.
3. Bring the liquid to the boil in the open pan and add the vegetables. Remember, they will expand and absorb water during cooking so do not fill the pan more than half full. Soda must not be added as it will discolour the pressure cooker.
4. Skim the liquid, lower the heat so that the contents boil gently but do not rise. Secure lid and weight and bring to High pressure.
5. At the end of the cooking time (see chart) allow pressure to reduce at room temperature.

Note: Times for pressure cooking pulses vary according to taste (see chart). Pressure cooking lentils or split peas is not recommended as they may block the vents in the pressure cooker. Do not cook 'Bean Mix' in your pressure cooker as the cooking times vary according to the ingredients. Overcooking of the lentils in the mix could cause the setting control or ventpipe to become blocked.

Baked Beans

Serves 8

Oven temp 140°C/275°F/Gas Mark 1

Freeze 6 months

	Metric	Imperial	American
Dried haricot (navy) beans	450 g	1 lb	1 lb
Small onion, chopped	1	1	1
230 g/8 oz can of plum tomatoes	1	1	1
Black treacle	100 ml	4 fl oz	½ cup
Brown sugar	15 ml	1 tbls	1 tbls
Tomato ketchup	30 ml	2 tbls	2 tbls
Chilli sauce (optional)	5 ml	1 tsp	1 tsp
Dry mustard	2.5 ml	½ tsp	½ tsp
Salt	5 ml	1 tsp	1 tsp

AVERAGE COOKING TIMES FOR PULSES

Name	Notes on Soaking	Cooking Times Saucepan	Pressure Cooker (High or 15 lb pressure)
Adzuki beans	Soak (1 hr if in boiling water)	45 minutes	10 minutes
Black-eyed beans	Soak (1 hr if in boiling water)	1–1½ hours	20 minutes
Borlotti beans	Soak (1 hr if in boiling water)	1–1½ hours	20 minutes
Butter beans	Soak at least 12 hours in cold water 2 hours in boiling water.	2–2½ hours	25 minutes
Haricot (navy) beans	Soak (1 hr if in boiling water)	1½–2 hours	20 minutes
Mung beans	Soak (1 hr if in boiling water)	30–45 minutes	10 minutes
Pinto beans	Soak (1 hr if in boiling water)	1–1½ hours	20 minutes
Red kidney beans	Soak (1 hr if in boiling water)	1–1½ hours	20 minutes
Soya (soy) beans	Soak at least 12 hours in cold water or 2 hours in boiling water. Keep refrigerated while soaking in cold water	2 hours	25 minutes
Chickpeas	Soak as for soya beans	2 hours	20 minutes
Split peas	No need to soak; if soaked, boil about 30 minutes only	1–1½ hours	Not recommended
Whole peas	Soak (2 hrs if in boiling water)	1½ hours	25 minutes
Split lentils	No need to soak; if soaked, boil about 20 minutes only	40 minutes	Not recommended
Whole lentils	Soak (1 hr if in boiling water)	45 minutes	Not recommended

1. Wash the beans well. Put them in a large saucepan. Cover them with 850 ml/1½ pt/ 3¾ cups boiling water. Boil for 2 minutes, then leave off the heat for 1 hour.
2. Return the pan of beans and soaking liquid to gentle heat. Bring to simmering point, cover and cook gently for 1–1½ hours until ready for oven-cooking. Add a little extra water while cooking if needed. To test for readiness, place a few beans on a spoon, and blow on them. If the skins break, they are ready.
3. Drain the beans when ready. Put them in a deep casserole or bean-pot. Mix in the onion, and the tomatoes with their juice. Chop the tomatoes when adding them if firm.
4. Mix together all the remaining ingredients and pour over the beans. Add enough fresh water to come level with the top of the beans.
5. Cover the casserole tightly, and bake at the temperature above for 6–8 hours. Add extra water occasionally if needed to prevent the beans drying out.
6. Serve hot, straight from the casserole.

Notes:
1. The quantities of sweetening and chilli sauce can be varied to taste.

2. It is not practical to make a small quantity of baked beans. They will reheat perfectly for a second meal, or can be frozen.

Variation
For Boston Baked Beans, omit the canned tomatoes and ketchup. Bury a 100 g/4 oz/¼ lb piece of blanched pickled pork among the boiled beans in the casserole so that the surface of the rind just shows. Bake as above, but uncover the casserole for the last 30 minutes of cooking time.

Chilli con Carne

Serves 4

Oven temp 180°C/350°F/Gas Mark 4

Freeze 2 months

	Metric	Imperial	American
Corn oil	30 ml	2 tbls	2 tbls
Beef mince	600 g	1¼ lb	1¼ lb
Medium onions, sliced	2	2	2
Chilli powder	10 ml	2 tsp	2 tsp
Dried basil	5 ml	1 tsp	1 tsp
Oregano	10 ml	2 tsp	2 tsp
Ground cumin	5 ml	1 tsp	1 tsp
Cayenne pepper	2.5–5 ml	½–1 tsp	½–1 tsp
Salt			
Tomato purée, (paste) to taste (optional)			
Cornflour (cornstarch)	15 g	½ oz	½ oz
Water	30 ml	2 tbls	2 tbls
Beef stock	450 ml	¾ pt	2 cups
Cooked red kidney beans (or use one 425 g/15 oz can, drained)	250 g	9 oz	9 oz

1. Heat the oil in a saucepan, and fry the beef mince, turning it over, until lightly browned all over. Add the onions and chilli powder, and fry for another 3 minutes.

2. Add the remaining seasonings and tomato purée. Blend the cornflour with the water and stir into the stock.
3. Transfer the contents of the pan to a casserole. Pour over the stock, cover and bake at the temperature above for 1 hour.
4. Stir the beans into the contents of the casserole. Cover again, and return to the oven for 40 minutes. Serve hot with Baked Maize (page 122).

Eastern-Bean Salad

Serves 4

Not suitable for freezing

	Metric	Imperial	American
Eggs	4	4	4
Small bunch of parsley	1	1	1
Olive oil	150 ml	¼ pt	⅔ cup
Tomato Sauce (page 90)	150 ml	¼ pt	⅔ cup
Lemons, quartered	2	2	2
Cold cooked brown beans (see note)	500 g	1 lb 2 oz	1 lb 2 oz
Large garlic cloves, halved	2	2	2
Salt and pepper			

1. Hard-boil (hard-cook) the eggs (page 139); drain when ready, and leave in cold water.

2. While boiling the eggs, chop the parsley finely, and put it in a small bowl. Pour the olive oil and Tomato Sauce into separate small jugs. Put the lemon quarters on a saucer. Place all these on a tray for serving.
3. Drain the beans if needed, and divide between 4 small bowls. Squeeze half a garlic clove over each helping, and stir in lightly.
4. Shell the eggs as soon as you can handle them. Place one on each pile of beans. Season lightly.
5. Serve one bowl to each person, and offer the tray of seasonings with it. Each person mashes the egg into the beans with seasonings.

Note: Brown beans are available canned; they are called *ful medames*. Canned red kidney beans (two 425 g/15 oz cans) can be substituted.

Pease Pudding

Serves 4

Freeze 3 months

	Metric	Imperial	American
Split peas	225 g	8 oz	½ lb
Bacon or ham scraps without rind	100 g	4 oz	¼ lb
Onion, skinned	½	½	½
Butter	25 g	1 oz	2 tbls
Egg, beaten	1	1	1
Pinch of sugar			

Ground black pepper
Salt
Chopped parsley (optional)

1. Wash and pick over the peas. Drain.
2. Tie the peas loosely in a cloth. Put in a pan, and cover with fresh cold water. Add the bacon or ham scraps and the onion to the pan.
3. Bring to the boil, skim, and boil gently with a lid on the pan for 1½–2 hours, or until tender.
4. Drain the peas thoroughly, reserving the onion, then process the peas in a blender or food processor with the butter, egg, sugar, a little pepper, and salt if needed. When smooth, add the parsley if you wish, and some or all of the onion (chopped).
5. Turn out onto a warmed dish. Serve with boiled ham, bacon or pickled pork instead of potatoes.

A colorful selection of dishes made from beans and pulses. From the left, Eastern Bean Salad served with Tomato Sauce (page 90) and olive oil, Pease Pudding and Chilli con Carne.

Boiled Lentils

Serves 4

Freeze 2 months

	Metric	Imperial	American
Lentils, whole or split	350 g	12 oz	¾ lb
Corn oil (for split lentils)	30 ml	2 tbls	2 tbls
Water	700 ml	1¼ pt	3 cups
A good grinding of pepper			
Pinch of cayenne pepper			
Pinch of one or more of the following spices: ground cumin, coriander, turmeric or allspice, garlic powder			
Sugar			
Salt			

1. Pick over the lentils, discarding any discoloured ones. Rinse the lentils thoroughly in a sieve.
2. Soak whole lentils overnight in cold water or for 1 hour in water poured on them boiling. Simmer split lentils for 3–4 minutes in the oil. Drain.
3. Drain soaked lentils. Put whole or split lentils in a large pan with the given quantity of fresh water. Bring to the boil over moderate heat, then reduce the heat to a gentle boil. Cover, and cook for about 45 minutes or until tender; test split lentils for readiness after 20 minutes.
4. Drain the lentils thoroughly when ready. Toss with the pepper, cayenne, chosen spices, sugar and salt. Serve as a side dish, or as the basis of a main dish with other ingredients; or cool, for use as a salad. Pulses such as lentils, combined with grains (see right), provide complete protein, the equivalent of meat.

Notes:
1. If the lentils will be served hot, and must wait, put them in a sieve over simmering water, covered with a damp cloth.
2. If the lentils will be used as part of another, spicy dish, toss them just with pepper, cayenne, sugar and salt.

Curried Beans

Serves 4

Freeze 1 month

	Metric	Imperial	American
Haricot (navy) beans	225 g	8 oz	½ lb
Medium onion, finely chopped	1	1	1
1 cm/½ in piece of fresh root ginger, chopped			
Garlic cloves, crushed	2	2	2
Corn oil or other pure vegetable oil (not olive oil)	30 ml	2 tbls	2 tbls
Cayenne pepper	2.5 ml	½ tsp	½ tsp
Ground cumin	2.5 ml	½ tsp	½ tsp
Ground coriander	5 ml	1 tsp	1 tsp
Ground turmeric	2.5 ml	½ tsp	½ tsp
Chilli powder	5 ml	1 tsp	1 tsp
Brown sugar	15 ml	1 tbls	1 tbls
400 g/14 oz can of plum tomatoes	1	1	1

1. Rinse, soak and cook the beans as suggested in the chart (page 115). To test for readiness, put a few beans on a spoon and blow on them gently. The skins should crack.
2. While cooking the beans, fry the onion, ginger and garlic gently in the oil, stirring all the time, for 5 minutes. Stir in the cayenne pepper and all the spices. Stir for 2 minutes. Add the sugar, and stir for 4 minutes longer.
3. Chop the tomatoes, and add them with their juice to the beans. Stir in the curry mixture gently.
4. Cover and simmer for 1 hour. Serve with Boiled Rice (opposite).

RICE AND OTHER GRAINS

(For sweet grain dishes, see pages 173 and 174.)

Rice

Rice is sold as whole grain in two forms. White rice has more starch and less protein, fat, and mineral content than any other cereal because it has been polished to remove all the fibre. Brown rice is unpolished, so retains its fibre and nutrients and has a distinctive flavour. It takes a little longer to cook than white rice, and is particularly good for savoury main dishes.

Boil-in-the-bag and 'instant' or 'minute' rice are now sold, which cook in a few minutes. Cooking directions for these are given on the packets.

There are several varieties of rice. Use a long grain variety such as Patna rice for savoury dishes because the grains stay separate during cooking. Use a short, round, thick grain rice such as Carolina rice for sweet dishes because the grain becomes soft and creamy when cooked long and slowly.

Ground rice is grain ground to a fine meal or coarse flour used mostly for puddings and cakes.

Other Grains

Oats are usually sold processed as rolled oats (used for porridge) and as coarse, medium or fine oatmeal. The meal is used for making porridge and puddings, oatcakes and other baked goods, and for coating foods before frying.

Barley is sold as Scotch barley, pearl barley (which is polished like white rice), or as barley flakes. Pearl barley is used in substantial soups and casseroles.

Rye is mostly made into a dark flour; it has very little gluten (page 206).

Maize is sold as whole grains on the cob, or scraped off them and canned or frozen. The yellow or white meal is called polenta in Italy and is used for the dishes of that name. In America, it is called cornmeal.

Wheat, besides being made into flour, is sold as whole grain, kibbled (coarsely chopped) grain, as semolina (from the first milling), and in forms such as cous-cous (fine semolina) used in Middle Eastern dishes.

Boiled Rice (white)

Rinse the rice well. Put it into fast-boiling water containing 5 ml/1 tsp salt and 5 ml/1 tsp lemon juice per 1 l/1¾ pt/4⅓ cups. Stir round once, then boil for 12–15 minutes. Drain in a sieve and rinse under hot water.

Serve the rice as it is, e.g. with curries, or reheat in a pan with a little melted butter or margarine, stirring with a fork to keep the grains separate.

Variations

1. For a *Ring of Boiled Rice*, boil 225 g/8 oz/½ lb long grain rice as above. Turn into a well-greased 18 cm/7¼ in ring mould and press down evenly. Stand the mould in a pan of hot water for 7–10 minutes to reheat the rice. Place a serving plate upside down on the mould and invert the plate and mould together. The rice ring should slip out of the mould easily without breaking. Fill with flaked fish, chopped meat or poultry or vegetables in a sauce, or cool and fill with a salad mixture.
2. For *Yellow Rice*, boil 200 g/7 oz rice in 700 ml/1¼ pt/ 3 cups water with a cinnamon stick, 2.5 ml/1 tsp ground turmeric, 5 ml/ 1 tsp salt and 15 ml/1 tbls butter or margarine. Cook until the rice is tender and the water almost all absorbed. Serve with roasts, grills or barbecued dishes, or cool and use as a rice salad.

Boiled Rice (brown)

Rinse the rice well. Put 250 g/9 oz rice in a saucepan with 500 ml/18 fl oz/2¼ cups water and 2.5 ml/½ tsp salt. Bring to the boil and cook for 3 minutes. Reduce the heat to simmering, cover and cook very gently for 35–45 minutes, adding a little more water after 25 minutes and at 10-minute intervals thereafter if needed. When ready and tender, the rice should have absorbed all the liquid and be quite dry. Remove from the heat, stir once, and leave to stand, covered, for 5 minutes.

Note: Brown rice keeps well in a refrigerator, and freezes perfectly.

Risotto (basic recipe)

Serves 4–6

Freeze 2 months

	Metric	Imperial	American
Onion, chopped	1	1	1
Butter or margarine	65 g	2½ oz	5 tbls
White rice	350 g	12 oz	¾ lb
White wine	75 ml	3 fl oz	⅓ cup
Chicken Stock (page 15), warmed	1 l	1¾ pt	4⅓ cups
Salt and pepper			
Grated Parmesan cheese	25 g	1 oz	¼ cup

1. In a fairly large saucepan, fry the onion gently in 40 g/1½ oz/3 tbls of the fat until soft. Add the rice, and stir until well coated but not browned.
2. Gradually stir in the wine and cook gently, stirring, until it is all absorbed.
3. Add about half the warmed stock. Bring to the boil, reduce the heat, and simmer until the liquid is all absorbed. Half cover and continue cooking, adding more stock in small quantities, until the rice is tender but still firm (about 15–20 minutes in all) and all the added stock has been absorbed.
4. Season well, and stir in the cheese and remaining butter. Serve hot and glistening.

Note: Do not use instant or minute rice for this dish.

Variations

1. Make the risotto with brown rice, using extra stock if necessary, and cooking 40–45 minutes.
2. Instead of cheese, add cooked vegetables or dried fruit, e.g. 30 ml/2 tbls each of peas, sliced green beans, sultanas, chopped pimento or button mushrooms, to the mixture about 10 minutes before the end of cooking time.

Rice Salad

Serves 4

Freeze 2 months

	Metric	Imperial	American
Long grain rice	100 g	4 oz	¼ lb
Salt			
French Dressing (page 132)	50–100 ml	2–4 fl oz	¼–½ cup
Carrot, grated	1	1	1
Cooked peas	50 g	2 oz	2 oz
Celery stalks, chopped	2	2	2
Red-skinned apple, cored, chopped and dipped in French Dressing	1	1	1
Chopped chives or spring onion (scallion)	10 ml	2 tsp	2 tsp
Chopped parsley	10 ml	2 tsp	2 tsp
Ground black pepper			

1. Cook the rice in boiling, salted water until tender. Drain well, and rinse under warm running water. Mix at once, while still warm, with enough dressing to moisten well.
2. Mix in the vegetables, apple, chives or onion and parsley. Season lightly.
3. Turn into a serving bowl. Chill lightly before serving.

Variations
1. Vary the salad by adding or substituting other vegetables. Include one pulse, e.g. cooked red kidney beans, if not using peas.
2. Risotto with added vegetables (page 119) can be used instead of plain boiled rice with added vegetables. Moisten with dressing.
3. For a more substantial salad, use brown rice, tomato wedges, sliced pepper and mushrooms and add peanuts and olives.

Below: *Rice Salad makes a colourful accompaniment to cold meat or fish, or served on its own, with the addition of cheese or nuts, it becomes a light lunch or supper dish.*

Opposite: *Corn Chowder and Semolina Gnocchi (page 122) are both suitable for winter lunch dishes.*

Corn Chowder

Serves 6

Not suitable for freezing

	Metric	Imperial	American
Sweetcorn kernels, canned or frozen	450 g	1 lb	1 lb
Potatoes	225 g	8 oz	½ lb
Salt and pepper			
Onion, coarsely chopped	1	1	1
Celery stalks, thinly sliced	2	2	2
Bacon fat or margarine	45 ml	3 tbls	3 tbls
Cooked bacon rashers (slices) without rind, chopped (optional)	2	2	2
Flour	25 g	1 oz	¼ cup
Milk	450 ml	¾ pt	2 cups
Butter	40 g	1½ oz	3 tbls

1. Drain, or thaw and drain, the corn. Keep aside.
2. Peel the potatoes and cut into 2 cm/¾ in dice. Place in a large pan and boil for 5 minutes in 450 ml/¾ pt/2 cups water. Add seasoning to taste, reduce the heat to simmering, cover the pan and simmer for 5–10 minutes, or until potato dice are tender. Take off the heat.
3. Fry the onion and celery in 30 ml/2 tbls of the fat in a saucepan until the onion is golden. Remove the vegetables with a slotted spoon, and add to the potatoes with the bacon if used.
4. Add the remaining 15 ml/1 tbls fat to the pan. Scatter in the flour, and cook for 2 minutes, stirring. Gradually add the milk to make a sauce. Bring to the boil and cook, stirring, for 1 minute. Add to the potatoes.
5. Stir the corn and butter into the chowder. Reheat gently for 5–6 minutes. Serve in soup bowls as a first course or complete supper dish.

Semolina Gnocchi

Serves 4

Oven temp 200°C/400°F/Gas Mark 6

Freeze 2 months (before baking)

	Metric	Imperial	American
Milk	575 ml	1 pt	2½ cups
Semolina	100 g	4 oz	¼ lb
Salt and pepper			
Grated nutmeg	1.5 ml	¼ tsp	¼ tsp
Egg, beaten	1	1	1
Grated cheese	125 g	4½ oz	4½ oz
Butter	40 g	1½ oz	3 tbls

1. Bring the milk to the boil in a fairly large saucepan. Sprinkle in the semolina, and stir over gentle heat until the mixture is very thick.
2. Stir in the seasonings, egg, and 75 g/3 oz of the cheese. Beat until well blended and smooth.
3. Spread the mixture evenly in a 2 cm/¾ in layer in a baking tin (pan) or dish. Leave until cold and set.
4. Cut the mixture into 2.5 cm/1 in squares or small rounds. Arrange in a greased, shallow ovenproof dish, in layers. Sprinkle with the remaining cheese, and dot with the butter.
5. Bake at the temperature above until the topping is golden-brown and the gnocchi are well heated. Serve hot.

Note: There are several kinds of gnocchi. One kind is made with spinach, another with potato, a third with cream cheese. Cooking methods vary almost as much as ingredients.

Baked Maize (Corn) Meal

Serves 4–6

Oven temp 180°C/350°F/Gas Mark 4

Not suitable for freezing

	Metric	Imperial	American
Milk	450 ml	¾ pt	2 cups
Maize meal (cornmeal, polenta)	100 g	4 oz	¼ lb
Melted butter or margarine	30 ml	2 tbls	2 tbls
Eggs, separated	3	3	3
Salt	5 ml	1 tsp	1 tsp
Baking powder	2.5 ml	½ tsp	½ tsp

1. Bring the milk to scalding point in a medium-large saucepan. Sprinkle in the meal, and stir over gentle heat until the mixture is very thick. Stir in the melted fat. Take the pan off the heat. Cool for 5 minutes.
2. Grease a 1.5 l/2½ pt/6¼ cup oven-to-table baking dish.
3. Beat the egg yolks and salt until light. Stir them into the maize meal mixture. Whisk the egg whites and baking powder together until stiff enough to hold soft peaks. Fold them into the maize meal mixture with a metal spoon.

4. Turn the mixture gently into the dish. Bake at the temperature above for 40 minutes, or until golden.
5. Serve from the dish with a spoonful of butter on each serving.

Note: This dish can be served instead of pasta or potatoes, or as a main dish with bacon or ham, tomatoes, etc.

Variation
Use semolina instead of maize meal.

Wheat-Stuffed Marrow

Serves 4–6

Oven temp 190°C/375°F/Gas Mark 5

Freeze 2 months (stuffing only)

	Metric	Imperial	American
1.1–1.4 kg/			
2½–3 lb vegetable			
marrow (squash) 1	*1*	*1*	
Butter or margarine 100 g	*4 oz*	*½ cup*	
Large onion,			
chopped	*1*	*1*	*1*
Celery stalk, finely			
chopped	*1*	*1*	*1*
Cracked wheat			
(bulgar)	*100 g*	*4 oz*	*¼ lb*
Chicken or vegetable			
stock	*150 ml*	*¼ pt*	*⅔ cup*
Dry (apple) cider	*150 ml*	*¼ pt*	*⅔ cup*
Salt and pepper			
Fresh sage leaves	*6*	*6*	*6*
Cooking (tart) apple	*1*	*1*	*1*
Seedless raisins	*50 g*	*2 oz*	*2 oz*

1. Split the marrow lengthways and remove the seeds. Spread the hollows with a little of the fat.
2. Melt 50 g/2 oz/¼ cup of the remaining fat in a deep pan, and fry the onion and celery until soft but not coloured.
3. Add the cracked wheat, stock and cider with a little seasoning. Stir round. Bring to simmering point, and cook gently for 15 minutes with a cover on the pan.
4. Chop the sage leaves; core and chop the apple with the raisins.
5. Add the sage, apples and raisins to the wheat mixture. Stir in thoroughly. Take the pan off the heat.
6. Place the marrow halves in a greased baking tin (pan), cut side up. Fill with the stuffing, piling it up in a centre ridge. Dot with some of the remaining fat, and put the rest into the tin (pan).
7. Cover the marrow halves loosely with greased foil. Bake at the temperature above for 1–1½ hours. Uncover for the last 15 minutes to brown. Serve hot.

PASTA

Cooking Pasta

Pasta can be boiled in salted water until tender or partly boiled, then finished in the oven. Boiled pasta is usually served just with a rich sauce, although vegetables, cheese etc. may be mixed with the pasta itself. Baked pasta is usually layered with a stuffing ingredient and a sauce.

Any shape of pasta can be used for any dish, but certain shapes are more practical for some dishes than others. A baked dish of pasta layered with a stuffing is best made with wide flat noodles such as lasagne. Wide tubes of pasta called cannelloni are used for filling with stuffing.

Tomatoes, mushrooms, eggs, cheese, garlic and basil feature largely in pasta dishes.

Use 50–75 g/2–3 oz uncooked pasta for each person for a first course, 25 g/1 oz extra for a main course.

To Boil Pasta

1. Bring a large pan of salted water to the boil. Add 15–30 ml/1–2 tbls olive oil to prevent the pasta sticking together.
2. Break long pasta into short lengths. Put them into the water and press them down gently as they soften. Drop elbow-cut pieces or small round pasta shapes into the water a few at a time, and stir round. Slide lasagne into the water one sheet at a time to prevent them sticking together. Drop bundled pasta into the water, leave to soften, then stir with a fork.
3. Cook the pasta until tender but not soggy. Most rods and flat ribbons, short cut lengths and fancy shapes will take 7–10 minutes (vermicelli and tiny shapes for soups 4–5 minutes, also 'quick' macaroni). Large, ridged and stuffed pasta shapes take 15–20 minutes.
4. Drain the pasta in a colander. Either return it to the empty pan if mixing it with a sauce or place in a warmed serving dish and add butter or a sauce as you wish. If the pasta must wait, keep it warm in a damp cloth in a colander over simmering water; then add butter or sauce. Serve hot.

To Bake Pasta (lasagne, dry cannelloni)

1. Cook by boiling as in step 2 above for 6–8 minutes (lasagne) or 13–14 minutes (dry cannelloni). Remove pasta pieces from water one at a time and lay side by side on a damp cloth to drain.
2. Heat oven to 200°C/400°F/Gas Mark 6 or as recipe directs. Prepare sauce and stuffing if not done beforehand. Layer lasagne with stuffing and sauce in a greased baking dish, or fill cannelloni with stuffing, lay side by side in the dish and cover with sauce and any topping.
3. Bake as the recipe directs. Serve hot.

Baked Lasagne with Cheese

Serves 4

Oven temp 200°C/400°F/Gas Mark 6

Freeze 2 months (ready for baking)

	Metric	Imperial	American
Lasagne rectangles	225 g	8 oz	½ lb
Olive oil	15 ml	1 tbls	1 tbls
Pouring White Sauce (page 84)	575 ml	1 pt	2½ cups
Grated Parmesan cheese	75 g	3 oz	¾ cup
Chopped parsley	45 ml	3 tbls	3 tbls
Cottage cheese	350 g	12 oz	¾ lb
Philadelphia soft cheese	75 g	3 oz	3 oz
Salt and pepper			
Dry white breadcrumbs or fine cracker crumbs	60 ml	4 tbls	4 tbls
Butter	20 ml	4 tsp	4 tsp

1. Boil the lasagne in 2 or 3 batches, in about 3.4 l/6 pt/7½ pt salted water and the oil; cook for 5–6 minutes only.
2. Wring out a tea-towel dipped in cold water, and lay it on a flat surface.
3. Drain the lasagne in a colander. Drop into cold water for 1 minute. Drain again, and lay the rectangles side by side on the cloth.
4. In a saucepan, warm the White Sauce without boiling. Stir in half the Parmesan cheese and all the parsley. Sieve in both soft cheeses, and stir until smooth. Season.
5. Grease an oven-to-table baking dish (approx 25 × 20 cm/10 × 8 in size). Sprinkle half the dry crumbs on the bottom. Cover with a third of the lasagne rectangles in an even layer.
6. Spread a third of the sauce over the pasta. Sprinkle with 15 g/½ oz/⅛ cup of the remaining Parmesan.
7. Repeat these layers twice more, using all the ingredients. Mix the remaining crumbs with the last 15 g/½ oz Parmesan cheese before sprinkling it on the sauce.
8. Dot the dish with the butter. Bake at the temperature above for 15–20 minutes until the dish is lightly browned. Serve hot.

Below: *Baked Lasagne with Cheese.*

Opposite: *Cannelloni with Spinach and Cheese.*

Cannelloni with Spinach and Cheese

Serves 4

Oven temp 180°C/350°F/Gas Mark 4

Freeze 1 month (ready for baking)

	Metric	Imperial	American
Dry wholemeal			
cannelloni tubes	8	8	8
Olive oil	15 ml	1 tbls	1 tbls
Frozen chopped			
spinach, thawed			
and drained	350 g	12 oz	¾ lb
Mozzarella cheese	225 g	8 oz	½ lb
Salt and pepper			
Pinch of grated			
nutmeg			
Smoked raw ham or			
beef	50 g	2 oz	2 oz
Pouring White			
Sauce			
(page 84)	575 ml	1 pt	2½ cups
Dry white			
breadcrumbs	25 g	1 oz	¼ cup
Grated Parmesan			
cheese	25 g	1 oz	¼ cup

1. Boil the cannelloni tubes, a few at a time, in about 3.4 l/6 pt/7½ pt salted water with 15 ml/1 tbls oil. Boil for 15 minutes, drain and dip in cold water for 1 minute. Drain again, and lay, separated, on a clean tea-towel wrung out in cold water.
2. Chop the spinach finely if needed. Grate or shred the Mozzarella cheese. Put 50 g/2 oz/ ½ cup cheese aside, and mix the rest with the spinach. Season with salt, pepper and nutmeg.
3. Holding each cannelloni tube open, spoon the spinach mixture into the tubes. Lay the filled tubes side by side in a greased, shallow oven-to-table dish. Spread any leftover stuffing over them.
4. Shred the smoked ham or beef. Sprinkle over the cannelloni.
5. Mix the reserved Mozzarella cheese into the White Sauce. Pour it over the dish. Bake at the temperature above for 20 minutes.
6. Mix together the breadcrumbs and Parmesan and place under moderate grill (broiler) heat for 2–3 minutes to brown. Serve at once.

Note: Fresh spinach may be used. Cook in a very little water and drain well.

Macaroni with Mushroom Sauce

Serves 4

Freeze 2 months

	Metric	Imperial	American
Long or short-cut			
(elbow) macaroni	450 g	1 lb	1 lb
Small onion	1	1	1
Garlic clove	½	½	½
Butter	15 ml	1 tbls	1 tbls
Oil	15 ml	1 tbls	1 tbls
Chopped parsley	10 ml	2 tsp	2 tsp
Flour			
Small mushrooms,			
finely sliced	275 g	10 oz	10 oz
Chicken stock (from			
cube)	75 ml	5 tbls	5 tbls
Salt and pepper			
Extra butter	10 ml	2 tsp	2 tsp

1. Boil the macaroni in salted water until just tender.
2. Meanwhile, chop the onion and garlic finely. Heat the butter and oil in a frying pan (skillet), and fry the onion and garlic until soft. Add the parsley.
3. Sprinkle the onion and garlic well with flour. Stir in the mushrooms and 60 ml/4 tbls of the stock. Simmer until the mushrooms soften. Add the remaining 15 ml/1 tbls stock if needed to make a slightly thickened sauce. Season.
4. Drain the macaroni, and turn into a warmed serving dish. Mix the extra butter into the mushroom sauce and spread on top. Serve hot.

Pasta Shells with Garlic Dressing

Serves 4

Not suitable for freezing

	Metric	Imperial	American
Garlic cloves	2	2	2
Pasta shells	350 g	12 oz	¾ lb
Olive oil	100 ml	4 fl oz	½ cup
Large parsley sprig			
(leaves only),			
finely chopped	1	1	1
Small green pepper,			
cored,			
de-seeded and			
finely chopped	1	1	1

1. Peel the garlic cloves and cut into thin slivers.
2. Boil the pasta shells in salted water until just tender.
3. Meanwhile, fry the garlic in the oil until brown. Add the parsley and pepper, and fry gently until soft and beginning to brown.
4. Drain the pasta shells and turn into a warmed serving bowl. Toss with the hot dressing. Serve hot as a first course.

Spaghetti Bolognese

Serves 4

Freeze 2 months

	Metric	Imperial	American
Streaky bacon			
without rind,			
chopped	50 g	2 oz	2 oz
Butter	15 ml	1 tbls	1 tbls
Onion, chopped	1	1	1
Carrot, chopped	1	1	1
Celery stalk,			
chopped	½	½	½
Beef mince	225 g	8 oz	½ lb
Chicken livers,			
chopped	100 g	4 oz	¼ lb
Tomato paste	15 ml	1 tbls	1 tbls
White wine	150 ml	¼ pt	⅔ cup
Salt and pepper			
Pinch of grated			
nutmeg			
Beef stock	225 ml	8 fl oz	1 cup
Spaghetti	450–600 g	1–1¼ lb	1–1¼ lb
Extra butter	10 ml	2 tsp	2 tsp
Grated Parmesan			
cheese			

1. First make the sauce. In a saucepan, cook the bacon gently in the butter, until brown. Add the onion, carrot and celery, and fry until tender and turning brown.
2. Stir in the mince and cook, stirring, until it is browned all over.
3. Add the chicken livers and cook, stirring, for 3 minutes. Gradually mix in the tomato paste and wine. Season with salt, pepper and nutmeg.
4. Stir in the stock. Bring to the boil, then reduce the heat to simmering. Cover the pan and simmer for 30 minutes, or until the sauce is thick and well-flavoured.
5. While simmering the sauce, cook the spaghetti in boiling salted water until just tender.
6. Drain the spaghetti, and turn into a warmed serving dish. Mix in the sauce. Top with the extra butter and with grated Parmesan cheese.

9
SALADS AND SALAD DRESSINGS

A salad can be made from any edible raw, blanched or cooked vegetable, pulse or fruit, used alone or mixed, and seasoned as a rule, with oil and vinegar or some other salad dressing. Herbs, nuts, or a starchy ingredient such as pasta can be added.

For sweet fruit salads served as desserts see page 195.

INGREDIENTS

Use your imagination and initiative in making salads. They should provide fragrance, crispness and flavours which freshen the palate, and colours which add vitality to the menu.

Try, for instance, shredded Chinese cabbage or young spinach instead of lettuce, or use blanched shredded chicory (endive) or red cabbage as a basis for a winter salad. Cooked dried beans make a colourful salad if you mix two or three of the types now available. Pickled vegetables such as cucumbers add zesty flavour, while smoked and other delicatessen meats and fish (e.g. salami or rollmop herrings) are popular main-course items. Cheeses, especially hard and blue cheeses, are used grated or cubed or may be crumbled into a dressing. Other popular salad flavourings are supplied by dressings made with a tangy ingredient such as yoghurt or soy sauce; by garlic, rubbed round the salad bowl before adding the salad or over toast cubes placed in the bottom of the bowl; or by fresh chopped herbs such as mint, parsley, chives or dill leaves.

Green leaf vegetables must be fresh and crisp. Remove stems, tough ribs and any wilted or yellowed leaves. Wash quickly and shake in a cloth or salad basket, to dry. Whenever possible, tear rather than cut the leaves into small pieces; cutting may dull the flavour and make the leaves limp. Wash, dry and pick over watercress carefully, cut off all root ends and any coarse stalks, and (unlike other leaves) crisp in a polythene bag in the refrigerator for 1 hour before use. Trim the stalks of small cress and wash off any small black seeds. Slice cucumbers, sprinkle with salt and drain on a tilted plate for 30 minutes to remove bitterness.

Raw vegetables such as carrots, celery, chicory (endive), cucumber, mild onions, spring onions (scal-lions), radishes and tomatoes: Top and tail, wash, and scrape or peel if needed. Slice, sliver, chop, or grate as appropriate. (Remove bitter core of chicory (endive) with a pointed knife, and separate into leaves or slice into rings.)

Blanched vegetables such as red or winter white cabbage, cauliflower sprigs, kohlrabi or leeks (used raw when young for some salads): Prepare like raw vegetables, then parboil for 2–3 minutes in salted water, drain well and cool.

Cooked vegetables and pulses: You can use firm leftover vegetables from the previous meal but not older ones. Do not use watery or very soft vegetables. When cooking vegetables for a salad, strip off all coarse parts such as the outer stalks of celery or sheaths of fennel bulbs. Avoid orange lentils which cook to a purée quickly. Peel and dress potatoes and pulses while still warm to let the dressing soak in.

Herbs and flavourings: Fresh chopped leaf herbs add fragrance and a tang to any salad. If using in a green salad served with meat or fish, suit the herbal flavours to the main dish; a dill-flavoured salad is ideal with fish, a tarragon-flavoured one with chicken. Do not overdo garlic; a hint of the flavour is best added as described left. Wash and dry any herbs before chopping them.

Fruit: Prepare fresh fruit as for stewing; dip any which may discolour quickly in French Dressing (page 132) or lemon juice. Drain canned or bottled fruits well ahead of the meal, so that they dry off; use fruit canned in natural juice if possible. Soak, rinse and dry dried fruits to plump them, and remove prune stones.

Nuts: Blanch and skin if possible. Chop whole nuts or put through a nut mill. Fry or toast flaked almonds or coarsely chopped hazelnuts if you wish.

Meat: Slice thinly, skinning delicatessen sausages, or dice; bacon can be cut into small strips or squares and fried lightly.

Fish: Drain canned fish thoroughly, and rinse lightly if in strong brine or flavoured oil. Dry well.

Cheese: Dice, grate, chop or crumble.

HINTS ON PREPARING SALADS

It is usual to dress a salad. All dressings can be classed as either thin (oil and vinegar) dressings or as thick (mayonnaise, potato, cream or yoghurt-based) dressings. The basic difference in preparing salads is how and when the ingredients are mixed with the dressing.

Salads Mixed with a Thin Dressing (green and mixed salads)

Mix all the ingredients lightly shortly before serving, and place in a clean salad bowl, preferably of well-seasoned wood kept only for salads or, if necessary, in a glass or china bowl. Do not use a metal bowl. At the table or just before, sprinkle the salad with the dressing and toss the ingredients in it lightly with 2 spoons. Do not dress the salad earlier as the dressing will trickle down to the bottom of the bowl, and make the lowest layers of salad soggy, while leaving the top ones limp.

Cooked Vegetable and Similar Salads Mixed with a Thick Dressing

Mix all the ingredients, and bind with the dressing, mixing carefully to avoid breaking the vegetables. Turn onto a bed of green salad, or into individual containers such as hollowed tomatoes; or arrange and garnish on small salad plates. Serve at once before the dressing dulls or forms a 'skin'.

Note: Meat or fish dressed with Chaudfroid Sauce (see Chaudfroid of Chicken or Turkey, page 82) are also usually served garnished with other salad ingredients as cold salads.

Moulded Salads

Salad vegetables, meat, fish or fruit can be mixed with aspic jelly, a thick dressing containing gelatine, or a very thick well-flavoured sauce. Generally, such salads are put in a mould, chilled until set, then turned out like a jelly (page 191) for serving.

WINTER SALADS

It is important to serve salads in winter because it is on sunless days that we need the vitamins in raw fruit and vegetables most. Now that imported salad ingredients are available in most supermarkets year-round, there is little excuse; lightly blanched and cooked winter vegetables and pulses such as carrots, cauliflower, chicory (endive), celeriac, red cabbage and lentils can be used to supplement them. Apples or pears, dried fruits and nuts can also be used to make interesting and colourful salads year-round.

Opposite: *Cole Slaw and Avocado-Orange Salad.*

Avocado-Orange Salad

Serves 4

Not suitable for freezing

	Metric	Imperial	American
Round lettuce	1	1	1
Avocados	2	2	2
French Dressing (page 132)	60 ml	4 tbls	4 tbls
Orange	1	1	1
Tomatoes, skinned	2	2	2
7.5 cm/3 in piece of cucumber (unpeeled)	1	1	1
Black (ripe) olives	8	8	8

1. Separate the lettuce leaves, rinse and dry quickly, and arrange on a salad plate.
2. Peel the avocados, halve them and remove the stones. Cut the flesh into small cubes. Dip at once in the dressing to prevent discoloration.
3. Peel the orange, and cut into segments without white skin, pith or pips. Slice both tomatoes and cucumber thinly. Halve and stone the olives.
4. Mix these ingredients with the avocado cubes lightly, and toss in the dressing. Arrange on the bed of lettuce.

Cole Slaw

Serves 4

Not suitable for freezing

	Metric	Imperial	American
Firm white cabbage	450 g	1 lb	1 lb
Carrots	100 g	4 oz	¼ lb
Small onion	1	1	1
Mayonnaise (page 134)	175 ml	6 fl oz	¾ cup
Pinch of dry mustard			
Pinch of sugar			
Salt and pepper			

1. Remove any coarse outside cabbage leaves and core. Shred the leaves finely. Rinse and drain well.
2. Scrape the carrots, top and tail and shred or grate coarsely. Skin and shred the onion.
3. Mix all the vegetables in a bowl. Season the mayonnaise with the mustard, sugar, salt and pepper. Add to the vegetables and toss lightly.

Potato Salad

Serves 4

Not suitable for freezing

	Metric	Imperial	American
New potatoes	450 g	1 lb	1 lb
French Dressing			
(page 132)	30 ml	2 tbls	2 tbls
Chopped chives	10 ml	2 tsp	2 tsp
Chopped parsley	15 ml	1 tbls	1 tbls
Chopped mint	5 ml	1 tsp	1 tsp
Mayonnaise			
(page 134)	150 ml	¼ pt	⅔ cup

1. Cook the potatoes without breaking them. Drain well.
2. While still warm, cut the potatoes into 1 cm/½ in dice. Mix with the French Dressing to let them absorb its flavours while cooling.
3. Mix the herbs with the mayonnaise and pour over the cooled potatoes. Mix lightly.

Fennel and Yoghurt Salad

Serves 4

Not suitable for freezing

	Metric	Imperial	American
Cucumber	200 g	7 oz	7 oz
Salt			
Fennel bulb with coarse outside sheaths removed	400 g	14 oz	14 oz
Sweet Red pepper	½	½	½
Spring onions (scallions) (green and white parts)	2	2	2
Chopped parsley	15 ml	1 tbls	1 tbls
Grated rind of 1 lemon			
A few drops of lemon juice			
A few drops of olive oil			
Black pepper			
Natural yoghurt	150 ml	¼ pt	⅔ cup

1. Slice the cucumber thickly without peeling, then cut the slices into quarters. Sprinkle with salt and leave on a tilted plate for 30 minutes.
2. Slice the fennel thickly. Blanch it in salted boiling water for 2 minutes. Drain and cool.
3. De-seed the pepper and chop finely. Put a few bits aside. Chop the green and white parts of the spring onions (scallions). Cut the cooled fennel into small strips.
4. Drain the cucumber. Mix with the fennel, pepper, onion and most of the parsley in a bowl. Sprinkle with the lemon rind, juice and oil. Grind a little black pepper over the salad.
5. Pile the salad in a shallow dish, and spoon the yoghurt over it. Sprinkle the reserved red pepper and chopped parsley on top.

Moulded Brown Rice Salad

Serves 6

Not suitable for freezing

	Metric	Imperial	American
Gelatine (unflavored gelatin)	10 ml	2 tsp	2 tsp
Chicken Stock (page 15) clarified (as on page 22)	175 ml	6 fl oz	¾ cup
Mayonnaise (page 134)	100 ml	4 fl oz	½ cup
Cooked brown rice (page 119)	500 g	1 lb 2 oz	3 cups
Green pepper, de-seeded and diced	75 g	3 oz	¾ cup
Finely chopped celery	65 g	2½ oz	½ cup
Radishes, chopped	3	3	3
Chopped parsley	30 ml	2 tbls	2 tbls
Chopped basil or chives	15 ml	1 tbls	1 tbls
Chopped tarragon (optional)	5 ml	1 tsp	1 tsp
Chopped watercress leaves			

1. Sprinkle the gelatine on the stock in a small saucepan. Leave until softened, then warm, stirring, until dissolved. Mix into the mayonnaise.
2. Mix all the other ingredients, except the watercress, in a large mixing bowl. Stir in the gelatine mixture.
3. Turn the salad into a wetted 1.4 l/2½ pt/6 cup mould. Cover and chill for 6 hours. Unmould onto a serving plate and garnish with chopped watercress.

Chef's Salad

Serves 4

Not suitable for freezing

	Metric	Imperial	American
Cos (Romaine) lettuce or small Chinese cabbage	½	½	½
French Dressing (page 132)	150 ml	¼ pt	⅔ cup
Cooked chicken	75 g	3 oz	3 oz
Cooked ham	75 g	3 oz	3 oz
Cooked tongue	75 g	3 oz	3 oz
Gruyère cheese	75 g	3 oz	3 oz
Hard-boiled (hard-cooked) eggs	2	2	2

1. Wash and dry the lettuce or cabbage and shred finely. Mix in the bottom of a salad bowl with a little of the dressing.
2. Cut all the meats into julienne strips (page 18). Dice the cheese. Mix the meats and cheese, and place on the lettuce. Slice the eggs, and use to cover the salad. Serve the remaining dressing in a jug.

Russian Salad

Serves 4

Not suitable for freezing

	Metric	Imperial	American
Small cauliflower, lightly cooked	1	1	1
Large potatoes, boiled or baked	2	2	2
Tomatoes	2	2	2
Small gherkins	3	3	3
Cooked peas	60 ml	4 tbls	4 tbls
Diced cooked carrot	45 ml	3 tbls	3 tbls
Diced cooked turnip	45 ml	3 tbls	3 tbls
Salt and pepper			
Mayonnaise (page 134)	45 ml	3 tbls	3 tbls

1. Cut the cauliflower into tiny florets. Peel and dice the potatoes. (Both should be cold.)
2. Skin, de-seed and chop the tomatoes. Chop the gherkins.
3. Mix all the salad ingredients in a bowl. Season the mayonnaise and mix lightly with the salad. Use as part of a mixed hors d'oeuvre (page 8), or to fill hollowed tomatoes, avocados, etc.

Waldorf Salad

Serves 4

Not suitable for freezing

	Metric	Imperial	American
Crisp red eating apples	4	4	4
Celery stalks	2	2	2
Chopped walnuts	25 g	1 oz	¼ cup
Mayonnaise (page 134)	75 ml	5 tbls	5 tbls
Lemon juice	30 ml	2 tbls	2 tbls
Pinch of salt			

1. Remove any blemishes from the apples. Core them without peeling, and dice or chop them.
2. Slice the celery finely. Mix with the apple and add the nuts.
3. Mix the mayonnaise, lemon juice and salt. Combine lightly with the salad.

Salade Niçoise

Serves 4

Not suitable for freezing

	Metric	Imperial	American
Sliced cooked French (green) beans	275 g	10 oz	10 oz
Hard-boiled (hard-cooked) eggs, quartered	2	2	2
Tomatoes, skinned and quartered	3	3	3
Garlic clove, crushed	1	1	1
Canned tuna in brine	225–250 g	8–9 oz	8–9 oz
Black (ripe) olives, stoned (pitted)	50 g	2 oz	2 oz
French Dressing (page 132)	60 ml	4 tbls	4 tbls
Round lettuce	1	1	1
Anchovy fillets, drained	50 g	2 oz	2 oz

1. Lightly mix together the beans, eggs, tomatoes and garlic.
2. Drain the tuna, divide into small pieces and add to the other ingredients with most of the olives. Pour the dressing over and toss lightly.
3. Separate the lettuce leaves, wash and dry, and use to cover a salad plate. Pile the salad on top. Garnish with the remaining olives and the anchovy fillets.

DRESSINGS FOR SALADS

There are two types of salad dressing, thin and thick. Most thin salad dressings consist of oil mixed with an acid ingredient such as vinegar or lemon juice, seasoned and often flavoured with herbs. French Dressing is the basic thin dressing and the one most often used on green leaf salads.

The thick type of salad dressing is usually made by whisking eggs into oil or a similar liquid until it is fully blended or emulsified and will not separate on standing. Mayonnaise is the basic and most commonly used thick dressing: it can be varied in many ways by adding flavourings such as garlic or other herbs or spices, e.g. curry powder. Cream dressings have cream added to the basic emulsion or are simply made with thick fresh or flavoured sour cream. Dressings based on natural yoghurt are increasingly popular.

French Dressing (basic thin dressing)

You will need surprisingly little dressing for most salads, but it stores well in a closed jar in the refrigerator so you can make quite a large quantity to use when needed. Use 15 ml/1 tbls white wine vinegar, lemon juice, wine or a mixture of these to each 45 ml/3 tbls good quality pure oil seasoned with salt and ground black pepper, a pinch of dry English mustard and a pinch of sugar (optional). Mix the oil and seasoning with a fork in a bowl, then whisk in the vinegar or other liquid drop by drop until emulsified. Alternatively, put all the ingredients in a small screw-topped jar, close it tightly and shake it briskly. Shake it again just before use.

Only dress a salad just before you eat it, preferably at the table, and use only enough dressing to moisten the salad lightly. If you add the dressing too early it will trickle down to the bottom of the salad bowl, and make the lowest layer of salad soggy; if you use too much dressing, it will make tender summer leaves in particular heavy and limp. To dress a green salad, sprinkle it lightly with dressing, then toss the leaves with 2 forks to distribute the dressing.

Variations
1. Use garlic oil (oil in which 1–2 garlic cloves have been steeped).
2. Use grapefruit or orange juice instead of vinegar in salads which contain grapefruit or orange.
3. Use tarragon or another herb-flavoured vinegar, and add a little of the fresh chopped herb to the dressing.
4. Make *Vinaigrette Sauce* by adding 2.5 ml/½ tsp each of chopped gherkin, capers, chives or shallot, parsley and fresh tarragon to 60 ml/4 tbls of the dressing.

Above: *A selection of Winter Salads served with French bread.*

Opposite: *Mayonnaise and French Dressing can be made with different oils and vinegars to vary their flavours to complement the accompanying salad.*

Mayonnaise

Makes 575 ml/1 pt/2½ cups (approx)

Not suitable for freezing

	Metric	Imperial	American
Egg yolks	3	3	3
White wine vinegar, herb-flavoured vinegar or lemon juice	15 ml	1 tbls	1 tbls
Salt	2.5 ml	½ tsp	½ tsp
Dry or prepared mustard	1.5 ml	¼ tsp	¼ tsp
Corn or olive oil	275 ml	½ pt	1¼ cups
Extra vinegar or lemon juice as needed			
Extra salt, mustard and a little pepper			

1. Bring all the ingredients to room temperature. Wash a mixing bowl and a hand whisk or electric beater with hot water, and dry them.
2. Whisk the egg yolks until thick. Add the vinegar or lemon juice, salt and mustard and beat well.
3. Begin adding the oil, drop by drop, beating constantly. Do not stop beating. When you have added about 100 ml/4 fl oz/½ cup the mixture will begin to thicken to a smooth cream. Pour in the oil a little faster, still beating constantly, until all the oil has been added and the mixture is fully blended and thick.
4. If the mayonnaise becomes too thick for your needs while beating, add a few drops more vinegar or lemon juice but DO NOT STOP BEATING.
5. Season the mayonnaise to taste. Cover the bowl until ready to use.

Notes:
1. For a coating consistency add a little milk or cream.
2. If the mayonnaise refuses to thicken or separates on standing, it is said to have 'turned'. To correct this, beat the mayonnaise little by little into another egg yolk. Add only 5 ml/1 tsp mayonnaise at a time.
3. The mayonnaise will store for several days in a screw-topped jar in the refrigerator.

Variations
1. For Aspic Mayonnaise add to the completed mayonnaise an equal quantity of stiff aspic jelly, melted and cooled until beginning to thicken.
2. For Chilli Mayonnaise, use chilli vinegar when making the mayonnaise.

3. For Curry Mayonnaise, add 1 clove squeezed garlic and 5 ml/1 tsp curry powder to 275 ml/½ pt/1¼ cups completed mayonnaise.

Salad Cream

Makes 150 ml/¼ pt/⅓ cup (approx)

Not suitable for freezing

	Metric	Imperial	American
Double (heavy) cream or evaporated milk	60 ml	4 tbls	4 tbls
Hard-boiled (hard-cooked) egg yolks	2	2	2
Prepared English mustard	5 ml	1 tsp	1 tsp
Worcestershire sauce	5 ml	1 tsp	1 tsp
Pinch of caster (superfine) sugar			
Salt and pepper			
White wine vinegar	15 ml	1 tbls	1 tbls
Corn or olive oil	30 ml	2 tbls	2 tbls

1. Whip the cream or evaporated milk lightly. (If using evaporated milk it should first be boiled in the unopened can for 20 minutes, then cooled.)
2. Sieve the egg yolks into a bowl. Beat in the mustard, Worcestershire sauce, sugar and seasoning. Add the vinegar and blend in.
3. Beat in the oil, drop by drop at first, as when making Mayonnaise.
4. Fold in the whipped cream or milk. Use at once.

Note: This dressing cannot be made in a blender or food processor.

Sour Cream or Yoghurt Salad Dressing

Makes 275 ml/½ pt/1¼ cups

Not suitable for freezing

	Metric	Imperial	American
Sour cream or natural yoghurt	275 ml	½ pt	1¼ cups
Salt and pepper			
Prepared English mustard	5 ml	1 tsp	1 tsp
Caster (superfine) sugar to taste			

1. Beat the cream or yoghurt in a bowl to liquefy it.
2. Stir in the flavourings.
3. Chill, covered, for 1 hour to firm up slightly.

10
CHEESE AND EGG DISHES

CHEESE

Storing Cheese

Cheese is a living food which goes on getting firmer and stronger-flavoured as it ages until it becomes overripe and unattractive to eat. Cheeses which have been pressed to squeeze out the liquid whey and water keep better than soft or young cheeses. Cheeses such as Brie, which ripen on the outside first, do so very rapidly.

Any cheese is best stored loosely wrapped in polythene or greaseproof paper. Leave a little air space inside to prevent any sweating or mouldiness. Keep the cheese in a cool place. Remember, however, if you keep it in a refrigerator to take it out at least an hour or two before serving to let the cheese recover its flavour; it will have been dulled by the chilling. Vacuum-packed cheeses should be kept cooler than unwrapped cheeses. If the surface of the cheese is wet when it is unwrapped, let it dry off naturally before you eat it. If a cheese remains unused for a time and becomes sharp-flavoured or begins to go mouldy, it need not be wasted. The only exceptions are the soft cheeses like Camembert which develop an ammonia-type smell and must then be thrown away. Any light mould on the harder cheeses can be scraped off, and the cheese can then be used at once. If hard cheese becomes dry with age, simply grate it. Then store it in a screw-topped jar for use in cooking. Grated Cheddar cheese can also be bought from delicatessen chilled cabinets but it does not keep well unless refrigerated.

Cheese and Spinach Cutlets

Serves 4

Freeze 1 month (before frying)

	Metric	Imperial	American
227 g/8 oz packets frozen chopped spinach	2	2	2
Butter or margarine	15 g	½ oz	1 tbls
Egg yolks, beaten	2	2	2
Cheddar cheese, grated	225 g	8 oz	½ lb
Salt and pepper			
Pinch of grated nutmeg			
Beaten egg yolk and breadcrumbs for coating			
Melted butter for sprinkling			

1. Put the frozen spinach in a saucepan. Heat for 4–5 minutes until thawed, turning once or twice. Bring to the boil, reduce the heat, and cook gently for 3 minutes or until tender and dry. Drain well, pressing out excess liquid. Stir in the fat.
2. Spread the spinach on a plate, and cool for 10 minutes. Mix in the egg yolks, cheese and seasonings.
3. Chill the cutlet mixture in the refrigerator for 15 minutes to firm up.
4. Shape the mixture into 8 oval patties. Pinch one end to make cutlet shapes. Coat with beaten egg, then with breadcrumbs, twice.
5. Place the cutlets on a greased grill (broiler) grid. Grill (broil) under moderate heat until golden-brown, turning once to brown the second side. Serve at once on a bed of mashed potato (page 99).

Variation

Cheese and potato balls: Use 450 g/1 lb mashed potato instead of spinach, and half quantities of fat and cheese. Omit the egg yolk in the mixture but add a little prepared mustard if you wish. Roll the potato mixture into balls, coat with egg and crumbs, and deep fry until golden-brown all over.

Baked Vegetables with Cheese

Baked Vegetables with Cheese.

Serves 4

Oven temp 190°C/375°F/Gas Mark 5

Not suitable for freezing

	Metric	Imperial	American
Large aubergine (eggplant), about 450 g/1 lb	1	1	1
Salt and pepper			
Seasoned flour	25 g	1 oz	¼ cup
Corn oil	150 ml	¼ pt	⅔ cup
Medium onions, chopped	2	2	2
Medium tomatoes, skinned and chopped	3	3	3
Garlic clove, crushed	1	1	1
Dried basil	1.5 ml	¼ tsp	¼ tsp
Chopped parsley	45 ml	3 tbls	3 tbls
Brown sherry or light port	50 ml	2 fl oz	¼ cup
Mozzarella cheese, shredded	350 g	12 oz	¾ lb
Grated Parmesan cheese	40 g	1½ oz	1½ oz

1. Peel the aubergine (eggplant) and cut it into 5 mm/¼ in slices. Sprinkle generously with salt and leave to stand for 30 minutes to draw out the bitter juices. Drain, rinse in cold water and pat dry with soft kitchen paper. Coat the aubergine slices with seasoned flour.
2. Heat the oil in a large frying pan (skillet), add the aubergine slices, and sauté until lightly browned on both sides. Sauté in 2 batches if necessary. Remove with a slotted spoon and place on soft paper to drain.
3. Add the onions, tomatoes, garlic and herbs to the pan, reduce the heat and simmer until mushy, to make a sauce; stirring often while cooking. Season, then stir in the sherry or port.
4. Pour a third of the sauce into a 1.1 1/2 pt/5 cup greased baking dish suitable for serving. Add half the aubergine slices in an even layer. Cover with 100 g/4 oz/¼ lb Mozzarella and half the Parmesan.
5. Repeat the layers of sauce, aubergine slices and cheeses, reserving the last third of the sauce and 100 g/4 oz/¼ lb Mozzarella.
6. Cover the dish with the reserved sauce. Bake at the temperature above for 30–35 minutes until the aubergine slices are soft when pierced with a skewer.
7. Cover with the remaining Mozzarella, and return to the oven until it melts. Serve at once.

Cheese Roll

Serves 6

Oven temp 180°C/350°F/Gas Mark 4

Not suitable for freezing

	Metric	Imperial	American
Oil for greasing			
Eggs	6	6	6
Salt and pepper			
Gruyère cheese, grated	175 g	6 oz	6 oz
Flour	25 g	1 oz	¼ cup
Butter	30 ml	2 tbls	2 tbls
Extra flour	30 ml	2 tbls	2 tbls
Milk	150 ml	¼ pt	⅔ cup
Double (heavy) cream	30 ml	2 tbls	2 tbls
Chopped parsley	30 ml	2 tbls	2 tbls

1. Oil a 32.5 × 22.5 cm/13 × 9 in Swiss (jelly) roll tin (pan). Line it with non-stick baking parchment and oil the paper lightly. Heat the oven to the temperature above.
2. Separate 5 of the eggs. Season the yolks lightly, and beat until thick and pale. Beat in 2/3 of the cheese and the 25 g/1 oz flour.

3. Whisk the egg whites with a pinch of salt until semi-stiff. Stir 2–3 tbls into the yolk mixture, then fold in the rest. Spread the mixture evenly in the prepared tin.
4. Bake in the oven for 16–17 minutes, until firm.
5. While baking, prepare the filling. Make a thick white sauce (page 84), with the butter, extra flour, milk and cream. Beat the remaining whole egg, and add it with the remaining 50 g/2 oz cheese and 15 ml/1 tbls parsley.
6. Remove the roll from the oven. Turn out of tin by inverting onto a double sheet of greaseproof (waxed) paper.
7. Remove the inverted tin, and peel the lining paper off the roll. Trim the ends of the roll if crisp.
8. Spread the filling all over the inverted roll, except for 2.5 cm/1 in at one end. Roll up from the covered end, so that the exposed cut end is underneath. Lift on the paper, and place on the tin.
9. Return the roll to the oven for 8–10 minutes to cook the filling. Serve at once, sprinkled with the remaining parsley.

Notes:
1. Swiss Emmenthal or mild Cheddar cheese can be used instead of Gruyère.
2. If you wish, sprinkle the roll with a little extra grated cheese before returning it to the oven.

Cheese Roll.

Cheese Pudding

Serves 4–6

Oven temp 180°C/350°F/Gas Mark 4

Not suitable for freezing

	Metric	Imperial	American
Milk	275 ml	½ pt	1¼ cups
Soft white breadcrumbs	50 g	2 oz	1 cup
Eggs, separated	2	2	2
Grated Cheshire cheese	40 g	1½ oz	1½ oz
Grated Parmesan cheese	40 g	1½ oz	1½ oz
Softened butter	15 ml	1 tbls	1 tbls
Salt and pepper			
Pinch of ground mace			

1. Grease a 700 ml/1¼ pt/3 cup deep pie dish or 4–6 individual ramekins (custard cups).
2. Bring the milk to the boil, and pour it over the breadcrumbs in a bowl. Leave to stand for 10 minutes.
3. Beat in the egg yolks, then the cheeses and butter. Season.
4. Whisk the egg whites until they just hold a soft shape. Stir one spoonful into the cheese mixture, then fold in the rest.
5. Turn the mixture gently into the dish or dishes. Bake at the temperature above for 30–35 minutes (ramekins 15–20 minutes). Serve immediately.

Note: Any other English hard cheese except the blue cheeses can be substituted for Cheshire in this recipe.

Cheese Soufflé

Serves 4

Oven temp 200°C/400°F/Gas Mark 6

Not suitable for freezing

	Metric	Imperial	American
Butter	25 g	1 oz	2 tbls
Flour	25 g	1 oz	¼ cup
Milk	150 ml	¼ pt	⅔ cup
Grated Cheddar or other hard cheese	75 g	3 oz	¾ cup
Eggs, separated	3	3	3
Salt and pepper			
Pinch of cayenne pepper			

1. Prepare a 15 cm/6 in soufflé dish by greasing the inside. You need not tie a paper band round it for this recipe. Heat the oven to the temperature above.
2. Make a white sauce with the fat, flour and milk. Cool slightly, then stir in the cheese. Beat in the egg yolks, one at a time. Season.
3. Whisk the egg whites until fairly stiff. Stir one spoonful into the cheese mixture, then fold in the rest.
4. Turn the mixture gently into the prepared soufflé dish. With a knife point, score a circular slit in the top of the mixture about 2 cm/¾ in in from the edge of the dish.
5. Bake for 25–30 minutes at the temperature above until the soufflé is well risen and browned. Do not underbake. Serve immediately, protecting the soufflé from a draught if you have to carry it any distance.

Welsh Rarebit

Serves 4

Not suitable for freezing

	Metric	Imperial	American
Butter or margarine	25 g	1 oz	2 tbls
Grated Cheddar or Cheshire cheese	175 g	6 oz	1½ cups
Salt, pepper and cayenne pepper			
Prepared English mustard			
Single (light) cream	15 ml	1 tbls	1 tbls
Slices of buttered toast	4	4	4

1. Melt the fat in a saucepan, and stir in the cheese, seasonings to taste and cream. Stir over low heat until smooth.
2. Spread the cheese mixture on the toast, brown under a hot grill (broiler), and serve at once.

Note: If you wish, stir in a well-beaten egg with the seasonings.

Variations
1. For a cheaper rarebit, make a sauce with the melted fat, 10 ml/2 tsp flour and a little milk before adding 100–150 g/4–5 oz/1–1¼ cups cheese only, seasoning to taste.
2. Make a sauce with the melted fat, 15 ml/ 1 tbls flour and 75 ml/5 tbls light ale. Take off the heat, and add 2.5 ml/½ tsp Worcestershire sauce and 1.5 ml/¼ tsp red wine vinegar instead of mustard. Use Cheshire cheese, and stir in 2 beaten eggs with the salt and pepper. Reheat until thick, without boiling, before pouring the mixture over the toast.

Macaroni Cheese

Serves 4

Oven temp 220°C/425°F/Gas Mark 7

Freeze 2 months

	Metric	Imperial	American
Long or short-cut			
(elbow) macaroni	*150 g*	*5 oz*	*5 oz*
Butter or margarine	*25 g*	*1 oz*	*2 tbls*
Flour	*25 g*	*1 oz*	*¼ cup*
Milk	*450 ml*	*¾ pt*	*2 cups*
Grated Cheddar			
cheese	*125 g*	*4 oz*	*1 cup*
Prepared English			
mustard	*2.5 ml*	*½ tsp*	*½ tsp*
Salt and pepper			
Browned			
breadcrumbs			

1. Grease a 700 ml/1¼ pt/3 cup oven-to-table baking dish.
2. Break long macaroni into 2 cm/¾ in lengths. Cook either macaroni in boiling salted water until tender. Drain, reserving 150 ml/¼ pt/ ⅔ cup of the cooking water.
3. Make a white sauce (page 84) with the fat, flour, milk and cooking water. Simmer for 3 minutes. Remove from the heat and add 75 g/3 oz/¾ cup of the grated cheese and seasonings.
4. Mix together the drained macaroni and sauce. Turn into the prepared dish.
5. Sprinkle the remaining cheese on top, then sprinkle lightly with browned breadcrumbs. Bake at the temperature above for 20 minutes. Serve at once.

Variations

1. Macaroni Cheese with Eggs: After turning the Macaroni Cheese into the baking dish, make 4 hollows in the mixture and break an egg into each hollow. Sprinkle each egg with salt and pepper, and top with a dab of butter or margarine. Sprinkle with the cheese and browned breadcrumbs, and bake for 15 minutes at the temperature above.
2. Macaroni Cheese with Eggs and Bacon: Instead of browned breadcrumbs, garnish the Macaroni Cheese with sliced hard-boiled eggs and grilled bacon rashers (slices) shortly before serving. Sprinkle with a little extra grated cheese and return to the oven for a few minutes to melt and brown it.
3. Macaroni Cheese with Tomatoes: After turning the Macaroni Cheese into the prepared dish, place 6–8 tomato halves on top, cut side up. Sprinkle them with salt and pepper and dab with butter or margarine. Sprinkle with the reserved cheese, and browned breadcrumbs, and bake for 20 minutes at the temperature above.

EGGS

There are a number of classic recipes, such as mayonnaise, hot and cold soufflés, ice creams and methods of cooking eggs which a comprehensive cookery book such as this must include. However it is recommended that whilst government guidelines for the use of fresh eggs are in existence these are followed and that anyone who could be at risk from salmonella should avoid eating raw or partially cooked eggs until advised it is safe to do so.

Frozen pasteurized eggs, dried egg and dried egg white are available and may be successfully substituted in recipes requiring beaten eggs and whisked egg whites. Follow the manufacturer's instructions.

Storing Eggs

Store eggs rounded end up in refrigerator, away from strong-flavoured foods. Bring to room temperature before use. Do not use cracked or damaged eggs.

To Bake Eggs

1. Grease individual ovenproof china, earthenware or glass ramekins (custard cups), cocottes or saucers with 2.5 ml/½ tsp butter each. Stand them on a baking sheet.
2. Break an egg into each container. Season lightly.
3. Cover loosely with greased paper, and bake at 180°C/350°F/Gas Mark 4 for 8–10 minutes (2–3 minutes longer in glass dishes).

To Boil Eggs

Soft-boiled (soft-cooked) eggs have tender whites and runny yolks. In medium-boiled eggs, the whites are firm and the yolks just set, and in hard-boiled eggs both whites and yolks are firm.

1. Use eggs brought to room temperature to prevent the shells cracking.
2. Place each egg in turn on a tablespoon and lower gently into just-simmering water. Do not crowd the eggs. If one cracks, add 15 ml/ 1 tbls vinegar or lemon juice to the water.
3. Simmer eggs for the minutes needed to give them the consistency you want (see below).
4. Drain. Run hard-boiled eggs under cold water to prevent a grey ring forming round the yolks, or cool completely in cold water.

	Soft-boiled	Medium-boiled	Hard-boiled
Sizes 1 and 2	*3½*	*5*	*12*
Sizes 3 and 4	*3¼*	*4¾*	*11*
Size 5	*3*	*4½*	*10*

Note: These times are for eggs bought in a shop. New-laid or fresh farm eggs may take slightly longer. If you use eggs stored for some time, put the eggs into simmering water and roll each over 2 or 3 times before adding the next to set some of the white around the yolk.

To Coddle Eggs

1. Prepare moulds for coddling as for baked eggs. The eggs should only fill three-quarters of the container. Cover each mould closely with greased foil to prevent water getting in.
2. Place the moulds in a saucepan, and pour in enough very hot water to come half-way up their sides. Cover the pan with a lid.
3. Place the pan over medium heat and boil gently for about 10 minutes, until the eggs are just set.
4. Remove with a cloth. Serve in the containers.

Notes:
1. Chopped cooked bacon, mushrooms or onion can be added to eggs when coddling them.
2. Specially-made china egg coddlers with metal screw-on lids can be purchased.

To Fry Eggs

1. Melt in a frying pan (skillet) enough bacon fat, dripping, butter or other fat or oil to cover the bottom completely. It should be hot but not sizzling.
2. Break eggs, one by one, into a saucer, and slide them into the fat, without breaking the yolk. Leave enough room between them to let you turn them over and remove them easily.
3. Cook the eggs very gently for 2–3 minutes, until the white is opaque.
4. If you wish, baste with the fat, and cook for 2 minutes only (veiled eggs). Alternatively, turn the eggs over with a broad spatula or slice, and cook for 1½ minutes more.
5. Remove with a slotted fish slice (spatula), and drain over the pan. Serve very hot.

To Scramble Eggs

Scrambled eggs should be soft and creamy, not solid or grainy. They must therefore be cooked very gently over low heat.

1. Beat the eggs well with a rotary beater or fork, adding a little single (light) cream and seasonings. Use 2 eggs for each person.
2. Melt 25 g/1 oz/2 tbls butter for each 4 eggs in a pan without letting it get very hot. Add the eggs and cook very gently, stirring continuously with a wooden spatula or a fork until the eggs are half set. Remove from the heat, and stir in a little more cold cream to stop the cooking. Continue stirring until the eggs are softly but fully set.
3. Turn the eggs onto a warmed dish or plate and serve immediately.

Note: Scrambled eggs can be served on hot buttered toast, or on a bed of spinach or another vegetable. Other ingredients can also be added to the eggs during cooking such as chopped or flaked meat or fish, a vegetable (e.g. chopped fried onion or sautéed mushrooms), grated cheese, or a flavouring such as chopped parsley or herbs. See Mushroom Scramble (page 143).

To Poach Eggs

1. Put about 5 cm/2 in stock, milk or water containing a little vinegar or lemon juice into a shallow pan. Bring it to simmering point.
2. Break one egg at a time onto a saucer and slide it into the pan. Immediately fold the white over the yolk with a spoon, then roll the egg over to make it a neat shape.
3. Cook until set, then remove with a slotted spoon. Serve at once.

Note: For evenly shaped poached eggs, put metal poaching rings or large pastry cutters into the liquid, and break one egg into each ring. Alternatively a special egg poacher or steamer can be used which has loose metal cups set in a metal sheet over a shallow pan. Grease the cups and break an egg into each after half-filling the pan with water. Place a lid on top, bring the pan of water to the boil and cook until the eggs are set. This method is suitable for chilled eggs with watery whites which float in wisps if placed in water.

OMELETS

There are 3 types of omelet:

1. a plain or savoury omelet is made with beaten whole eggs and seasoning, covered with a filling, then folded in half or into three;
2. a thick or Spanish omelet is made with beaten whole eggs, with chopped additions added to the mixture; the top of the omelet is browned under the grill, and it is then served unfolded;
3. a sweet omelet is generally made with beaten egg yolks, the whites being whisked separately and folded in to make a light, puffy omelet; it is generally covered with a sweet filling, then folded in half (page 183).

The general method for making all three types of omelet is the same.

Opposite: *Boiled, poached and coddled eggs.*

Above: *A plain savoury Omelet.*

To Make an Omelet

1. Use a thick, flat-based pan with sloping sides which has been well seasoned. A 15 cm/6 in pan is suitable for an omelet using 2–3 eggs, an 18 cm/7 in pan for one using 4 eggs; the omelet will then be neither thin and leathery nor thick and lumpy.
2. Unlike other egg dishes, an omelet must be cooked quickly, and served immediately the egg mixture has just set. For easy handling and serving, use a fairly small pan and make one omelet for each person.
3. Cook any filling ingredients before making the omelet. They can often be fried in the omelet pan, and removed to a plate, leaving the fat in the pan for cooking the omelet.
4. Beat the eggs in a bowl with salt and pepper for a savoury or Spanish omelet. Beat the yolks only for a sweet omelet, then whisk the whites separately and fold them into the yolks with sweetening as the recipe directs. A little water added to the eggs or yolks while beating makes an omelet lighter.
5. Use unsalted butter or margarine and ½–1 tbls oil. Heat the pan first, then melt the fat in it, tilting the pan to cover the bottom evenly. Do not let the fat brown. Pour in the beaten eggs, leave for a few seconds, then lift the egg mixture from the sides of the pan towards the centre as it sets, letting the egg in the centre run to the sides. Repeat the process if needed; in a moment or two the egg will set, and after a few more seconds, it will be golden underneath.
6. Take the pan off the heat at once, and loosen the omelet by shaking the pan gently, and by running a palette knife round the sides and underneath. Sprinkle with any filling not already incorporated. Tilting the pan slightly, fold a savoury or sweet omelet, and slide it onto a warmed plate. Place a Spanish omelet under the grill for a few moments, until lightly browned, then serve from a warmed serving dish.

For recipes, see pages 146, 183.

SOUFFLÉS

A soufflé consists of a purée or flavoured thick sauce or panada (page 84) lightened with whisked egg whites. Strictly, it is a hot dish, usually baked (although it can be steamed) to set the egg whites. Most so-called cold soufflés are in fact more like mousses because whipped cream as well as whisked egg white is used to lighten them, and they are set with gelatine.

Most (but not all) hot soufflés are savoury, and most cold ones are sweet. Cold soufflés are therefore described on page 189 in the chapter on cold desserts.

Since you must work quickly when making any soufflé to get it into the oven or refrigerator before the egg whites lose the air whisked into them, you must always prepare the dish for it before starting work on the ingredients.

A soufflé is usually cooked or 'set' in a special straight-sided dish made of ovenproof glass or fluted porcelain, brought to table for serving. Traditionally the dish is prepared by tying a doubled paper band around it, rising 7–8 cm/3 in above its rim. The band holds the soufflé up as it rises and until it has set. It is peeled off with a knife blade before serving so that the soufflé rises proudly above the rim of the dish when presented.

Preparing a soufflé dish in this way needs care since it must be secured so that it fits tightly, uncreased, around the dish. It must also be removed from a hot soufflé quickly and expertly, so that the soufflé can be served before it sinks. Most baked soufflés are therefore served simply in a deep decorative straight-sided dish a little larger than if a paper band is used. A soufflé made in an 850 ml/1½ pt/3¾ cup dish with a band needs a 1 l/1¾ pt/4½ cup dish without one.

The method of making a paper band is described on page 183 because it is used much more often for cold soufflés than for hot ones.

Hot savoury soufflés – general method

A hot soufflé can be baked or steamed, either in one large dish or in individual ones. Set the oven to heat or prepare a steamer. Prepare a dish with a band (page 183) for a steamed soufflé, or grease a dish or dishes for a baked soufflé and dust with fine dry breadcrumbs.

1. Prepare a very thick, well-cooked panada (page 84), beating it until it leaves the sides of the pan. Cook it just enough to let you beat in the required egg yolks without 'scrambling' them.
2. Chop any solid flavourings finely: large bits will sink. Add flavourings to the panada generously; the whisked egg whites will mute the flavour.
3. Whisk the required egg whites until they hold soft peaks. Stir 1–2 spoonfuls into the panada, then fold in the rest lightly but thoroughly.
4. Turn the mixture into the prepared dish. If using a band, the mixture can fill the dish. If not, the dish must only be three-quarters full.
   Alternatively, fill a dish without a band seven-eighths full, and make a deep circular cut in the mixture 2 cm/¾ in from the edge all round; the centre of the soufflé will rise above the rest as it bakes.
5. If baking the soufflé, put it in the centre of the oven, close the oven door gently and do not open it until you think the soufflé is ready. Any draught will make the soufflé fall. Test whether it is done by shaking it without taking it out of the oven; the crust should hardly move in the centre. Take it out of the oven, and protect it on the way to the table.
6. If steaming the soufflé, use a dish with a band (page 183). Cover the top with a circle of greased paper to prevent water drops falling

on the soufflé. Only let the water simmer very gently. When done, the soufflé should be well risen but not inflated, and the centre should be firm.

Eggs with Maître d'Hôtel Butter

Serves 4

Not suitable for freezing

Oven temp 180°C/350°F/Gas Mark 4

	Metric	Imperial	American
Butter or margarine for greasing	15 g	½ oz	1 tbls
Eggs	4	4	4
Salt and pepper			
Butter or margarine for garnishing	25 g	1 oz	2 tbls
A few drops of lemon juice			
Chopped parsley	5 ml	1 tsp	1 tsp

1. Grease a shallow ovenproof dish with the 15 g/½ oz/1 tbls butter or margarine.
2. Break each egg in turn onto a saucer, and tip them into the dish, side by side. Season well.
3. Cover loosely with greased foil and bake at the temperature above for 10–20 minutes.
4. Melt the fat for garnishing, add seasoning, lemon juice and parsley, and pour over the eggs. Serve at once.

Variation
Eggs Florentine: Thaw, cook and thoroughly drain 2 x 225 g/8 oz packets frozen chopped spinach. Spread it over a shallow ovenproof dish greased as above, and make 4 hollows in it. Break one egg into each hollow, then complete the recipe.

Eggs Mornay

Serves 4

Not suitable for freezing

	Metric	Imperial	American
Eggs	4	4	4
White Sauce (coating consistency), (page 84)	275 ml	½ pt	1¼ cups
Grated Cheddar cheese	50 g	2 oz	½ cup
French mustard	1.5 ml	¼ tsp	¼ tsp
Small fried bread dice, to garnish			

1. Put the eggs into cold water, bring to the boil and cook for 7–8 minutes. Drain and plunge into cold water for 1 minute.
2. Shell the eggs carefully, holding them in a cloth. Place in a flameproof dish.
3. Heat the White Sauce thoroughly and add two-thirds of the cheese and the mustard. Do not allow to boil after adding the cheese. Pour the cheese sauce over the eggs.
4. Sprinkle with the remaining cheese. Brown under the grill (broiler) or in the oven. Serve at once, garnished with fried bread dice.

Mushroom Scramble

Serves 2

Not suitable for freezing

	Metric	Imperial	American
Eggs	4	4	4
Single (light) cream or milk	30 ml	2 tbls	2 tbls
Salt and pepper			
Butter or margarine	25 g	1 oz	2 tbls
Cooked, or drained canned, button mushrooms, chopped	50 g	2 oz	2 oz
Chopped parsley	10 ml	2 tsp	2 tsp

1. Beat together in a bowl the eggs, 15 ml/1 tbls of the cream or milk, and seasoning to taste.
2. Melt the fat in a frying pan (skillet) over low heat. Add the mushrooms, and stir round. Pour in the eggs, and continue stirring until the mixture has partly set.
3. Take the pan off the heat, and stir in the parsley and the second spoonful of cream. Stir quickly, until the mixture is evenly set and creamy. Serve immediately.

Variations
Cheese Scramble: Add 50 g/2 oz/½ cup grated cheese when beating the eggs.
Lunch Scramble: Add 50 g/2 oz/¼ cup cooked ham or tongue, finely shredded, when beating the eggs.
Fish Scramble: Add 50 g/2 oz/¼ cup flaked cooked smoked haddock, canned salmon or chopped cooked shelled shrimps when beating the eggs.

Piperade

Serves 4

Not suitable for freezing

	Metric	Imperial	American
Green peppers	2	2	2
Tomatoes	450 g	1 lb	1 lb
Butter	50 g	2 oz	¼ cup
Onions, thinly sliced	2	2	2
Garlic clove, crushed	1	1	1
Salt and pepper			
Eggs	6	6	6
Milk or water	45 ml	3 tbls	3 tbls
Fried bacon rashers (slices)	4	4	4

1. Quarter and de-seed the peppers, and cut into fine strips. Skin, de-seed and chop the tomatoes.
2. Melt the butter in a large pan, and fry the peppers gently for 4 minutes. Add the onions and garlic, and continue frying, stirring often, for 4–5 minutes until all the vegetables are soft. Add the tomatoes and cook for 3–4 minutes longer until mushy. Season well while cooking.
3. Beat the eggs in a bowl with the milk or water. Pour them over the vegetables and cook gently, stirring with a fork, until they are almost set. Top with the bacon rashers and serve at once.

Curried Eggs

Serves 2

Not suitable for freezing

	Metric	Imperial	American
Curry Sauce (page 90)			
Hard-boiled (hard-cooked) eggs	3	3	3
Boiled rice (page 119)	275–350 g	10–12 oz	10–12 oz

1. Reheat the Curry Sauce if necessary.
2. Quarter the eggs and fold into the sauce.
3. Turn into a serving dish, and serve surrounded by boiled rice.

Opposite: *Piperade is a colourful light lunch dish.*

Below: *Stuffed Eggs (page 147) make a substantial starter.*

Savoury Omelet

Serves 1

Not suitable for freezing

	Metric	Imperial	American
Filling (see below)			
Eggs	*2*	*2*	*2*
Salt and pepper			
Water	*15 ml*	*1 tbls*	*1 tbls*
Unsalted butter or			
margarine	*15 ml*	*1 tbls*	*1 tbls*
Oil	*10 ml*	*2 tsp*	*2 tsp*

1. Prepare filling, e.g. grate cheese, chop parsley, sauté chopped onion. Keep aside.
2. Beat the eggs with the salt and pepper and the water until well mixed but not frothy. Add any filling from List 1.
3. Make the omelet as described on page 141, using the fat for frying.
4. When nearly set, sprinkle with any filling from List 2. Fold in half, slide onto a warmed plate, and serve at once.

Fillings
List 1
a. Cheese Omelet: 40 g/1½ oz grated cheese (add 25 g/1 oz to eggs, sprinkle rest over.)
b. Herb Omelet: 2.5 ml/½ tsp each of chopped tarragon, chives, chervil and parsley, or 5 ml/1 tsp dried mixed herbs.
c. Ham Omelet: 25 g/1 oz finely chopped ham, gammon, pork luncheon meat, or tongue.
d. Onion Omelet: 25 g/1 oz finely chopped onion, sautéed gently in the pan before adding the eggs.

List 2
a. Mushroom Omelet: 50 g/2 oz finely sliced mushrooms sautéed in butter, or canned mushrooms in white sauce, heated.
b. Seafood omelet: 50 g/2 oz chopped shrimps or prawns sautéed in butter in a saucepan.
c. Dinner Omelet: 40 g/1½ oz chopped cooked chicken, ham, bacon or cooked mixed vegetables heated in a little white sauce.

Scotch Eggs

Serves 4

	Metric	Imperial	American
Sausagemeat or			
skinless sausages	*350 g*	*12 oz*	*¾ lb*
Flour			
Hard-boiled			
(hard-cooked)			
eggs	*4*	*4*	*4*
Large egg, beaten	*1*	*1*	*1*
Dry white			
breadcrumbs	*50 g*	*2 oz*	*½ cup*
Oil for deep frying			

1. Mash the sausagemeat, or sausages, smoothing any lumps. Gather into a ball and divide into 4 equal portions.
2. Roll out each portion on a lightly floured surface into a round 13 cm/5 in across.
3. Shell the eggs. Pat dry and dust with flour. Place 1 egg in the centre of each sausagemeat round. Mould the sausagemeat round the egg, enclosing it completely.
4. Coat the covered eggs with beaten egg, then with crumbs, pressing them on firmly.
5. Fry gently in deep hot oil until golden-brown; allow enough time for the raw meat to cook.
6. Drain on soft kitchen paper. Serve hot or cold, cut in half.

Spanish Omelet

Serves 2

Not suitable for freezing

	Metric	Imperial	American
Large potatoes,			
parboiled and			
peeled	*2*	*2*	*2*
Large onions,			
coarsely chopped	*2*	*2*	*2*
Olive oil	*45–60 ml*	*3–4 tbls*	*3–4 tbls*
Salt			
Eggs	*4*	*4*	*4*

1. Cut the potatoes into 2 cm/¾ in cubes. Mix with the onion.
2. Heat the oil gently in an 18–20 cm/7–8 in frying pan (skillet). Add the potatoes and onion, and stir to coat them. Sprinkle well with salt. Put a lid on the pan, reduce the heat, and stew the vegetables until soft, stirring occasionally. Meanwhile, beat the eggs in a bowl.
3. Remove the vegetables with a slotted spoon, draining well over the pan. Add them to the eggs.
4. Pour out some of the oil if needed, leaving just enough in the pan to make the omelet. Pour in the egg mixture, covering the base of the pan.
5. Raise the heat if needed, and cook the omelet, as described on page 142, until just browned underneath, shaking the pan once or twice to prevent it sticking.
6. Slide the pan under medium grill (broiler) heat, to 'set' the top and brown it lightly. Serve at once, or cool and serve cold with salad.

Note: Cooked vegetables such as peas, chopped pepper, sliced green beans or cooked chopped spinach can be added to the omelet with the onion and potato; so can chopped cooked chicken, chopped ham or shredded continental sausage.

Stuffed Eggs

Serves 4

Not suitable for freezing

	Metric	Imperial	American
Hard-boiled (hard-cooked) eggs	4	4	4
Softened butter	25 g	1 oz	2 tbls
Mayonnaise or double (thick) cream	15 ml	1 tbls	1 tbls
Salt and pepper			
Finely chopped parsley or paprika			

1. Shell the eggs when cold. Halve them lengthways and remove the yolks to a bowl. Cut a thin sliver off the rounded side of each halved egg to make it stand level and steady.
2. Mash or pound the yolks with the butter, mayonnaise or cream and seasoning, to make a smooth paste.
3. Pile the mixture back in the hollowed white halves; or put it in a forcing (pastry) bag fitted with a small star nozzle, and pipe it into the egg white hollows.
4. Arrange on a platter and garnish each halved egg with parsley or paprika. Serve as a first course or as part of a buffet salad.

Variations
1. Add 15 ml/1 tbls chicken or ham paste, or smooth liver sausage without skin, to the egg yolk paste.
2. Add 5 ml/1 tsp anchovy essence to the egg yolk paste, and garnish each halved egg with a curled anchovy fillet.

Baked Savoury Soufflé

Serves 2–3

Oven temp 190°C/375°F/Gas Mark 5

Not suitable for freezing

	Metric	Imperial	American
Butter or margarine	25 g	1 oz	2 tbls
Flour	30 ml	2 tbls	2 tbls
Milk	150 ml	¼ pt	⅔ cup
Filling or flavouring (see below)			
Salt and pepper			
Eggs	3	3	3

1. Prepare a 15 cm/6 in soufflé dish (without a paper band).
2. In a fairly large saucepan, melt the fat, stir in the flour, and cook for 2 minutes without letting the flour colour. Gradually stir in the milk, and bring to the boil, stirring all the time. Cook until very thick. Cool slightly.
3. Add the filling or flavouring and season well.
4. Separate the eggs, beating each egg yolk in turn into the panada when separating them.
5. Whisk the egg whites until they hold soft peaks. Stir 1 spoonful into the flavoured mixture, then fold in the rest. Turn the mixture gently into the prepared dish. Make a circular cut all round the top 2 cm/¾ in in from the edge.
6. Bake at the temperature above for 30 minutes, until well risen and browned. Serve without delay.

Fillings/flavourings
Use 75 g/3 oz finely chopped or mashed canned meat (e.g. pork luncheon meat), or fish (e.g. canned salmon) or well-drained chopped sautéed mushrooms.

11
HOME-MADE PASTRY AND PIZZA DOUGH

General Rules for Pastry Making

All pastry except hot water crust should be as light and crisp as possible. To make light pastry, you must incorporate air when making the pastry, use the right proportions of fat and water, keep the ingredients cool and handle the pastry as little as possible.

a. Work on a cool surface, e.g. a stone or marble slab. Keep everything cool, including your hands (by running cold water over your wrists).

b. Always sift the flour and salt after measuring to lighten the pastry.

c. When rubbing (cutting) fat into the flour, work with your fingertips, and lift your hands so that air is mixed into the flour as it falls back into the bowl.

d. Flour varies in the amount of water it needs to make it stick together. Do not use too much water or the pastry will be hard. Mix it in evenly with a round-bladed knife.

e. Handle the pastry as little as possible and work quickly.

f. Chill the pastry or 'rest' it in a cool place for 30 minutes after making it.

g. Use only a little flour for rolling out, and brush off any surplus afterwards. Roll the pastry quickly, lightly and evenly. Roll away from you, not from side to side. Do not roll off the edge or you will squash the air out of the pastry. Never turn the pastry over.

h. Use the rolled side of the pastry for the outside of a flan case, pie or tart shell, or pie crust. Do not stretch the pastry to make it fit; it will shrink back. There is no need to grease the tin (pan) or baking sheet except for choux pastry, sweet pastry and suet crust pastry.

i. Bake the pastry in a fairly hot oven. The richer the pastry, the hotter it must be, at least to start with.

j. If pastry is not used at once, store it closely wrapped in the refrigerator.

k. Use frozen shortcrust (basic pie dough), puff or strudel pastry as the directions on the packet suggest.

To bake 'blind': A pastry tart or flan case (pie shell) is often partly or fully baked before being filled. Prick the bottom of the case with a fork. Cover it with a round of greaseproof (waxed) paper, then fill the case with dried beans. Bake the case at the usual temperature for the type of pastry for 8–12 minutes for a partly-baked case, about 20 minutes for a fully baked one. Remove the beans and paper, and return the case to the oven for 5–6 minutes to dry out. The dried beans can be re-used whenever you need them.

If the edge of the pastry case is cooked and browned before removing the beans and paper, dry it out at a low temperature.

A partly baked tart or flan case is used if the filling needs to be cooked at a low heat or just for a short time. A fully baked case is used if the filling only needs reheating or will be served as it is. If possible, place a fully baked flan case made in a ring on its serving plate before filling it, as the weight of the filling may crack the pastry if it is lifted afterwards. After removing the flan ring, slide the case from the baking sheet onto the plate.

Small tarts or tartlets are baked in deep or shallow tartlet or patty tins (pans). Roll out the pastry and cut into rounds big enough to line the tins, allowing for their depth. Use a plain cutter if the tartlets will have lids, a fluted if not. Cut lids to fit the tops of the tins. Tartlet tins are often moulded in a single metal sheet. If individual tins or foil pans are used, they must be placed on a baking sheet.

A cool kitchen and a light touch are the secrets of successful pastry making.

Shortcrust Pastry

Makes 375 g/13 oz pastry (approx)

Freeze 4 months (unbaked), 6 months (baked)

	Metric	Imperial	American
Plain (all-purpose) flour	225 g	8 oz	2 cups
Pinch of salt			
Butter or margarine	50 g	2 oz	¼ cup
Lard (shortening)	50 g	2 oz	¼ cup
Cold water to mix			

1. Sift together the flour and salt into a bowl.
2. Cut the fat into small pieces with a knife and add it to the flour.
3. Rub (cut) the fat into the flour until the mixture is like fine breadcrumbs.
4. Add a little cold water (about 45 ml/3 tbls) and mix to a stiff dough.
5. Turn out onto a lightly floured board, knead a little and gather into a ball. 'Rest' the pastry for 30 minutes, then roll out or wrap and store as required.

Variation
For Wholemeal Shortcrust Pastry, use half wholemeal and half plain white flour and about 15 ml/1 tbls more water.

Cheese Pastry

Makes 225 g/8 oz pastry (approx)

Freeze 1 month (unbaked), 2 months (baked)

	Metric	Imperial	American
Plain (all-purpose) flour	100 g	4 oz	1 cup
Salt and pepper			
A few grains of cayenne pepper			
Butter or margarine	50 g	2 oz	¼ cup
Grated Cheddar or other hard or semi-hard cheese	75 g	3 oz	¾ cup
Egg yolk	1	1	1
Water			

1. Sift together the flour, salt and pepper, and cayenne into a bowl.
2. Rub (cut) in the fat until the mixture is like fine breadcrumbs.
3. Add the cheese. Beat the egg yolk with about 15 ml/1 tbls water. Use some or all of it to bind the mixture to a stiff dough. (Keep leftover egg wash for glazing the pastry.)
4. Knead the dough lightly on a slightly floured surface, then gather into a ball. Roll out or wrap and store as required.

Rough Puff Pastry

Makes 900 g/2 lb pastry (approx)

Freeze 4 months (unbaked), 6 months (baked)

	Metric	Imperial	American
Plain (all-purpose) flour	450 g	1 lb	4 cups
Pinch of salt			
Butter or margarine	175 g	6 oz	¾ cup
Lard (shortening)	175 g	6 oz	¾ cup
Lemon juice	5 ml	1 tsp	1 tsp
Cold water to mix			

1. Sift together the flour and salt into a bowl. Add the fat cut into walnut-sized pieces.
2. Stir the knobs of fat into the flour with the lemon juice and enough cold water to make a stiff dough.
3. Turn onto a well-floured surface and roll into an oblong 3 mm/⅛ in thick with a short side nearest you.
4. Fold the one-third of the pastry nearest you over the centre third, and the top one-third down over it.
5. Press the edges of the pastry hard to enclose the air, and press three equally spaced 'ribs' in the pastry surface to distribute the air. 'Rest' the pastry for 15 minutes.
6. Give the pastry a half-turn to the right, roll it into an oblong again, and repeat steps 4 and 5. Repeat again twice more, making four rollings, foldings, rests and half-turns in all.
7. Roll the pastry out for use or wrap and store as required.

Flaky Pastry

Makes 900 g/2 lb pastry (approx)

Freeze 4 months (unbaked), 6 months (baked)

	Metric	Imperial	American
Plain (all-purpose) flour	450 g	1 lb	4 cups
Pinch of salt			
Butter or margarine	175 g	6 oz	¾ cup
Lard (shortening)	175 g	6 oz	¾ cup
Lemon juice	5 ml	1 tsp	1 tsp
Cold water to mix			

1. Sift together the flour and salt into a bowl.
2. Blend the fats on a plate, and cut into 4 equal portions.
3. Rub (cut) one portion into the flour until the mixture is like fine breadcrumbs. Bind with the lemon juice and enough water to make a very stiff dough.
4. Turn the dough onto a lightly-floured surface and roll into an oblong strip with one short side towards you.

5. Distribute the second portion of fat in small pats, placed in even rows over the two-thirds of the pastry furthest from you. Leave 2.5 cm/1 in of the pastry edge uncovered.
6. Fold the nearest one-third of the pastry over the centre one-third, then fold the furthest one-third down over it. Give this three-layer pastry 'sandwich' a half turn to the right.
7. Seal the edges by pressing hard on them with the rolling pin. Then press three 'ribs' in the pastry to distribute the air. 'Rest' the pastry for 15 minutes.
8. Repeat Steps 5–7 twice, using the two remaining portions of fat. Then roll and fold once more (4 times in all).
9. 'Rest' the pastry for at least 30 minutes. Then roll out for use or wrap and store, as required.

Puff Pastry

Makes 1 kg/2¼ lb pastry (approx)

Freeze 4 months (unbaked), 6 months (baked)

	Metric	Imperial	American
Plain (all-purpose)			
flour	450 g	1 lb	4 cups
Salt	1.5 ml	¼ tsp	¼ tsp
Lemon juice	5 ml	1 tsp	1 tsp
Cold water to mix			
Butter, chilled	450 g	1 lb	2 cups

1. Sift together the flour and salt into a bowl.
2. Mix the lemon juice and 175 ml/6 fl oz/¾ cup cold water. Use to bind the flour, adding enough extra water to make a firm dough.
3. Place the dough on a lightly-floured surface, and knead until smooth and elastic.
4. Wrap the butter loosely in a folded dry cloth, and squeeze out any moisture. Press the butter into a flat square slab.
5. Roll out the dough into a rectangle slightly more than twice as long as the butter slab, and a little wider.
6. Place the butter on one half of the dough, and fold the other half over it. Press the pastry edges to seal them.
7. Proceed as in Steps 4–7 of making Rough Puff Pastry (opposite) but give the puff pastry 7 rollings and foldings. 'Rest' the pastry for several hours before rolling it for use.

Hot Water Crust Pastry

Makes 500 g/18 oz pastry (approx)

Not suitable for freezing

	Metric	Imperial	American
Plain (all-purpose)			
flour	350 g	12 oz	3 cups
Salt	1.5 ml	¼ tsp	¼ tsp
Lard (shortening)	100 g	4 oz	½ cup
Water	100 ml	4 fl oz	½ cup

1. Sift together the flour and salt into a warmed bowl.
2. Melt the lard gently in a saucepan, add the water when just melted and bring to the boil.
3. Stir the liquid into the flour with a wooden spoon and mix quickly until blended.
4. Turn onto a lightly-floured surface and knead until smooth. Do not allow to cool, use at once.
5. Use for raised pies following the instructions given below and the recipe for Raised Pork Pie given on page 54.

Raised Pie (made with hot water crust pastry):

The pie can be moulded by hand on a baking sheet, or the warm pastry can be moulded over a suitable-sized inverted jar or cake tin (pan). Alternatively, the pie can be made in a hinged oval or round pie mould or a loose-based deep cake tin (pan). A 17.5 cm/7 in pie mould or cake tin will require pastry made with 350 g/12 oz/3 cups flour (above).

Reserve one quarter of the pastry for a lid, and leave it in a warm place covered with greased polythene. Grease and flour the outside of an inverted mould or the inside of a pie mould or cake tin. Roll out the pastry 5 mm/¼ in thick.

Lay the pastry over an inverted jar or tin, and mould the pastry round it, making sure that you do not stretch the pastry and that it is an even thickness all over. Leave to cool, then ease the hardened pastry shell off the mould, stand it right way up on a baking sheet and fill it. Tie a doubled thickness of greaseproof (waxed) paper round it to prevent it bursting during baking.

Alternatively, lay the pastry in a hinged mould or loose-bottomed cake tin, press it into place and fill it at once. In either case, roll out the reserved pastry to fit the top of the pie shell, put it on the filling, and pinch the edges of the dampened pastry shell and lid together to seal. Make a hole in the centre of the lid and decorate if you wish. Bake as your recipe directs. If the pie is baked in a hinged mould or loose-bottomed cake tin, remove it from the container about 30 minutes before the end of the cooking time, brush it all over with beaten egg, and complete the cooking on a baking sheet.

Suet Crust Pastry

Makes 400 g/14 oz pastry (approx)

Freeze 4 months (unbaked), 6 months (baked)

	Metric	Imperial	American
Plain (all-purpose) or self-raising flour	*225 g*	*8 oz*	*2 cups*
Baking powder (with plain flour)	*5 ml*	*1 tsp*	*1 tsp*
Pinch of salt			
Butcher's suet (see note)	*100 g*	*4 oz*	*¼ lb*
Cold water to mix			

1. Sift together the flour, baking powder if used, and salt into a bowl.
2. Remove any skin from the suet, shred and chop it finely. Sprinkle a little of the flour over it while chopping.
3. Add the prepared suet to the flour.
4. Mix with cold water to a soft dough. Roll out for use, or wrap and store as required.
5. Use for savoury and sweet steamed and boiled puddings, dumplings, etc. following the instructions given below and the recipes given on pages 69 and 180.

Note: 75 g/3 oz ready-shredded suet from a bought packet can be used instead of butcher's suet.

Suet Crust Pastry Pudding:

This is usually made in a deep heatproof pudding basin (mixing bowl) if the pudding will be boiled or steamed, although a charlotte mould or cake tin (pan) can be used for a baked pudding. An 850 ml/1½ pt/3¾ cup pudding basin will need pastry made with 225 g/8 oz/2 cups flour (see left).

Cut off rather more than a quarter of the pastry for the lid. Grease the inside of the basin. Roll out the remaining pastry into a round 1 cm/½ in larger than the top of the basin. Place it in the basin carefully so that the centre of the pastry round is in the centre of the basin. Press with your fingertips from the centre of the pastry, to cover first the bottom, then the sides of the basin evenly with pastry, working up the sides to the top. Put in the filling. Roll out the pastry for the top into a round the same size as the top of the basin. Damp the rim of the basin, and fit on the top crust; seal it to the edge of the lining pastry. Then cover the basin as described on page 180.

Opposite: *Vol-au-vent cases filled with a selection of fillings.*

Below: *Suet Crust Pastry is used for both sweet and savoury puddings.*

Yeast Pastry

Makes 400 g/14 oz pastry (approx)

Not suitable for freezing

	Metric	Imperial	American
Bread dough (page 208) using 225 g/8 oz flour			
Butter or margarine	50 g	2 oz	¼ cup
Lard (shortening)	50 g	2 oz	¼ cup

1. Roll out the dough on a lightly floured surface into an oblong, with one short side towards you.
2. Mix the fats and divide into 4 equal portions.
3. Proceed as in Steps 5–8 of making Flaky Pastry (page 150), giving the pastry 4 rollings and 4 turns.
4. Wrap the pastry in greased paper and a cloth, and leave in a cool place overnight.
5. Next day, roll out to the thickness required for your chosen recipe.
6. Leave in a warm place to prove before baking. Bake at 220°C/425°F/Gas Mark 7.
7. Use in traditional recipes as an alternative to flaky pastry.

VOL-AU-VENT AND PATTY CASES

(made with puff, rough puff or flaky pastry)

Note: Small flattish double-crust pies made with shortcrust pastry (basic pie dough) and baked in shallow tartlet tins or small saucers are also called patties.

Small Vol-au-Vent or Bouchée Cases (for cocktail or buffet snacks and petits four)

Makes 12–16

Oven temp 220°C/425°F/Gas Mark 7

Freeze 2 months (unfilled)

½ recipe quantity Puff Pastry (page 151)
Beaten egg to glaze

1. Roll out the pastry 7 mm/⅓ in thick. Make sure it is evenly rolled, or the risen pastry cases will fall over.
2. Cut out about 14 rounds, using a 5 cm/2 in cutter. With a 3 cm/1¼ in cutter, make a cut in the centre of each round, cutting only half-way through the depth of the pastry.
3. Brush the surface with beaten egg, avoiding the edges and the cut in the centre.
4. Place on a dampened baking sheet. Bake at the temperature above for 10 minutes.
5. With a knife-point, remove the centre top of each vol-au-vent for a lid. Take out any soft pastry inside without piercing the bottom. Fill with a hot mixture or cool the cases and fill with a cold one. Replace the lids if you wish.

Vol-au-vent Case – Large

Makes one 18 cm/7 in case

Oven temp 230°C/450°F/Gas Mark 8

Freeze 6 months (unfilled)

½ recipe quantity Puff Pastry (page 151)
Beaten egg to glaze

1. Roll out the pastry to an even thickness of 2 cm/¾ in, if possible in an oval shape. Using a vol-au-vent cutter or cutting round an oval salad plate, cut out an oval 18 cm/7 in long.
2. With a smaller cutter or judging by eye, make a cut about 2 cm/¾ in inside the edge, cutting about half-way through the depth of the pastry.
3. Place the pastry oval on a dampened baking sheet. Brush the top with beaten egg, taking care not to cover the edges or the cut marking the lid.
4. Bake at the temperature above for 20 minutes or until risen, crisp and golden-brown.
5. With a knife-point, remove the centre oval of crisp pastry inside the cut, and lay aside. Remove the soft pastry inside, taking care not to pierce the bottom. Keep warm if serving hot.
6. Fill the case with any savoury or sweet filling. Replace the pastry 'lid' on a hot filling.

Note: A vol-au-vent case is generally used as a container for a delicately flavoured mixture such as shellfish or chicken in a cream sauce.

Patty Cases

Makes 12 x 7 cm/4½ × 2¾ in patty cases

Oven temp 220°C/425°F/Gas Mark 7

Freeze 2 months (unfilled)

½ recipe quantity Rough Puff, Puff or Flaky Pastry
(pages 150, 151)
Beaten egg to glaze

1. Roll out the pastry about 3 mm/⅛ in thick, and cut into 24 rounds with a 7 cm/2¾ in cutter.
2. Remove the centres of half the rounds with a 4 cm/1½ in cutter. Keep aside.
3. Dampen the edges of the uncut rounds, and place the cut rings on top. Prick the centres of the cases inside the rings with a poultry skewer.
4. Place the cases and the buttons of pastry cut out on a dampened baking sheet. Leave to stand for 10 minutes.

5. Brush the tops of the cases and the buttons with beaten egg. Bake at the temperature above for 10 minutes or until risen, crisp and golden-brown. Fill like small vol-au-vent cases, and top with the pastry buttons as lids.

SWEET PASTRY RECIPES

Sweet Pastry (Rich Short Crust Pastry)

Makes 350 g/12 oz pastry (approx)

Freeze 3 months (unbaked), 4 months (baked)

	Metric	Imperial	American
Plain (all-purpose) flour	175 g	6 oz	1½ cups
Pinch of salt			
Margarine	50 g	2 oz	¼ cup
Lard (shortening)	50 g	2 oz	¼ cup
Caster (superfine) sugar	15–25 g	½–1 oz	1–2 tbls
Egg yolk, beaten	1	1	1

1. Sift together the flour and salt into a bowl.
2. Cut the fat into small pieces with a knife and add to the flour.
3. Rub (cut) the fat into the flour until the mixture is like fine breadcrumbs.
4. Add the sugar. Then work in the beaten egg to make a smooth dough.
5. Turn out onto a lightly floured board, knead lightly, and gather into a ball. 'Rest' the pastry for 30 minutes, then roll out or wrap and store as required.
6. Use for open tarts, flans and tartlets.

Note: This pastry is also sometimes called Fleur Pastry or Pâte Sucrée.

Choux Pastry

	Metric	Imperial	American
Water	275 ml	½ pt	1¼ cups
Butter	80 g	3½ oz	7 tbls
Pinch of salt			
Plain (all-purpose) flour	150 g	5 oz	1¼ cups
Small eggs	4	4	4

1. Heat the water, fat and salt gently in a medium-sized saucepan until the fat melts. Raise the heat and bring to the boil.
2. Immediately take the pan off the heat and tip in all the flour at once. Beat briskly with a spoon until it forms a single mass. If at all wet, return to very low heat and beat until

the paste begins to leave a thin film on the bottom of the pan.

3. Take off the heat, and beat in the eggs one at a time, incorporating each thoroughly; the paste should be smooth and glossy.
4. Use while still warm if possible, for cocktail puffs or cream buns, profiteroles, éclairs etc. (page 166).

Note: Beat in an extra egg white if you have a spare one; it will make light, dry puffs, easy to store.

Crumb Crusts

Instead of pastry, dry biscuit or other crumbs mixed with fat and flavourings can be used to make a flan or tart shell, or as a base for cheesecakes. Dry cracker crumbs flavoured with cheese or herbs are the type most often used for savoury quiches or flan cases. Sweet cases are more varied. Semi-sweet or sweet biscuits such as digestive biscuits (graham crackers) or ginger nuts are popular for their texture and flavour, but plain crumbs flavoured with spice, nuts or an essence are often used. Rolled oats, corn flakes or ground nuts can be used instead of some of the crumbs for texture interest. Honey, treacle or syrup can be used instead of sugar for sweetening and chocolate can be used instead of some of the fat for binding the crumbs.

The usual proportions of crumbs, fat and sugar (for sweet dishes) are 100 g/4 oz/1 cup crumbs to 50 g/2 oz/¼ cup fat and 25 g/1 oz/3 tbls sugar, but fatty or very sweet crumbs may need less fat and sweetening, while very dry crumbs may need more fat. The general method of making any crumb crust is as follows: The crumbs are made by crushing broken biscuits, bits of cake etc. with a rolling pin or in a food processor. They must be fine and even to make sure they stick together properly. The fat can be softened and worked into them with the sugar and any flavouring, or the dry foods can be mixed together then bound with melted fat. Alternatively, the sugar can be melted with the fat used to bind the crumbs. The crumb mixture is then pressed into place firmly with a knife-blade or the back of a spoon. If making a tart or flan case, it is applied in quite a thick layer, say 7 mm/⅓ in, evenly all over the base and sides. The top rim is levelled off by running a sharp knife over the surface, any loose crumbs then being brushed off. Finally, the case is chilled thoroughly until firm if the filling will be cold; or it may be baked at 180°C/350°F/Gas Mark 4 for about 15 minutes until firm and crisp, then chilled before being filled. A baked case can be re-baked if the filling needs cooking.

A sweetened crumb crust mixture is most often used as a base for a cheesecake, often today served as a dessert or fancy gâteau. An example using a crumb crust is given on page 162.

PIZZA

There are many shapes, sizes and types of pizza. The best known, the Neapolitan pizza, has a colourful topping of tomatoes, herbs, cheese and black (ripe) olives. Other toppings include ham, salami, bacon, eggs, mushrooms, fish or shellfish.

A good time to prepare a pizza for baking is when you are making bread. You will need 450 g/1 lb risen bread dough, white or wholemeal. If you do not want to bake the pizza at once, you can freeze the dough . However, if you want to make a pizza when you have no frozen bread dough in stock (see Freezing Hints, page 255), use the following basic dough mix and make up following White Bread recipe on page 208.

Basic Pizza Dough

	Metric	Imperial	American
Yeast Liquid			
Fresh (compressed)			
yeast	7 g	¼ oz	¼ cake
OR dried (active			
dry) yeast	5 ml	1 tsp	1 tsp
Sugar (if using			
dried yeast)	5 ml	1 tsp	1 tsp
Warm water	150 ml	¼ pt	⅔ cup
Dough-mix			
Bread flour, white			
or wholemeal	225 g	8 oz	2 cups
Salt	5 ml	1 tsp	1 tsp
Lard (shortening)	7.5 ml	1½ tsp	1½ tsp
To Make Pizza			
Risen bread dough			
(see above)	450 g	1 lb	1 lb
	(approx)	*(approx)*	*(approx)*
Corn oil for			
brushing			
Filling			
Mozzarella or mild			
Cheddar cheese	350 g	12 oz	¾ lb
	(approx)	*(approx)*	*(approx)*
Sliced fresh or			
canned tomatoes	350 g	12 oz	¾ lb
Ground black			
pepper			
Fresh or dried			
thyme,			
marjoram,			
oregano or basil	10 ml	2 tsp	2 tsp
Anchovy fillets			
Black (ripe) olives,			
halved and stoned			

1. Lightly oil four 15–18 cm/6–7 in flat pie plates or a Swiss (jelly) roll tin (pan) about 32.5 × 22.5 cm/13 × 9 in in size. Crumble, shred or grate the cheese and keep aside.
2. Turn the risen dough onto a lightly floured surface. Flatten it with your knuckles or a

rolling pin into a long strip. Brush it lightly with oil, roll it up like a Swiss (jelly) roll.

3. Repeat the flattening, and rolling up twice more.

4. Cut the dough into 4 equal-sized pieces if making individual pizza, and roll them into flat circles to fit the places; OR roll out the single piece of dough to fit the tin. Pinch up a small rim of dough all round.

5. Brush the dough with oil. Scatter about two-thirds of the cheese all over it except the rim; top with the tomatoes in an even layer. Sprinkle with pepper, then with the chosen herb. Scatter the remaining cheese on top.

6. Garnish with a lattice of anchovy fillets, with black olives between them (see note 1).

7. Bake for 20–30 minutes at 230°C/450°F/Gas Mark 8.

Notes:

1. If you will freeze the unbaked pizzas, only add the anchovy fillets and olives after thawing, just before baking.

2. You need not raise the dough a second time, but if possible let a pizza stand for 30 minutes in a cool place before baking.

Variations

1. Use 25 g/1 oz/¼ cup Parmesan instead of 25 g/1 oz/¼ cup of the Mozzarella.

2. Add a layer of 100–150 g/4–5 oz, sliced salami, cold ham or pork luncheon meat, or the same quantity of drained mashed tuna fish, over the tomato layer.

3. Scatter chopped fried onions or mushrooms over the tomato layer.

4. Instead of anchovy fillets, make a lattice of thin strips of rindless bacon, and use halved pickled walnuts, stoned prunes or capers instead of olives.

Individual Pizzas topped with onions, cheese and tomato purée are served with a mixed salad for a favourite snack.

12

PASTRY PIES AND PUDDINGS

DEEP FRUIT PIES AND TARTS

Traditional English Apple Pie

Serves 6

Oven temp 200°C/400°F/Gas Mark 6
180°C/350°F/Gas Mark 4

Freeze 1 month (unbaked or baked)

	Metric	Imperial	American
Cooking (tart) apples, peeled, cored, and sliced	600 g	1¼ lb	1¼ lb
Caster (superfine) sugar	100 g (approx)	4 oz (approx)	⅔ cup (approx)
Grated lemon rind	2.5 ml	½ tsp	½ tsp
Shortcrust pastry (basic pie dough) using 225 g/8 oz flour (page 150)			
Caster (superfine) sugar for dredging			

1. Mix together the fruit, sugar to taste (depending on the tartness of the apples) and lemon rind. Put into an 850 ml/1½ pt/ 3¾ cup pie dish with a pie funnel.
2. Roll out the pastry into an oval 1 cm/½ in bigger than the top of the pie dish. Trim off a strip 1 cm/½ in wide all round the edge.
3. Dampen the rim of the pie dish, and fit on the pastry strip.
4. Dampen the strip, and lay the pastry oval on top. Seal the edge to the strip, and trim if required.
5. Brush lightly with water and dredge with sugar. Bake at the first temperature above for 20 minutes, then reduce the heat and bake at the second temperature for another 20 minutes. Serve hot or cold with pouring custard (page 174) or cream.

Note: The freezing time suggested is shorter than for most baked deep fruit pies because apples tend to discolour after a few weeks.

Variations
Other fruit can be mixed with the apples or can be used instead of them. For *Blackberry and Apple Pie* use 350 g/12 oz/¾ lb of each fruit.

Damsons, gooseberries, plums or rhubarb are popular alternatives to apples but any prepared fresh or bottled fruit can be used, or fruit canned in natural juice. Prepare fresh fruit as for stewing. Drain bottled or canned fruit thoroughly. Omit the lemon rind unless the fruit is very sweet. Dried fruits such as apple rings or apricots can also be used if soaked overnight and stewed until almost soft and cooled.

OPEN TARTS, FLANS AND PLATE PIES

American Apple Pie

Serves 6

Oven temp 200°C/400°F/Gas Mark 6

Freeze 2 months (unbaked), 4 months (baked)

	Metric	Imperial	American
Shortcrust pastry (basic pie dough) using 350 g/12 oz/¾ lb flour (page 150)			
Egg white, beaten	1	1	1
Cooking (tart) apples, peeled, cored and sliced	275 g	10 oz	10 oz
Caster (superfine) sugar	50–100 g	2–4 oz	¼–½ cup

1. Roll out the pastry into 2 rounds to fit a 22.5 cm/9 in pie plate (page 148). Line the plate with one round. Brush the bottom of the pastry with some of the egg white. (This prevents sogginess.)
2. Arrange half the apple slices in the pastry shell. Sprinkle with sugar to taste (depending on the sweetness of the apples). Cover with the remaining apples.
3. Dampen the edges of the pastry lining. Cover with the second pastry round. Press the edges of the lid and lining together to seal. Trim the edges.

4. Make a small hole in the centre of the lid or cut triangular slits in it at intervals to let steam escape.
5. Bake for 50 minutes at the temperature above. If you wish, remove the pie from the oven 10 minutes before the end of the cooking time, brush the top crust with any remaining egg white, sprinkle with sugar and return to the oven to complete the cooking.
6. Serve hot or cold with cream.

Variations
1. For a 17.5 cm/7 in pie to serve 4, use pastry made with 225 g/8 oz/2 cups flour and 225 g/8 oz/½ lb apples. Reduce the sugar to 40–75 g/1½–3 oz/3–6 tbls.
2. For *Apple and Sultana Pie*, add 50 g/2 oz/⅓ cup sultanas and a little grated lemon rind for each 275 g/10 oz/1½ cups prepared apples.
3. For other fruit pies, use the same quantities as above of any fresh or bottled fruit, thawed frozen fruit or fruit canned in natural juice. Drain juice from bottled or canned fruit and thicken with cornflour (cornstarch) or arrowroot to make a fruit sauce to serve with the pie. Dried fruit can also be used for a pie if soaked, stewed and drained.

Open Fruit Tart or Flan

Serves 6

Oven temp 200°C/400°F/Gas Mark 6

Freeze 6 months (unfilled), 2 months (filled)

	Metric	Imperial	American
Shortcrust pastry (basic pie dough) or sweet pastry using 175 g/6 oz/ 1½ cups flour (page 150)			
Egg white (optional)	1	1	1
Stewed fruit, (frozen, thawed, bottled, or canned fruit in natural juice)	450 g	1 lb	1 lb
Arrowroot or cornflour (cornstarch) as needed			
Extra sugar or lemon juice if needed			
Whipped cream, to decorate (optional)			

1. Roll out the pastry and use to line a 22.5 cm/9 in pie plate or flan ring placed on a baking sheet (page 148).
2. If using a pie plate, cut the trimmings of pastry into small rounds with a fluted cutter. Brush round the edge of the pastry case with water or egg white and arrange the rounds on it in an overlapping ring, making a raised rim.
3. Prick the centre of the pastry case, place a round of greaseproof (waxed) paper on it and cover with dried beans.
4. Bake blind (page 148) for 20–25 minutes at the temperature above. Remove the beans and paper, and return to the oven for 5–8 minutes. Cool.
5. Drain the fruit over a saucepan while cooling the case. Arrange the fruit in the case. Thicken the juice with 5 ml/1 tsp arrowroot or cornflour (cornstarch) per 275 ml/½ pt/1¼ cups juice, and sweeten to taste. (Fruit stewed or bottled in syrup should not need sweetening, but may need a few drops of lemon juice.)
6. Just before the juice sets, pour it evenly over the fruit; leave until quite cold. Decorate with whipped cream if you wish.

Notes:
1. Instead of thickening the fruit juice with arrowroot or cornflour, you can 'set' the liquid of a flan filling with gelatine (unflavored gelatin). Use 7.5 ml/1½ tsp gelatine for each 275 ml/½ pt/1¼ cups juice. Soften and dissolve the gelatine in a little water, then stir it into the sweetened warmed juice. Cool. When cold but not yet set, pour the liquid jelly evenly over the fruit in the pastry case.
2. The fruit juice can be tinted with a few drops of food colouring if you wish.

Variation
Meringue-Topped Fruit Tart or Flan: Use fresh soft fruit, e.g. raspberries, for filling. Arrange in the cooled pastry case, and sprinkle with sugar to taste. Whisk 2 egg whites until stiff, fold in 50 g/2 oz/¼ cup caster (superfine) sugar and pile the meringue on the fruit, sealing it to the edges of the pastry. Sprinkle with a little extra sugar. Bake at 150°C/300°F/Gas Mark 2 for 15 minutes until the meringue has set and is slightly browned.

Bakewell Tart

Serves 4–5

Oven temp 190°C/375°F/Gas Mark 5

Freeze 2 months

	Metric	Imperial	American
Shortcrust pastry (basic pie dough) using 100 g/4 oz/ 1 cup flour (page 150)			
Blackcurrant jam			
Butter or margarine	50 g	2 oz	¼ cup
Caster (superfine) sugar	50 g	2 oz	⅓ cup
Eggs, separated	2	2	2
Ground almonds	75 g	3 oz	¾ cup
Plain cake crumbs, e.g. Madeira	75 g	3 oz	1½ cups
Grated rind of ½ lemon			
Almond essence			

1. Use the rolled-out pastry to line a 20 cm/8 in sandwich cake tin (layer pan). Cover the bottom with a thin layer of blackcurrant jam.
2. Beat together the fat and sugar. Beat in the egg yolks, one at a time.
3. Add the ground almonds, cake crumbs, lemon rind and almond essence. Beat well.
4. Whisk the egg white fairly stiffly. Stir 1–2 tbls into the tart filling, then fold in the rest.
5. Spread the mixture evenly over the jam. Bake at the temperature above for 40 minutes. Serve hot or cold.

Variation

Gainsborough Tart: Make the pastry case and spread it with raspberry jam. For the filling, melt 25 g/1 oz/2 tbls butter or margarine, and stir in 1 beaten egg, 50 g/2 oz/¼ cup caster (superfine) sugar, and 100 g/4 oz/1⅓ cups desiccated (shredded) coconut mixed with 1.5 ml/¼ tsp baking powder. Pour the mixture into the case, and bake at the temperature above for 30 minutes only.

Treacle Tart

Serves 6

Oven temp 200°C/400°F/Gas Mark 6

Freeze 3 months

	Metric	Imperial	American
Shortcrust pastry (basic pie dough) using 175 g/6 oz/ 1½ cups flour (page 150)			
Breadcrumbs or plain cake crumbs	25–50 g	1–2 oz	½–1 cup
Golden (light corn) syrup	225 g	8 oz	½ lb
Lemon juice or ground ginger			

1. Roll out the pastry 2.5–4 cm/1–1½ in larger than a 22.5 cm/9 in pie plate. Cut off the extra strip of pastry and cut it in half lengthways. Dampen the edge of the plate and lay one strip round the edge. Keep the other aside, with any trimmings.
2. Dampen the strip on the plate. Line the plate with the pastry round, so that the edge covers the strip. Sprinkle the bottom of the pastry case with crumbs.
3. Warm the syrup in a saucepan until liquid. Stir in the remaining crumbs and lemon juice or ginger. Pour into the case.
4. Roll out the reserved pastry strip and trimmings thinly. Cut into 1 cm/½ in strips to fit across the tart at equally spaced intervals. Arrange them in a lattice on top of the tart.
5. Bake at the temperature above for 30 minutes. Serve hot or cold.

Jam Tart

Serves 6

Oven temp 200°C/400°F/Gas Mark 6

Freeze 3 months

	Metric	Imperial	American
Shortcrust pastry (basic pie dough) using 175 g/6 oz/ 1½ cups flour (page 150)			
Firm or whole fruit jam (see note)	175 g	6 oz	½ cup
Beaten egg yolk and water for glazing			

1. Use the rolled-out pastry to line a 22.5 cm/9 in pie plate (page 148).
2. Trim the edges. Cut the trimmings into small rounds with a fluted cutter. Dampen the edge of the pastry and arrange the rounds on it.
3. Spread the jam evenly over the pastry. Brush the pastry edge with beaten egg and water.
4. Bake at the temperature above for 20–25 minutes. Serve hot or cold.

Note: Do not use a thin, watery jam. Cover a whole fruit or thick jam loosely with greaseproof (waxed) paper while cooking if it shows any sign of scorching.

Lemon Meringue Pie

Serves 6

Oven temp 160°C/325°F/Gas Mark 3

Not suitable for freezing

	Metric	Imperial	American
22.5 cm/9 in baked flan case made with shortcrust pastry (basic pie dough) using 175 g/6 oz/ 1½ cups flour (pages 148 and 150)			
Cornflour (cornstarch)	40 g	1½ oz	1½ oz
Caster (superfine) sugar	100 g	4 oz	⅔ cup
Salt	1.5 ml	¼ tsp	¼ tsp
Boiling water	350 ml	12 fl oz	1½ cups
Lemon juice	50 ml	2 fl oz	¼ cup
Grated rind of 1 lemon			
Butter, well softened	25 g	1 oz	2 tbls
Eggs, separated	3	3	3
Extra sugar for meringue	100 g	4 oz	⅔ cup

1. Mix the cornflour (cornstarch), sugar and salt in a saucepan. Add the boiling water, and stir until blended.
2. Stir over gentle heat for 3 minutes or until the mixture thickens.
3. Take the pan off the heat, and stir in the lemon juice and rind, then the fat. Stir until melted and blended.
4. Beat the egg yolks until liquid. Beat in a little of the hot mixture. Pour the egg mixture into the saucepan.
5. Return the pan to very gentle heat, and cook, stirring constantly, until well thickened. Take off the heat and cool.
6. Whisk the egg whites until stiff, and fold in 75 g/3 oz/6 tbls of the sugar to make a meringue. Pour the lemon custard mixture into the flan case, and pile the meringue on top, sealing the edges to the pastry. Sprinkle with the remaining sugar.
7. Bake at the temperature above for 20 minutes until the meringue is set and slightly browned. Cool before cutting.

OTHER PUDDINGS MADE WITH PASTRY

Apple Meringue Pudding

Serves 6

Oven temp 180°C/350°F/Gas Mark 4
140°C/275°F/Gas Mark 1

Not suitable for freezing

	Metric	Imperial	American
Shortcrust pastry (basic pie dough) using 175 g/6 oz/ 1½ cups flour (page 150)			
Large cooking (tart) apples	600 g	1¼ lb	1¼ lb
Water	30 ml	2 tbls	2 tbls
Caster (superfine) sugar	75 g	3 oz	½ cup
Butter or margarine	50 g	2 oz	¼ cup
Grated rind and juice of 1 lemon			
Large eggs, separated	2	2	2
Extra caster (superfine) sugar	15 ml	1 tbls	1 tbls
Glacé (candied) cherries and angelica			

1. Use the rolled-out pastry to line an 850 ml/ 1½ pt/3¾ cup pie dish. Decorate the edges with trimmings.
2. Peel, core and slice the apples. Simmer with the water until soft. Sieve or purée in a food processor. Return to the stewpan and reheat until hand-hot.
3. Add the sugar, fat, grated rind and juice. Stir in the egg yolks thoroughly.
4. Turn the mixture into the pastry shell. Bake at the temperature above for 30 minutes.
5. While baking, whisk the egg whites until stiff. Fold in the extra sugar. Pile the meringue on the pudding inside the pastry rim. Decorate with glacé (candied) cherries and angelica.
6. Return the dish to the oven and bake at the second temperature above for 25–30 minutes to set the meringue. Serve hot with cream.

Opposite: *Lemon Meringue Pie with a crisp pastry crust, tangy filling and meringue topping is always a popular dessert.*

13
CHEESECAKES AND SMALL PASTRIES

CHEESECAKES

Basically, a cheesecake is a mixture of eggs, soft cheese or curds and fresh or slightly soured cream in a pastry case or on a crumb crust base. Large cheesecakes may be baked to set the eggs like a baked custard, or unbaked and set with gelatine or flavoured jelly (jello) from a packet. Either type may be flat like a tart or flan, or light and fluffy like a gâteau. The most usual flavouring for any cheesecake is lemon juice. The flat, more solid cheesecakes may also contain dried fruit or spice. Light fluffy American-style cheesecakes are usually flavoured with fresh or canned fruit, chocolate, coffee or a liqueur.

Cheesecake bases may be made from pastry, sponge cake or a crumb crust mixture and flavoured with chocolate or spices to complement the flavour of the topping.

Lemon cheese is an old name for lemon curd which is a thick, lemon-flavoured egg custard. A fruit cheese, e.g. plum cheese, is a fresh fruit paste, made like jam but boiled until thicker.

American Lemon Cheesecake (unbaked)

Serves 6–8

Freeze 2 months (undecorated)

	Metric	Imperial	American
Ingredients as for American Lemon Cheesecake (baked), except nuts			
Gelatine (1 envelope unflavored gelatin)	15 g	½ oz	2 tbls
Cold water	30 ml	2 tbls	2 tbls
Whipped cream for decoration			
Candied lemon slices (small bought sweets) for decoration			

1. Prepare a 20cm/8 in loose-based cake tin (pan) and make the crumb base as for American Lemon Cheesecake (baked). Chill.
2. Soften the gelatine in the water in a small heatproof jug, then stand the jug in hot water and stir until the gelatine dissolves. Remove from the heat. Cool slowly without allowing gelatine to set.
3. Beat the egg yolks and sugar for the filling in a heatproof bowl until well blended. Balance the bowl over simmering water, and whisk until the mixture is light and thick. Remove from the heat and continue whisking until the mixture is barely warm.
4. Sieve the cheese, and fold it into the mixture with the lemon rind and juice.
5. Whip the cream until it just holds soft peaks. Fold in gently. Then stir in the cooled gelatine little by little to prevent it forming lumps.
6. Whisk the egg whites like the cream, and fold them in.
7. Turn the mixture into the chilled crumb case, and chill for several hours or overnight.
8. Remove from the tin and decorate with whipped cream and sweets just before serving.

American Lemon Cheesecake (baked)

Serves 6–8

Oven temp 160°C/325°F/Gas Mark 3

Freeze 2 months

	Metric	Imperial	American
Base			
Butter	50 g	2 oz	¼ cup
Digestive biscuit (graham cracker) crumbs	225 g	8 oz	3 cups
Caster (superfine) sugar	25 g	1 oz	3 tbls
Ground cinnamon	7.5 ml	1½ tsp	1½ tsp
Filling			
Eggs, separated	2	2	2
Caster (superfine) sugar	100 g	4 oz	⅔ cup

	Metric	Imperial	American
Full fat soft cheese	350 g	12 oz	3/4 lb
Grated rind and juice of 1 lemon			
Double (heavy) cream	150 ml	1/4 pt	2/3 cup
Chopped mixed nuts	25 g	1 oz	1/4 cup

1. Grease the inside of a 17.5 cm/7 in loose-based cake tin (pan).
2. Make the crumb base. Melt the butter and work in 175 g/6 oz/2¼ cups of the crumbs, all the sugar and the spice. Press the mixture evenly all over the base of the tin. Coat the sides with the remaining 50 g/2 oz/¾ cup crumbs. Chill.
3. Make the filling. Beat the egg yolks and sugar together until thick. Sieve in the cheese, add the lemon rind and juice, and beat well.
4. Whisk the egg whites until they just hold soft peaks, and fold them into the mixture. Whip the cream until stiff and fold in. Turn the mixture gently onto the chilled crumb base in the tin.
5. Bake the cheesecake at the temperature above for 45 minutes. Sprinkle the nuts on top without moving cheesecake, if possible for another 15–20 minutes.
6. Cool the cheesecake in the turned-off oven so that it cools slowly, free from draughts. (This helps to prevent it cracking.)
7. When quite cold, remove from the tin. Chill for at least 4 hours before cutting.

Variation
For a less rich cheesecake use cottage cheese and single (light) cream for the filling.

SMALL PASTRIES

Custard Tarts

Makes 12 deep tarts

Oven temp 200°C/400°F/Gas Mark 6

Not suitable for freezing

	Metric	Imperial	American
Shortcrust pastry (basic pie dough) using 100 g/4 oz/ 1 cup flour (page 150)			
Caster (superfine) sugar	15 g	1/2 oz	1 tbls
Egg, lightly beaten	1	1	1
Warm milk	150 ml	1/4 pt	2/3 cup
Pinch of salt			
Sprinkling of grated nutmeg			

1. Roll out the pastry and use to line 12 deep tartlet tins or small bun tins.
2. Add the sugar to the lightly beaten egg. Stir in the warm milk with a pinch of salt.
3. Pour the mixture into the pastry cases. Sprinkle nutmeg on top.
4. Bake at the temperature above for 20 minutes. Cool in the tins.

Mince Pies

Makes 12 small pies (approx)

Oven temp 230°C/450°F/Gas Mark 8

Freeze 2 months

	Metric	Imperial	American
Shortcrust (basic pie dough) using 350 g/12 oz/3 cups flour (page 150) or Puff Pastry using 225 g/8 oz/2 cups flour (page 151)			
Mincemeat (page 240)	275–350 g	10–12 oz	1¼–1½ cups
Icing (confectioners') sugar for dredging			
Brandy Butter (page 188)			

1. Roll out the pastry, and cut out rounds with a plain cutter to line 12 deep tartlet tins or small bun tins. Cut out 12 slightly smaller rounds for lids. If using puff pastry, cut out the lids first, so that any re-rolled pastry is used for the linings.
2. Line the tins with the larger rounds.
3. Fill the pastry cases three-quarters full with mincemeat.
4. Dampen the edges of the pastry, put on the lids and seal the edges. Cut 2–3 small slits in each lid to let steam escape.
5. Bake at the temperature above for 15–20 minutes.
6. Serve hot or cold, dredged with sugar and with brandy butter as an accompaniment.

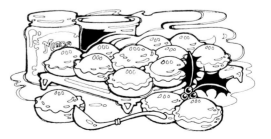

Fresh Fruit Tarts

Makes 6

Oven temp 220°C/425°F/Gas Mark 7

Freeze 1 month

1. Make the pastry cases with any type of short pastry, made with 175 g/6 oz/1½ cups flour. To make the cases, roll out the pastry fairly thickly, and cut out rounds which will fit lightly greased individual flan tins.
2. Bake at 220°C/425°F/Gas Mark 7 for about 10 minutes until lightly browned. Cool in the tins, then ease out the pastry cases.
3. Spoon a little thick coating custard (page 186) or confectioners' custard (page 240) into each cooled case. Cover with fresh stone or soft fruit, prepared as for fruit salad (page 195). Pile the fruit in the cases, sprinkle with sugar or honey and cap with whipped cream.
4. Alternatively, fill the cases only three-quarters full. Make a glaze by blending 10 ml/2 tsp arrowroot or cornflour (cornstarch) with 30 ml/2 tbls fruit juice or water taken from a measured 150 ml/¼ pt/ ⅔ cup, sweetened to suit the flavour of the fruit. Stir the blended arrowroot or cornflour into the remaining liquid and bring to the boil, stirring constantly. Boil for 2 minutes until the glaze thickens and clears. Tint with a few drops of food colouring if you wish.
5. Spoon a little glaze over the fruit in each case, and cool, then cap with whipped cream.
6. If fresh fruit is scarce or expensive, use fruit canned in natural or fruit juice. One 285 g/ 11½ oz can yields 175 g/6 oz fruit and 125 ml/4 fl oz/½ cup juice. This quantity will half-fill 4–6 pastry cases. For the glaze, blend the arrowroot or cornflour (cornstarch) with water and add to the juice from the can.

Vanilla Slices

Makes 16

Oven temp 230°C/450°F/Gas Mark 8

Freeze 4–6 months (unfilled, without icing)

	Metric	Imperial	American
Puff Pastry using 225 g/8 oz/2 cups flour (page 151)			
Vanilla-flavoured confectioners' custard (page 240)	275 ml	½ pt	1¼ cups
Vanilla-flavoured glacé icing as needed (page 237)			

1. Roll out the pastry thinly, to an oblong 20 cm/8 in long and 16 cm/6 in wide. Cut the oblong in half across, then cut into strips 10 cm/4 in long and 2 cm/¾ in wide.
2. Place the strips on a dampened baking sheet. Bake at the temperature above for 10–14 minutes until well risen and cooked through. Cool on a wire rack.
3. When cold, sandwich with the confectioners' custard. Ice the tops with glacé icing.

Note: Traditionally the pastry is rolled thickly, and split through the middle to make layers for the filling, but it is tricky to do.

Jam Puffs

For this recipes, use trimmings of Puff or Rough Puff Pastry (pages 150 and 151). The other ingredients are sieved jam, beaten egg white and caster sugar.

Oven temp 230°C/450°F/Gas Mark 8

Freeze 1 month

1. Gather the trimmings into a ball and roll out thinly. Cut into 10 cm/4 in rounds with a fluted cutter.
2. Place 2.5 ml/½ tsp jam in the centre of each round.
3. Dampen the edges of the pastry with beaten egg white or water. Pull the edges up together and form into a three-cornered shape; seal the edges of the flaps together in the centre. Twist the corners.
4. Brush with egg white and sprinkle with caster sugar.
5. Bake at temperature above for about 10 minutes until cooked through and browned. Cool on a wire rack.

Opposite: *A selection of Fresh Fruit Tarts make a tempting display. Small berries can be used whole but larger fruit should be quartered or sliced.*

Eclairs, Cream Buns and Profiteroles

Makes 10–12

Oven temp 190°C/375°F/Gas Mark 5

Freeze 3 months (baked, unfilled)

	Metric	Imperial	American
½ recipe quantity Choux pastry (page 154)			
Double (heavy) or whipping cream	150 ml	¼ pt	⅔ cup
Caster (superfine) and icing (confectioners') sugar mixed	10 ml	2 tsp	2 tsp
Vanilla essence			
Plain (semi-sweet dark) chocolate	50 g	2 oz	2 squares
Butter	15 g	½ oz	1 tbls
Water	20 ml	4 tsp	4 tsp
Icing (confectioners') sugar	25 g	1 oz	¼ cup

1. For éclairs use a forcing (pastry) bag fitted with a plain 2 cm/¾ in nozzle; pipe 10–12 lengths of choux pastry on a lightly greased baking sheet, spaced well apart.
2. Bake at the temperature above for about 35 minutes. The éclairs should be well risen, golden-brown and dry.
3. Place on a wire rack, and slit one side of each éclair to let steam escape. Soop out any uncooked filling with a teaspoon and leave to dry and cool. If at all damp, return on the baking sheet to a cool oven for a few minutes to dry the insides.
4. Whip the cream with mixed sugars and essence. Spoon into the cooled éclairs.
5. Melt the chocolate and butter with the water in a small pan over a low heat, stirring constantly. Sift the sugar into a bowl, and beat in the hot chocolate mixture until smooth. Cool, then spread on top of each éclair.
6. For large choux puffs (cream buns), make and bake the pastry as for éclairs but pipe it in 5 cm/2 in balls. Slit and remove uncooked filling as for éclairs. Fill with sweetened whipped cream, but top with sprinkled icing sugar instead of chocolate icing.

Notes:
1. Éclairs or puffs can be filled with plain or chocolate-flavoured confectioners' custard (page 240) instead of cream.
2. Small éclairs make good cocktail snacks if filled with thick cheese sauce (page 88) or can be used as sweet petits fours if filled with confectioners' custard and iced as above. Use a 1 cm/½ in nozzle or slightly smaller, and pipe in 3.5–5 cm/1½–2 in lengths. Bake at the temperature above for 20–25 minutes only.

Variation
Profiteroles (small puffs): Pipe pastry in 2.5 cm/1 in balls, making about 25 small puffs. Bake like small éclairs (note 2 above). Shortly before serving, fill the puffs with sweetened whipped cream, and pile them in a pyramid on a flat serving dish. Cover them with hot or cold Chocolate Sauce (page 187).

Little Orange Cheesecakes

Makes 18 tartlets

Oven temp 190°C/375°F/Gas Mark 5

Freeze 2 months

	Metric	Imperial	American
Frozen puff pastry, thawed	175 g	6 oz	6 oz
Boudoir biscuits (lady fingers)	3	3	3
Grated rind and juice of ½ large orange			
Butter, softened	75 g	3 oz	⅓ cup
Icing (confectioners') sugar to taste			
Pinch of ground cinnamon			
Lemon juice to taste			
Low fat soft cheese	50 g	2 oz	2 oz
Single (light) cream	45 ml	3 tbls	3 tbls
Egg, beaten	1	1	1

1. Roll out the pastry and use to line 18 shallow tartlet tins (pans). Chill.
2. Crush the biscuits to fine crumbs. Mix in the orange rind, then work in the butter, a little sugar and the spice.
3. Mix in the orange juice, and a little lemon juice to sharpen.
4. Sieve the cheese into a second bowl. Blend in the cream, then the beaten egg.
5. Beat the cheese mixture into the butter-orange mixture until smoothly blended.
6. Divide the mixture between the pastry cases. Bake at the temperature above for 20 minutes. Cool in the turned-off oven.

14
BATTERS, PANCAKES AND CRÊPES

RECIPE FOR BATTER

Basic Batter for Puddings

Makes 450 ml/¾ pt/2 cups

	Metric	Imperial	American
Plain (all-purpose) flour	100 g	4 oz	1 cup
Salt	1.5 ml	¼ tsp	¼ tsp
Egg	1	1	1
Milk or half milk and half water	275 ml	½ pt	1¼ cups

1. Sift together the flour and salt into a bowl.
2. Make a well in the centre and break in the egg. Mix with a wooden spoon, adding about half the liquid, a little at a time. Draw in the flour to make a smooth batter.
3. When all the flour has been incorporated, beat briskly until air bubbles rise.
4. Stir in the rest of the liquid.
5. Leave in a cool place for about 1 hour, to let the starch grains swell and burst. Use as required for puddings, pancakes, etc. (see pages 53, 169). For Coating Batters, see page 170.

RECIPES FOR BATTER DISHES

Batter Pudding (Yorkshire Pudding)

Serves 4

Oven temp 220°C/425°F/Gas Mark 7

Not suitable for freezing

	Metric	Imperial	American
Cooking fat or dripping	25 g	1 oz	2 tbls
Recipe quantity of Basic Batter (above)			

1. Heat the oven to the temperature above. Put the fat in an 18 x 27.5 cm/7 x 11 in baking tin (pan).
2. Heat the tin in the oven for 5 minutes or until very hot.
3. Pour in the batter quickly, and return to the oven for 30–35 minutes.
4. Cut in squares to serve.

Notes:
1. Although best known as Yorkshire Pudding, the traditional accompaniment to roast beef, batter pudding may be served with gravy or a meat sauce as a main savoury dish, or with golden (light corn) syrup or treacle as a sweet one.
2. *Yorkshire Pudding* can be baked in a single tin as above, or in individual deep bun or patty tins. For *individual Yorkshire Puddings*, put about 5 ml/1 tsp lard (shortening) into each tin, and place them in the oven heated to 220°C/425°F/Gas Mark 7 until very hot. Half-fill with batter and bake for at least 20 minutes. The batter will puff up above the tins like soufflés, and will be almost hollow inside. Do not underbake.

Variations
1. For a lighter pudding batter use more water than milk.
2. For a richer pudding batter, e.g. for Yorkshire Pudding, include a second egg.
3. Instead of milk or milk and water, add 15 ml/1 tbls cooking oil or cooled melted butter with the egg and use 275 ml/½ pt/1¼ cups mild beer as the liquid. Beat well. Use for savoury puddings.
4. Flavoured savoury batter pudding to eat without meat can be made by adding 50 g/2 oz/½ cup grated cheese or sautéed onion or mushrooms to the basic batter. Sprinkle extra grated cheese over a cheese batter pudding before baking.
5. *Savoury Herb Batter*: Add one medium chopped cooked onion, 5 ml/1 tsp chopped parsley, and a pinch each of mixed dried herbs and pepper to the basic batter.

Pancakes and Crêpes

Makes 8 × 13–15 cm/5–6 in pancakes (crêpes)

Freeze 6 months

1. Make a Basic Batter (page 167). Whisk briefly just before use and pour into a jug.
2. Heat just enough margarine or lard (shortening) in a 15 cm/6 in shallow frying pan (skillet) to film the bottom well. Heat until moderately hot.
3. Pour in enough batter to film the bottom of the pan. Tilt the pan quickly in all directions to run the batter over the whole surface, and rotate it to swirl the batter around the edge. The pancake should be paper-thin (see note).
4. Cook the pancake until the surface is dry and the underside is patched with brown. Run a palette knife under the pancake, and shake the pan to loosen it.
5. Do not try to toss the pancake unless you are expert. Turn it with the palette knife to brown the second side.
6. As soon as it is patched with brown, lay it flat on a plate, cover loosely with greaseproof (waxed) paper and keep warm.
7. Add a little more fat to the pan, and repeat the process until all the pancakes have been fried, stacking them on the plate as you make them. Then use as desired.

Notes:
1. Pancakes can be used in many ways, for both savoury and sweet dishes. Thicker pancakes are generally kept for savoury dishes, the thinner (more successful) ones for sweet dishes.
2. *Savoury pancakes* are generally rolled around a fairly solid mixture such as fish or chopped chicken in a cream sauce. They are laid side by side in a shallow dish, covered with a savoury cream sauce or grated cheese (or both) and reheated briefly. Alternatively, the pancakes can be stacked one on another with a savoury filling or two or three different fillings, spread between them. The stack is topped with sauce or cheese and can then either be browned under a moderate grill or heated in a moderate oven.
3. *Sweet pancakes* are most often sprinkled with sugar and lemon juice, rolled up and served with extra sugar and lemon wedges for squeezing. But they can also be rolled around a solid fruit or mincemeat filling, or confectioners' custard. Very thin pancakes (called crêpes) can also be served in a sauce as in Crêpes Suzette (opposite).

4. Pancakes are ideal standbys for freezing. Make a double recipe quantity of batter. Instead of keeping the completed pancakes warm on a plate, lay them in two piles on soft kitchen paper; place thin pancakes on one pile, thicker ones on the other. When cold, package in piles of six or eight pancakes, labelling each pile as either savoury (thick) pancakes or sweet (dessert) pancakes. Freeze until needed.

Crêpes Suzette

Makes 8 pancakes

Freeze 2 months (pancakes and filling separately)

	Metric	Imperial	American
Basic Batter (page 167)	275 ml	½ pt	1¼ cups
Melted butter, cooled	15 ml	1 tbls	1 tbls
Unsalted butter	100 g	4 oz	½ cup
Caster (superfine) sugar	50 g	2 oz	⅓ cup
Grated rind and juice of 1 orange			
Lemon juice	5 ml	1 tsp	1 tsp
Orange liqueur (optional)	10 ml	2 tsp	2 tsp
Brandy	50 ml	2 fl oz	¼ cup

1. Make the batter, and beat the melted butter into it. While it stands, make the orange butter.
2. Cream the unsalted butter and sugar. Beat in the orange rind, lemon juice, and liqueur if used. Add enough orange juice to make the butter soft and creamy.
3. Make 8 very thin pancakes with the batter (left). Spread the orange butter over them. Fold each pancake in half, then in half again, like handkerchiefs.
4. Heat 4 folded pancakes in the greased frying pan (skillet) over fairly high heat until the filling melts. Spoon it over the pancakes. Tip in half the brandy, tilt the pan, and ignite it.
5. Lift out the pancakes onto warmed plates and spoon the sauce over them. Serve at once.
6. Repeat the process to prepare the remaining 4 pancakes.

Pancakes can be used for a variety of sweet and savoury dishes. Pictured here are rolled pancakes with lemon and sugar and Crêpes Suzette.

Coating Batter

Makes 275 ml/½ pt/1½ cups

	Metric	Imperial	American
Plain (all-purpose) flour	100 g	4 oz	1 cup
Pinch of salt			
Egg	1	1	1
Milk or half milk and half water	150 ml	¼ pt	⅔ cup

1. Sift together the flour and salt into a bowl.
2. Add the egg and stir to make a smooth batter, adding the milk or milk and water gradually.
3. Beat well, and leave in a cool place for 1 hour. Use as required.
4. This is a fairly firm batter, suitable for fish fillets, fishcakes and meat slices.

Variation
For a quicker and cheaper batter, use 2.5 ml/½ tsp baking powder instead of an egg and mix with milk. Use at once.

Coating Batter with Egg White

Makes 275 ml/½ pt/1¼ cups (approx)

	Metric	Imperial	American
Plain (all-purpose) flour	100 g	4 oz	1 cup
Pinch of salt			
Cooking oil or melted butter	30 ml	2 tbls	2 tbls
Water	150 ml	¼ pt	⅔ cup
Egg whites	2	2	2

1. Sift together the flour and salt into a bowl. Add the oil or butter and some of the water, and mix to a batter. Add the remaining water and beat well. Use at once, or cover and chill. If chilled, whisk before use.
2. Just before using, whisk the egg whites fairly stiffly and fold into batter.
3. This makes a crisp light batter suitable for kromeskis, fruit fritters or small fish fillets.

Variation
For a thicker, rich batter, mix the egg yolks into the oil or fat. Use only 125 ml/4 fl oz/½ cup water.

Coating Batter with Yeast

Makes 450 ml/¾ pt/2 cups

	Metric	Imperial	American
Plain (all-purpose) flour	100 g	4 oz	1 cup
Pinch of salt			
Milk	150 ml	¼ pt	⅔ cup
Butter or margarine	25 g	1 oz	2 tbls
Dried yeast (active dry yeast)	5 ml	1 tsp	1 tsp
Caster (superfine) sugar	1.5 ml	¼ tsp	¼ tsp

1. Sift together the flour and salt into a mixing bowl, and warm slightly.
2. Warm the milk and fat until the fat melts. Cool to tepid.
3. Sprinkle the yeast and sugar on the milk, and stir in with a fork. Leave for 15 minutes.
4. Pour the yeast mixture into the flour, and whisk to make a thick batter. Leave for 15 minutes until well risen.
5. This makes a crisp batter suitable for coating fish or meat, or large pieces of vegetables such as cauliflower florets.

FRITTERS

Most fritters consist of small pieces of food coated with batter, or mixed with batter (if very small, such as sweetcorn kernels). Soufflé fritters just consist of spoonfuls of batter or choux pastry.

Almost always, fritters are fried in deep hot oil. Only a few fritters should be fried at a time so that the fat does not cool by having a lot of cold food added at once; cool fat soaks into the batter before it is sealed by the frying, and makes greasy fritters.

Coated foods such as fritters should not be fried in a frying basket because they will stick to it. They should be put straight into the hot fat, and removed with a slotted spoon when they rise to the surface and are browned all over. Raw foods are usually fried at a lower temperature than cooked foods because they must be cooked through, not just reheated.

Most foods in batter should be fried in oil heated to 175–180°C/340–350°F. The temperature can be measured by using a fat thermometer, or by dropping a bread cube into the hot oil; it will brown in 1 minute at 180°C/350°F. Thick raw pieces of fish, meat or poultry are fried at a slightly lower temperature, rissoles or kromeskies at a slightly higher one. Average frying times are:

Sliced raw vegetables and fruits	2–3 minutes
Parboiled vegetables, apple rings	3–4 minutes
Fish fillets or portions	3–5 minutes
Raw meat, poultry or game (cubes, slices or thin portions)	4–7 minutes
Cooked meat, poultry or game as above, also rissoles croquettes, kromeskies, etc. made with minced meat	2–4 minutes
Egg croquettes, bread-and-butter fritters	2–3 minutes

Safety Recommendations for Deep Fat Frying

1. Use a deep pan.
2. Never fill the pan more than one-third full with fat or oil.
3. Do not overload the pan by trying to fry too much food at one time. The pan should never be more than two-thirds full with food and fat or oil.
4. Dry uncoated food thoroughly on soft kitchen paper before frying, and lower food slowly into the hot fat or oil.
5. Keep the outside of the pan clean and free from streaks of fat or oil.

General Method

Prepare a batter thick enough to coat the back of a spoon. Heat enough fat or oil in a large heavy pan to cover the food. It must be hot enough to seal the batter coating at once, but not hot enough to burn it before the food is cooked through. Spear each piece of food in turn on a skewer and dip in the chosen batter; lift it and let any excess batter drip back into the jug or bowl. Drop the fritter into the hot fat. When it rises to the surface, turn it over if needed, to brown both sides. Lift out fritters with a slotted spoon when ready, and transfer to soft kitchen paper. Turn over to blot off all excess fat. Keep warm in a single layer until frying is completed. Bring fat or oil back to the correct frying temperature before frying each small batch of fritters.

Preparation – Vegetable Fritters

Raw vegetables: Prepare and quarter or slice the vegetables. Pat dry with soft paper.

Blanched, frozen or lightly cooked vegetables: Cool or thaw vegetables. Drain, then quarter or slice if needed. Dry thoroughly. Dust with seasoned flour if you wish before dipping in batter. See Cauliflower Fritters (right).

Chopped or small vegetables, e.g. garden peas: Prepare and dry well. Mix vegetables into Coating Batter with Egg White made with egg yolk and only 125 ml/4 fl oz/½ cup liquid.

Preparation – Fruit Fritters

Apples: Peel, core and cut into rings. Sprinkle with lemon juice, and with sugar if tart.

Bananas: Peel fruit. Cut in half across, then in half lengthways. Sprinkle with lemon juice or rum.

Oranges: Dip in boiling water, then peel and scrape off white skin. Divide into pieces of 2 or 3 segments each. Take out pips, breaking the skin as little as possible.

Pineapple: Drain slices or cubes of canned pineapple thoroughly.

Cauliflower Fritters

Serves 4

Not suitable for freezing

	Metric	Imperial	American
Medium cauliflower	1	1	1
Seasoned flour			
Oil for deep frying			
Recipe quantity Coating Batter with Egg White (left)			

1. Prepare the cauliflower, and cook whole (page 101) until almost soft. Drain well, and cool completely.
2. Divide the cauliflower into florets, and dip in seasoned flour. Shake off excess. Heat the oil.
3. Prepare the batter. Dip the florets in batter one by one. Fry a few at a time in the hot oil until golden-brown.
4. Remove with a slotted spoon, drain and mop dry with soft kitchen paper. Keep warm in one layer until all the florets are fried. Serve as soon as possible.

Sweet Soufflé Fritters or Beignets

Serves 4

Not suitable for freezing

Recipe quantity Choux
  Pastry (page 154)
Oil for deep frying
Icing (confectioners')
  sugar, sifted

1. Make the choux pastry. Heat the oil in a large deep saucepan.
2. Drop heaped teaspoonfuls of pastry into the hot fat, a few at a time. They swell, and rise to the surface in about 1 minute, puffed and golden. Turn over if not evenly browned and fry for another moment.
3. Remove to soft kitchen paper with a slotted spoon. Keep warm while frying remaining beignets.
4. Serve immediately, dusted with icing sugar.

Note: *Cheese beignets* are made by adding 50 g/2 oz/½ cup grated cheese to the pastry when making it. Sprinkle with Parmesan cheese when fried.

15
TRADITIONAL HOT PUDDINGS

MILK PUDDINGS

Baked Cereal Milk Pudding 1.

Serves 4

Oven temp 140°C/275°F/Gas Mark 1

Not suitable for freezing

	Metric	Imperial	American
Rice (white or brown), sago, tapioca, short-cut (elbow) macaroni (15 g/½ oz extra)	40 g	1½ oz	¼ cup
Milk	575 ml	1 pt	2½ cups
Sugar	25 g	1 oz	2 tbls
Pinch of salt			
Strip of lemon rind or ½ bay leaf (optional)			
Flaked butter (optional)	15 g	½ oz	1 tbls
Grated nutmeg			

1. Wash the cereal. Put in a well-greased 1 l/1¾ pt/4⅓ cup deep pie dish with the milk, sugar, salt and lemon rind or bay leaf if used. Leave to stand for 20 minutes. Remove the flavouring.
2. Stir round. Sprinkle with flaked butter if you wish, and with grated nutmeg.
3. Bake at the temperature above for at least 3 hours until the pudding is soft, creamy and browned on top.

Variation (with eggs)
Put the washed cereal in the top of a double boiler with the milk. Cook it gently until tender (about 1 hour). Cool slightly. Separate 1 egg. Stir the yolk, sugar and salt into the cooled pudding. Whisk the white, and fold in. Turn the pudding into the greased pie dish, sprinkle with butter and nutmeg, bake at 160°C/325°F/Gas Mark 3 for 45 minutes.

Opposite: *Bread and Butter Pudding (page 175) and Baked Rice Pudding.*

Baked Cereal Milk Pudding 2.

Serves 4

Oven temp 140°C/275°F/Gas Mark 1

Not suitable for freezing

	Metric	Imperial	American
Milk	575 ml	1 pt	2½ cups
Strip of lemon rind or ½ bay leaf (optional)			
Semolina, coarse oatmeal, burghal cornmeal, etc.	50 g	2 oz	⅓ cup
Pinch of salt			
Sugar	25 g	1 oz	2 tbls
Flaked butter (optional)	15 g	½ oz	1 tbls
Grated nutmeg			

1. Warm the milk in a saucepan. Soak the flavouring in it, if used, for 20 minutes. Remove it.
2. Sprinkle the cereal into the milk, stirring briskly.
3. Stirring constantly, bring to simmering point. Cook, still stirring, for 15–20 minutes until the grain is transparent. Stir in the salt and sugar.
4. Serve the pudding as it is, with stewed fruit or with jam or syrup and cream: or turn it into a well-greased 1 l/1¾ pt/4⅓ cup deep pie dish, sprinkle with butter if you wish and with nutmeg, and bake at the temperature above for 40–45 minutes.

Variation (with eggs)
Make the pudding as above but with only 40 g/1½ oz grain. Cool slightly before adding sugar, then whisk in the yolk of 1 egg after the sugar. Whisk the white, and fold in. Then bake as above.

Baked Finely Ground Cereal Pudding

Serves 4

Oven temp 140°C/275°F/Gas Mark 1

Not suitable for freezing

	Metric	Imperial	American
Cereal e.g. cornflour, (cornstarch) ground rice, arrowroot, etc.	40 g	1½ oz	1½ oz
Milk	575 ml	1 pt	2½ cups
Strip of lemon rind or ½ bay leaf (optional)			
Pinch of salt			
Sugar	25 g	1 oz	2 tbls

1. Blend the cereal to a paste with a little of the cold milk.
2. Warm the remaining milk and soak the flavouring in it, if used, for 20 minutes. Remove it.
3. Bring the milk to the boil with the salt, and stir gradually into the blended cereal without letting lumps form.
4. Return the mixture to the pan, and cook for a few minutes until thick, stirring constantly. Stir in the sugar.
5. Serve the pudding as it is, or turn it into a well-greased 1 l/1¾ pt/4⅓ cup deep pie dish, and bake at the temperature above for 40 minutes or until browned on top.

Variation (with eggs)
Make the pudding as above without salt, and cool slightly before adding sugar. Separate 1 or 2 eggs. Whisk the yolks into the pudding with the salt and sugar. Whisk the egg whites and fold in, then bake as above.

Egg Custard (for pouring)

Makes 575 ml/1 pt/2½ cups

Not suitable for freezing

	Metric	Imperial	American
Milk	575 ml	1 pt	2½ cups
Eggs	2–3	2–3	2–3
Caster (superfine) sugar (for sweet custards)	25 g	1 oz	2 tbls
Flavouring (optional)			

1. Warm the milk slightly.
2. Beat the eggs until liquid, with the sugar if used. Stir in the milk.

3. Strain the milk into a bowl placed over simmering water.
4. Stir with a wooden spoon over gentle heat for 15–25 minutes until the custard is as thick as thin single (light) cream. Stir well round the base of the bowl to prevent lumps forming. If the custard shows any signs of curdling, stand the bowl in cold water and beat briskly.
5. As soon as the custard thickens, turn it into a clean bowl or jug. Cool, covered with damp greaseproof (waxed) paper, foil or film to prevent a skin forming. For serving hot, stand the bowl or jug in hot water (but do not overheat).

Note: This custard with extra sugar can be used as the basis for Custard Ice Cream (page 199).

Variation
Egg Custard (for coating): Use 4 whole eggs (or 3 eggs and 2 yolks) for a richer, thicker, more velvety custard.

Baked Custard

Serves 4

Oven temp 160°C/325°F/Gas Mark 3

Not suitable for freezing

	Metric	Imperial	American
Milk	575 ml	1 pt	2½ cups
Eggs (see recipe)	2–3	2–3	2–3
Pinch of salt			
Sugar	25 g	1 oz	2 tbls
Flavouring, e.g. grated nutmeg, ground cinnamon, strip of or grated lemon rind, rum or rum essence			

1. Warm the milk to about 66°C/150°F. Infuse any solid flavouring, e.g. lemon rind, for 10–15 minutes. Remove it.
2. Beat the eggs until fully blended; use 2 eggs for a soft custard, 3 for a firmer one.
3. Stir the milk, salt and sugar into the beaten egg. Add any liquid flavouring (e.g. rum). Strain into a greased 700 ml/1¼ pt/3¼ cup deep pie dish. Sprinkle any grated or powdered flavouring (e.g. lemon rind or grated nutmeg) over the custard.
4. Bake at the temperature above for 1 hour or until the custard is set in the centre.

Note: The cooking time of a baked custard can be shortened slightly if the milk is heated before mixing it with the eggs, but it must be stirred in gradually to prevent curdling.

Cornflour Custard (pouring)

Makes 575 ml/1 pt/2½ cups

Not suitable for freezing

	Metric	Imperial	American
Cornflour (cornstarch)	10 ml	2 tsp	2 tsp
Milk	575 ml	1 pt	2½ cups
Sugar (optional)	25 g	1 oz	2 tbls
Eggs	2	2	2
Flavouring (optional)			

1. Blend the cornflour (cornstarch) to a cream with a little milk.
2. Heat the remaining milk until steaming. Pour it, stirring constantly, onto the cornflour.
3. Return the mixture to the saucepan, and bring to the boil over moderate heat, stirring all the time. Take care not to let lumps form on the base of the pan.
4. Take the pan off the heat, stir in the sugar if used, and allow to cool. While cooling, beat the eggs lightly.
5. Pour 2–3 spoonfuls of cornflour sauce onto the beaten eggs and stir in.
6. Pour the mixture into the pan of cornflour sauce, stir well and replace over low heat. Stir for 2–3 minutes until the eggs thicken the sauce.
7. Keep warm as for Egg Custard or serve cold as a pouring sauce.

Caramel Custard

Serves 4

Oven temp 160°C/325°F/Gas Mark 3

Not suitable for freezing

	Metric	Imperial	American
Caramel			
Sugar	100 g	4 oz	¼ lb
Water	175 ml	6 fl oz	¾ cup
Custard			
Milk	450 ml	¾ pt	2 cups
Eggs	3	3	3
Caster (superfine) sugar	25 g	1 oz	2 tbls
Vanilla essence			

1. Tie a strong paper band round a 15 cm/6 in round cake tin (pan) or charlotte mould, securing it firmly. Heat in the oven.
2. Heat the caramel ingredients gently in a saucepan until the sugar dissolves, stirring occasionally. Then boil without stirring until the syrup is light gold (no darker).

3. Pour the caramel into the hot dry tin or mould and swirl it round to coat evenly the base and sides of the container. The paper will protect your hands and prevent drips when you coat the edge of the container. Leave until the caramel is set, remove paper.
4. Warm the milk. Beat the eggs and pour in the warmed milk while beating. Add the sugar, and essence to taste.
5. Strain the custard into the prepared tin or mould. Cover it closely with greased foil or paper.
6. Either steam the custard over simmering water for 40–45 minutes until firm in the centre; or stand the container in a baking tin of hot water which comes halfway up its sides and bake at the temperature above for 1 hour.
7. Remove the container from the heat, and leave to stand for a moment or two. Invert a wetted plate on top and turn over both together. Lift off the container. The caramel will run off as a sauce surrounding the set custard.

Bread and Butter Pudding

Serves 4

Oven temp 150°C/300°F/Gas Mark 2

Not suitable for freezing

	Metric	Imperial	American
Butter for greasing and spreading			
Thin square slices of bread without crusts	100 g	4 oz	¼ lb
Sultanas or raisins	50 g	2 oz	⅓ cup
Grated nutmeg or ground cinnamon as needed			
Milk	425 ml	¾ pt	2 cups
Eggs	2	2	2
Granulated sugar	25 g	1 oz	2 tbls
Demerara (light brown) sugar for sprinkling			

1. Grease a 1 l/1¾ pt/4⅓ cup deep pie dish.
2. Spread the slices of bread with butter. Cut into triangles. Arrange in layers in the dish, buttered side up, sprinkling each layer with dried fruit and a little spice. Arrange the top layer of slices in an attractive pattern, and sprinkle with the last of the fruit.
3. Warm the milk slightly. Beat the eggs with the granulated sugar, and slowly stir in the warmed milk. Strain over the bread.
4. Sprinkle the top of the pudding with the Demerara sugar.
5. Bake at the temperature above for 1½ hours until set and lightly browned on top.

BAKED, STEAMED AND BOILED PUDDINGS

All these puddings have a starchy base such as flour or breadcrumbs, mixed with a raising agent such as baking powder and with butter, margarine or suet. Sugar is the most usual sweetening. The ingredient proportions of many puddings are very like those of cakes, and the fat used is incorporated in the same ways: by 'rubbing (cutting) in', 'creaming' or occasionally by melting (page 228). Suet crust pastry (page 152) is used for some boiled and steamed puddings, and breadcrumbs are often substituted for some of the flour to make a lighter pudding.

The pudding mixture is usually moistened with water or milk, and sometimes with beaten eggs.

General Cooking Method

The pie dish, pudding basin, charlotte mould or other container should always be prepared before the pudding mixture is made. It should be greased with clarified fat or oil inside, and a foil cover should also be prepared and greased if required. Some pudding mixtures can be cooked in small individual bowls, dariole moulds or ramekins (custard cups) if preferred.

A *baked pudding* is generally made in a deep pie dish or oven-to-table baking dish, which is placed on a flat baking sheet in the oven to make removing the pudding easier. A charlotte is baked in a charlotte mould (a flower-pot shape with almost vertical sides) or in a deep round casserole.

A *steamed pudding* is generally made in a deep pudding basin (heatproof mixing bowl) covered with a cloth secured with string or with greased foil pleated around the edge, to keep the pudding dry. There must be room under the covering for the pudding to swell. For the same reason, the basin should only be three-quarters filled. It can either be put in the perforated top part of a steamer over simmering water, or can stand on a trivet or thick cloth in a saucepan with gently boiling or simmering water which comes half-way up the basin's sides. In either case, the pan lid must fit tightly, and the pan must be kept topped up with boiling water throughout the cooking. Most puddings are left to 'rest' for a few minutes in the basin after cooking, and are then turned out for serving. A fruit pudding should be turned out into a shallow dish, not onto a plate, as juice may run out of it.

A pudding can also be steamed in the oven in a casserole or pot-roaster containing boiling water and closely covered with a lid. It will take about the same time as a pudding cooked on top of the cooker, although it may take slightly longer if cooked under another dish as part of an automatically controlled meal. If steamed alone in the oven, it should be placed in the centre at a temperature of 160°C/325°F/Gas Mark 3.

A *boiled pudding* can be cooked in a basin (bowl) as for a steamed pudding; it should fill the basin and be securely covered as the pudding will be immersed in boiling water. Otherwise, boil the pudding in a scalded, floured cloth or greased, doubled leakproof foil. Roly-poly puddings are cooked in this way; secure the ends of a cloth or foil so that there is space for the pudding to swell. Immerse the pudding in rapidly-boiling water, then reduce the heat to let it simmer until cooked through. Let the pudding remain covered for a few minutes after removing it from the water, then undo the covering and tip the pudding onto a serving dish. Serve with custard or a sweet sauce.

BAKED PUDDINGS

Baked Apples

Serves 6

Oven temp 200°C/400°F/Gas Mark 6

Not suitable for freezing

	Metric	Imperial	American
Large cooking (tart) apples	6	6	6
Brown sugar	50 g	2 oz	1/3 cup
Butter	50 g	2 oz	1/4 cup
Demerara (light brown) sugar			
Boiling water			

1. Wipe and core the apples.
2. Slit the skin of each apple all round, midway between the stem end and base. Place upright in a shallow ovenproof dish or baking tin (pan).
3. Mix the brown sugar and butter and spoon into the core holes. Sprinkle a little Demerara sugar on top of each apple.
4. Pour a little boiling water into the dish or tin. Bake at the temperature above until the apples are tender. The time will depend on the size and type of apples, but 50–60 minutes is the average.

Alternative fillings
1. Chopped dates mixed with golden syrup.
2. Marmalade or apricot jam.
3. Sultanas or raisins mixed with honey.

Note: To make Apple Snow, scrape the pulp out of the skins of the baked apples and beat until smooth. Whisk 2 egg whites stiffly, adding sugar to taste and fold into the apple pulp. Serve in individual glasses with cream or with 275 ml/$\frac{1}{2}$ pt/1$\frac{1}{4}$ cups cornflour custard (page 175).

Opposite: *Baked Apples filled with sultanas, butter and sugar.*

Apple Charlotte

Serves 6

Oven temp 180°C/350°F/Gas Mark 4

Freeze 2 months

	Metric	Imperial	American
Cooking (tart) apples	450 g	1 lb	1 lb
Grated rind and juice of 1 lemon			
Caster (superfine) sugar	100 g	4 oz	½ cup
Butter for greasing			
Butter, melted	75 g	3 oz	⅓ cup
Large thin slices of white bread	10	10	10
Caster (superfine) sugar for sprinkling			

1. Peel core and slice the apples. Simmer them with the lemon rind, lemon juice and sugar to a thick purée.
2. Grease thickly with butter a 1 l/1¾ pt/4⅓ cup charlotte mould or soufflé dish. Cut the crusts off the bread slices. Cut one slice into a round to fit the bottom of the mould or dish, and dip it in the melted butter. Put it in the dish, and put other small pieces of bread dipped in butter around it to cover the bottom.
3. Cut another round of bread to cover the top of the mould and keep it aside. Dip the remaining slices in butter and use to line the sides of the mould or dish closely. Turn in the cooled purée.
4. Cover the top of the dish with the reserved bread round and any bits needed to fill the gaps, all dipped in butter.
5. Cover the dish loosely with greased foil. Bake at the temperature above for 40 minutes.
6. Turn out and sprinkle with caster (superfine) sugar. The bread slices should be golden and slightly crisp. Serve with cream.

Note: The pudding can be made with slices of bread and butter instead of melted butter. Place the lining slices with the buttered side towards the mould, and the covering ones buttered side up.

Variation
Layer the apple mixture with the butter-dipped slices or bread and butter instead of lining the mould or dish. Begin and end with bread slices. Serve from the dish.

Baked Apple Dumplings

Serves 4

Oven temp 200°C/400°F/Gas Mark 6

Freeze 1 month

	Metric	Imperial	American
Plain (all-purpose) flour	275 g	10 oz	2½ cups
Pinch of salt			
Fat (half lard (shortening) and half butter or hard margarine)	150 g	5 oz	10 tbls
Sugar	5 ml	1 tsp	1 tsp
Cooking (tart) apples, peeled and cored	4	4	4
Light soft brown sugar			
Pinch of ground cinnamon			

1. Make shortcrust pastry (basic pie dough) with the flour, salt, fat and sugar (page 150).
2. Roll out the pastry and cut into 4 rounds, each large enough to cover an apple completely.
3. Place one apple in the centre of each pastry round. Fill the core holes with mixed sugar and cinnamon.
4. Dampen the edges of the pastry, and draw it up to cover each apple, pinching the edges at the top to seal.
5. Place the dumplings, sealed side down, on a greased baking sheet.
6. Bake in the centre of the oven at the temperature above for 40 minutes.

Note: The dumplings can be brushed lightly with milk and dredged with caster (superfine) sugar before baking if you wish.

Fruit Crumble

Serves 4

Oven temp 180°C/350°F/Gas Mark 4

Freeze 2 months

	Metric	Imperial	American
Prepared or drained stewed fruit (see note)	450 g	1 lb	1 lb
Light soft brown sugar if needed			
Ground cinnamon or ginger	1.5 ml	¼ tsp	¼ tsp
Butter or margarine	60 g	2½ oz	5 tbls

	Metric	Imperial	American
Plain (all-purpose) or self-raising flour	150 g	5 oz	1¼ cups
Baking powder (with plain flour)	1.5 ml	¼ tsp	¼ tsp
Caster (superfine) sugar	40 g	1½ oz	3 tbls
Pinch of salt			

1. Put the fruit into a greased 850 ml/1½ pt/3¾ cup deep pie dish. Sweeten with brown sugar if required. Sprinkle with cinnamon or ginger.
2. Rub (cut) the fat into the mixed flour and baking powder. Add the caster sugar and salt.
3. Spread the mixture over the fruit. Bake at the temperature above for 30 minutes or until the crumble is golden.

Note: Stewed cooking apples, damsons, gooseberries or rhubarb, or fresh prepared soft fruit are suitable.

Golden Pudding

Serves 4

Oven temp 180°C/350°F/Gas Mark 4

Freeze 4 months

	Metric	Imperial	American
Warm golden (light corn) syrup (see method)	45 ml	3 tbls	3 tbls
Water	30 ml	2 tbls	2 tbls
Butter or margarine	100 g	4 oz	½ cup
Caster (superfine) sugar	100 g	4 oz	½ cup
Eggs, beaten	2	2	2
Plain or self-raising flour	100 g	4 oz	1 cup
Pinch of salt			
Baking powder (with plain flour)	2.5 ml	½ tsp	½ tsp

1. Grease an 850 ml/1½ pt/3¾ cup ovenproof bowl or charlotte mould.
2. Warm the syrup in the oven before measuring. Mix with the water, and pour into the bowl. Cool.
3. Beat the fat and sugar together until creamy. Beat in the eggs, one at a time, and mix well.
4. Sift together the flour, salt and baking powder if used. Stir into the mixture.
5. Cover the syrup with the pudding mixture, gently but evenly, taking it to the edges of the basin. Bake at the temperature above for 45 minutes. Leave to stand for 5 minutes, then turn out onto a warmed serving dish. Serve with custard (page 175) or warmed golden syrup mixed with a little ginger syrup from a jar of preserved ginger.

STEAMED PUDDINGS (MADE WITH SUET)

Steamed Suet Pudding

Serves 6

Freeze 4 months

	Metric	Imperial	American
Plain (all-purpose) or self-raising flour	125 g	4 oz	1 cup
Baking powder (with plain flour)	5 ml	1 tsp	1 tsp
Pinch of salt			
Fresh white breadcrumbs	100 g	4 oz	2 cups
Shredded suet or home-prepared suet, finely chopped	100 g	4 oz	¾ cup
Caster (superfine) sugar	50 g	2 oz	¼ cup
Egg, beaten	1	1	1
Milk			

1. Mix all the dry ingredients in a bowl.
2. Mix in the egg and enough milk to make a mixture which drops easily from the spoon.
3. Turn into a greased 1 1/1¾ pt/4⅓ cup heat-proof pudding basin (mixing bowl). Cover securely with greased foil.
4. Steam as on page 176 for 2½ hours.
5. Leave for 10 minutes to firm up. Then turn out if you wish.

Variations
1. Add 50–175 g/2–6 oz/⅓–1 cup dried fruit such as raisins, chopped dates or figs, or a mixture. Use brown sugar.
2. Boil the pudding for 2 hours (or for 2½ hours if using 175 g/6 oz/1 cup dried fruit) instead of steaming it.
3. If making the pudding with figs, add 15 ml/1 tbls black treacle (dark molasses) and use 2.5 ml/½ tsp bicarbonate of soda (baking soda) instead of baking powder.
4. Use butter or margarine instead of suet for a lighter pudding.

Steamed Fresh Fruit Pudding

Serves 6

Freeze 4 months

	Metric	Imperial	American
Fresh fruit	450 g	1 lb	1 lb
Caster (superfine) sugar	50 g (approx)	2 oz (approx)	¼ cup (approx)
Recipe quantity Suet Crust Pastry (page 152)			

1. Prepare the fruit as on page 194. Mix with sugar to taste.
2. Grease an 850 ml/1½ pt/3¾ cup heatproof pudding basin (mixing bowl). Line it with about three-quarters of the pastry as described on page 152. Fill to the top with fruit, and moisten with 15 ml/1 tbls cold water. Dampen the top edge of the pastry.
3. Roll out the remaining pastry and cover the pudding with it, sealing the edges.
4. Cover the pudding with greased foil or paper, and steam for 2½ hours or slightly longer.
5. Serve from the basin (bowl), or leave at room temperature, then turn out into a shallow dish.

Notes:
1. Apples, blackberries, damsons, gooseberries, plums and rhubarb are all suitable on their own or as a mixture. Apples and blackberries are a popular 'mix'.
2. Vary the quantity of sugar to suit the sweetness of the fruit.

Variation

The pudding can also be baked. Sprinkle an 850 ml/1½ pt/3¾ cup deep pie dish with light soft brown sugar after greasing it, and before lining it with pastry. Fill and cover with pastry as above. Cover with greased foil or paper. Bake at 190°C/375°F/Gas Mark 5 for 1 hour.

Steamed Fresh Fruit Pudding filled with sliced apples and raisins.

Ginger Pudding

Ginger Pudding steamed in individual moulds.

Serves 4

Freeze 4 months

	Metric	Imperial	American
Plain (all-purpose) flour	225 g	8 oz	2 cups
Pinch of salt			
Ground ginger	5 ml	1 tsp	1 tsp
Shredded suet	75 g	3 oz	½ cup
Caster (superfine) sugar	50 g	2 oz	¼ cup
Golden (light corn) syrup, warmed	100 g	4 oz	⅓ cup
Egg, beaten	1	1	1
Bicarbonate of soda (baking soda)	1.5 ml	¼ tsp	¼ tsp
Milk, warmed	45 ml	3 tbls	3 tbls
Extra syrup	45 ml	3 tbls	3 tbls

1. Sift together the flour, salt and ginger. Mix in the suet and sugar.
2. Mix the warmed syrup and beaten egg, and use to bind the mixture.
3. Dissolve the soda in the milk and mix in. Add extra milk if needed to give a soft dropping consistency.
4. Grease a 1.1 1/2 pt/5 cup pudding basin (heat-proof mixing bowl) and add enough extra syrup to coat the bottom of the basin. Turn in the mixture. Cover securely.
5. Steam as on page 176 for 1¾–2 hours.
6. Leave to stand for 10 minutes, then turn out onto a warmed dessert plate.

Notes:
1. If you wish, put a little chopped preserved ginger in the bottom of the basin before turning in the mixture.
2. Steam the mixture in 4 small individual pudding basins for 1 hour if you prefer, or for 30 minutes in 8 dariole moulds.
3. *Spice Pudding:* Substitute ground mixed spice (ground allspice) and a small pinch of ground cinnamon for the ginger.

Christmas Pudding

Serves 8

Freeze 4 months

	Metric	Imperial	American
Plain (all-purpose) flour	50 g	2 oz	½ cup
Pinch of salt			
Fresh breadcrumbs	100 g	4 oz	2 cups
Mixed spice	10 ml	2 tsp	2 tsp
Shredded suet	100 g	4 oz	¾ cup
Soft brown sugar	175 g	6 oz	1 cup
Chopped mixed (candied) peel	50 g	2 oz	¼ cup
Sultanas (golden raisins)	175 g	6 oz	1 cup
Currants	175 g	6 oz	1 cup
Raisins	225 g	8 oz	1¼ cups
Chopped blanched almonds	50 g	2 oz	¼ cup
Grated lemon rind	5 ml	1 tsp	1 tsp
Grated orange rind	5 ml	1 tsp	1 tsp
Black treacle (molasses)	30 ml	2 tbls	2 tbls
Brandy	45 ml	3 tbls	3 tbls
Stout or orange juice	30 ml	2 tbls	2 tbls
Egg	1	1	1

1. Grease a 1.1 1/2 pt/5 cup pudding basin (heat-proof mixing bowl).
2. Sift the flour, salt and spices into a bowl. Add the remaining ingredients and mix well. Cover and leave to stand overnight.
3. Stir the mixture and put into the pudding basin. Cover securely with greased, greaseproof (waxed) paper and a pudding cloth.
4. Steam the pudding for 4 hours. Cover with clean coverings and store in a cool, dry place. Steam for a further 2 hours before serving with Rich Brandy Sauce (page 185) or Hard Sauce (Brandy Butter) (page 188).

STEAMED PUDDINGS (MADE WITH BUTTER OR MARGARINE)

Canary Pudding

Serves 4–6

Freeze 4 months (before or after steaming)

	Metric	Imperial	American
Butter or margarine, softened	100 g	4 oz	½ cup
Caster (superfine) sugar	100 g	4 oz	½ cup
Eggs	2	2	2
Grated lemon rind	10 ml	2 tsp	2 tsp
Plain (all-purpose) or self-raising flour	175 g	6 oz	1½ cups
Baking powder (with plain flour)	5 ml	1 tsp	1 tsp
Milk	30 ml	2 tbls	2 tbls

1. Grease an 850 ml/1½ pt/3¾ cup pudding basin (heatproof mixing bowl).
2. Beat together the fat and sugar until light. Beat in the eggs and lemon rind.
3. Sift together the flour and baking powder, and fold into the batter with the milk.
4. Turn into the basin. Cover with greased foil, pleating it round the rim to make it fit tightly, and leaving room on top for the pudding to swell. Secure with a rubber band if required.
5. Put a folded thick cloth or trivet in a large pan. Lower the pudding into the pan.
6. Pour into the pan enough boiling water to reach half-way up the sides of the basin. Cover the pan and steam for 1¼ hours, topping up the water if needed.
7. Remove from the water, and leave to stand in the basin for 5 minutes. Then unmould onto a warmed dish.
8. Serve with pouring custard (page 174) or a sweet sauce.

Note: This pudding can be oven-steamed if you prefer (see page 176).

Variations
1. *Steamed Chocolate Pudding*: Substitute 25 g/1 oz/ ¼ cup cocoa powder (unsweetened cocoa) for 25 g/1 oz/¼ cup of the flour.
2. *Gold Cap or Red Cap Pudding*: Before turning the pudding mixture into the basin, put in 30 ml/2 tbls golden (light corn) syrup or red jam. Serve the pudding with the same-flavoured sauce. For *Lemon Curd Pudding* or *Marmalade Pudding*, substitute 30 ml/2 tbls lemon curd or fine-cut jelly marmalade.
3. *Ginger Madeira Pudding*: Add 100 g/4 oz chopped stem (preserved) ginger with the flour.
4. *Sultana Sponge Pudding*: Use half the above quantities of all the ingredients and 50–75 g/2–3 oz/½ cup sultanas (golden raisins). Put a few sultanas in the bottom of the basin before putting in the mixture. Add the rest with the flour. Steam for the same time as Canary Pudding. Serves 3–4.

Note: Any other type of firm fruit or dried fruit, or a flavouring spice or essence can be used instead of sultanas.

Guards' Pudding

Serves 4–6

Freeze 4 months

	Metric	Imperial	American
Butter or margarine	100 g	4 oz	½ cup
Soft brown sugar	100 g	4 oz	⅔ cup
Sieved raspberry jam	45 ml	3 tbls	3 tbls
Beaten eggs	2	2	2
Pinch of salt			
Fresh brown (not wholemeal) breadcrumbs	175 g	6 oz	3 cups
Bicarbonate of soda (baking soda)	2.5 ml	½ tsp	½ tsp
Warm water	10 ml	2 tsp	2 tsp

1. Grease a 1.1 1/2 pt/5 cup pudding basin (heatproof mixing bowl).
2. Cream the fat and sugar. Beat in the jam.
3. Mix in the eggs. Sprinkle the salt on the breadcrumbs, and stir them into the mixture.
4. Dissolve the soda in the water, and mix in thoroughly.
5. Turn the pudding into the prepared basin. Cover securely and steam for 3 hours. Leave at room temperature for 5 minutes, then turn out. Serve with warm sieved raspberry jam.

SWEET SOUFFLÉS

Hot Sweet Soufflés
Follow the general method for hot savoury soufflés on page 142. Prepare a paper band (see below) if you will steam the soufflé. If you grease a dish or dishes for a sweet baked soufflé, dust with caster (superfine) sugar instead of dry crumbs.

Peel a paper band off a sweet steamed soufflé in the same way as for a cold soufflé. See page 190.

To Prepare a Paper Band for a Hot (or Cold) Soufflé

Cut a piece of doubled greaseproof (waxed) paper, non-stick baking parchment or uncreased foil, 7.5 cm/3 in taller than the dish and long enough to go all round it and overlap at the ends. Tie it round the dish with tape, both above and below the rim if there is one. If you wish, oil the inside of the dish and band. Some cooks say it helps the soufflé to rise and makes removing the band easier; others say it merely leaves unsightly traces of oil on the sides of the soufflé. (For Sweet Baked Soufflés see page 184).

Sweet Soufflé Omelet

Serves 1

Not suitable for freezing

	Metric	Imperial	American
Eggs, separated	2	2	2
Caster (superfine) sugar	15 g	½ oz	1 tbls
A few drops of vanilla essence			
Pinch of salt			
Butter	15 ml	1 tbls	1 tbls
Icing (confectioners') sugar			
Filling (see below)			

1. Beat together the egg yolks, sugar and vanilla. Heat an 18 cm/7 in omelet pan on top of the cooker, and heat the grill (broiler).
2. Add the salt to the egg whites and whisk stiffly. Fold into the yolk mixture.
3. Put the butter in the heated pan, and swirl it as it melts to coat the bottom.
4. Spread the omelet mixture gently in the pan to cover it. Cook until pale gold underneath. Loosen the omelet around the edge with a palette knife, and cut into it a few times with the end of the knife, but do not stir.
5. Place the omelet under the grill (broiler) for a few minutes to brown the top.
6. Slide the omelet onto sugared paper. Cover half with your chosen filling, then lift the paper to tip the uncovered half over it. Lift the omelet on the palette knife to a warmed plate and serve at once.

Fillings
1. *Jam*: Spread 30 ml/2 tbls warmed jam over the omelet.
2. *Lemon curd*: Spread 45 ml/3 tbls Lemon Curd mixed with 15 ml/1 tbls lemon juice over the omelet.
3. *Raspberry*: Spread 30 ml/2 tbls warmed raspberry purée or Melba Sauce (page 188) over the omelet.
4. *Strawberry*: Mash 6 ripe strawberries with icing (confectioners') sugar and Kirsch and spread over the omelet.
5. *Rum*: Add 15 ml/1 tbls rum to the egg yolks before making the omelet.
6. *Banana and Rum*: Mash a small banana with brown sugar until smooth and spread over a rum flavoured omelet.
7. *Chocolate*: Sprinkle omelet with grated plain chocolate before folding.

Hot Baked Soufflé

Hot Chocolate Soufflé.

Serves 4

Oven temp 190°C/375°F/Gas Mark 5

Not suitable for freezing

	Metric	Imperial	American
Butter	*75 g*	*3 oz*	*6 tbls*
Plain (all-purpose) flour	*50 g*	*2 oz*	*½ cup*
Milk	*450 ml*	*¾ pt*	*2 cups*
Flavouring (see variations)			
Large eggs, separated	*4*	*4*	*4*
Caster (superfine) sugar	*50 g*	*2 oz*	*¼ cup*

1. Prepare a suitable 1.1 1/2 pt/5 cup dish as described on page 183.
2. Melt the butter in a medium-sized saucepan. Stir in the flour, and blend well without colouring. Stir in the milk gradually, and continue stirring until it makes a thick smooth sauce. Take off the heat.
3. Cool the sauce slightly, then beat in any flavouring (see below). Beat the egg yolks until thick and pale, then beat them into the sauce thoroughly.
4. Whisk the egg whites lightly then whisk in the sugar gradually and whisk again until the whites hold soft peaks. Fold into the sauce.
5. Turn the soufflé mixture into the prepared dish. Stand it in a roasting tin (pan) half-filled with water. Bake at the temperature above for 45 minutes or until the soufflé is well risen with a slight crust on top. Serve immediately, with care (see page 142).

Variations
1. *Chocolate Soufflé:* Add 15 ml/1 tbls cocoa powder (unsweetened cocoa) and a pinch of cinnamon with the flour. Decorate with sieved icing (confectioners') sugar before serving.
2. *Coffee Soufflé:* Dissolve 30 ml/2 tbls instant coffee in the milk and add a few drops of vanilla essence.
3. *Fruit Soufflé:* Add 175 g/6 oz/¾ cup smooth fruit purée, e.g. apricot or sieved raspberry, to the completed sauce before adding the egg yolks.

16
SWEET SAUCES

HOT SWEET SAUCES

Rich Brandy Sauce

Makes 175 ml/6 fl oz/¾ cup (approx)

Not suitable for freezing

	Metric	Imperial	American
Cornflour			
(cornstarch)	*5 ml*	*1 tsp*	*1 tsp*
Milk	*150 ml*	*¼ pt*	*⅔ cup*
White sugar	*5 ml*	*1 tsp*	*1 tsp*
Egg yolk, beaten	*1*	*1*	*1*
Brandy	*50 ml*	*2 fl oz*	*¼ cup*

1. Mix the cornflour to a smooth cream with a little of the milk.
2. Bring the rest of the milk to the boil. Off the heat, stir the cornflour into the boiling milk.
3. Return to the heat and boil, stirring constantly, for 2 minutes. Stir in the sugar. Leave to cool slightly.
4. Whisk in the egg yolk and brandy. Return to low heat, and stir constantly WITHOUT BOILING until the sauce thickens. Serve hot.

Rich Brandy Sauce poured over Christmas Pudding.

Arrowroot Sauce

Makes 275 ml/½ pt/1¼ cups (approx)

Not suitable for freezing

	Metric	Imperial	American
Arrowroot	10 ml	2 tsp	2 tsp
Water or half water and half strained grapefruit, lemon or orange juice	275 ml	½ pt	1¼ cups
Thinly pared rind of ½ lemon or orange if using juice			
White sugar or clear honey	75–100 g	3–4 oz	⅓–½ cup
Flavouring if using water (see method)			

1. Mix the arrowroot to a smooth cream with a little of the water or diluted fruit juice.
2. Bring the rest of the liquid to the boil in a small saucepan, add the lemon or orange rind if used, and simmer for 5 minutes. Remove the rind, and stir in the sugar or honey. Bring back to the boil and simmer until the sweetening dissolves.
3. Pour the boiling liquid over the blended arrowroot. Return to the pan.
4. Cook gently, stirring constantly, until the arrowroot thickens. Add vanilla or other essence, or a little ground mixed spice or grated nutmeg if not using fruit juice. Serve hot.

Variations
1. For *Brandy Sauce* or *Rum Sauce*, use 15 ml/ 1 tbls brandy or rum as flavouring.
2. For *Butterscotch Sauce*, make the sauce with 5 ml/1 tsp arrowroot and 150 ml/¼ pt/⅔ cup water only. Use 100 g/4 oz/⅔ cup Demerara (light brown) sugar as sweetening, and add 15–25 g/½–1 oz/1–2 tbls butter with it. Use vanilla essence to flavour at the end.

Cornflour Sauce

Makes 275 ml/½ pt/1¼ cups (approx)

Not suitable for freezing

	Metric	Imperial	American
Cornflour (cornstarch)	20 ml	4 tsp	4 tsp
Milk	275 ml	½ pt	1¼ cups
White sugar	15–30 ml	1–2 tbls	1–2 tbls
Vanilla essence or other flavouring			

1. Mix the cornflour to a smooth cream with a little of the milk.
2. Bring the rest of the milk to the boil in a clean saucepan.
3. Pour the boiling milk over the cornflour. Return to the heat and simmer, still stirring, for 2–3 minutes until the sauce thickens. Stir in the sugar and flavouring. Serve hot.

Other flavourings
1. Add 10 ml/2 tsp ground ginger or 5 ml/1 tsp ground cinnamon or grated nutmeg to the cooked sauce.
2. For *Coffee Sauce*, add 10 ml/2 tsp instant coffee dissolved in 10 ml/2 tsp boiling water to the cooked sauce.
3. Add 15–30 ml/1–2 tbls brandy or rum to the cooked sauce. Serve as a hot alternative to Hard Sauce (page 188) with Christmas Pudding.

Variations
1. For *Rich Cornflour Sauce*, whisk 1 beaten egg yolk and 15 ml/1 tbls single (light) cream into the basic sauce. Reheat the sauce WITHOUT BOILING, stirring constantly.
2. For a quick, inexpensive *Custard Sauce*, make the sauce with 7 g/1½ tsp cornflour and 575 ml/1 pt/2½ cups milk. Do not flavour. Cool the sauce slightly, then whisk in 1 beaten egg, and reheat, stirring, WITHOUT BOILING, until the sauce thickens. (For Custard Sauce using eggs only, see below.)
3. For *Custard Powder Sauce*, make the sauce with 7 g/1½ tsp custard powder or as the maker's instructions direct, using only 10 ml/2 tsp sugar.

Custard Sauce made with Eggs

Makes 275 ml/½ pt/1¼ cups (approx)

Not suitable for freezing

	Metric	Imperial	American
Milk	275 ml	½ pt	1¼ cups
Egg	1	1	1
White sugar	15 g	½ oz	1 tbls
Flavouring (see method)			

1. Heat the milk but do not boil.
2. Whisk together the egg and sugar. Pour on the hot milk, stirring constantly. Pour into a bowl.
3. Rinse the pan, and strain the custard back into it.
4. Heat below the boil, stirring constantly, until the sauce thickens.
5. Add a few drops of flavouring essence, concentrated fruit juice or a liqueur. Serve at once.

Notes:
1. For a thicker sauce, use 2 eggs.
2. Custard Sauce can be served cold. Stir occasionally while cooling to prevent a skin forming.

Variation

Caramel Sauce: Dissolve 50 g/2 oz loaf sugar (sugar cubes) in 150 ml/¼ pt/⅔ cup water. Stir until it melts, then boil without stirring until it is golden-brown. Add 150 ml/¼ pt/⅔ cup cold water, and strain into 275 ml/½ pt/1¼ cups hot Custard Sauce. Serve hot.

Sweet White Sauce

Make Basic White Pouring Sauce as on page 84, using milk as the liquid and omitting pepper from the seasoning. Stir 5 ml/1 tsp caster (superfine) sugar into 275 ml/½ pt/1¼ cups sauce, and flavour to taste with essence or spice. Serve hot.

For *Melted Butter Sauce*, use 25 g/1 oz/2 tbls butter when making the sauce.

Chocolate Sauce (coating)

Makes 275 ml/½ pt/1¼ cups

Not suitable for freezing

	Metric	Imperial	American
Plain (semi-sweet dark) chocolate, grated	50 g	2 oz	2 squares
Water	45 ml	3 tbls	3 tbls
Cornflour (cornstarch)	10 ml	2 tsp	2 tsp
Caster (superfine) sugar	10 ml	2 tsp	2 tsp
Milk	150 ml	¼ pt	⅔ cup
Single (light) cream	60 ml	4 tbls	4 tbls
A few drops of vanilla essence			

1. Melt the chocolate in the water in a saucepan over gentle heat.
2. Blend the cornflour and sugar with a little of the milk, stir in the remaining milk, and pour into the chocolate and water. Stir to blend.
3. Continue stirring until the sauce comes to the boil and thickens. Remove from the heat and cool slightly.
4. Stir in the cream and vanilla. Use hot or cold over profiteroles, cold rice desserts, etc.

Notes:
1. A few drops of rum or brandy can be added to the sauce if you wish.
2. For a hot chocolate sauce to serve over ice cream, see page 199.

Chocolate Sauce (pouring)

Makes 275 ml/½ pt/1¼ cups

Freeze 1 month

	Metric	Imperial	American
Plain (semi-sweet dark) chocolate, grated	50 g	2 oz	2 squares
Caster (superfine) sugar	25 g	1 oz	2 tbls
Milk	275 ml	½ pt	1¼ cups
Cornflour (cornstarch)	15 ml	1 tbls	1 tbls
Vanilla essence			

1. Grate the chocolate and put in a saucepan with the sugar.
2. Mix 15 ml/1 tbls of the milk with the cornflour until blended. Add the rest to the saucepan.
3. Heat the milk, chocolate and sugar gently until the chocolate melts.
4. Stir in the cornflour, raise the heat and bring to the boil. Boil for 3 minutes, stirring constantly. Add the vanilla.
5. Strain into a warmed jug. Serve hot, or cover and cool, stirring occasionally, then freeze if you wish.

Hot Sabayon Sauce

Makes 225 ml/8 fl oz/1 cup (approx)

Not suitable for freezing

	Metric	Imperial	American
Egg yolks	2	2	2
White sugar	10 ml	2 tsp	2 tsp
Medium sweet sherry or Madeira	30 ml	2 tbls	2 tbls
Small piece of lemon rind			

1. Beat the egg yolks and sugar together in a heatproof bowl. Add the sherry or wine, and lemon rind.
2. Place the bowl over simmering water, and whisk steadily until the sauce is thick, creamy and frothy (about 10 minutes).
3. Take out the lemon rind. Serve at once.

Peach Melba (page 200) topped with Raspberry Sauce.

COLD SWEET SAUCES

Hard Sauce (Brandy Butter)

Makes 225–275 g/8–10 oz/1–1¼ cups

Freeze 6 months

	Metric	Imperial	American
Softened butter	*100 g*	*4 oz*	*½ cup*
Caster (superfine)			
sugar	*100 g*	*4 oz*	*½ cup*
Brandy	*15 ml*	*1 tbls*	*1 tbls*
Ground almonds	*50 g*	*2 oz*	*½ cup*

1. Beat the butter and sugar to a cream.
2. Gradually beat in the brandy and almonds. Beat vigorously until light and spongy. Chill before serving.

Variation

For *Rum Butter*, use soft brown sugar and rum instead of brandy; omit the almonds.

Raspberry (Melba) Sauce

Makes 125 ml/4 fl oz/½ cup (approx)

Freeze 3 months

	Metric	Imperial	American
Fresh hulled			
raspberries	*225 g*	*8 oz*	*½ lb*
Icing			
(confectioners')			
sugar	*45 ml*	*3 tbls*	*3 tbls*
White wine			
(optional)			

1. Place the raspberries in a nylon sieve placed over a heatproof bowl. Crush them with a wooden spoon. Add the sugar, and sieve into the bowl.
2. Place the bowl in a pan of simmering water, and stir for 2 minutes to dissolve the sugar.
3. Add a little wine if the sauce is too thick. It should just coat the back of the spoon. Chill before serving.
4. Serve over Peach Melba (page 200), meringues or creamed rice.

Variation

For *Strawberry Sauce*, substitute strawberries for raspberries.

17

COLD DESSERTS, MERINGUES AND ICES

Cold Soufflés

A cold soufflé, savoury or sweet, is nearly always set in a soufflé dish with a paper band round it, which is peeled off with a knife blade dipped in hot water. The sides of the soufflé above the dish are then decorated as a rule with golden toast crumbs or grated cheese (savoury soufflés) or with chopped nuts, cake or biscuit crumbs, or toasted coconut (sweet soufflés). The top of a savoury soufflé may be garnished with chopped parsley, that of a sweet soufflé may be decorated with whipped cream, crystallised fruits, or nuts.

To Make a Cold Soufflé – General Method

1. Prepare a soufflé dish with a paper band, and make a place for it in the refrigerator.

2. Soften the required quantity of gelatine (unfla- voured gelatin) by sprinkling it on cold water in a heatproof bowl. Stand the bowl in warm water and stir until the gelatine dissolves.

3. Whisk egg yolks, flavourings and sugar if used in a bowl placed over fairly hot water until the mixture thickens; drips from the raised whisk should leave a trail for a moment or two. Mix a little egg mixture into the dissolved gelatine, then whisk the gelatine into the main egg mixture. Chill until the mixture begins to set at the edges.

4. Whip the cream lightly. Whisk the egg whites until they hold soft peaks.

Cold Lemon Soufflé (page 190).

5. Fold the cream into the soufflé mixture. Then stir 1–2 spoonfuls of whisked egg white into the mixture, and fold in the rest.
6. Turn the mixture into the prepared dish and chill until set.
7. Undo any fastenings around the paper band. Peel it off by sliding a hot wet knife-blade down between the paper and soufflé, then sliding it round the soufflé. Stand the soufflé on a sheet of strong paper.
8. Press crumbs, nuts, coconut or other similar garnishings or decorations onto the sides of the soufflé, with the palms of your hands, letting any loose bits fall onto the paper. Garnish or decorate the top of the soufflé as you wish.

Cold Lemon Soufflé

Serves 4

	Metric	Imperial	American
Eggs, separated	3	3	3
Caster (superfine) sugar	100 g	4 oz	½ cup
Grated rind and juice of 2 lemons			
Gelatine (unflavored gelatin)	15 ml	1 tbls	1 tbls
Cold water	60 ml	4 tbls	4 tbls
Double (heavy) cream	150 ml	¼ pt	⅔ cup
Finely chopped nuts			
Whipped cream			

1. Prepare a 575 ml/1 pt/2½ cup soufflé dish with a paper band (page 183).
2. Put the egg yolks, sugar, lemon rind and juice in a heatproof bowl. Place the bowl over a pan of hot water on very low heat; the water must not touch the bowl or boil.
3. Whisk the egg yolk mixture for 10 minutes or until thick and pale. Take off the heat and whisk until cool.
4. Soften the gelatine in the cold water in a second heatproof bowl. Stand the bowl in hot water and stir the gelatine until dissolved.
5. Fold 30 ml/2 tbls of the custard into the dissolved gelatine. Whisk the gelatine mixture into the egg mixture. Chill until about to set.
6. While chilling, whip the cream lightly, and whisk the egg whites until they hold soft peaks.
7. Fold the whipped cream into the gelatine-egg mixture. Then fold in the whisked egg whites. Turn gently into the prepared dish, and chill until set.
8. Peel off the paper band as described above, and decorate with the chopped nuts and whipped cream.

Variations
1. *Chocolate Soufflé*: Whisk the egg yolks with only 75 g/3 oz/6 tbls sugar and with 30 ml/2 tbls water instead of lemon juice. Melt 75 g/3 oz/3 squares plain (semi-sweet dark) chocolate in a bowl over simmering water, and whisk it into the cooled egg yolk mixture before the gelatine. Decorate as the Lemon Soufflé.
2. *Coffee-Rum Soufflé*: Use 4 eggs. Whisk 30 ml/2 tbls strong black coffee, 30 ml/2 tbls rum and a few drops of vanilla essence into the egg yolk mixture when removed from the heat. Decorate the completed soufflé with grated chocolate on the sides and top.
3. *Orange Soufflé*: Whisk the egg yolks with 75 g/3 oz/6 tbls sugar only, and with the rind and juice of 2 oranges instead of lemons. Dissolve the gelatine in 30 ml/2 tbls orange juice and 15 ml/1 tbls water.

Chocolate Mousse

Serves 4

Not suitable for freezing

	Metric	Imperial	American
Plain (semi-sweet dark) chocolate	100 g	4 oz	4 squares
Water	60 ml	4 tbls	4 tbls
Gelatine (unflavored gelatin)	10 ml	2 tsp	2 tsp
Eggs, separated	3	3	3
Vanilla essence			
Double (heavy) cream	100 ml	4 fl oz	½ cup
Grated milk chocolate, to decorate			

1. Grate the chocolate into a large heatproof bowl. Add the water and sprinkle in the gelatine.
2. Stand the bowl over a pan of hot water. Heat gently until the chocolate has melted and the gelatine dissolved. Take off the heat, and stir until smooth.
3. Beat in the egg yolks and a few drops of vanilla.
4. Whip the cream lightly and fold into the chocolate-egg mixture.
5. Whisk the egg whites until they hold soft peaks. Fold into the mousse mixture.
6. Rinse a deep 700 ml/1¼ pt/3 cup dish with cold water. Turn in the mousse mixture and chill until set.
7. Decorate with coarsely grated milk chocolate and whipped cream.

Variation
If you wish, substitute strained orange juice for the water. Serve with crisp ginger biscuits.

MOULDED DESSERTS — JELLIES, CUSTARDS AND CREAMS

Most moulded desserts need gelatine (unflavored gelatin) to make them hold together. A jelly is basically just a liquid such as fruit juice, fruit purée or milk set with gelatine even if it has small solid bits suspended in it. Creams, too, are set with a little gelatine because their main ingredients are semi-liquid. They are made either with flavoured pure cream, a pouring egg custard (page 174) mixed with cream and flavouring (sometimes called a Bavarian cream), or with equal parts of custard, cream and fruit purée (called a fruit cream).

Moulding and unmoulding any of these is done the same way. Choose a china, glass or metal mould and rinse it out with cold water. A cold mould makes a smoother, better-shaped dessert. Pour in the mixture from a height or shake it slightly unless very delicate to fill every bit of a decorative mould. To unmould, have ready a basin of very hot water. Run a pointed knife tip round the edge of the dessert to loosen it from the mould, then dip the mould quickly in the hot water almost to the rim. Lift it out and invert a flat wetted dish or plate over the mould and turn over both together. Shake them gently to dislodge the dessert from the mould and make it drop onto the plate. Then lift off the mould. Repeat the dipping process if the dessert 'sticks'.

Fruit Cream

Serves 4

Not suitable for freezing

	Metric	Imperial	American
Fruit purée made from soft, stewed or canned fruit (see note)	225 ml	8 fl oz	1 cup
Milk	225 ml	8 fl oz	1 cup
Eggs	3	3	3
Egg yolk	1	1	1
Caster (superfine) sugar	20–50 g	1–2 oz	2–4 tbls
Lemon juice (optional)			
Gelatine (unflavored gelatin)	10 ml	2 tsp	2 tsp
Water	60 ml	4 tbls	4 tbls
Whipping cream	225 ml	8 fl oz	1 cup

1. Rinse an 850 ml/1½ pt/3¾ cup deep dessert bowl or mould. Sieve the purée if it contains any pips.
2. Make a custard as on page 186 with the milk, eggs, yolk and 25 g/1 oz/2 tbls sugar. Strain it into a large bowl. Cool.
3. Mix in the fruit purée. Add extra sugar and a little lemon juice if needed.

4. Soften the gelatine in the water, then dissolve it by warming the water slightly while stirring. Stir it thoroughly into the custard. Cool or chill until beginning to set. stirring occasionally.
5. Whip the cream lightly and fold it into the mixture. Turn into the bowl or mould, and chill until set (2–3 hours). Turn out onto a wetted dessert plate if you wish.

Note: Poach fresh fruit with very little sugar or use fruit canned in natural juice.

Traditional Trifle

Serves 6

Not suitable for freezing

	Metric	Imperial	American
Individual trifle sponge cakes, bought or homemade	6	6	6
Raspberry jam			
Apricot jam			
Macaroons (page 222)	6	6	6
Flaked (slivered) almonds	25 g	1 oz	¼ cup
Grated lemon rind	15 ml	1 tbls	1 tbls
Sweet sherry	100 ml	4 fl oz	½ cup
Hot Coating Custard (page 174)	275 ml	½ pt	1¼ cups
Double (heavy) cream	275 ml	½ pt	1¼ cups
Caster (superfine) sugar	25 g	1 oz	2 tbls
Glacé (candied) cherries and angelica to decorate			

1. Split the sponge cakes lengthways. Spread half the cut sides with raspberry jam and half with apricot jam. Crush the macaroons.
2. Cut the split sponge cakes in half across. Layer the pieces and the crushed macaroons in a deep glass bowl, sprinkling each layer with almonds and lemon rind. The layers should fill three-quarters of the bowl. Pour the sherry over them.
3. Pour the custard over the cake layers. Cover closely with dampened greaseproof (waxed) paper, clingfilm or foil and leave to cool.
4. Whip the cream until stiff, gradually adding the sugar while whipping. Spread it over the trifle, and decorate with glacé (candied) cherries and angelica.

Variation
For a special occasion top with ratafias and pipe cream around edge of dish.

Lemon Jelly

Serves 6–8

Not suitable for freezing

	Metric	Imperial	American
Thinly peeled rind and juice of 2 lemons			
Lemon juice (extra)	150 ml	¼ pt	⅔ cup
Water	1 l	1¾ pt	4½ cups
Gelatine (unflavored gelatin)	40 g	1½ oz	3 tbls
Caster (superfine) sugar	150–175 g	5–6 oz	⅔–¾ cup
Small stick of cinnamon or ½ bay leaf			
Whites and shells of 2 eggs			

1. Put the rind and juice in a large saucepan, add about 275 ml/½ pt/1¼ cups of the water and sprinkle in the gelatine little by little to prevent lumps forming. Leave to soak for 20 minutes.
2. Add the remaining water, the sugar and the cinnamon stick or bay leaf.
3. Whisk the egg whites fairly stiffly and crush the shells. Add to the pan.
4. Bring nearly to the boil over low heat, whisking constantly.
5. Remove the whisk and leave the pan on the heat for 2–3 minutes, without boiling. Take the pan off the heat and leave to stand for 10 minutes to settle. Under the crust of scum, which is used as a filter, the jelly should be clear. Do not disturb the crust.
6. Scald (see note) a jelly bag or folded muslin (cheesecloth) lining a round-bottomed metal strainer (see note). Place over a bowl.
7. Carefully slide or tip the crust into the hot bag or cloth. Pour the jelly through the crust and let it drip into the bowl. Pour into a scalded, wet 1.2 l/2¼ pt/5½ cup mould and leave to set.

Notes:
1. To scald the bag or cloth, pour boiling water through it. Use it while hot so that the jelly stays liquid. Scalding removes grease, so, for sparkling clear jelly, scald all the equipment you use, including the saucepan.
2. Lemon jelly is used as the basis or decoration of many other desserts, e.g. for lining a mould which will contain a 'set' cream filling.

Opposite: *Traditional Trifle (page 191) makes a special occasion dessert.*

Variations
1. *Cleared Orange Jelly*: Use 2 oranges instead of lemons, and 150 ml/¼ pt/⅔ cup orange or lemon juice. Omit the cinnamon or bay leaf.
2. *Wine Jelly*: Substitute about 175 ml/6 fl oz/¾ cup white or red wine, sherry or port for the same quantity of water. Omit cinnamon or bay leaf.

Bavarian Cream

Serves 4–6

Not suitable for freezing

	Metric	Imperial	American
Grated milk chocolate	50 g	2 oz	2 squares
Strong black coffee	100 ml	4 fl oz	½ cup
Milk	175 ml	6 fl oz	¾ cup
Egg yolks	4	4	4
Caster (superfine) sugar	50 g	2 oz	¼ cup
Gelatine (unflavored gelatin)	10 ml	2 tsp	2 tsp
Cold water	60 ml	4 tbls	4 tbls
Whipping cream, or half double (heavy) and half single (light) cream	275 ml	½ pt	1¼ cups
Whipped cream or finely grated plain (semi-sweet dark) chocolate			

1. Prepare and rinse an 850 ml/1½ pt/3¾ cup mould.
2. Melt the chocolate with the coffee in the milk. Only warm the milk gently.
3. Beat together the egg yolks and sugar until pale and fluffy. Slowly stir in the milk. Strain the mixture into a heatproof bowl over simmering water.
4. Stir gently until custard thickens; it must cook very slowly. Strain it into a large bowl; cool.
5. Sprinkle the gelatine on the water in a heatproof jug. Stand the jug in hot water, and stir until the gelatine dissolves. Stir in 1–2 spoonfuls of custard, then mix the diluted gelatine into the rest of the custard.
6. Leave in a cool place until setting at the edges. Stir occasionally to prevent a skin forming.
7. Whip the cream (or both creams) lightly. Fold into the custard thoroughly. Turn into the wetted mould, and leave to set. Unmould before serving.
8. Decorate with whipped cream or finely grated plain chocolate.

Note: 1 whole egg and 2 yolks can be used instead of 4 yolks.

Junket

Serves 4

Not suitable for freezing

	Metric	Imperial	American
Milk (not longlife, skimmed, sterilised or U.H.T. milk)	575 ml	1 pt	2½ cups
Caster (superfine) sugar	15 ml	1 tbls	1 tbls
Vanilla essence			
Liquid rennet (or unflavoured rennet tablet)	5 ml	1 tsp	1 tsp
Ground cinnamon (optional)			

1. Warm the milk to blood heat (37°C/98°F). Stir in the sugar and essence.
2. Stir in the crushed tablet or liquid rennet.
3. Pour at once, gently, into a single large dish or 4 individual dishes, standing in a warm place where they need not be moved.
4. Leave for at least 1 hour. Sprinkle with cinnamon if you wish.
5. Serve with cream, flavoured with rum or brandy (if liked).

Variations
1. *Chocolate junket*: Grate 25 g/1 oz/1 square plain chocolate into the milk before warming it, and dissolve it in the milk. Sprinkle the completed junket with grated chocolate instead of ground cinnamon.
2. *Coffee junket*: Blend 5–10 ml/1–2 tsp instant coffee with a little of the milk before warming it. Sprinkle the completed junket with crushed flaked (slivered) almonds instead of ground cinnamon.

COLD FRUIT DESSERTS

To Prepare Fresh Fruit (for Fruit Salad and other dishes)

Apples: Quarter and core. Peel if skins are tough or blemished. Cube or slice. Dip in lemon juice or put into fruit syrup at once (see right).

Apricots, nectarines, peaches: Peel, halve and stone. Cut in pieces. Put in syrup at once.

Bananas: Peel, slice and dip in lemon juice or put in syrup at once. Only peel shortly before use, to prevent browning.

Cherries: Remove stalks, wash and stone. Halve if you wish.

Grapes: Wash, halve and remove pips.

Kiwi Fruit: Peel and slice.

Lychees: Peel, halve and stone.

Mangoes: Peel, slice and stone.

Melon: Halve, scrape out seeds and fibres, cut flesh into cubes or balls.

Oranges, grapefruit, tangerines etc.: Dip in boiling water for 2 minutes. Drain and peel, removing all pith. Cut into segments without the skins which enclose them. Discard pips and centre pith.

Pears: Peel, halve, core, then cube or slice. Dip in lemon juice or put into fruit syrup at once.

Pineapple: Peel and remove 'eyes'. Quarter lengthways and remove hard core. Cut flesh into small pieces.

Soft fruits: Hull, clean, and add to syrup shortly before serving.

Fruit Syrup

To 575 ml/1 pt/2½ cups water or fruit juice, add 75 g/3 oz/6 tbls sugar and the juice of 1 or more lemons. Also add, if you wish, some sweet liqueur or whole spices, e.g. a piece of cinnamon stick or a few whole cloves. Heat gently in a saucepan until the sugar dissolves, then boil until the syrup is reduced by one third. Strain and use at once, or cool before use.

STEWED FRUIT

To Prepare Fruit

Apples and pears: Peel, removing any bruised parts, and core. Leave whole if small, quarter if large.

Gooseberries: Top and tail, removing a scrap of skin to let syrup seep in.

Peaches and apricots: Peel, halve or quarter and remove stones.

Plums and other stone fruits: Wash, remove stalks. Halve and remove stones if you wish.

Rhubarb: String or skin old garden rhubarb. Wipe young or forced rhubarb. Cut off root ends and any leaf. Cut into short lengths.

Soft fruits and currants: Hull or remove strings and stalks. Clean.

Dried fruits: Wash well in tepid water to remove grit, sand etc.

To Cook Whole Fruits

Make a syrup with sugar or other sweetening and water or other liquid, with added flavouring if you wish. The quantity of sugar will depend on the sweetness of the fruit, but on average allow 100 g/4 oz/½ cup per 450 g/1 lb fruit. For most fruits use 275 ml/½ pt/1¼ cups liquid per 450 g/1 lb fruit, but juicy fruits, e.g. soft fruits, only need 150 ml/¼ pt/⅔ cup liquid, and hard cooking pears, which need long cooking, need at least 575 ml/1 pt/2½ cups. To make the syrup, bring the ingredients to the boil, and simmer for 5 minutes. Skim and use as below.

To stew the fruit, cook it in a covered saucepan over low heat, or in a covered casserole in the oven at 160°C/325°F/Gas Mark 3, until the fruit is soft but not broken. The second method takes longer but the fruit keeps its shape better. Lift out the fruit with a slotted spoon, put it in a dessert bowl or dish, and reduce the syrup by boiling. Pour the syrup over the fruit. Serve hot or cold.

Soft fruits or currants should simply be put into very hot reduced syrup and left to stand. Gooseberries should be cooked just until the skins crack.

An alternative stewing method for harder fruit is to put it in a casserole with sweetening and only a little liquid and to cook it at 180°C/350°F/Gas Mark 4 until tender.

To Cook Fruit to Purée

Put the prepared fruit in a saucepan with sweetening and only enough water to prevent burning. Add any flavouring, e.g. grated lemon rind, vanilla essence, whole or ground spices or chopped herbs. Cook in the covered pan until the fruit is very soft and pulpy. Beat until smooth, or process in a food processor or blender. Sieve any fruit with pips, e.g. raspberries or tomatoes, if you want a very smooth purée.

To Cook Dried Fruit

Wash thoroughly, then put in a large bowl with 850 ml/1½ pt/3¾ cups water per 450 g/1 lb fruit. Soak for 12–24 hours. Drain over a bowl. Weigh the fruit. Put it in a saucepan with 275 ml/½ pt/1¼ cups of the soaking liquid per 450 g/1 lb soaked fruit. Add at least 15 g/½ oz/1 tbls sugar for each 275 ml/½ pt/1¼ cups liquid. (Firm fruits, e.g. apple rings, may need 4–5 times as much.) Cover the pan, and simmer until the fruit is tender.

If you prefer, soak the fruit for 1 hour only in boiling water.

As an alternative to saucepan cooking, put the fruit, sugar and liquid in a casserole, cover, and oven-cook at 160°C/325°F/Gas Mark 3.

Notes:
1. Granulated sugar is the cheapest sweetening. Brown sugar is pleasant if you like the slightly different flavour. It darkens the fruit a little. Honey or golden (light corn) syrup can be used, but have the same effect as brown sugar.
2. To serve bottled fruit hot, drain off the juice into a saucepan, add extra sugar if needed and bring to the boil. Put the fruit in an ovenproof dish, pour the boiling syrup over the fruit, and put into a warm oven for a few minutes before serving. This prevents the skins toughening.

To Use Spare Syrup from Stewed or Bottled Fruit

1. Substitute syrup for water in making jellies;
2. Soak sponge cakes in syrup when making trifle (page 191);
3. Add syrup to the mixture for ice cream;
4. Add to fresh fruit salad;
5. Boil down until syrupy to use as a sauce, e.g. for ice cream;
6. Add lemon juice, and mix with soda water, lemonade or milk as the basis of a fruit drink or milk shake.

Fruit Salad

Not suitable for freezing

Use fresh, bottled, canned, frozen or dried fruit, or a mixture, with fruit syrup and any spice or liqueur flavouring.

Prepare fresh fruit (page 194) and put into syrup.

Drain canned fruit: if canned in natural juice, use it to make the syrup; if canned in syrup, dilute and flavour it instead of making syrup.

Soak dried fruit as for stewed dried fruit (left). Add to other fruits in the syrup.

Note: Avoid fruits that may discolour the syrup, e.g. canned raspberries

Fruit Salad Basket

Use a melon or pineapple for the 'basket' and a choice of brightly coloured fruits as above. Put the fruit into cooled syrup.

Cut a thick slice off one end of a melon or the top of a pineapple. Make sure a melon will stand level on the uncut end by paring off a thin slice. Scoop out the seeds, Cut the centre core out of pineapple without piercing the bottom. Remove the inner flesh of either fruit, leaving a firm shell. Cut up the flesh and add to the syrup.

Drain the fruit from the syrup, and put into the 'basket', putting brightly coloured fruits, e.g. cherries, tangerine segments, on top. Place the 'basket' on a dessert plate and surround with extra fruit.

Variation
If you prefer, cut the melon or pineapple in half lengthways, and serve as a 'boat' instead of a 'basket'. Prepare in the same way.

Fruit Fool

Serves 4

Freeze 1 month (made with cream)

	Metric	Imperial	American
Unsweetened stewed fruit (page 194) or raw soft fruit	450 g	1 lb	1 lb
Caster (superfine) sugar to taste (depending on sweetness of fruit)	100 g (approx)	4 oz (approx)	½ cup (approx)
Food colouring (optional)			
Whipping cream or half double (heavy) cream and half cold Coating Custard (page 174)	200–225 ml	7–8 fl oz	1 cup (approx)

1. Sieve the fruit into a bowl. Add the sugar and whisk until blended in.
2. If the fruit is pale, whisk in a few drops of food colouring. Remember that the colour will be paler when the cream has been added.
3. Whip the cream lightly. Whip it more stiffly if using half cream and half custard. Fold cream and custard together.
4. Fold the cream or cream mixture into the puréed fruit. For a more interesting appearance, leave a few streaks of cream unblended in the fool mixture.
5. Spoon the fool into four individual dessert glasses. Chill. Serve with thin sweet biscuits.

Summer Pudding

Serves 6

Freeze 2 months

	Metric	Imperial	American
Mixed rich-coloured soft fruit, e.g. black- and redcurrants, blackberries, raspberries, damsons	900 g	2 lb	2 lb
Sugar	100–175 g	4–6 oz	½–¾ cup
Large slices of white bread, 5 mm/¼ in thick	10	10	10

1. Prepare the fruit as on page 194. Put it in a bowl with the sugar overnight.
2. Turn the fruit and sugar into a saucepan, and simmer for 3–4 minutes. Keep aside.
3. Cut the crusts off the bread. Cut a round of bread to fit the bottom of a 1.1 1/2 pt/5 cup pudding basin or deep bowl. Use the remaining bread to line the basin completely; use bits of bread to fill any gaps. Keep enough bread to cover the top of the basin.
4. Fill the bread case with the fruit. Cover with bread.
5. Put a plate on the pudding which just fits inside the basin rim. Put a weight on top and leave for 12–24 hours.
6. Turn out onto a dessert plate. Serve with pouring custard (page 174).

Note: This recipe can also be made in six individual bowls, holding 175 ml/6 fl oz/¾ cup each. Use 12 slices of bread.

Variation
Use canned fruit in natural juice when soft fruit is out of season. Use one 300 g/11 oz can each of blackberries, blackcurrants and raspberries. Mix the fruit and leave to stand for 1 hour, then strain off the juice. Make as above in individual bowls, omitting the sugar. Stack the bowls one on another with a 225 g/8 oz/½ lb weight on top.

Strawberry Shortcake

Serves 4–6

Oven temp 190°C/375°F/Gas Mark 5

Freeze 3 months (without filling)

	Metric	Imperial	American
Self-raising flour	225 g	8 oz	2 cups
Baking powder	5 ml	1 tsp	1 tsp
Pinch of salt			
Butter or margarine	75 g	3 oz	6 tbls
Caster (superfine) sugar	50 g	2 oz	¼ cup
Small eggs, beaten (see note)	2	2	2
Filling			
Fresh strawberries	175 g	6 oz	6 oz
Caster (superfine) sugar	30 ml	2 tbls	2 tbls
Double (heavy) cream	150 ml	¼ pt	⅔ cup

1. Grease two 18 cm/7 in sandwich cake tins (layer cake pans).
2. Mix and sift together the flour, baking powder and salt. Rub (cut) in fat until the mixture is like breadcrumbs. Stir in sugar.
3. Mix in the beaten eggs little by little to make a 'short' dough. Knead it lightly until it can be rolled.

4. Divide the dough in half. Roll or pat out each portion evenly into an 18 cm/7 in round. Put one round in each tin. Press lightly so that the edges fit the sides of the tin.
5. Bake at the temperature above for 15 minutes. Cool on a wire rack.
6. While cooling, hull and rinse the strawberries. Pat dry. Keep 6 for decoration and slice the rest, sprinkling them with 15 ml/1 tbls sugar.
7. Whip the cream stiffly with the remaining sugar. Mix two-thirds of the cream with the sliced fruit.
8. When the shortcake layers are cold, spread one with the cream and sliced fruit mixture. Cover with the second layer and decorate with the remaining cream and reserved strawberries.

Note: You can use 1 large egg and 1 yolk instead of 2 small eggs. Add the unused egg white to the cream and whip together.

Variations
1. For a lighter shortcake, use an 18 cm/7 in sponge cake split horizontally or 2 sponge cake layers (page 231). Cover with extra whipped cream to make a Strawberry Gâteau.
2. Other fruits, e.g. sliced apricots or crushed well-drained pineapple, can be used instead of strawberries.

MERINGUE DESSERTS

Meringue for Shells or Cases

Makes 12 shells, 24 petits fours (baby shells) or 1 × 20 cm/8 in round case

Oven temp 100–110°C/200–225°F/Gas Mark ¼

Not suitable for freezing

	Metric	Imperial	American
Egg whites	*4*	*4*	*4*
Pinch of salt			
Pinch of cream of tartar			
Caster (superfine) sugar	*250 g*	*9 oz*	*9 oz*

1. Thoroughly rinse and dry a large bowl and a whisk.
2. Place the egg whites in the bowl. Add the salt and cream of tartar.
3. Whisk the egg whites very stiffly, until they remain in the bowl if it is inverted for a moment. They should stand in dry peaks.
4. Whisk in 15 ml/1 tbls sugar until the mixture is as stiff as before. Repeat, whisking in 15 ml/1 tbls sugar at a time until 100 g/4 oz/½ cup has been added. Put 25 g/1 oz/2 tbls of the remaining sugar aside.
5. Sprinkle the remaining sugar over the surface of the meringue and fold in very lightly with a metal spoon.
6. Place a doubled sheet of greaseproof (waxed) paper or non-stick baking parchment on a baking sheet. For a meringue case, draw a 20 cm/8 in circle on the paper. Oil the paper lightly.
7. Shape meringue shells with 2 dessertspoons or place the meringue in a forcing (pastry) bag fitted with a plain or star nozzle and pipe in the shapes and sizes you want. For a case, spread a layer of meringue over the circle on the sheet, then pipe a border of close-set rosettes around its edge to make the sides of the case. Dust the shells or case with some or all of the reserved sugar.
8. Bake at the temperature above until dry. Do not let the meringue colour. When shells are dry on top, turn them gently on their sides with a knife-blade to dry underneath. Press in the centres of large meringues underneath, then finish drying.
9. Cool on a wire rack. Store unfilled in an airtight tin for up to two weeks.

Fillings for meringue shells or cases
Sweetened vanilla-flavoured whipped cream (Chantilly Cream) is the most usual filling for meringue shells, but you can use other flavourings or fillings to suit the flavour of the meringue (see Variation 2 below). For instance, you could flavour whipped cream with a sweet liqueur, or use Confectioners' Custard (page 240) or a Butter Icing (page 238).
To make Chantilly Cream for the quantity of meringue above, use 150 ml/¼ pt/⅔ cup double (heavy) or whipping cream with 5 ml/1 tsp caster (superfine) sugar and 1–2 drops vanilla essence. Whip the cream lightly with the sugar and essence until it holds its shape when the beater is lifted. Sandwich meringue shells together in pairs with the cream.
Meringue cases usually have fruit mixed with the cream filling.

Variations
1. *Cooked meringue:* Use the same ingredients and general method as above, but whisk the egg whites and sugar in a bowl over simmering water until very thick. The meringues will be easier to shape, and will store longer. Use cooked meringue for cases.
2. Flavour the meringue with a little lemon juice or with almond or other essence instead of vanilla if you wish. Coffee essence or a liqueur are other choices. Cooked meringue can also have chopped or ground nuts folded into it.
3. Baby meringues can be used singly without filling to decorate desserts or small cakes instead of cream rosettes. They can also be included in a petit four selection.

Meringue for Topping Pies, Flans etc.

Make like meringue previous page, but with only 25–40 g/1–1½ oz/2–3 tbls sugar for each egg white. Whisk the whites stiffly, then fold in all the sugar. Spread over a baked pie or flan a few minutes before the end of the cooking time, sealing it to the edges. Flick up the meringue in small peaks. Return to the oven to finish baking at the temperature given in the recipe concerned.

Meringue topping made with 4 egg whites will cover a 20–22 cm/8–9 in pie or flan.

Pavlova

Serves 4

Oven temp 140°C/275°F/Gas Mark 1

Not suitable for freezing

	Metric	Imperial	American
Egg whites	3	3	3
Pinch of salt			
Caster (superfine)			
sugar	150 g	5 oz	⅔ cup
Cornflour			
(cornstarch)	15 ml	1 tbls	1 tbls
White vinegar	5 ml	1 tsp	1 tsp
Double (heavy)			
cream	150 ml	¼ pt	⅔ cup
Prepared fruit (page			
194) as below	350 g	12 oz	¾ lb

1. Draw one 18 cm/7 in and one 12.5 cm/5 in circle on non-stick baking parchment. Lay the paper on a baking sheet.
2. Put the egg whites and salt in a rinsed, dry bowl. Whisk until stiff and dry.
3. Whisk in 85 g/3½ oz/7 tbls sugar, a little at a time, whisking the whites until stiff each time.
4. Mix the remaining sugar and cornflour. Fold into the meringue with the vinegar.
5. Spread a layer of meringue 5 mm/¼ in thick on each circle. Put the remaining meringue in a forcing (pastry) bag with a 7 mm/⅓ in star nozzle, and pipe swirls around the edge of each circle, making 2 cases.
6. Bake at the temperature above for 1 hour or until the pavlova cases are dry to touch. Cool in the turned-off oven with the door closed.
7. Shortly before serving, whip the cream fairly stiffly. Slice about two-thirds of the fruit. Place the larger pavlova case on a serving dish and fill three-quarters full with a layer of cream. Put the sliced fruit in an even layer on top. Cover with the smaller pavlova case, and decorate it with whole fruits and any cream not used.

Suggested fruit combinations:
1. Sliced kiwi fruits, strawberries and pineapple bits (fresh or canned).
2. Sliced apricots and black grapes.
3. Sliced bananas and maraschino cherries.
4. Sliced canned guava halves and blackcurrants in fruit juice.

Note: This pavlova should be used on the day it is made or not more than 24 hours afterwards.

ICE CREAMS

Ice cream is easy to make in a home freezer or the ice-making compartment of a refrigerator. Set the dial to 'fast freeze' or to the coldest setting 1 hour before use. If possible, freeze the mixture (except for water ices) in a container in which it can be beaten once or twice during freezing, to break down any ice crystals; it should have a lid or be easily sealed with foil. If necessary, turn the mixture into a chilled bowl for beating. After beating, the mixture can be put in a serving dish or mould or in a storage container, covered and frozen until firm; then the dial should be returned to its normal setting.

If you use an electric ice cream maker or churn freezer follow the manufacturer's instructions.

The main types of ice cream are water ices, made from a fruit or flavoured sugar syrup, sorbets which are water ices with added whisked egg whites or gelatine, real cream ices made with pure cream, and custard ice creams which are the commonest type. They can be simple or very rich indeed, depending on how many eggs are used in the custard and how much cream is added; as a rule, 2 parts of custard are used to 1 part cream. Mousses are iced cream or custard mixtures made with whisked egg whites to lighten them.

Ice cream desserts include *bombes*, made in a bowl-shaped mould, lined with a cream or custard ice mixture and filled with a differently-flavoured mousse mixture; *cassata* which has diced crystallised fruits, nuts or biscuits mixed into the centre of the bombe; coupes and sundaes which consist of fruit, nuts, chocolate or biscuit crumbs mixed with ice cream, and topped with whipped cream and a sweet sauce. Vanilla ice cream is the most popular flavour for making assembled ice cream desserts, milk shakes etc. and therefore the most convenient to make for storage.

Ingredients

Use *double (heavy) cream* if possible or combine single cream with a really rich custard. *Caster (superfine) or icing (confectioners') sugar* is generally used for ice creams, often as sugar syrup. Use with care; too much sugar makes gritty ice cream, and too little makes hard tasteless ice cream. Add extra when beating if required. *Fruit purées* (which should be smooth without pips) should be sweetened as their flavour requires, and any solid bits of fruit should stay soft when frozen; stem (preserved) ginger, washed glacé (candied) cherries and shaved chocolate all freeze well.

You can serve any ice cream with a hot or cold sweet sauce which complements its own flavour; use a fruit sauce with fruit-flavoured ice cream, Chocolate Sauce (below) or Butterscotch Sauce with most other types of ice cream.

Fruit-Flavoured Cream Ice

Makes 575 ml/1 pt/2½ cups

	Metric	Imperial	American
Cold puréed soft or stewed fruit, sweetened to taste	275 ml	½ pt	1¼ cups
Double (heavy) cream	275 ml	½ pt	1¼ cups
Lemon juice			
Food colouring if needed			

1. Sieve the fruit purée if it contains any lumps or pips.
2. Half-whip the cream.
3. Blend in the purée, lemon juice to taste and any colouring.
4. Pour into a container and freeze as described above for 1 hour.
5. Turn out and beat until smooth. Return to the container or a serving dish, and complete freezing.

Notes:
1. Any well-flavoured fruit purée or sieved bananas can be used.
2. 30–45 ml/2–3 tbls fruit syrup can be used with each 275 ml/½ pt/1¼ cups cream instead of purée.

Vanilla Ice Cream

Makes 850 ml/1½ pt/3¾ cups

	Metric	Imperial	American
Double (heavy) cream	275 ml	½ pt	1¼ cups
Cold Egg Custard (page 174) made with 2 eggs and 100 g/4 oz/½ cup sugar	575 ml	1 pt	2½ cups
Vanilla essence	7.5 ml	1½ tsp	1½ tsp

1. Half-whip the cream.
2. Mix lightly with the other ingredients.
3. Turn into a cold container, chill, then freeze as described above. Beat once during freezing.
4. Store covered, and use as required.

Note: If you wish, you can use custard made with a brand custard powder for this ice cream.

Variations
1. *Coffee Ice Cream:* Substitute 30–45 ml/2–3 tbls strong black coffee for the vanilla.
2. *Ginger Ice Cream:* Instead of vanilla, use 75 g/3 oz/⅓ cup preserved ginger in syrup with about 60 ml/4 tbls of the syrup and a little ground ginger.

Chocolate Ice Cream

Serves 6–8

	Metric	Imperial	American
Egg yolks	4	4	4
Caster (superfine) sugar	100 g	4 oz	½ cup
Milk	575 ml	1 pt	2½ cups
Plain (semi-sweet dark) chocolate	75 g	3 oz	3 squares
Vanilla essence	5 ml	1 tsp	1 tsp
Double (heavy) cream	150 ml	¼ pt	⅔ cup

1. Make a custard like Egg Custard for Pouring (page 174) with the egg yolks, sugar and milk.
2. Grate the chocolate into the hot custard, add the vanilla, and whisk until smooth. Cool.
3. Whip the cream lightly, and fold into the cold custard. Pour the mixture into a metal container. Freeze at 'fast freeze' in a home freezer or at the coldest temperature in the ice-making compartment of a refrigerator.
4. Beat 2 or 3 times before the ice cream hardens.

Variations
1. For Chocolate Walnut Ice Cream, add 75 g/3 oz/¾ cup chopped walnuts to the ice cream before freezing, and decorate when serving with walnut halves.
2. Serve the ice cream with a topping made by melting together 50 g/2 oz/2 squares plain chocolate in small pieces, 60 ml/4 tbls golden syrup and 15 ml/1 tbls butter. Beat quickly when melted, and pour over the ice cream while hot. Serve at once.

Peach Melba

Serves 6

	Metric	Imperial	American
Fresh peaches	3–6	3–6	3–6
Syrup for stewing fruit (page 194)			
Vanilla essence			
Vanilla ice cream (page 199)	575 ml (approx)	1 pt (approx)	2½ cups (approx)
Raspberry (Melba) Sauce (page 188)	275 ml	½ pt	1¼ cups

1. Halve, stone and skin the peaches. Poach them in syrup flavoured with a little vanilla. Cool completely.
2. Divide the ice cream between 6 chilled individual dessert glasses. Drain the peaches well, and put 1 or 2 halves on each portion of ice cream, cut side down. Coat with the Melba Sauce.

Ice Cream Gâteau

Serves 6

	Metric	Imperial	American
Vanilla ice cream (page 199)	1.1 l	2 pt	5 cups
Mixture for Victoria Sandwich Cake (page 231) using 1½ times recipe quantities			
Jam (see note)			
Sliced fresh or well-drained canned fruit (see note), (optional)			
Whipped cream			

1. Freeze the ice cream after beating it in 2 × 18 cm/7 in sandwich cake tins (layer cake pans).
2. Make the sandwich cake in 3 × 18 cm/7 in sandwich cake tins. Cool.
3. Warm and sieve enough jam to cover the 3 sandwich cake layers. Slice the tops off the cake layers to level them if needed, and spread 2 of them with jam, and with a flat layer of sliced fruit if using it.
4. Place one jam-covered cake layer on a dessert plate. Cover it with a layer of ice cream and place the second jam-covered cake layer on top. Place the second ice cream layer on top of this, and top with the uncovered cake layer.
5. Cover the top, or the whole, of the dessert with whipped cream. Decorate with sliced fruit.

Note: Strawberries or whole raspberries are the most popular fruits for this gâteau because of their vivid colour, but fresh poached or canned peaches, apricots or kiwi fruit are also suitable. Choose an appropriately flavoured jam. As an alternative to jam and fruit, you could sprinkle the cake layers with grated chocolate, reserving a little to decorate the top of the gâteau.

18
VOLS-AU-VENT, CANAPÉS AND OTHER SAVOURIES

Bases for Savouries

Almost all cocktail savouries and many larger after-dinner ones are served on bread or pastry 'carriers'. The commonest ones are:

Canapés or croûtes: Small rounds, squares or fingers of toasted or fried bread or pastry, or similar small unsweetened biscuits.

Croustades: Fried bread cases. Cut day-old bread into slices 3.5 cm/1½ in thick. Cut into rounds and coat with egg and breadcrumbs. Press a smaller cutter half-way down into each round from the centre top. Fry the rounds briefly in deep hot oil and drain well. Then remove the centre portion and scoop out the soft bread to make a case. Fill with a savoury mixture, replace the fried bread 'lid' and serve at once. (If the cases must be made ahead and reheated, take care that they do not get too crisp to cut easily.)

Small pastry cases: Make small vol-au-vent or patty cases (pages 153, 154). Fill while hot (or reheated) with a hot mixture or cool and fill with a cold one.

Small puffs: Make puffs as described for profiteroles (page 166) and fill with any smooth hot or cold savoury filling; or make small éclairs and fill as described on page 166.

COCKTAIL SAVOURIES

Salted Almonds

Freeze 2 months

	Metric	Imperial	American
Whole shelled almonds			
Corn oil for frying			
Salt and pepper			
Cayenne pepper			

1. Blanch the almonds in boiling water. Drain, and rub off the brown skins.
2. Heat a little oil in a frying pan (skillet). Sauté the almonds, stirring and turning them constantly, until brown. Scoop out with a slotted spoon at once, and scatter on soft kitchen paper to drain. Blot dry.
3. While still warm, tip the almonds into a metal sieve (strainer), and sprinkle with salt, pepper and cayenne to taste. Toss to coat well.
4. Scatter the nuts on a dry baking sheet and leave in a warm place to dry off. Store in an airtight tin for 1–2 weeks if required.

Note: Celery salt or coarse sea salt can be substituted for table salt, and paprika can be used instead of cayenne.

Cheese Straws

Makes about 42 straws and 8 rings

Oven temp 180°C/350°F/Gas Mark 4

Freeze 2 months

	Metric	Imperial	American
Recipe quantity *Cheese Pastry* *(page 150)*			

1. Roll out the pastry into a strip 7.5 cm/3 in wide and 3–5 mm/⅛–¼ in thick.
2. Place the pastry strip on an inverted baking tin (pan) or a flat baking sheet without a rim. Trim the edges of the strip into a neat rectangle. Reserve the trimmings.
3. With a sharp knife, cut the strip across into narrow ribbons about 5 mm/¼ in wide. Push them apart with the knife, to avoid spoiling their shape.
4. Re-roll the trimmings and any leftover pastry to the same thickness. Cut out 4–6 rounds 3.5–5 cm/1½–2 in diameter. Cut out the centres with a 2–3 cm/¾–1¼ in cutter. Carefully lift the rings onto the baking tin or sheet with a palette knife.
5. Bake at the temperature above for 10–12 minutes, until golden and crisp.
6. Since the straws are very brittle when newly baked, cool on the baking tin or sheet. When cold, slide 4–6 straws into each ring. Serve cold.

Cheese Biscuits

Makes 15–20 biscuits

Oven temp 180°C/350°F/Gas Mark 4

Freeze 2 months

	Metric	Imperial	American
Recipe quantity *Cheese Pastry* *(page 150)*			

1. Roll out the pastry 5 mm/¼ in thick on a lightly floured surface. Cut into rounds with a 3 cm/1¼ in cutter.
2. Place on an ungreased baking sheet and bake at the temperature above for 8–10 minutes. Serve hot or cold.

Cheese Cream Fingers

Makes 12 fingers

Not suitable for freezing

	Metric	Imperial	American
Bread slices from *large tin loaf,* *with crusts cut* *off (see note 1)*	4	4	4
Double (heavy) *cream*	60 ml	4 tbls	4 tbls
Grated Parmesan *cheese*	60 ml	4 tbls	4 tbls
Salt and pepper			
Cayenne pepper			
Anchovy fillets, *drained (see* *note 2)*	6	6	6

1. Toast the bread, then cut each slice into 2 fingers.
2. Whip the cream fairly stiffly. Blend in enough cheese to make a thick, well-flavoured paste. Season with salt, pepper and cayenne.
3. Spread the mixture thickly on the toast fingers.
4. Cut the anchovy fillets in half lengthways. Lay one half fillet along the length of each toast finger. Serve cold.

Notes:
1. Small oblong crackers or fingers of cheese pastry can be used instead of toast.
2. If you prefer, garnish the fingers with chopped parsley and paprika instead of anchovy fillets.

Celery Cream Biscuits

Makes 12 biscuits

Not suitable for freezing

	Metric	Imperial	American
Cheese Biscuits *(left)*	12	12	12
Double (heavy) *cream*	60 ml	4 tbls	4 tbls
Celery salt			
Salt, pepper and *cayenne pepper*			
Canned celery *heart, well* *drained*	1	1	1
A few small celery *leaves*			
Paprika			

1. If using freshly-made biscuits, make sure they are quite cold.
2. Whip the cream fairly stiffly, seasoning with the salts, pepper and cayenne to taste.
3. Finely chop enough celery heart to give the cream a fairly solid texture. Blend it into the cream.
4. Pile the mixture on the biscuits in small mounds or pyramids. Garnish with celery leaves and sprinkle with paprika.

Note: The mixture can also be used on toast or pastry fingers or small oblong or round crackers.

Cocktail Vols-au-Vent (hot or cold)

Very small or bite-sized vols-au-vent or bouchées are one of the most popular cocktail and buffet party snacks. They can be given many different fillings, and can be served hot or cold, depending on the type of filling. A filling which melts and drips through the pastry base when heated must obviously be served cold.

Cold bouchées can be filled with a cold savoury mixture shortly before serving, but for hot bouchées, pastry cases and filling should be heated separately, and combined at the last moment.

The following fillings will each fill 24–30 baby vols-au-vent or bouchées made as on page 153.

Hot Fillings

Make a thick coating white sauce (page 84) with 25 g/1 oz/2 tbls butter, 45 ml/3 tbls flour and 150 ml/¼ pt/⅔ cup milk and single (light) cream mixed. Add:
1. 75 g/3 oz/⅔ cup chopped button mushrooms sautéed in butter, and a drop of Worcestershire sauce (Mushroom Filling).
2. 1 small onion, finely chopped and sautéed, and 100 g/4 oz/⅔ cup diced chicken or turkey meat, heated in the sauce. Substitute a little cayenne pepper for Worcestershire sauce (Chicken Filling).

3. 100 g/4 oz/¼ lb cooked shelled prawns or shrimps, 2.5 ml/½ tsp chopped parsley and a drop of lemon juice (Shellfish Filling).

Cold Fillings

1. Cream 100 g/4 oz/½ cup full fat soft cheese (plain or flavoured with herbs) with 50 g/2 oz/¼ softened butter, 5 ml/1 tsp lemon juice and a little salt and pepper.
2. As (1) but use plain soft cheese and substitute 10 ml/2 tsp tomato paste and a few drops of Worcestershire sauce for the lemon juice.
3. Mix 150 ml/¼ pt/⅔ cup whipped double (heavy) cream with 100 g/4 oz/⅔ cup finely diced cooked chicken and about 2.5 ml/½ tsp finely chopped parsley or cress. Add seasoning to taste.

Canapés

Almost any savoury paste mixture can be spread on toast, sliced bread or pastry fingers or small biscuits. Try for instance, a soft cheese mixture such as the cold filling (1) for bouchées (above), a savoury butter, or any well-flavoured bought pâté softened with the back of a spoon.

AFTER-DINNER SAVOURIES

Bacon and Pineapple Rarebit

Serves 4

Not suitable for freezing

	Metric	Imperial	American
Back bacon rashers (slices) without rind	4	4	4
227 g/8 oz can of pineapple rings in natural juice, drained	1	1	1
Butter or margarine	20 ml	4 tsp	4 tsp
Finely grated Cheddar cheese	100 g	4 oz	¼ lb
Prepared mustard	5 ml	1 tsp	1 tsp
Salt			
A few grains of cayenne pepper			
A few drops of Worcestershire sauce			
Square slices of bread from large tin loaf	4	4	4

1. Grill the bacon until as crisp as you wish. Place bacon and pineapple rings on a warmed plate.

2. Blend together the fat and cheese with the back of a spoon, and add seasonings and Worcestershire sauce to taste.
3. Cut the crusts off the bread, and toast one side lightly. Turn over, and spread the other side with cheese mixture.
4. Grill the cheese mixture until browned and bubbling. Top each helping with a pineapple ring and a slice of bacon. Serve at once.

Cheese Canapés

Makes 8 (4 servings)

Oven temp 190°C/375°F/Gas Mark 5

Not suitable for freezing

	Metric	Imperial	American
Grated hard cheese (e.g. Cheddar, Lancashire, etc.)	100 g	4 oz	¼ lb
Soft white breadcrumbs	50 g	2 oz	1 cup
Butter or margarine, melted	25 g	1 oz	2 tbls
Milk	10 ml	2 tsp	2 tsp
Egg yolk	1	1	1
Salt			
A few grains of cayenne pepper			
Canapés (page 201)	8	8	8
Paprika			

1. Mix together the cheese, breadcrumbs, melted fat, milk, egg yolk and seasonings. Blend well.
2. Make the canapés if not made ahead. Pile the cheese mixture thickly on top, shaping it into a peak.
3. Heat in the oven at the temperature above for 10 minutes, or until well browned.
4. Sprinkle with paprika and serve hot.

Notes:
1. The canapés have a pleasant rosy colour if made with red Cheshire or Leicester cheese.
2. The savouries can be prepared ahead, and slipped into the oven while you eat the main course.
3. Other cheese recipes suitable for after-dinner savouries, are in the section on Cheese Dishes (pages 135–139) and in the section on Fritters (pages 170–171).

Herring Roes on Toast

Serves 4

Not suitable for freezing

	Metric	Imperial	American
Bread slices from large tin loaf, crusts removed	2	2	2
Thyme Butter (page 12)			
Soft herring roes	12	12	12
Seasoned flour	15 ml	1 tbls	1 tbls
Butter for shallow frying			
Lemon juice			
Cayenne pepper			
Paprika			

1. Toast the bread slices lightly on both sides. Spread one side with Thyme Butter, then cut each slice in half into 2 croûtes. Keep warm.
2. Wash the roes and pat dry. Dust with seasoned flour.
3. Fry the roes gently in the butter, turning over constantly, for 6–8 minutes, or until cooked through but not hardened.
4. Place 3 roes on each croûte, season with a small squeeze of lemon juice, and dust lightly with cayenne and paprika. Serve very hot.

Sardine Toasts

Serves 6

Not suitable for freezing

	Metric	Imperial	American
120 g/4 oz cans sardines in tomato sauce	2	2	2
Bread slices from small tin loaf	6	6	6
Butter or margarine for spreading			
Tomato ketchup			
Grated Cheddar or processed cheese	50 g	2 oz	½ cup

1. Open the cans of sardines without damaging the fish.
2. Cut the crusts off the bread and toast the slices lightly on both sides.
3. Spread the slices with fat on one side, then with a very little ketchup.
4. Lay one sardine on each toast slice from corner to corner, and trickle a little juice from the can over it.
5. Sprinkle the sardines with cheese. Grill under gentle heat until the cheese melts. Serve at once.

Note: Wholemeal bread gives a good flavour and texture contrast to the fish.

Scotch Woodcock

Serves 4

Not suitable for freezing

	Metric	Imperial	American
Bread slices from large tin loaf	2	2	2
Butter for spreading			
Butter	25 g	1 oz	2 tbls
Eggs, beaten	3	3	3
Milk	30 ml	2 tbls	2 tbls
Salt and pepper			
Anchovy fillets, drained	8	8	8
Capers, rinsed and drained	8	8	8

1. Cut the crusts off the bread, and toast the slices lightly on each side. Butter one side and cut each slice into 4 squares. Keep warm.
2. Warm the 25 g/1 oz/2 tbls butter gently in a frying pan (skillet). Mix together the eggs, milk and seasoning. Turn into the pan, and stir over low heat until the eggs are scrambled.
3. Arrange the scrambled egg on the toast quarters. Cut the anchovy fillets in half across. Arrange 2 half fillets in the form of a cross on each pile of egg, and top with a caper in the centre. Serve at once.

Note: If you prefer, spread the toast with anchovy paste instead of butter, and omit the fillets on top.

Ham Vols-au-Vent or Croustades

Serves 6

Oven temp 130°C/250°F/Gas Mark ½

Freeze 2 months (pastry cases and filling separately: do not freeze croustades)

	Metric	Imperial	American
Individual vols-au-vent, home-made (page 153) or bought, or freshly-made croustades 6 cm/ 2½ in across (page 201)			
Small, onion, chopped	1	1	1
Butter or margarine	15 g	½ oz	1 tbls
Ham, minced (ground) or chopped	175 g	6 oz	6 oz
Egg yolks	2	2	2
Double (heavy) cream or thick coating White Sauce (page 84)	15 ml	1 tbls	1 tbls
Chopped parsley	2.5 ml	½ tsp	½ tsp
Cayenne pepper			

1. Place the pastry cases or croustades in the preheated oven to warm through.
2. Fry the onion in the fat until soft and golden. Add the ham, and stir over low heat until very hot.
3. Beat the egg yolks lightly with the cream or white sauce. Stir into the ham and cook slowly, stirring constantly, until thickened.
4. Stir in the parsley and season lightly with cayenne.
5. Spoon the mixture into the pastry cases or croustades. Serve very hot.

Devils on Horseback

Serves 4

Oven temp 220°C/425°F/Gas Mark 7

Not suitable for freezing

	Metric	Imperial	American
Prunes, soaked overnight	8	8	8
Thin bacon rashers (slices), without rinds	8	8	8
Bread slices from large tin loaf	4	4	4
Butter or margarine	40–50 g	1½–2 oz	3–4 tbls

1. Stone the prunes. Stretch the bacon with the flat of a knife, then roll a prune in each slice. Secure with wooden cocktail picks.
2. Place the prune rolls, with the cut edge underneath, on a baking sheet. Bake for 8 minutes at the temperature above, or until the bacon is crisp.
3. While baking the rolls, cut the crusts off the bread, and cut the slices in half across. Fry in the fat, turning once, until golden on each side.
4. Remove the cocktail picks and place one bacon roll on each croûte. Serve 2 to each person.

Note: The prunes can be stuffed with fried chicken livers, skinned fried almonds, or stuffed olives if you wish. Use 2 chicken livers, quartered, 8 whole shelled almonds, or 8 olives.

Mushrooms on Toast

Serves 4

Not suitable for freezing

	Metric	Imperial	American
Rounds cut out of large square bread slices	4	4	4
Butter for spreading			
Button or small cup mushrooms	225 g	8 oz	½ lb
Lemon juice	10 ml	2 tsp	2 tsp
Worcestershire sauce	2.5 ml	½ tsp	½ tsp
Butter	25 g	1 oz	2 tbls
Salt and pepper			
Single (light) cream	30 ml	2 tbls	2 tbls
Chopped parsley			

1. Toast the bread rounds lightly on both sides. Butter one side lightly. Keep warm.
2. Roughly chop the mushrooms. Put them in a small saucepan. Season with the lemon juice and Worcestershire sauce. Add the butter and about 5 cm/2 in depth of warm water.
3. Place the pan over low heat and boil gently until the water has almost evaporated. Check that the mushrooms are tender by piercing with a skewer.
4. Stir in the cream, and heat for a moment or two.
5. Pile the mushrooms on the toast rounds, and sprinkle with chopped parsley.

19
BREADS AND ROLLS

Most breads, and a good many other flour-based goods, are leavened, or raised, by means of yeast to make them light and spongy. This chapter describes mainly how to handle yeast and make yeasted goods. The various types of flour and other ingredients are described and the basic recipes for bread and rolls follow. A recipe for Soda Bread which is raised with bicarbonate of soda (baking soda) is also included.

NOTES ON YEAST

Yeast is a living organism. When warm, moistened and fed it produces carbon dioxide gas which 'blows up' a dough. Its action is slowed down by cold, salt or too much sugar or fat, and it is killed by high heat.

Yeast is adaptable, convenient and economical to use in cooking. It can be made to raise a dough quickly or slowly as you wish, and it increases the volume and yield of baked goods without eggs and using very little fat and sugar. It also adds B vitamins, essential for health, to them. A wide range of different flours can be used to make variously flavoured breads, rolls and buns, cakes and batters.

Types of Yeast

Today, special bakers' yeast is used for cooking, available in both fresh (compressed) and dried (active dry) forms. Either is easy to use although they are handled slightly differently. Twice as much fresh yeast is needed as dried yeast.

Fresh (compressed) yeast is usually sold as a small compact cream-coloured or greyish 'cake' rather like putty. It should be cool, smell slightly beery and be easy to break up. It is not always easy to buy in cities, although healthfood stores sometimes stock it; in country areas a neighbourhood craft baker will often supply it if asked. It can be refrigerated, wrapped in polythene, for 4–5 days, and can be frozen for 1 month. To use it, simply blend it into a warm liquid, then add the liquid to the flour, etc., being used for the recipe.

Dried (active dry) yeast is sold in tins or smaller packets, as grains of varying size. It keeps for at least 6 months in an unopened container, or for 2–3 months once opened. Since it keeps less well if there is much air space in the container, transfer it from a large tin to a smaller one if necessary. It is

sold in most fair-sized supermarkets and neighbourhood grocery stores. To use it, prepare a hand-hot liquid containing 2.5–5 ml/½–1 tsp sugar. Sprinkle on the yeast and leave to stand in a warm place for 10–20 minutes until the yeast rises and 'froths'. If it does not react within 30 minutes, it is stale and should be thrown away. Once the yeast 'froths' it should be added at once to the flour, etc., being used in the recipe.

Some dried yeast now contains an activating agent (vitamin C) and does not need soaking with sweetening. It is simply sprinkled into the dry ingredients and is activated by the liquid used to make the dough.

OTHER INGREDIENTS USED IN YEAST COOKERY

Flour: Wheat flour is most often used for bread-making because it contains more gluten than most other cereal flours. Gluten is a protein substance in flour which becomes elastic when combined with water, and it becomes stronger (springier) as the flour and water dough is kneaded (see right). Yeast or any other raising agent stretches the gluten, puffing it out into small pockets which give the dough a spongy texture; when baked, the heat 'sets' the dough in this spongy form.

For best results in bread-making, use a *strong* flour, sometimes called bread flour, which has a higher gluten content than ordinary, softer flour. It absorbs more liquid and, when kneaded, gives a more elastic dough and a bigger volume of raised dough. Ordinary plain (all-purpose) flour can be used but the loaves will not be as light or as large.

Wholemeal, wholewheat, granary, wheatmeal and other forms of wheat flour are available as strong or bread flour. As a rule, they absorb slightly more liquid than white flour, and give a slightly denser loaf because of the fat, sugar and bran which they contain. (Fat and sugar soften gluten.)

Other cereal flours such as rye, barley or lentil flour which contain little or no gluten are generally mixed with wholemeal or white strong flour if used for bread-making.

Salt: A little salt is used to flavour breads and to prevent the yeast fermenting too quickly. Too much salt, however, kills the yeast.

Sugar is a food for yeast, but concentrated sugar kills it. If you 'cream' fresh yeast with sugar, some of the yeast cells may be destroyed, and will give a yeasty flavour to the bread made from that batch of dough.

Fat enriches a dough, softens and colours the baked crumb and delays staling.

Liquid: The liquid may be water or milk, or a mixture. The quantity depends both on the type of flour used, and on the recipe. Flours vary in their capacity to absorb water, but slightly less than 275 ml/½ pt/1¼ cups liquid to 450 g/1 lb strong flour can be used as a rough guide.

Milk breads have extra food value, and a better keeping quality and crust colour.

MAKING YEASTED DOUGHS

Mixing the Dough

Prepare the yeast as described above. Sift the basic dry ingredients into a large mixing bowl, and (as a rule) rub (cut) in any fat at this stage. Add the yeast liquid to the dry ingredients and mix to a soft dough. Turn onto a lightly floured surface for kneading.

Kneading

Any yeasted dough must be kneaded or beaten well to develop and strengthen the gluten, and make the dough rise well. Very soft doughs are beaten; all others are kneaded.

To knead a dough by hand, pat the dough into a cushion shape. Fold it over towards you, then push downward and away from you with the heel of your hand. Give the dough a quarter turn, and repeat. Continue kneading like this, with a rocking rhythm, until – sometimes quite suddenly – the dough ceases to feel sticky, and is springy and elastic.

Note: Mixing and kneading can be done in one operation if using an electric mixer. Put the yeast liquid in the bowl, then the dry goods. Attach the dough hook to the machine, and mix at the lowest speed to combine the ingredients. Then mix as the manufacturer's pamphlet recommends, usually for a few minutes only. Then, if necessary, knead by hand to get the dough together in one piece.

Rising

Any yeasted dough must be left to rise at least once before baking, to give the yeast time to do its work. As a rule, bread has a more even texture if it rises twice: the second rising is generally called proving and takes place after shaping the dough. The dough must be covered while it rises to prevent it losing heat or drying out and forming a skin, but it must not be held down by its covering. Put it in a lightly greased container with a lid, such

as a casserole, with plenty of headspace between the lid and the dough, or put it in a bowl inside a large, lightly greased polythene bag. If necessary, the bowl can then be put in a larger bowl containing hot water for quick rising.

Rising times vary with the temperature of the dough and its surroundings. Within limits, you can use a temperature to suit your convenience, but take care not to raise a dough too quickly. Slow rising through controlled yeast growth gives a better, more even-textured loaf: so if you are short of time, rather refrigerate the dough and retard its rising until you can deal with it, than force it to rise fast. If the rising place is too warm, the loaf will be dry and will soon stale. Worse still, the yeast may be over-activated, and may over-stretch the gluten. If that happens the loaf may collapse in the oven, and will smell sour or yeasty. Average rising times are:

45–60 minutes in a warm place;
1½–2 hours at room temperature (18–21°C/64–70°F)
8–12 hours in a cold room or larder
up to 24 hours in a refrigerator, depending on the temperature.

Note: Let refrigerated dough return to room temperature before shaping it.

Leave dough to rise until it has doubled in bulk and springs back when lightly pressed with your finger.

Shaping and Proving (Second Rising)

A bread loaf will have a better, more even texture and shape if it is 'knocked back' ('punched down') to get rid of air bubbles, and allowed to rise again when shaped. To 'knock back' ('punch down') flatten the dough firmly with your knuckles, and knead as before to firm the dough for shaping.

Use very little flour on the board this time, because too much will spoil the colour of the bread crust. Follow your recipe instructions for shaping the dough.

To 'prove' the dough, place the shaped dough in its tin or on its baking sheet inside a lightly greased polythene bag, loosely tied, and leave to rise as before until doubled in bulk and resilient when pressed.

Baking

Any yeasted dough should be baked for at least 10 minutes in a very hot oven to kill the yeast and prevent it overstretching the dough in the heat. Bake plain white or wholemeal bread at 230°C/450°F/Gas Mark 8. Bake enriched breads (see recipes) at 190–220°C/375–425°F/Gas Mark 5–7.

When done, a bread loaf will have shrunk slightly from the sides of a tin if used, and will sound hollow if you tap the bottom.

Cool any yeasted baked goods on a wire rack.

Note: Except for unbaked bread, the freezing times suggested in the following recipes are for baked goods.

RECIPES FOR BREADS AND ROLLS

White Bread or Rolls

Makes two 900 g/2 lb loaves OR four 450 g/1 lb loaves OR about 36 rolls (see note)

Oven temp 230°C/450°F/Gas Mark 8

Freeze 6 weeks (baked bread); 8 weeks (unbaked dough); 4 weeks (pre-sliced baked bread or rolls)

	Metric	Imperial	American
Yeast Liquid			
Fresh (compressed) yeast	25 g	1 oz	1 cake
OR dried (active dry) yeast	15 ml	1 tbls	1 tbls
Sugar (if using dried yeast)	5 ml	1 tsp	1 tsp
Warm water	850 ml	1½ pt	3¾ cups
Dry Mix			
White bread flour	1.4 kg	3 lb	3 lb
Salt	30 ml	2 tbls	2 tbls
Lard (shortening)	25 g	1 oz	2 tbls

1. Blend the fresh yeast to a thin cream with a little of the water, then add to the rest of the water; OR sprinkle the sugar into the water and stir to dissolve it, then stir in the dried yeast and leave for 10–15 minutes until frothing.
2. Sift the flour and salt into a large bowl. Rub (cut) in the fat.
3. Mix the yeast liquid into the dry ingredients with a wooden spoon, then with your hands. Add extra flour if needed. Work to a firm dough which leaves the sides of the bowl cleanly.
4. Turn the dough onto a lightly floured surface, and knead thoroughly as described above until the dough feels elastic and no longer sticky. Shape into a ball.
5. Place the dough in a large lightly greased polythene bag, tie the bag loosely with headspace for the dough to rise, and leave to rise until doubled in bulk and resilient when pressed. Leave in a warm or cool place or refrigerate depending on how fast you want the dough to rise, i.e. when you want to make the bread.
6. For two large loaves, grease two 900 g/2 lb loaf tins (pans). Knock back (punch down) and re-knead the dough until firm. Divide the dough in half, and form it into two equal-sized loaf shapes to fit the tins. Smooth the tops, and fit into the tins. For 4 small loaves, grease four 450 g/1 lb loaf tins, divide the kneaded dough into quarters, and handle as above. For rolls, shape the kneaded dough into 36 lightly flattened small balls or sausage shapes (for oval rolls), weighing about 50 g/2 oz each. Place 2.5 cm/1 in apart on lightly floured baking sheets.
7. Replace the tins or baking sheets inside one or more lightly greased polythene bags as before, and leave loaves to prove for 1–1½ hours or longer if refrigerated. The dough should reach the tops of the tins. Leave rolls to prove for 40–50 minutes until puffy.
8. Remove from the polythene, and bake at the temperature above for:

    35–50 minutes (large loaves)
    25–35 minutes (small loaves)
    18–20 minutes (rolls)

    Turn out loaves and tap on the bottom; they should sound hollow. Cool on a wire rack.

Notes:
1. If you prefer, shape small loaves into rounds like large rolls. Cut a deep cross in the top of each and bake on a greased baking sheet.
2. If you prefer, make one large or two small loaves, and 18 rolls, or one large and one small loaf, and 9 rolls.
3. Brush the surface of loaves or rolls with water or milk for a crisp crust, or with beaten egg and water or milk and a pinch of sugar for a richly-coloured one. Sprinkle with a few poppy seeds if you wish.

Variation
Milk Bread: Use milk instead of water. Rub (cut) 50 g/2 oz butter, margarine or lard (shortening) into the dry mix. This gives a slightly softer crumb with a better crust colour, which keeps a little longer than plain bread. (For Milk Rolls, see next recipe.)

Wholemeal Bread or Rolls

Use 50 g/2 oz/2 cakes fresh (compressed) yeast or 30 ml/2 tbls dried (active dry) yeast for a dry mix based on 1.4 kg/3 lb wholemeal bread flour. Add 30 ml/2 tbls sugar to the dry mix.

Seeds such as sesame, caraway or sunflower, chopped nuts or cracked wheat may be added to the wholemeal flour, or sprinkled on to the risen bread or rolls before baking.

Otherwise, use the same quantities, and make and bake exactly like white bread and rolls. Brush the tops of bread loaves with salt water before proving.

Opposite: *Wholemeal bread may be cooked in a loaf tin or shaped into rounds. For a textured crust the loaves are sprinkled with cracked wheat.*

Milk Rolls

Makes 32 small rolls

Oven temp 220°C/425°F/Gas Mark 7

Freeze 4 weeks (baked)

	Metric	Imperial	American
Yeast Liquid			
Fresh (compressed)			
yeast	15 g	½ oz	½ cake
OR dried (active			
dry) yeast	10 ml	2 tsp	2 tsp
Sugar (if using			
dried yeast)	5 ml	1 tsp	1 tsp
Warm milk	450 ml	¾ pt	2 cups
Dry Mix			
White bread flour	700 g	1½ lb	1½ lb
Salt	7.5 ml	1½ tsp	1½ tsp
Butter, margarine			
or lard			
(shortening)	50 g	2 oz	¼ cup

1. Make like White Bread Rolls, but prove on lightly greased baking sheets instead of floured ones.
2. Bake at the temperature above for 15–20 minutes only.

Soda Bread

Makes 1 round loaf

Cooking time 45 minutes

Oven temp 220°C/425°F/Gas Mark 7

Freeze 6 weeks

	Metric	Imperial	American
Plain (all-purpose)			
flour	450 g	1 lb	1 lb
Salt	5 ml	1 tsp	1 tsp
Bicarbonate of			
soda (baking			
soda)	5 ml	1 tsp	1 tsp
Butter, margarine			
or lard			
(shortening)			
(optional)	50 g	2 oz	¼ cup
Soured milk or			
buttermilk	275 ml approx	½ pt approx	1¾ cups approx

1. Sift together the flour, salt and soda into a bowl.
2. Rub (cut) in the fat if used. (It improves the flavour and keeping quality.)
3. Mix in enough soured milk or buttermilk to make a soft but not sticky dough. The exact quantity will depend on the consistency of the liquid.
4. Shape into a flattish round cake or bun shape on a greased baking sheet. Score 3 lines across the top.
5. Bake at the temperature above for 30 minutes. Cool on a wire rack.

Variation
Use wholemeal flour, and rub (cut) in bacon fat or lard (shortening).

20

TRADITIONAL TEA BREADS, BUNS AND SCONES

Currant Bread

Makes two 450 g/1 lb loaves

Oven temp 220°C/425°F/Gas Mark 7

Freeze 2 months

	Metric	Imperial	American
Yeast Liquid			
Fresh (compressed)			
yeast	25 g	1 oz	1 cake
OR dried (active			
dry) yeast	15 ml	1 tbls	1 tbls
Sugar (if using			
dried yeast)	5 ml	1 tsp	1 tsp
Warm milk and			
water, mixed	275 ml	½ pt	1¼ cups
Dry Mix			
White bread flour	400 g	14 oz	3½ cups
White sugar	25 g	1 oz	2 tbls
Salt	5 ml	1 tsp	1 tsp
Margarine	25 g	1 oz	2 tbls
Currants	100 g	4 oz	¾ cup
Honey for brushing			

1. Prepare the yeast liquid as for White Bread (page 208).
2. Mix the flour, sugar and salt in a large bowl, rub (cut) in the fat and add the fruit.
3. Blend in the yeast liquid to make a firm dough. Add extra flour if needed until the dough leaves the sides of the bowl cleanly.
4. Turn the dough onto a lightly floured surface, and knead as described on page 207 until the dough is elastic.
5. Lightly grease two 450 g/1 lb loaf tins (pans). Divide the dough into 2 equal portions. Flatten each piece into a rectangle the same width as the length of the tins. Roll up each piece like a Swiss roll and fit it into a tin.
6. Place the tins in lightly greased polythene bags, tie loosely and leave until the dough reaches the tops of the tins or springs back when lightly pressed.
7. Bake at the temperature above for 30–35 minutes.
8. Brush the tops of the loaves with a wet brush dipped in honey. Cool on a wire rack.

Sally Lunn

Makes two 15 cm/6 in Sally Lunns

Oven temp 220°C/425°F/Gas Mark 7

Freeze for 2 months

	Metric	Imperial	American
Yeast Batter			
Bread flour	150 g	5 oz	1¼ cups
Sugar	5 ml	1 tsp	1 tsp
Fresh (compressed)			
yeast	15 g	½ oz	½ cake
OR dried (active			
dry) yeast	10 ml	2 tsp	2 tsp
Warm milk	375 ml	13 fl oz	1⅔ cups
Other Ingredients			
Bread flour	300 g	11 oz	2¾ cups
Salt	10 ml	2 tsp	2 tsp
Eggs, beaten	2	2	2
Butter, melted	50 g	2 oz	¼ cup
Glaze			
Water	15 ml	1 tbls	1 tbls
Sugar	15 ml	1 tbls	1 tbls

1. Mix the flour and sugar for the batter. Blend fresh yeast into some of the milk or stir dried yeast into it. Mix the yeast liquid with the remaining milk, and leave until frothy.
2. Add the remaining flour, salt, eggs and melted butter. Beat until smooth.
3. Grease two 15 cm/6 in round cake tins (pans). Pour in the batter. Cover with greased polythene and leave to rise until the mixture has doubled in size, and comes almost to the tops of the tins (about 1½ hours in a warm place).
4. Bake at the temperature above for 20–25 minutes until golden-brown.
5. While baking, boil the sugar and water for the glaze for 2 minutes. Brush over the Sally Lunns.
6. To serve, split a Sally Lunn across into 3 layers, and toast each lightly on both sides. Spread with clotted cream, re-shape the cake and serve cut in wedges.

Banana Bread

Makes one 900 g/2 lb loaf

Oven temp 160°C/325°F/Gas Mark 3

Freeze 2 months

	Metric	Imperial	American
Self-raising flour	275 g	10 oz	2½ cups
Shredded suet	100 g	4 oz	¾ cup
Eggs, beaten	2	2	2
Large ripe bananas, mashed	2	2	2
Walnut pieces, chopped	50 g	2 oz	½ cup
Soft brown sugar	175 g	6 oz	1 cup
Natural yoghurt	150 ml	¼ pt	⅔ cup
Bicarbonate of soda (baking soda)	5 ml	1 tsp	1 tsp

1. Grease a 900 g/2 lb loaf tin (pan), and line the base with greaseproof (waxed) paper.
2. Mix all the ingredients thoroughly in a large bowl. Turn into the tin and level the top.
3. Bake at the temperature above for 1–1¼ hours until risen and golden. Cool for 15 minutes in the tin, then turn onto a wire rack to finish cooling. Serve cut in slices with butter.

Bath Buns

Makes 18–20

Oven temp 220°C/425°F/Gas Mark 7

Freeze 4 weeks

	Metric	Imperial	American
Yeast Batter (liquid and flour)			
Bread flour	100 g	4 oz	1 cup
Sugar	5 ml	1 tsp	1 tsp
Fresh (compressed) yeast	25 g	1 oz	1 cake
OR dried (active dry) yeast	15 ml	1 tbls	1 tbls
Warm milk	150 ml	¼ pt	⅔ cup
Warm water	75 ml	3 fl oz	⅓ cup
Dough Mix			
Bread flour	350 g	12 oz	3 cups
Salt	5 ml	1 tsp	1 tsp
Butter or margarine	50 g	2 oz	¼ cup
Sugar	50 g	2 oz	¼ cup
Egg, beaten	1	1	1

Banana Bread makes a tea time treat.

Filling

Egg, beaten	1	1	1
Sugar	25 g	1 oz	2 tbls
Sultanas (golden raisins)	175 g	6 oz	1 cup
Chopped peel	50 g	2 oz	⅓ cup

To finish
Egg wash
Crushed lump
  sugar (cubes)

1. Mix the flour and sugar for the batter. Blend fresh yeast into some of the milk or stir dried yeast into it. Mix the yeast liquid and the remaining milk and water with the flour and sugar. Leave for 20–30 minutes until spongy.
2. Sift together the flour and salt for the dough mix into a bowl. Rub (cut) in the fat. Add the sugar and egg, and blend to mix.
3. Mix the yeast batter into the dough mix, together with the filling ingredients.
4. Turn the dough onto a lightly floured surface, and knead (page 207) until elastic and no longer sticky.
5. Put back in the bowl to rise in a lightly greased polythene bag, loosely tied with space to spare inside. Leave to rise for 1–1½ hours at room temperature (see page 207). If refrigerated, return the dough to room temperature before shaping.

Hot Cross Buns are flavoured with dried fruit and spice.

6. When risen, beat with a wooden spoon to knock out air bubbles.
7. Place 50–60 g/2–2½ oz portions of dough well apart on lightly floured baking sheets. Put back in the greased bag and leave for 30 minutes or until the dough is springy.
8. Remove from the bag, brush with egg wash and crushed lump sugar. Bake at the temperature above for 15–20 minutes.
9. Cool on a wire rack.

Variation
Hot Cross Buns: Add to the dough mix, 7.5 ml/1½ tsp mixed spice (ground allspice), 2.5 ml/½ tsp ground cinnamon, 2.5 ml/½ tsp grated nutmeg, 100 g/4 oz/¾ cup currants and 25 g/1 oz/3 tbls chopped peel. When the dough has risen, turn it onto a floured surface, knock back (punch down) and knead until firm. Divide into 6–8 equal-sized pieces and shape into small balls. Place on a floured baking sheet and prove. Cut a deep cross in the top of each bun, then bake as above. Instead of egg wash, boil 50 g/2 oz/¼ cup sugar in 60 ml/4 tbls water for 2 minutes to make a glaze, and brush over buns after baking.

Savarin

Serves 4–6

Oven temp 200°C/400°F/Gas Mark 6

Freeze 3 months (with or without syrup)

	Metric	Imperial	American
Yeast Liquid			
Fresh (compressed)			
yeast	*10 g*	*¼ oz*	*¼ cake*
OR dried (active			
dry) yeast	*5 ml*	*1 tsp*	*1 tsp*
Sugar (if using			
dried yeast)	*1.5 ml*	*¼ tsp*	*¼ tsp*
Warm milk	*60 ml*	*4 tbls*	*4 tbls*
Other Ingredients			
Bread or plain			
(all-purpose)			
flour	*100 g*	*4 oz*	*1 cup*
Eggs	*2*	*2*	*2*
Softened butter	*65 g*	*2½ oz*	*5 tbls*
Syrup, glaze and			
filling as below			

1. Grease an 18 cm/7 in savarin or ring mould.
2. Blend the fresh yeast into the warm milk or stir in dried yeast and sugar and leave until frothy.
3. Sift the flour into a bowl. Stir in the yeast liquid and leave in a warm place for 20 minutes, until light and spongy.
4. Beat in the eggs, with the well-softened butter.
5. Turn the mixture into the prepared mould, cover with lightly greased polythene and leave in a warm place until the mixture almost reaches the top of the mould.
6. Take off the polythene. Bake the savarin at the temperature above for about 30 minutes or until springy and golden. Turn out onto a wire rack, and finish as below.

Note: The savarin mixture can be baked in 8 individual baba moulds to make *Rum Babas*.

To Complete a Savarin or Babas

A basic savarin is used for several fancy desserts. It is most often soaked in a rum syrup then glazed and served without a filling, but it can be filled with any rich sweet mixture such as flavoured whipped cream or a fruit purée or compote flavoured with a liqueur.

Jam Doughnuts

Makes 8–9

Freeze 4 weeks

	Metric	Imperial	American
Ingredients as for			
Chelsea Buns			
(below), except			
for melted butter			
and filling			
ingredients			
Thick jam for filling			
Oil for deep frying			
Caster (superfine)			
sugar	*50 g*	*2 oz*	*¼ cup*
Ground cinnamon	*2.5 ml*	*½ tsp*	*½ tsp*

1. For the dough, follow steps 1–5 of the recipe for Bath Buns (page 212) without adding any filling ingredients.
2. Turn the risen dough onto a lightly floured surface and knead well to knock out air bubbles and firm up.
3. Divide the dough into 50 g/2 oz pieces and roll each into a ball with lightly oiled hands. Poke a hole on each ball and put in a dab of jam. Cover the hole by squeezing and smoothing the dough over it.
4. Place on a floured tray, put in a large greased polythene bag and leave to prove until the balls are light and puffy.
5. Heat the oil for deep frying to 185°C/360°F. Deep fry the doughnuts until golden all over. Drain on soft kitchen paper.
6. Roll the doughnuts in a mixture of the sugar and cinnamon.

Chelsea Buns

Makes 9

Oven temp 190°C/375°F/Gas Mark 5

Freeze 4 weeks

	Metric	Imperial	American
Yeast Batter			
Bread flour	*50 g*	*2 oz*	*½ cup*
Sugar	*2.5 ml*	*½ tsp*	*½ tsp*
Fresh (compressed)			
yeast	*15 g*	*½ oz*	*½ cake*
OR dried (active			
dry) yeast	*10 ml*	*2 tsp*	*2 tsp*
Warm milk	*100 ml*	*4 fl oz*	*½ cup*
Dough Mix			
Bread flour	*175 g*	*6 oz*	*1½ cups*
Salt	*2.5 ml*	*½ tsp*	*½ tsp*
Butter, margarine			
or lard			
(shortening)	*15 g*	*½ oz*	*1 tbls*

Egg, beaten	1	1	1
Melted butter for brushing			

Filling

Mixed dried fruit	75 g	3 oz	½ cup
Chopped peel	25 g	1 oz	3 tbls
Soft brown sugar	50 g	2 oz	⅓ cup
Honey for brushing			

1. Follow steps 1–5 of the recipe for Bath Buns (page 212), i.e until the shaping stage, but do not add the filling to the mixture.
2. After kneading the dough well, roll into a rectangle 33 × 23 cm/13 × 9 in in size. Brush with melted butter, and spread with filling.
3. Roll up from one long side like a Swiss (jelly) roll, and seal the edge.
4. Cut the filled roll of dough into 9 equal-sized slices. Place well apart, cut side down, on lightly greased baking sheets. Place in a greased polythene bag and leave to prove until the dough is springy.
5. Bake at the temperature above for 20–25 minutes.
6. Brush the still-warm buns with honey, and cool on a wire rack.

Cup Cakes (Fairy Cakes)

Makes 12–16

Oven temp 190°C/375°F/Gas Mark 5

Freeze 3 months

	Metric	Imperial	American
Butter or margarine	100 g	4 oz	½ cup
Caster (superfine) sugar	100 g	4 oz	¼ cup
Eggs, beaten	2	2	2
Plain (all-purpose) or self-raising flour	100 g	4 oz	1 cup
Pinch of salt			
Baking powder if using plain flour	2.5 ml	½ tsp	½ tsp

1. Grease small bun tins (muffin pans) or put paper cases in dry bun tins.
2. Cream together the fat and sugar. Beat in the eggs a little at a time.
3. Sift in together the flour, salt and baking powder if used. Stir in lightly.
4. Turn the mixture into the prepared cases, filling only three-quarters full.
5. Bake at the temperature above for 15–20 minutes until firm. Cool on a wire rack.

Variations

Cherry Cupcakes: Add 50 g/2 oz glacé (candied) cherries, washed, dried and quartered, with the flour mixture.

Chocolate Cupcakes: Add 15 ml/1 tbls milk with the eggs, and 30 ml/2 tbls cocoa powder (unsweetened cocoa) with the flour.

Coconut Cakes: Add 30 ml/2 tbls milk with the eggs, and 50 g/2 oz/¾ cup desiccated (shredded) coconut with the flour.

Queen Cakes: Add 75 g/3 oz/½ cup currants or sultanas (golden raisins) with the flour.

Butterfly Cakes: Cut the tops off the baked cooled cakes and cut the tops in half. Whip 150 ml/¼ pt/⅔ cup double (heavy) cream with 5 ml/1 tsp caster (superfine) sugar and vanilla essence to taste. Pipe a rosette on each cake, and fix the 2 cut halves on the top, cut edge down, standing upright in the cream like wings. Dust with icing (confectioners') sugar.

Raspberry Buns

Makes 12

Oven temp 190°C/375°F/Gas Mark 5

Freeze 3 months

	Metric	Imperial	American
Plain (all-purpose) or self-raising flour	225 g	8 oz	2 cups
Pinch of salt			
Baking powder if using plain flour	5 ml	1 tsp	1 tsp
Butter or margarine	75 g	3 oz	6 tbls
Caster (superfine) sugar	75 g	3 oz	6 tbls
Grated lemon rind	2.5 ml	½ tsp	½ tsp
Egg, beaten	1	1	1
Milk	30–45 ml	2–3 tbls	2–3 tbls
Raspberry jam			
Egg white, beaten	1	1	1
Caster (superfine) sugar for sprinkling			

1. Grease 1 or 2 baking sheets.
2. Sift together the flour, salt and baking powder if used. Rub (cut) in the fat. Add the sugar and lemon rind.
3. Mix in the egg, and enough milk to make a soft dough.
4. Divide the dough into 12 equal-sized pieces. Roll each into a ball and flatten slightly. Put a dab of jam in the centre and gather up the dough round it, to enclose it. Smooth out creases. Place, smooth side up on the baking sheets.
5. Brush the buns with beaten egg white and sprinkle with sugar.
6. Bake at the temperature above for about 20 minutes. Buns made with self-raising flour may need slightly less time.
7. Cool on a wire rack.

Rock Buns

Makes 12

Oven temp 200°C/400°F/Gas Mark 6

Freeze 4 months

	Metric	Imperial	American
Plain (all-purpose) or self-raising flour	225 g	8 oz	2 cups
Pinch of salt			
Baking powder if using plain flour	10 ml	2 tsp	2 tsp
Ground mixed spice (allspice)	2.5 ml	½ tsp	½ tsp
Butter or margarine	50 g	2 oz	¼ cup
Lard (shortening)	50 g	2 oz	¼ cup
Demerara (light brown) sugar	100 g	4 oz	⅔ cup
Grated rind of ½ lemon			
Currants	75 g	3 oz	½ cup
Chopped peel	25 g	1 oz	3 tbls
Egg, beaten	1	1	1
Milk	5 ml	1 tsp	1 tsp

Above: *Rock Buns, Tea Bread and Chocolate Cake (page 232) topped with vanilla butter icing.*

Opposite: *Plain Scones and Sultana Scones.*

1. Grease a baking sheet. Sift together the flour, salt, baking powder if used, and spice.
2. Rub (cut) in the fats until the mixture resembles fine crumbs.
3. Mix in the sugar, lemon rind, currants and peel. Use the egg and milk to bind to a stiff dough. Add a very little more milk if needed.
4. Put the mixture in small rough piles on the prepared baking sheet, well spaced apart. Bake at the temperature above for 15 minutes or until firm and tipped with brown. Cool on a wire rack.

Variation

Fruit Tea Bread: Preheat oven to 160°C/350°F/Gas Mark 3.
Replace currants with raisins soaked for 30 minutes in 150 ml/¼ pt/⅔ cup tea. Melt fat and stir into sifted ingredients with raisins and tea and remaining ingredients. Cook in a lined and greased 450 g/1 lb loaf tin for 1¼ to 1½ hours. Slice and butter.

SCONES

Plain Scones

Makes 10–12

Oven Temp 220°C/425°F/Gas Mark 7

Freeze 2 months

	Metric	Imperial	American
Plain (all-purpose) flour	225 g	8 oz	2 cups
Cream of tartar	5 ml	1 tsp	1 tsp
Bicarbonate of soda (baking soda)	2.5 ml	½ tsp	½ tsp
Salt	2.5 ml	½ tsp	½ tsp
Butter, margarine or lard (shortening)	50 g	2 oz	¼ cup
Milk	150 ml	¼ pt	⅔ cup
Beaten egg or milk for brushing			

1. Sift together the flour, cream of tartar, bicarbonate of soda and salt into a bowl. Rub (cut) in the fat.
2. Using a knife, mix to a pliant dough with the milk.
3. Turn onto a floured surface and knead lightly. Roll or pat out into a sheet 1–2 cm/ ½–¾ in thick.
4. Cut into rounds with a 5–6 cm/2–2½ in cutter.
   Re-roll and cut trimmings.
5. Put the rounds on an ungreased baking sheet. Brush tops with egg or milk if you wish. Bake at the temperature above for 8–10 minutes.

Notes:
1. Serve freshly baked scones, split, with a selection of jams and jellies (pages 243 to 245), and double (heavy) cream if liked.
2. You can use sour milk, buttermilk or natural yoghurt as the liquid, if you wish. Reduce the cream of tartar to 2.5 ml/½ tsp.

Variations
Sweet Scones: Add 50 g/2 oz/¼ cup caster sugar before mixing with milk.
Sultana Scones: Add 50 g/2 oz/⅓ cup sultanas and 50 g/2 oz/¼ cup caster sugar before mixing with milk.
Brown Scones: Use half wholemeal flour and half white flour.
Cheese Scones: Add 75 g/3 oz/¾ cup grated Cheddar or other hard cheese, a pinch of dry mustard and a few grains of cayenne pepper before mixing with milk.

Muffins

Makes about 14

Freeze 6 months

	Metric	Imperial	American
Yeast Batter			
Fresh (compressed) yeast	15 g	½ oz	½ cake
OR dried (active dry) yeast	10 ml	2 tsp	2 tsp
Pinch of sugar (if using dried yeast)			
Warm milk	225 ml	8 fl oz	1 cup
Egg, beaten	1	1	1
Dough Mix			
Bread flour	400 g	14 oz	3½ cups
Salt	5 ml	1 tsp	1 tsp
Butter or margarine	25 g	1 oz	2 tbls

1. Blend the fresh yeast into a little of the milk until a thin cream, then mix into the rest of the milk; OR stir the dried yeast and sugar into the warm milk. Leave until frothy.
2. Sift together the flour and salt into a bowl, and rub (cut) in the fat.
3. Beat the egg into the yeast liquid. Stir the liquid into the flour mixture to make a soft dough. Beat well for 5–8 minutes with a wooden spoon.
4. Put the bowl in a large, lightly greased polythene bag, and leave to rise until almost doubled in bulk. (About 1½ hours in a fairly warm place.)
5. Beat the dough again lightly. Then roll out on a well floured surface to 1 cm/½ in thickness. Cut into 7.5 cm/3 in rounds with a floured cutter.
6. Place the rounds of a floured tray, cover loosely with greased polythene and leave to prove until puffy (45–60 minutes).
7. Lightly grease a griddle or large, thick-based frying pan (skillet). Heat well until very hot. Cook the muffins for about 8 minutes, turning once, until golden-brown on both sides. Cool.
8. To serve, split muffins around the sides almost to the centre. Toast gently on both sides until heated through. Pull open, fill with butter and sandwich together again. Serve hot.

Scotch Pancakes (Drop Scones)

Makes 24 pancakes (approx)

Freeze 2 months

	Metric	Imperial	American
Plain (all-purpose) flour	225 g	8 oz	2 cups
Salt			
Cream of tartar	5 ml	1 tsp	1 tsp
Bicarbonate of soda (baking soda)	2.5 ml	½ tsp	½ tsp
Egg	1	1	1
Milk	225 ml (approx)	8 fl oz (approx)	1 cup (approx)
Caster (superfine) sugar	15 ml	1 tbls	1 tbls

1. Sift together the flour, salt, cream of tartar and bicarbonate of soda into a bowl.
2. Make a well in the centre, break in the egg and about 45 ml/3 tbls milk. Mix thoroughly, adding more milk gradually until you have a thick smooth batter (see note). Mix in the sugar.
3. Lightly grease a large heavy frying pan (skillet) or griddle with a piece of pork rind or lard. Heat it well.
4. Using a dessertspoon (10 ml spoon), drop 2–3 spoonfuls of the batter on the greased surface, spaced well apart. Cook for about 3 minutes or until small bubbles rise to the surface and burst. Turn over quickly with a palette knife, and cook for 1–2 minutes until the undersides are golden-brown. Take off, and place in a folded dry cloth.
5. Repeat the frying, adding more fat when needed, until all the batter is used. Cool the pan or griddle slightly between batches; if it gets too hot, it will scorch the outsides of the scones before the insides are cooked.

Note: Some cooks like to make thinner drop scones by using up to 275 ml/½ pt/1¼ cups milk.

21
PLAIN AND SWEET BISCUITS AND COOKIES

BISCUITS AND COOKIES

Biscuits and cookies (soft biscuits, fingers etc.) are made by the same methods as cakes and can be baked on greased baking sheets or on sheets lined with non-stick baking paper. There are 5 main ways of shaping them. The unbaked dough may be rolled out like pastry, then cut into shapes with a metal or plastic cutter. Alternatively, it may be shaped into balls or other shapes by hand: or it may be formed into a long roll, then chilled or frozen and later sliced. If soft, it can be piped, or dropped, in small separate portions directly onto the baking sheets. Bar and wedge cookies are baked in a single piece or slab, then cut into the desired shapes after baking.

Digestive Biscuits

Makes 24

Oven temp 180°C/350°F/Gas Mark 4

Freeze unbaked dough 2 months; baked biscuits 4 months

	Metric	Imperial	American
Plain (all-purpose) wholemeal flour	175 g	6 oz	1½ cups
Plain (all-purpose) white flour	50 g	2 oz	½ cups
Medium oatmeal	50 g	2 oz	⅓ cup
Salt	2. 5 ml	½ tsp	½ tsp
Baking powder	5 ml	1 tsp	1 tsp
Butter or margarine	100 g	4 oz	½ cup
Light soft brown sugar, sifted	30 ml	2 tbls	2 tbls
Milk	60 ml	4 tbls	4 tbls

1. Mix together both flours, the oatmeal, salt and baking powder. Rub in the fat, then mix in the sugar.
2. Add the milk and mix to a dough. Knead well.
3. Roll out on a lightly floured surface into a sheet 5 mm/¼ in thick or very slightly thicker.

4. Cut into rounds with a 6 cm/2¼ in plain cutter. Place on greased baking sheets.
5. Bake at the temperature above for 12–15 minutes.

Oatcakes

Makes 8 large or 16 small

Oven temp 180°C/350°F/Gas Mark 4

Freeze unbaked dough 2 months; baked biscuits 4 months

	Metric	Imperial	American
Medium oatmeal	175 g	6 oz	1 cup
Plain (all-purpose) flour	50 g	2 oz	½ cup
Salt	2.5 ml	½ tsp	½ tsp
Bicarbonate of soda (baking soda)	1.5 ml	¼ tsp	¼ tsp
Bacon fat or lard (shortening)	25 g	1 oz	2 tbls
Hot water	75–125 ml	3–4 fl oz	⅓–½ cup
Fine oatmeal for dusting			

1. Mix together the oatmeal, flour, salt and soda.
2. Melt the fat, and add to the dry ingredients with enough hot water to make a fairly stiff dough. Turn onto a board dusted with fine oatmeal and knead well.
3. Divide the mixture into 2 equal portions. Roll out as thinly as possible into large rounds, dusting well with fine oatmeal to prevent sticking. Pinch the edges to keep them even.
4. Cut into quarters, then cut each quarter across into 2 small triangles if making small oatcakes (to serve with soup).
5. Place on an ungreased baking sheet dusted with fine oatmeal. Bake at the temperature above for about 20 minutes until the edges curl, and the cakes begin to brown. Cool on the sheets and store in an airtight tin.
6. To serve, dust with fine oatmeal, then toast lightly under a moderate grill (broiler). Serve warm or cold with soup or cheese, grilled or fried fish, or with honey for tea.

ROLLED-OUT SWEET BISCUITS AND COOKIES

Basic Creamed Biscuits (Shrewsbury Biscuits)

Makes 26–30

Oven temp 180°C/350°F/Gas Mark 4

Freeze unbaked dough 2 months, baked biscuits 4 months

	Metric	Imperial	American
Butter	100 g	4 oz	½ cup
Caster (superfine) sugar	100 g	4 oz	½ cup
Egg yolk	1	1	1
Plain (all-purpose) flour	225 g	8 oz	2 cups
Baking powder	5 ml	1 tsp	1 tsp
Grated lemon rind	5 ml	1 tsp	1 tsp

1. Beat the butter and sugar together until light and fluffy. Beat in the egg yolk.
2. Sift together the flour and baking powder. Mix with the lemon rind. Mix into the butter-sugar mixture using a fork, then your fingers. Knead lightly to make the mixture stick together.
3. Roll out evenly 5 mm/¼ in thick. Cut in rounds with a 6 cm/2¼ in cutter. Re-roll and cut out the trimmings.
4. Place the biscuits well apart on a greased baking sheet. Prick each with a fork.
5. Bake at the temperature above for 15 minutes or until pale fawn. Loosen, then cool on the sheet and store in an airtight tin.

Variations
Almond Rings: Cut out with a 6.5 cm/2¼ in fluted cutter, then use a 1.5 cm/¾ in cutter to make a hole in the centre of each. Re-roll and re-cut all the trimmings. Bake for 10 minutes, then lightly brush the tops of the biscuits with egg white and sprinkle with a few crushed flaked almonds and a little caster sugar. Complete baking.
Cherry Rings: Make as almond rings, but mix 60 ml/4 tbls finely chopped, washed glacé (candied) cherries into the dough. Bind with a little milk.
Easter Biscuits: Sift 2.5 ml/½ tsp ground cinnamon, 2.5 ml/½ tsp ground mixed spice (ground allspice) and 2.5 ml/½ tsp salt with the flour. Mix in as above then add 45 ml/3 tbls currants and 30 ml/2 tbls chopped mixed peel. Mix in 30 ml/2 tbls milk to bind. Cut out and bake as above.
Raspberry Rings: Make and cut out the basic biscuits. Cut out the centres of half the biscuits with a 2.5 cm/1 in cutter. Bake as above. When cooled, spread the complete rounds with warmed raspberry jam. Sandwich with the rings so that the jam shows through.

Gingerbread Men

Makes about 12

Oven temp 180°C/350°F/Gas Mark 4

Freeze 3 months

	Metric	Imperial	American
Plain (all-purpose) flour	350 g	12 oz	¾ lb
Pinch of salt			
Baking powder	15 ml	1 tbls	1 tbls
Ground ginger	5 ml	1 tsp	1 tsp
Butter or margarine	50 g	2 oz	¼ cup
Golden (light corn) syrup	50 ml	2 fl oz	¼ cup
Treacle (black molasses)	50 ml	2 fl oz	¼ cup
Egg, beaten	1	1	1
Light soft brown sugar	50 g	2 oz	⅓ cup

1. Sift together the flour, salt, baking powder and ginger into a mixing bowl. Heat the oven and warm the fat and the syrup and treacle in the opened cans.
2. When the fat is melted but not hot, add it to the egg. Measure and add the syrup, treacle and sugar.
3. Pour the egg, fat and sweetening into the dry ingredients and mix to a pliable dough.
4. Turn onto a lightly floured board and roll out to 5 mm/¼ in thick. Form into gingerbread men: Either use a gingerbread-man cutter, or shape bodies 5 cm/2 in long, legs and arms 3 cm/1½ in long, heads 2.5 cm/1 in diameter.
5. Make eyes from currants, mouths and hair from shredded peel, angelica, etc.
6. Place on greased baking sheets and bake at the temperature above for about 12 minutes, or until firm. The time will depend on the size of the 'men'.

Note: If wished, instead of making gingerbread men the dough can be put into heart-shapes or stars and the cooked biscuits decorated with coloured icing.

A mouth-watering selection of biscuits. From left, Shrewsbury Biscuits, Pinwheel Biscuits (page 225), Brandy Snaps (page 222), Chocolate Date and Nut Fingers (page 222), Raspberry Rings and Romany Creams (page 223).

DROPPED OR PIPED BISCUITS AND COOKIES

Brandy Snaps

Makes 16

Oven temp 160°C/325°F/Gas Mark 3

Freeze unbaked dough 2 months;   baked biscuits 4 months

	Metric	Imperial	American
Butter or margarine	50 g	2 oz	¼ cup
Golden (light corn) syrup	50 g	2 oz	¼ cup
Soft brown sugar	50 g	2 oz	⅓ cup
Lemon juice	2.5 ml	½ tsp	½ tsp
Plain (all-purpose) flour, sifted	50 g	2 oz	½ cup
Pinch of salt			
Ground ginger	1.5 ml	¼ tsp	¼ tsp

1. Melt together gently the fat, syrup, sugar and lemon juice
2. Mix in the sifted flour, salt and ginger.
3. Drop teaspoonfuls of the mixture 10 cm/4 in apart on greased baking sheets. Bake at the temperature above for 8 minutes.
4. Quickly lift each brandy snap in turn off the sheet with a palette knife and roll it quickly round the greased handle of a wooden spoon. Slip it off as soon as it sets. If the snaps harden while waiting their turn, put them back in the oven for a moment or two to soften them.
5. When cold, the snaps can be filled with whipped cream.

Macaroons

Makes 12 small macaroons

Oven temp 180°C/350°F/Gas Mark 4

Freeze 4 months (baked macaroons only)

	Metric	Imperial	American
Rice paper			
Egg white	1	1	1
Pinch of salt			
Caster (superfine) sugar	100 g	4 oz	½ cup
Ground almonds	50 g	2 oz	½ cup
Split almonds	12	12	12

1. Spread rice paper on a greased baking sheet.
2. Whisk the egg white and salt until stiff. Fold in the sugar and ground almonds.
3. Drop teaspoonfuls, well spaced apart, on the rice paper. Brush each with water to glaze. Top with a split almond.
4. Bake at the temperature above for 15–20 minutes. Cool on a wire rack.

BAR AND WEDGE BISCUITS AND COOKIES

Chocolate, Date and Nut Fingers

Makes 24

Oven temp 180°C/350°F/Gas Mark 4

Freeze 2 months

	Metric	Imperial	American
Plain (all-purpose) flour	150 g	5 oz	1¼ cups
Pinch of salt			
Baking powder	5 ml	1 tsp	1 tsp
Cocoa powder (unsweetened)	20 ml	4 tsp	4 tsp
Butter or margarine	100 g	4 oz	½ cup
Soft brown sugar	100 g	4 oz	⅔ cup
Egg, well beaten	1	1	1
Block stoneless (pitted) dates, finely chopped	75 g	3 oz	½ cup
Chopped mixed nuts	25 g	1 oz	¼ cup
Vanilla essence			

1. Grease the inside of a shallow oblong baking tin (pan), 30 x 22.5 cm/12 x 9 in in size and 2–2.5 cm/¾–1 in deep.
2. Sift together the flour, salt, baking powder and cocoa. Keep aside.
3. Melt the fat in a medium-sized saucepan, add the sugar and bring to the boil. Cool to tepid, stirring occasionally.
4. Whisk in the beaten egg thoroughly. Add the sifted ingredients and mix in well. Then mix in the chopped dates and nuts. Add vanilla to taste.
5. Spread the mixture evenly in the prepared tin (pan) with the back of a spoon. Work quickly before the mixture stiffens. Bake for 30 minutes at the temperature above. Cool in the tin.
6. Before the cake is quite cold, cut it into three equal strips lengthways. Then cut each strip across into eight 3.5 cm/1½ in fingers.

Flapjacks

Makes 16 fingers or square cookies

Oven temp 190°C/375°F/Gas Mark 5

Freeze unbaked dough 2 months; baked
    biscuits 4 months

	Metric	Imperial	American
Butter or margarine	175 g	6 oz	¾ cup
Demerara (light			
brown) sugar	175 g	6 oz	1 cup
Rolled oats			
(porridge oats)	225 g	8 oz	2⅔ cups
Pinch of salt			

1. Grease a 30 x 22.5 cm/12 x 9 in Swiss (jelly) roll tin (pan).
2. Cream the fat until very soft.
3. Mix together the sugar, rolled oats and salt. Stir them into the fat.
4. Spread the mixture evenly in the prepared tin. Bake at the temperature above for 20–25 minutes.
5. Leave to stand for 5–10 minutes in the tin, then cut into fingers or squares.

Shortbread Biscuits

Makes about 36

Oven temp 160°C/325°F/Gas Mark 3

Freeze unbaked dough 2 months; baked
    biscuits 4 months

	Metric	Imperial	American
Plain (all-purpose)			
flour (see note)	350 g	12 oz	3 cups
Pinch of salt			
Caster (superfine)			
sugar	100 g	4 oz	½ cup
Butter or			
margarine, cut in			
small pieces	225 g	8 oz	1 cup

1. Sift together the flour and salt. Add the sugar and the fat.
2. Work all together with the back of a spoon or your hands until fully blended. Knead until smooth. Chill well.
3. Roll out on a floured surface to 5 mm/¼ in thickness. Cut into rounds with a 5 cm/2 in fluted cutter.
4. Bake on ungreased baking sheets at the temperature above for 16–18 minutes. Allow to firm, then cool on a wire rack.

Note: If you wish, use 225 g/8 oz/2 cups flour and 100 g/4 oz/1 cup rice flour or ground rice instead of flour alone. Rice flour gives softer textured biscuits, ground rice grainier ones.

SHAPED BISCUITS AND COOKIES

Romany Creams

Makes 9 sandwich biscuits (18 single biscuits)

Oven temp 160°C/325°F/Gas Mark 3

Freeze unbaked dough 2 months; baked
    biscuits 4 months

	Metric	Imperial	American
Lard (shortening)	25 g	1 oz	2 tbls
Butter or margarine	25 g	1 oz	2 tbls
Caster (superfine)			
or light soft			
brown sugar	50 g	2 oz	¼/⅓ cup
Golden (light corn)			
syrup	2.5 ml	½ tsp	½ tsp
Plain (all-purpose)			
or self-raising			
flour	50 g	2 oz	½ cup
Pinch of salt			
Rolled oats			
(porridge oats)	25 g	1 oz	¼ cup
Ground mixed spice			
(allspice)	2.5 ml	½ tsp	½ tsp
Bicarbonate of soda			
(baking soda) if			
using plain flour	2.5 ml	½ tsp	½ tsp
Boiling water	10 ml	2 tsp	2 tsp
Butter Icing			
(frosting),			
page 238			

1. Cream together the fats and sugar, then beat in the syrup.
2. Sift in the flour and salt. Add the rolled oats and spice. Mix well.
3. Dissolve the soda in the boiling water if used. Mix the dry ingredients with the water to make a firm dough.
4. Shape into 18 equal-sized small balls. Place on greased baking sheets, spaced well apart. Flatten slightly with your palm.
5. Bake at the temperature above for 13–15 minutes. Loosen, then cool on the sheets.
6. When cold, sandwich pairs of biscuits together with butter icing.

Melting Moments

Makes 16

Oven temp 180°C/350°F/Gas Mark 4

Freeze unbaked dough 2 months; baked
    biscuits 4 months

	Metric	Imperial	American
Butter or margarine	100 g	4 oz	½ cup

	Metric	Imperial	American
Caster (superfine) sugar	75 g	3 oz	½ cup
Beaten egg	20–25 ml	4–5 tsp	4–5 tsp
Plain (all-purpose) or self-raising flour	150 g	5 oz	1¼ cups
Pinch of salt			
Baking powder if using plain flour	10 ml	2 tsp	2 tsp
Glacé (candied) cherries, washed, dried and cut into small pieces			

1. Cream together the fat and sugar. Beat in the egg, 30 ml/2 tbls flour and the salt.
2. Stir in the remaining flour and baking powder if using. Knead if required to make a smooth soft dough.
3. Shape the dough into 16 equal-sized small balls.
4. Place the balls, well spaced apart, on greased baking sheets. Flatten slightly, and top each with a piece of cherry.
5. Bake at the temperature above for 16–18 minutes. Loosen, and leave for 5 minutes on the sheets, then finish cooling on a wire rack.

CHILLED AND CUT BISCUITS (REFRIGERATOR COOKIES)

Pinwheel Biscuits

Makes 24

Oven temp 180°C/350°F/Gas Mark 4

Freeze 4 months (before or after baking)

	Metric	Imperial	American
Plain (all-purpose) flour	175 g	6 oz	1½ cups
Baking powder	5 ml	1 tsp	1 tsp
Pinch of salt			
Butter	75 g	3 oz	6 tbls
Caster (superfine) sugar	75 g	3 oz	⅓ cup
Vanilla essence			
Water	20–25 ml	4–5 tsp	4–5 tsp
Cocoa powder (unsweetened)	10 ml	2 tsp	2 tsp

1. Sift together the flour, baking powder and salt into a bowl.
2. Rub (cut) in the butter until the mixture resembles crumbs. Stir in the sugar.

Opposite: *Shortbread Biscuits and Flapjacks (page 223).*

3. Mix to a smooth workable dough with the vanilla and water. Shape it into an even block and cut in half.
4. Sprinkle one half with the cocoa, and work it in evenly.
5. Roll out the uncoloured dough into an oblong 25 x 18 cm/10 x 7 in in size with a long side towards you. Roll out the chocolate dough to the same size and lay it on top. Roll lightly to make the two pieces stick together.
6. Roll up the slab tightly from one long side like a Swiss (jelly) roll. Chill it with the cut edge underneath until firm enough to slice (or freeze if you wish).
7. Cut the roll of dough into slices 1 cm/½ in thick. Pat into neat rounds if misshapen. Place, cut side down, on a greased baking sheet, well apart. Bake for 15 minutes or until the white dough is golden.

Butterscotch Crisps

Makes about 48

Oven temp 190°C/375°F/Gas Mark 5

Freeze unbaked dough 2 months; baked biscuits 4 months

	Metric	Imperial	American
Butter or margarine	100 g	4 oz	½ cup
Dark soft brown sugar	100 g	4 oz	⅓ cup
Egg	1	1	1
Vanilla essence	1.5 ml	¼ tsp	¼ tsp
Plain (all-purpose) flour, sifted	225 g	8 oz	2 cups
Baking powder	7.5 ml	1½ tsp	1½ tsp
Salt	1.5 ml	¼ tsp	¼ tsp

1. Cream together the fat and sugar until light. Beat in the egg and vanilla essence.
2. Sift together the flour, baking powder and salt. Mix them into the creamed mixture a little at a time.
3. On a greaseproof (waxed) paper, shape the dough into 3 rolls about 5 cm/2 in in diameter. Chill for 4 hours or overnight.
4. Cut into slices 3 mm/⅛ in thick. Place on ungreased baking sheets and bake at the temperature above for about 10 minutes or until lightly browned.

Notes:
1. Freeze the dough if you wish. If you only want to bake a few biscuits, cut off the number of slices you want with a freezer or electrically powered knife, and return the rest to the freezer.
2. Most rolled-out biscuit doughs can be formed into rolls, then chilled and sliced as above. A dough containing rolled oats, dried fruit or nuts is not suitable, however.

22
BASIC CAKE MAKING

INGREDIENTS USED IN CAKES

Flour

Plain (all-purpose) flour is better for cakes than strong (bread) flour. It should be sifted before making light sponge cakes or when you wish to combine baking powder or spices with the flour before use.

Self-raising flour which already has a raising agent added can be used for a good many cakes because it makes them light and open-textured. It should not be used for a cake which contains more than one or two beaten eggs because the egg and raising agent combined will make the cake rise too fast and sink again before the oven heat can set it. It should not be used either where the weight of fat or sugar is more than three-quarters the weight of the flour, or for a rich fruit cake unless the recipe requires it.

Wholemeal flour is available as both plain and self-raising flour. Stone-ground flour in particular may be slightly more variable than white flour and need a little more liquid. 81% and 85% extraction flours are slightly more refined than 100% wholemeal flour. Rye flour, barley flour and soya flour are not as a rule used for cakes as they have a distinctive flavour and make a heavy dough even when mixed with white or brown flour.

Cornflour (cornstarch) or rice flour is sometimes added to white flour to make a soft-textured cake. Oatmeal is used for special baked goods such as Parkin (page 234).

Raising Agents

Air, e.g. in whisked egg whites, is a natural raising agent. It expands with heat, pushing the dough upward and so makes a cake larger and lighter for its size.

The commonest chemical raising agent used with or instead of whisked egg whites is *baking powder*. It contains an acid and an alkali (cream of tartar and bicarbonate of soda/baking soda); when moistened, they produce a gas, carbon dioxide, which acts like air on the cake dough. Instead of baking powder, 2 parts of *cream of tartar* to 1 part *bicarbonate of soda/baking soda* can be used in scone mixtures but this causes a very fast rise; or you can make a home-made baking powder using 25 g/1 oz bicarbonate of soda, 50 g/2 oz cream of tartar and 75 g/3 oz rice flour (as a filler to keep the mixture dry.)

Sour milk with bicarbonate of soda is used to raise some cakes and scones. Bicarbonate of soda may also be used alone in cakes made with syrup or treacle, lemon juice, vinegar etc. It tends to make the crumb yellowish.

Salt

Brings out the flavour of most cakes.

Fats

Fat enriches a cake and keeps it moist when stored. *Butter and hard block margarine* are the fats mainly used. *Lard* (shortening) is only used for some syrup cakes and special, regional 'lardy' cakes. *Clarified dripping* is also used for a few traditional cakes. Soft margarine or oil can be used for cakes made by the special all-in-one method (page 228).

Sweetening

Sugar is by far the most common sweetening used. *Caster* (superfine) sugar is better than *granulated* sugar for cakes made by the creaming method since it dissolves more quickly. (See notes opposite.) Most *brown* sugars are only slightly less refined than white sugars although some raw sugars do contain nutrients, so flavouring and colouring a cake. So do *honey, natural maple syrup* and *black molasses*. *Golden (light corn) syrup* and *black treacle (dark molasses)* are sometimes used to sweeten gingerbreads in particular.

Icing (confectioners') sugar is used mainly for decorating and icing cakes.

Eggs

The more eggs that are used, the lighter the cake will be, so it will need less baking powder or other raising agent. Break each egg into a cup before adding it to make sure it is fresh.

A spoonful or two of flour from the measured

quantity can be added with eggs to a creamed mixture to prevent it curdling.

Size 3 eggs are used for all the cakes in this book. If large eggs are used, a little more flour than stated may be needed, and if small eggs are used a little milk or water can be added.

Liquid

The liquid added to a cake mixture is usually milk, but water is sometimes used especially for sponge cakes because it makes them lighter. Strong cold coffee may be substituted for some of the liquid to make a coffee cake. Lemon or orange juice are not used as a rule, even for lemon or orange flavoured cakes, as they tend to make a heavy mixture.

Dried Fruit

Almost any dried, candied or crystallised fruits can be used. They must be dry, and chopped in small pieces if large, or they will sink in the cake and make a heavy, soggy layer at the bottom. Any stones, pips or stems must also be removed. Most dried fruit is now seeded and cleaned before sale, but many cooks like to rinse and dry packeted fruit before using it.

Surplus sugar must be removed from candied or crystallised fruits before use, and they must be washed if sticky (e.g. glacé/candied cherries), chopped and sprinkled with a little flour to keep the pieces separate. Use a knife dipped in hot water for chopping the fruit.

Seeded raisins (raisins with seeds) are larger and juicier than seedless ones.

Packeted block cooking dates are better than dessert dates for use in cakes although they must be chopped;

Prunes should be stoned, easier if they can be soaked first; they also need chopping, as do figs and dried apple rings.

Nuts

Almonds are usually sold shelled, either in their skins or already blanched. Blanched almonds are sold whole, flaked, split, slivered or nibbed (chopped).

To blanch almonds: Put them in a saucepan of cold water, bring to the boil, drain at once under running cold water, pinch off the skins and dry in a cloth.

To split almonds: Prise in half with a sharp knife while still warm after blanching.

To brown almonds: Place blanched almonds in a thin layer on a baking sheet in the oven or on the grill (broiler) pan. Use medium heat, and shake the nuts frequently to prevent them scorching in spots.

To toast almonds or fry them: Treat as for browning, sprinkled with a little pure oil or clarified butter, or fry briefly in a little butter, stirring constantly; tip onto soft kitchen paper as soon as lightly gilded, and pat with paper to remove the hot fat.

Desiccated coconut is sold ready for use, but can be coloured or toasted for decorating cakes. It is used in cake or biscuit mixtures or can be used over jam as a covering instead of icing.

Hazelnuts, peanuts and pistachios need skinning before use. Place on a baking sheet or grill pan, and bake or grill, then rub off skins in a paper bag or cloth. (always use unsalted peanuts for cakes). Most other nuts are sold ready blanched and skinned or do not (e.g. walnuts, pecans) need skinning.

Spices

Ground spices are normally used in cakes. They should be replaced if they remain unused for some time as the flavour diminishes subtly until they smell and taste musty.

Flavourings

Chocolate: Block chocolate should be grated and melted, if required, on a plate over simmering water or in a pan with liquid if the recipe directs it; a microwave oven may also be used.

Vanilla: Vanilla pods (beans) can be used to flavour milk by being infused in it. If washed and dried, the pods can be re-used. They can also be put in a jar of white sugar to flavour it.

Essences: Keep bottles tightly closed. Use essences sparingly; always pour the essence into the bottle cap and drip it into the mixture from the cap.

Notes on the ingredients used in this book:
1. Where self-raising flour can be used instead of plain flour, it is stated in the recipe list. Do not use it otherwise.
2. Hard block margarine should be used for all cakes except those made by the all-in-one method. Where soft tub margarine can be used it is stated in the recipe list.
3. Caster (superfine) sugar is recommended for all cakes made with white sugar.
4. Use size 3 eggs in all the recipes unless otherwise stated.

METHODS USED FOR MAKING CAKE MIXTURES

Rubbing in (Cutting in) Method

Used for plain cakes, scones, buns, biscuits, etc. where the weight of fat is not more than half that of the flour, e.g. 100 g/4 oz/½ cup fat to 225 g/8 oz/2 cups flour.

Put the flour, salt and baking powder into a bowl. Add the fat cut in small pieces. Rub in the fat with the fingertips, moving the thumbs from the little fingers towards the first fingers to break up the fat. Lift the hands high each time you pick up a little fat and flour, to incorporate air in the mixture as it falls back into the bowl. Keep your hands cool so that the fat is evenly mixed in, not melted. Rub until the mixture is like fine breadcrumbs. Then add other ingredients as the recipe directs.

Melting Method

Used for gingerbreads, parkins, some fruit cakes and sweet breads.

The fat and sweetening are melted in a saucepan, and mixed into the dry goods in a bowl. Eggs and other ingredients are added separately.

Creaming Method

Used for rich cakes, e.g. where equal quantities of flour, sugar and fat are used.

Put the fat and sugar into a bowl, and beat by hand or with a beater until light, fluffy and pale. Beat in the eggs, one at a time, with a little of the flour. If the mixture 'curdles', add a little more flour and beat briskly until it smooths out. Fold in the remaining flour and other ingredients as the recipe directs.

As air is incorporated during creaming, less raising agent is needed than for plain cakes; very rich fruit cakes need none at all.

Most cake mixtures made by this method should be stiff enough to cling to the spoon unless shaken off briskly. Very rich fruit cake mixtures may be so stiff that a spoon will stand upright in the mixture.

Whisking Method

Used for sponge cakes without fat. The eggs and sugar are whisked together (over hot water if whisked by hand), until very light and pale; the other ingredients are then folded in. (This method is also used for Genoese sponges which contain melted butter. Victoria sponges or sandwich cakes which also contain fat are made by the creaming method given above.)

All-in-One Method

Used for cakes made with oil or soft tub margarine. All the ingredients are put in a bowl together and whisked rapidly until the mixture is smooth and creamy.

CHOOSING AND PREPARING TINS (PANS) FOR CAKES

Round and Square Tins

Round tins, 7.5 cm/3 in deep are suggested for most large cakes in this book. However, you can equally easily use a square tin if it is more convenient, e.g. if you lack the right size of round tin. A cake baked in a square tin is easier to slice and to store.

A square tin holds the same quantity of mixture

as a round tin 2–2.5 cm/¾–1 in larger in diameter, e.g. an 18 cm/7 in square tin holds the same quantity of mixture as a 20 cm/8 in round tin of the same depth.

Larger or Smaller Round Tins

Cake tins may vary slightly in size, depending on their make and country of origin. As a rule a 5 mm/¼ in deviation does not matter, e.g. you can make an 18 cm/7 in cake in a 19 cm/7¼ in tin. If a tin is 2.5 cm/1 in too big or too small, however, you must adapt the cooking time accordingly.

Shallow sandwich tins (layer cake pans) also vary in depth. To distinguish them, the shallower ones, 2–2.5 cm/¾–1 in deep, are called layer tins or pans in this book and the deeper ones, 3.5 cm/1⅜ in deep are called sandwich tins.

The depth of the mixture determines its baking time. If you use a smaller, deeper tin than the one suggested you must bake the cake for longer than the recipe states. If you use a larger tin, you can shorten the cooking time. It is important, however, that the mixture should not spill over as it rises or rise to a sharp peak and crack. When risen, the layer of mixture should almost fill the tin. If, therefore, you have to use a smaller tin than suggested but of the same depth, use some of the mixture to make small cakes in paper cases. If you have to use a larger tin, set a greased jam jar in the centre of the tin, and bake a ring cake.

Preparing a Cake Tin (Pan)

For most cakes, buns, cookies and biscuits, tins (pans) should be greased, then either coated or lined as follows:
a. Tins for small cakes or buns and baking sheets for biscuits should be greased. Paper cases can be used for some small cakes, and baking sheets should be dusted with flour after greasing for some biscuits. Tins for sponge cakes should be lightly greased then dusted with equal quantities of flour and caster sugar or lined with a circle of paper;
b. tins for large plain (rubbed-in) cakes, should be greased, then lined on the bottom with greased greaseproof (waxed) paper or non-stick baking parchment.
c. tins for rich cakes (creamed mixtures), gingerbreads and Swiss (jelly) rolls should be fully lined after greasing. A tin for a rich fruit cake needing long baking can be lined with foil instead of paper. A long strip of foil or paper stretching across the bottom of a loaf tin and up both sides makes the cake easier to remove from the tin.

To Line a Cake Tin (Round or Square)

a. Cut a single or double piece of greaseproof (waxed) paper to fit the bottom of the tin exactly.
b. Cut a single or double strip long enough to go all round the tin with a small overlap; cut it 5 cm/2 in deeper than the sides of the tin.

c. Fold a 2 cm/¾ in turn-up like a hem right along one long edge of the strip. Make diagonal cuts in the turn-up at 1 cm/½ in intervals for a round tin. A square tin only needs cutting at the four corners.

d. Fit the long strip inside the greased tin, to line the sides, with the turn-up at the bottom. Smooth down the turn-up so that it fits flat against the bottom of the tin. Fit the piece you have cut for the bottom into the tin, covering the whole base including the cut edge of the turn-up.

Note: Line a Swiss (jelly) roll tin by cutting a rectangle of paper which will cover the base and sides of the tin exactly. Slit the corners. Fit the paper into the greased tin, overlapping the edges of the slits so that it fits neatly at the corners.

WHEN A CAKE GOES WRONG

If a cake does not rise:
a. too little raising agent was used or the mixture was over-mixed (flour should be folded in, not beaten);
b. the oven temperature was too high and the cake mixture 'set' before it was fully stretched;
c. too much liquid was added.

If a cake rises to a peak and cracks on top:
a. the fat and sugar were not creamed enough;
b. the oven was too hot or the cake was cooked too near the top;
c. the cake tin was too small or too deep.

If a cake sinks in the centre:
a. too much raising agent was used, so the dough got over-stretched and collapsed before it 'set';
b. the oven heat was too cool to 'set' the cake mixture;
c. the fat, or the whole mixture, was too soft, sometimes due to over-creaming a rich cake mixture;
d. too much moisture was added to the cake mixture, perhaps in the form of damp fruit, too many eggs or too much liquid;
e. the oven door was opened, cooling the air inside, or the cake was taken out before it was properly set or fully cooked.

If fruit has sunk to the bottom of the cake:
a. the mixture was too soft to support it;
b. the fruit was too large and heavy;
c. the oven was too cool to set the mixture soon enough to hold the fruit suspended.

If a cake has a thick crust:
a. the oven heat was a bit too hot;
b. the cake was cooked too long;
c. the cake tin was not lined thickly enough;
d. the tin was too large for the mixture;
e. too much sugar was added.

If a cake over-browns:
a. the cake was cooked too near the top of the oven;
b. a rich cake cooked for some time should have been covered loosely with paper or foil for part of the time.

How to Test When a Cake is Fully Baked

A fully baked cake is evenly browned on top and should have shrunk slightly from the sides of the tin. The top crust should be resilient when lightly pressed with your finger, or, in the case of a fruit cake, should be firm; return a spongy fruit cake to the oven for a short time. If you want to be doubly sure a cake is fully baked, run a thin warm skewer into it; the skewer should come out clean. If it has crumbs or sticky wet mixture sticking to it, the cake is not yet ready.

How to Turn Out (unmould) a Cake

a. Let the cake cool slightly in the tin or it may break when turned out. If you leave the cake in the tin, it will cool too slowly. Steam condensing as the cake cools cannot escape and may make the cake 'sad'.
b. Run a sharp, pointed knife round the inside of the tin between the tin and the cake or lining paper.
c. If the tin has been lined, lift out the lining paper with the cake in it, and place the cake on a wire rack.
d. If the tin has not been lined, place the tin gently on its side and ease out the cake, then set it right way up on the rack.
e. If the tin has a removable base, push the cake upwards from the bottom with one hand and turn it gently into a cloth; slide a knife between the cake and the base of the tin, remove the cake from the base and set it on the rack.
f. If a springform cake tin has been used, release the clip and remove the sides of the tin; remove the cake from the base before putting it on the rack.

23
SPONGES AND SWISS (JELLY) ROLLS

RECIPES FOR SPONGE CAKES, SWISS (JELLY) ROLLS AND SMALL SPONGE CAKES

Classic sponge cakes are made by the whisking method (below) and contain no fat. Three slightly different methods are given below. Genoese sponge cakes which contain melted butter are also made by the whisking method; a general basic recipe is given opposite. A Victoria sandwich or layer cake mixture is called a butter sponge, but is made by the creaming method like rich cakes; see recipe opposite.

Sponge Cake

Makes one 18 cm/7 in single sponge cake; two 15 cm/6 in sandwich layers or 14 sponge fingers

Oven temp See end of recipe

Freeze 4 months without filling or icing

	Metric	Imperial	American
Plain (all-purpose) flour	75 g	3 oz	¾ cup
Pinch of salt			
Pinch of baking powder			
Eggs	3	3	3
Caster (superfine) sugar	75 g	3 oz	6 tbls

1. Prepare a tin (pan) or tins for the type and size of cake you will make, as above. Preheat the oven.
2. Mix together the flour, salt and baking powder.
3. Whisk the eggs in a heatproof bowl until blended, add the sugar and place the bowl over a pan of hot water; it must not touch the water. Continue whisking for 10–12 minutes until the mixture is thick and pale.
4. Remove from the hot water, and continue whisking until cool.
5. Sift in a little of the flour mixture; fold it in gently without losing any of the whisked-in air. Sift in the remaining flour in small portions, folding each in gently.
6. Turn the mixture into the prepared tin or tins. Bake for the appropriate time given below.
7. Leave to cool in the tin for a few minutes, then turn out onto a wire rack to finish cooling. Fill, ice or decorate as you wish when quite cold.

Note: If you whisk the eggs and sugar with an electric beater, you need not do it over hot water; the beater creates enough heat itself. Do not use the beater to incorporate the flour mixture.

Baking temperature and times:
Single large cake 180°C/350°F/Gas Mark 4 for 40 minutes
Sandwich layers 180°C/350°F/Gas Mark 4 for 25 minutes
Sponge fingers on sheet 180°C/350°F/Gas Mark 4 for 8–10 minutes
Sponge fingers in tins 180°C/350°F/Gas Mark 4 for 10–12 minutes

Variation:
Swiss (Jelly) Roll: Grease and line a 30 × 20 cm/12 × 8 in Swiss Roll tin (page 229). Heat the oven to 200°C/400°F/Gas Mark 6. Make the sponge mixture as above, using 2.5 ml/½ tsp baking powder with the flour and salt. Bake for 8–10 minutes or until the sheet of sponge is just lightly gilded. While baking, cut a sheet of greaseproof (waxed) or non-stick bakewell paper a little larger than the Swiss roll. Cut out a second sheet and grease it if the roll will be filled with buttercream or whipped cream.
When the roll is baked, loosen the edges from the tin with a knife-point. Sprinkle it with caster (superfine) sugar and lay the ungreased sheet of paper on top. Holding the paper and tin together at each side, invert the roll onto a flat surface with the paper underneath it. Remove the tin, and the lining paper on the roll. Trim the edges if crusty. Spread with warmed jam and roll up tightly, then cool. Alternatively, cover with the greased paper and roll up; unroll carefully when cold, and fill with buttercream, whipped cream or chopped fruit and cream, then re-roll.

Chocolate Swiss (Jelly) Roll: Sift 75 g/1 oz/¼ cup cocoa powder with the flour. Make the sponge mixture as above, then fold in the flour and cocoa mixture with 1 tablespoon of water. Bake as left.

Victoria Sandwich Cake

Makes two 18 cm/7 in cake layers

Oven temp 180°C/350°F/Gas Mark 4

Freeze 4 months without filling or icing

	Metric	Imperial	American
Butter or margarine	100 g	4 oz	½ cup
Caster (superfine) sugar	100 g	4 oz	½ cup
Eggs, beaten	2	2	2
Plain (all-purpose) or self-raising flour	100 g	4 oz	1 cup
Pinch of salt			
Baking powder if using plain flour	2.5 ml	½ tsp	½ tsp
Filling (see below)			
Icing (confectioners') sugar			

1. Grease and line two 18 cm 7 in sandwich tins (layer pans).
2. Cream together the fat and sugar until light and creamy. Beat in the eggs in 2 or 3 portions, beating each in thoroughly. Add a spoonful of the measured flour if the mixture looks like curdling.
3. Sift together the flour, salt and baking powder, if used. Add to the mixture and mix in lightly.
4. Divide the mixture between the prepared tins. Level the tops. Bake at the temperature above for 25–30 minutes until the layers are resilient and lightly browned. Cool on a wire rack.
5. When cold, cover one layer with any filling you wish. Place the second layer on top. Dredge with icing (confectioners') sugar.

Variations
Large Sandwich Cake: Use 175 g/6 oz each fat, sugar and flour, 3 eggs and 5 ml/1 tsp baking powder. Bake in 19–20 cm/7½–8 in tins.
Lemon or Orange Sandwich Cake: Add the grated rind of 1 small or ½ large lemon or orange to the mixture before adding the eggs. Fill with Lemon or Orange Butter Icing (page 238).
Coffee Sandwich Cake: Add 10 ml/2 tsp instant coffee dissolved in 10 ml/2 tsp water and a few drops of vanilla essence to the mixture. Fill with Coffee Butter Icing (page 238).

Genoese Sponge (Pastry)

Makes one 30 x 20 cm/12 x 10 in sponge

Oven temp 180°C/350°F/Gas Mark 4

Freeze 4 months without filling or icing

	Metric	Imperial	American
Butter or margarine	75 g	3 oz	⅓ cup
Self-raising flour	75 g	3 oz	¾ cup
Pinch of salt			
Eggs	3	3	3
Caster (superfine) sugar	100 g	4 oz	½ cup

1. Grease and line a 30 × 20 cm/12 × 10 in deep Swiss (jelly) roll or shallow baking tin (pan) as for a Swiss roll (page 229).
2. Melt the fat without letting it get hot, and put aside to cool.
3. Sift together the flour and salt and leave in a warm place.
4. Whisk together the eggs and sugar over hot water as for Sponge Cake (Step 3). Whisk for about 10 minutes until the mixture is light, thick and pale. Remove from the heat and continue whisking until the mixture is tepid. Check that the fat is at about the same temperature.
5. Sift half the flour over the mixture, then add half the fat in a thin trickle. Fold in. Repeat, using the remaining flour and fat.
6. Turn gently into the prepared tin. Bake at the temperature above for 20–30 minutes.
7. Cool on a wire rack, then cut into shapes or use as desired.

Uses for Genoese sponge
1. Cut into pieces and use for making a trifle (page 192), or as the base for a cheesecake.
2. Cut into small squares or diamond shapes. Coat with glacé or other icing. Dry on a wire rack with paper spread underneath to catch drips of icing. When dry, decorate with nuts, quartered glacé (candied) cherries, piped butter icing or other decoration. Serve as petits fours.
3. Cut the slab of sponge in half, then sandwich the two halves together with jam or other filling. Cut into fingers and ice or decorate if you wish.

24
PLAIN CAKES, CHOCOLATE CAKES AND GINGERBREADS

Madeira Cake

Makes one 18 cm/7 in cake

Oven temp 180°C/350°F/Gas Mark 4

Freeze 2 months

	Metric	Imperial	American
Plain (all-purpose) flour	225 g	8 oz	2 cups
Baking powder	5 ml	1 tsp	1 tsp
Butter or hard block margarine, softened	175 g	6 oz	¾ cup
Caster (superfine) sugar	175 g	6 oz	¾ cup
Grated lemon rind	1.5 ml	¼ tsp	¼ tsp
Eggs (size 3)	3	3	3
Milk	15 ml	1 tbls	1 tbls
Thin slices of candied citron peel			

1. Grease and line a deep 18 cm/7 in round cake tin.
2. Sift together the flour and baking powder.
3. Cream together the fat, sugar and lemon rind until pale and light in texture. Beat in the eggs, one at a time, blending each in thoroughly. Add a spoonful of the measured flour if the mixture looks like curdling.
4. Re-sift the flour and stir into the creamed mixture a little at a time.
5. Turn the mixture into the prepared tin, and bake at the above temperature for 20 minutes. Lay the citron peel on top of the cake, and continue baking for another 50 minutes or until resilient and golden. Cool on a wire rack.

Variations
Orange Cake: Add the grated rind of 2 oranges as well as lemon rind with the fat and sugar. Omit citron peel.
Rich Seed Cake: Add 10 ml/2 tsp caraway seeds with the flour. Omit the citron peel.
Walnut Cake: Add 75 g/3 oz chopped walnut pieces with the flour. Use 5 ml/1 tsp vanilla essence instead of lemon rind. Decorate with walnut halves instead of citron peel. Bake at

180°C/350°F/Gas Mark 4 for 1½ hours.
Genoa Cake: Omit the baking powder. Stir in, after the flour, 150 g/5 oz/⅞ cup each of sultanas (golden raisins) and currants, 50 g/2 oz½ cup 8 flaked (slivered) almonds washed, dried and quartered glacé (candied) cherries, and 100 g/4 oz/¾ cup chopped mixed peel. Turn into the prepared tin. Smooth the top of the cake with the back of a spoon dipped in milk and scatter 25 g/1 oz/¾ cup flaked (slivered) almonds on top instead of citron peel. Bake at 150°C/300°F/Gas Mark 2 for 2½ hours.

Chocolate Cake

Makes one 20 cm/8 in cake

Oven temp 190°C/375°F/Gas Mark 5

Freeze 2 months (without icing)

	Metric	Imperial	American
Margarine, softened	175 g	6 oz	¾ cup
Caster (superfine) or soft brown sugar	175 g	6 oz	¾/1 cup
Eggs (size 2 or 3)	3	3	3
Plain (all-purpose) or self-raising flour	150 g	5 oz	1¼ cups
Baking powder if using plain flour	15 ml	1 tbls	1 tbls
Cocoa powder (unsweetened)	25 g	1 oz	¼ cup
Milk or orange juice if needed			
Chocolate Icing (page 238) using given quantities			

1. Grease and line a deep 18–19 cm/7–7½ in cake tin, and lightly grease the lining paper.
2. Cream the margarine and sugar until pale and soft; use an electric beater if possible. Beat in the eggs, one at a time, with 15 ml/1 tbls of the flour.

3. Sift together the flour and cocoa, then fold into the batter. The mixture should have a soft dropping consistency. If stiff, add a little milk or orange juice.
4. Turn the mixture gently into the prepared tin. Bake at the temperature above for 55 minutes.
5. Cool on a wire rack, then cover the top and sides with icing.

Note: This mixture is also used for Chocolate Victoria Sandwich Cake and for Chocolate Buns.

Variation
For an 18 cm/7 in cake, use 2 eggs, 100 g/4 oz/ ½ cup sugar, 100 g/4 oz/½ cup margarine, 85 g/ 3½ oz/¾ cup self-raising flour, 15 g/½ oz/3 tsp cocoa. If using plain flour, use 10 ml/2 tsp baking powder.

Chocolate Layer Cake

Makes one 3-layer 23 cm/9 in cake

Oven temp 190°C/375°F/Gas Mark 5

Freeze 2 months (without filling or icing)

	Metric	Imperial	American
Plain (all-purpose) flour	225 g	8 oz	2 cups
Salt	2.5 ml	½ tsp	½ tsp
Baking powder	15 ml	1 tbls	1 tbls
Plain (dark semi-sweet) chocolate, grated	100 g	4 oz	4 squares
Milk	275 ml	½ pt	1¼ cups
Butter or margarine, softened	100 g	4 oz	½ cup
Caster (superfine) sugar	250 g	9 oz	1¼ cups
Eggs, separated	4	4	4
Vanilla essence	5 ml	1 tsp	1 tsp

1. Grease and line three 23 cm/9 in layer cake tins (pans).
2. Sift the flour, salt and baking powder together. Keep aside.
3. Melt the chocolate with 15 ml/1 tbls of the milk in a heatproof bowl over simmering water or in microwave oven.
4. Cream the fat and sugar until light and fluffy. Beat in the egg yolks, then the melted chocolate.
5. Add the sifted ingredients in 3 parts, alternately with the milk, mixing in each addition thoroughly. Add the vanilla.
6. Whisk the egg whites until stiff. Stir 15 ml/ 1 tbls into the mixture, then fold in the rest.
7. Pour the mixture into the prepared tins. Bake each cake at the temperature above for 20–30 minutes. Cool on a wire rack.

8. When cooled, sandwich the layers together with Butter Icing (page 238), Confectioner's Custard (page 240) or whipped cream (for a party gâteau). Cover and decorate with butter icing or as you wish.

Variations
1. To vary the flavour, substitute 15 ml/1 tbls strong black coffee or the grated rind of ½ orange for the vanilla. Use the same flavoured icing.
2. For Milk Chocolate Cake, use 75 g/3 oz/ 3 squares milk (sweet) chocolate and 15 g/ ½ oz/½ square plain (dark semi-sweet) chocolate. Use only 225 g/8 oz/1 cup sugar.

Walnut Cake

Makes one 18 cm/7 in round or square cake

Oven temp 180°C/350°F/Gas Mark 4

Freeze 2 months

	Metric	Imperial	American
Butter or margarine, softened	175 g	6 oz	¾ cup
Caster (superfine) sugar	175 g	6 oz	¾ cup
Eggs (large)	3	3	3
Plain (all-purpose) or self-raising flour	275 g	10 oz	2½ cups
Pinch of salt			
Baking powder if using plain flour	5 ml	1 tsp	1 tsp
Chopped walnut pieces	50 g	2 oz	½ cup
Milk	45 ml	3 tbls	3 tbls
Vanilla essence	2.5 ml	½ tsp	½ tsp

1. Grease and line an 18 cm/7 in round or square cake tin.
2. Cream together the fat and sugar until creamy. Beat in the eggs, one at a time, with 15 ml/1 tbls of the flour.
3. Sift together the remaining flour, salt and baking powder. Stir them into the cake mixture, followed by the walnuts and the milk mixed with a few drops of vanilla.
4. Turn into the prepared tin, and level the top. Bake at the temperature above for about 1½ hours.
5. Cool on a wire rack.

Variations
Cherry Cake: Substitute 50 g/2 oz/¼ cup glacé (candied) cherries, quartered, washed and dried, for the walnuts.
Ginger Cake: Use 4 eggs. Add 2.5 ml/½ tsp ground ginger and a little grated lemon rind with

the flour. Use 75 g/3 oz/⅓ cup chopped preserved stem ginger and 15 ml/1 tbls syrup from jar of ginger instead of walnut pieces and milk.

Rich Fruit or Three Pound Cake: Instead of walnuts, use 450 g/1 lb/3 cups currants and sultanas mixed, 100 g/4 oz/⅓ cup chopped mixed peel and 5 ml/1 tsp grated lemon rind. Use bicarbonate of soda (baking soda) dissolved in the milk instead of baking powder. Do *not* use self-raising flour. Bake in a 20 cm/8 in tin for 2¼ hours at 160°C/325°F/Gas Mark 3.

Parkin

Makes one 28 x 23 cm/11 x 9 in parkin

Oven temp 150°C/300°F/Gas Mark 2

Freeze 2 months

	Metric	Imperial	American
Golden (light corn) syrup or syrup and black treacle (dark molasses) mixed	225 g	8 oz	⅔ cup
Caster (superfine) or light soft brown sugar	100 g	4 oz	½/¾ cup
Lard (shortening)	75 g	3 oz	⅓ cup
Milk	175 ml	6 fl oz	¾ cup
Plain (all-purpose) or self-raising flour	225 g	8 oz	2 cups
Pinch of salt			
Ground ginger	2.5 ml	½ tsp	½ tsp
Medium oatmeal	225 g	8 oz	1⅓ cups
Bicarbonate of soda (baking soda) if using plain flour	2.5 ml	½ tsp	½ tsp

1. Grease and line a 28 x 23 cm/11 x 9 in baking tin (pan) 5 cm/2 in deep.
2. Heat the oven with the opened tin of syrup in it to make measuring easier. Measure the syrup into a pan placed on the scale, adding the weight of the syrup to that of the pan.
3. Add the sugar and lard to the syrup and a little of the milk. Warm gently until melted. Cool slightly.
4. While melting, sift together the flour, salt and ginger and add the oatmeal. Mix well.
5. Dissolve the bicarbonate of soda, if used, in the rest of the milk.
6. Mix the melted ingredients into the flour mixture and add the milk and soda.
7. Turn the mixture evenly into the prepared tin. Bake at the temperature above for 1 hour 20 minutes.
8. Cool in the tin. Leave for at least 24 hours before cutting into squares or fingers.

Treacle Gingerbread

Makes one 26 × 20 cm/10½ × 8 in gingerbread

Oven temp 180°C/350°F/Gas Mark 4

Freeze 2 months

	Metric	Imperial	American
Black treacle (dark molasses)	225 g	8 oz	⅔ cup
Plain (all-purpose) or self-raising flour	225 g	8 oz	2 cups
Pinch of salt			
Ground mixed spice (allspice)	2.5 ml	½ tsp	½ tsp
Ground ginger	5 ml	1 tsp	1 tsp
Bicarbonate of soda (baking soda) if using plain flour	2.5 ml	½ tsp	½ tsp
Milk	30 ml	2 tbls	2 tbls
Lard (shortening)	100 g	4 oz	½ cup
Demerara (light brown) sugar	100 g	4 oz	¾ cup
Eggs, separated	2	2	2
Raisins (optional)	175 g	6 oz	1 cup

1. Grease and line a 26 x 20 cm/10½ x 8 in baking tin (pan) about 5 cm/2 in deep.
2. Warm the can of treacle, uncovered, in the oven. Sift together the flour, salt and spices, and keep aside. Dissolve the bicarbonate of soda, if using, in the milk.
3. Cream together the lard and sugar, and beat in the egg yolks. Mix in the soda and milk, then the warmed treacle. Add the sifted ingredients in 2 or 3 portions, stirring each in well. Stir in the raisins, if used.
4. Whisk the egg whites until they hold soft peaks. Stir 30 ml/2 tbls into the mixture to loosen it, then fold in the rest.
5. Turn the mixture into the prepared tin and level the surface. Bake at the temperature above for 50 minutes. Cool in the tin, then cut into squares.

Note: Substitute 50 g/2 oz flaked almonds for 50 g/2 oz of the raisins if you wish.

25
FRUIT CAKES

Fruit Cake

Makes one 20 cm/8 in round cake

Oven temp 150°C/300°F/Gas Mark 2

Freeze 4 months without almond paste or icing

	Metric	Imperial	American
Plain (all-purpose) flour	225 g	8 oz	2 cups
Baking powder	2.5 ml	½ tsp	½ tsp
Pinch of salt			
Butter or margarine,	225 g	8 oz	1 cup
Caster (superfine) sugar	225 g	8 oz	1 cup
Eggs	4	4	4
Grated rind of 2 lemons			
Sultanas (golden raisins)	100 g	4 oz	⅔ cup
Currants	100 g	4 oz	⅔ cup
Chopped (candied) peel	100 g	4 oz	⅔ cup
Glacé (candied) cherries	100 g	4 oz	⅔ cup
Chopped blanched almonds	50 g	2 oz	½ cup
Brandy (optional)	50 ml	2 fl oz	¼ cup

1. Grease and line a deep 20 cm/8 in cake tin.
2. Sift together the flour and salt.
3. Cream together the fat and sugar. Beat in the eggs one at a time, adding a spoonful of the measured flour if the mixture looks like curdling.
4. Add the sifted flour and salt to the creamed mixture in 2 or 3 portions with the other ingredients, mixing each portion in thoroughly.
5. Transfer the mixture to the prepared tin. Level the top. Bake at the temperature above for 2¾ hours. Cool for 20 minutes in the tin, then finish cooling on a wire rack.

Note: If more convenient, bake the cake at 180°C/350°F/Gas Mark 4 for 1 hour, then at 140°C/275°F/Gas Mark 1 or on the lowest oven shelf for another 2 hours, e.g. if using the oven for another dish.

Variation
Birthday Cake: Cover the completed cooled cake with Almond Paste and Royal Icing (page 239).

Plain Slab Fruit Cake

Makes one oblong 30 x 25 cm/12 x 10 in slab cake

Oven temp 180°C/350°F/Gas Mark 4

Freeze 4 months

	Metric	Imperial	American
Plain (all-purpose) or self-raising flour	275 g	10 oz	2½ cups
Pinch of salt			
Baking powder if using plain flour	12.5 ml	2½ tsp	2½ tsp
Butter or margarine, softened	175 g	6 oz	¾ cup
Caster (superfine) sugar	175 g	6 oz	¾ cup
Eggs	2	2	2
Milk	20 ml	4 tsp	4 tsp
Sultanas (golden raisins) or other dried fruit	175 g	6 oz	1 cup
Chopped (washed and dried) glacé (candied) cherries	25 g	1 oz	¼ cup

1. Grease and line a 30 x 25 cm/12 x 10 in roasting tin (pan).
2. Sift together the flour, salt and baking powder if used.
3. Cream together the fat and sugar. Beat in the eggs, one at a time, adding a spoonful of the measured flour if the mixture looks like curdling.
4. Stir in the flour mixture and mix with the milk to a dropping consistency. Mix in the fruit.
5. Turn the mixture into the prepared tin and level the top. Bake for about 40 minutes. Cool for 15 minutes in the tin, then finish cooling on a wire rack.

Spiced Prune Cake

Makes one 23 cm/9 in ring cake

Oven temp 180°C/350°F/Gas Mark 4

Freeze 2 months

	Metric	Imperial	American
Stewed prunes	450 g	1 lb	1 lb
Butter or margarine, softened	225 g	8 oz	1 cup
Light soft brown sugar	175 g	6 oz	1 cup
Eggs	2	2	2
Plain (all-purpose) flour	175 g	6 oz	1½ cups
Bicarbonate of soda (baking soda)	7.5 ml	1½ tsp	1½ tsp
Ground cinnamon	5 ml	1 tsp	1 tsp
Ground cloves	2.5 ml	½ tsp	½ tsp
Salt	2.5 ml	½ tsp	½ tsp
Butter milk	100 ml	4 fl oz	½ cup
Lemon Glacé Icing (opposite)			

1. Grease and line a 23 cm/9 in cake tin (pan), stand a greased narrow jam jar in the centre, or grease and flour a deep 23 cm/9 in heatproof ring mould.
2. Stone and sieve the prunes to give about 225 g/8 oz/1 cup purée.
3. Cream together the fat and sugar until light and creamy. Beat in the eggs, one at a time. Stir in the prune purée.
4. Sift together the flour, soda, spices and salt. Beat into the prune mixture in three parts, alternately with the butter milk. Beat well each time.
5. Turn the mixture into the prepared tin without disturbing the jar, if used. Bake at the temperature above for 1–1¼ hours. Cool in the tin for 15–20 minutes, then finish cooling on a wire rack. Cover the top of the ring or the whole cake with icing.

Variation
The cake can also be baked in two 23 cm/9 in layers as a sandwich cake. Fill with Lemon Butter Icing (page 238), or as you prefer.

Christmas Cake

Makes one 23 cm/9 in round or 20 cm/8 in square cake

Oven temp 140°C/275°F/Gas Mark 1

	Metric	Imperial	American
Butter, softened	350 g	12 oz	1½ cups
Soft brown sugar	350 g	12 oz	2 cups
Eggs	6	6	6
Plain (all-purpose) flour	450 g	1 lb	4 cups
Salt	1.5 ml	¼ tsp	¼ tsp
Ground mixed spice (allspice)	5 ml	1 tsp	1 tsp
Sultanas (golden raisins)	450 g	1 lb	1 lb
Currants	450 g	1 lb	1 lb
Raisins	100 g	4 oz	¾ cup
Chopped (candied) peel	175 g	6 oz	1 cup
Glacé (candied) cherries	50 g	2 oz	½ cup
Blanched almonds	100 g	4 oz	1 cup
Black treacle (molasses)	30 ml	2 tbls	2 tbls
Brandy	30 ml	2 tbls	2 tbls

1. Cream the fat until it is soft and then add the sugar and continue creaming until the sugar begins to dissolve.
2. Beat in the eggs one at a time.
3. Add the sifted flour and salt with the rest of the ingredients and mix well.
4. Transfer to the greased and lined tin.
5. Bake for about 6½ hours.
6. When completely cooled, store the cake for a minimum of 2 weeks to allow it to mature.
7. A week before you plan to ice it, cover with Almond Paste (page 239).
8. Cover loosely with foil and store the cake to allow the almond paste to dry out then cover with Royal Icing (page 239) and decorate.

26
ICINGS, FROSTINGS AND FILLINGS

ICINGS

The simplest icing to make is Basic Glacé Icing. It consists of sugar and warm or hot water, flavoured and coloured, if desired, or with an optional addition such as chocolate. It is used mostly for coating, and should be applied when still stiff enough to coat thickly the back of a wooden spoon. Once made, it must be applied immediately or covered with dampened greaseproof (waxed) paper to prevent crystallising. Scrape off any crystallised surface before use. Add decorations at once before the icing sets, except for any which may melt or stain the icing if damp, such as crystallised flowers or sweets. Put these on after the icing hardens.

The slightly raw taste of icing sugar can be eliminated if the icing is made with boiling water. It is then sometimes called Boiling Water Icing.

Butter Icing is popular because it can be used for covering, filling or decorating, and (unlike icings without fat) can be frozen. It consists basically of butter and icing (confectioners') sugar with cold or (better) hot or boiling liquid such as milk, cream or fruit juice whisked in, and colouring or extra flavouring if desired. The butter must be well softened or creamed before use, and the icing must be used when soft to prevent it pulling off cake crumbs and looking speckled. The icing can be refrigerated before use, but must be well softened by beating before being applied. (For freezing, see Freezing Hints, Chapter 29.)

American Frosting is fluffier than Glacé or Butter Icing, and is usually spread thickly or swirled in peaks. Apply when soft and spreadable.

Plain cakes can also be covered with a brushed-on covering of warmed apricot glaze, then covered with cake or biscuit crumbs or chopped nuts, pressed on firmly.

Almond icing or paste can be used to cover or fill a cake or pastry, and for decorations. It is used under Royal Icing on rich fruit cakes, such as wedding cakes, to give a flat, even surface. It should be applied over a brushed-on coating of warm apricot glaze.

Royal Icing is the classic hard icing, both for covering and for piped decorations. It is always used over a base of almond paste, which must be left to set for 2–5 days before icing; otherwise the almond oil may seep into the icing and cause discoloration. Two coats of icing are usually needed and the icing must be quite hard and dry before decorations are added. Royal Icing can also be flicked up in small peaks, to make a Christmas Cake "snow scene".

Basic Glacé Icing

Covers the top of one 18 cm/7 in cake

Not suitable for freezing

	Metric	Imperial	American
Icing (confectioners') sugar	100 g	4 oz	¾ cup
Tepid, hot or boiling water	15 ml	1 tbls	1 tbls
Flavouring (optional)			
Colouring (optional)			

1. Sift the icing sugar into a bowl.
2. Add the water, a little at a time, stirring with a wooden spoon, until a smooth coating consistency is obtained. (If the icing is too thin, sift in a little extra sugar.)
3. Add flavouring and colouring to taste. Pour over the cake and spread with a knife dipped in hot water. Do not move the cake until the icing has set.

Variations
Almond Icing: Use Almond essence and a few drops of lemon juice as flavouring.
Lemon Icing: Add grated lemon rind and lemon juice, and a few drops of yellow food colouring.
Orange Icing: Make like lemon icing, substituting orange for lemon and adding orange colouring.
Pineapple Icing: Add pineapple essence and a little yellow colouring.

Basic Butter Icing

Covers 2 layers of one 18–20 cm/7–8 in cake

Freeze 2–3 months

	Metric	Imperial	American
Icing (confectioners') sugar	275 g	10 oz	2 cups
Softened butter	100 g	4 oz	½ cup
Liquid, e.g. milk, single (light) cream or fruit juice, hot or cold	15 ml	1 tbls	1 tbls

1. Sift the icing sugar and add gradually to the butter with the liquid.
2. Beat until the icing is smooth and of a soft spreading consistency.

Variations
Coffee Butter Icing: Dissolve 5 ml/1 tsp instant coffee in 15 ml/1 tbls hot water. Allow to cool and use instead of the liquid in the plain butter icing.

Lemon or Orange Butter Icing: Use 15 ml/1 tbls lemon or orange juice as the liquid and add a little grated rind.

Walnut or Hazelnut Butter Icing: Add 25 g/1 oz/ 2 tbls of either chopped walnuts or chopped skinned hazelnuts.

Rich Butter Icing

Covers two 20 cm/8 in cakes

Freeze 2–3 months

	Metric	Imperial	American
Butter or margarine, softened	50 g	2 oz	¼ cup
Salt	1.5 ml	¼ tsp	¼ tsp
Icing (confectioners') sugar	450 g	1 lb	3⅓ cups
Double (heavy) cream	75–100 ml	3–4 fl oz	⅓–½ cup
Vanilla essence	5 ml	1 tsp	1 tsp

1. Cream the butter or margarine with the salt. Sift the icing sugar. Heat the cream gently, but do not boil.
2. Beat the sugar and hot cream into the butter alternately, blending well. Beat in the vanilla and continue beating until the icing is cold, creamy and thick enough to spread.

Note: If you need a stiffer icing, use a little less cream.

Variation
Browned Butter Icing: Heat the butter or margarine until brown. Remove from the heat and add salt. Beat in the sugar and cold cream. Omit the vanilla.

American Frosting

Covers top and sides of one 15 cm/6 in cake

Not suitable for freezing

	Metric	Imperial	American
Granulated (white) sugar	175 g	6 oz	¾ cup
Water	30 ml	2 tbls	2 tbls
Pinch of cream of tartar			
Egg white	1	1	1
Flavouring to taste (optional)			
Colouring (optional)			

1. Put the sugar and water in a large heatproof bowl over a pan of hot water. Stir until the sugar dissolves. Add the cream of tartar and egg white.
2. Place the pan over heat and bring to the boil. Whisk for 5–7 minutes, or until it forms peaks. Take the bowl off the pan, and add flavouring and colouring if desired.
3. Continue whisking until the frosting has the consistency required, either for a thick coating or for a swirled and peaked one.
4. Have the cake ready on a turntable, pour on the frosting and spread with a round-bladed knife.

Variation
Seafoam Frosting: Make as above, using 400g/ 14 oz/2 cups soft brown sugar, 150 ml/¼ pt/ ⅔ cup water, 1.5 ml/¼ tsp cream of tartar, 2 egg whites, and 5 ml/1 tsp vanilla essence.

Chocolate Icing

Covers tops of two 18–20 cm/7–8 in cakes or layers of one sandwich (layer) cake

Freeze 2 months

	Metric	Imperial	American
Plain (semi-sweet dark) chocolate, grated	50 g	2 oz	2 squares
Milk	15 ml	1 tbls	1 tbls

	Metric	Imperial	American
Icing (confectioners') sugar	275 g	10 oz	2 cups
Softened butter	100 g	4 oz	½ cup
Vanilla essence			

1. Place the chocolate in a heatproof bowl over hot water. Add the milk, stir until the chocolate has melted, then cool.
2. Sift the icing sugar and beat gradually into the chocolate mixture.
3. Beat in the softened butter and vanilla essence and use at once.

Mocha Icing

Covers two 20 cm/8 in cakes (approx)

Freeze 2–3 months

	Metric	Imperial	American
Butter or margarine	175 g	6 oz	¾ cup
Sifted icing (confectioners') sugar	350 g	12 oz	2½ cups
Unsweetened Cocoa powder	15 ml	1 tbls	1 tbls
Vanilla essence	5 ml	1 tsp	1 tsp
Strong coffee	75 ml	5 tbls	5 tbls

1. Cream the butter or margarine. Mix the sugar and cocoa and add to the creamed fat. Beat until light and fluffy.
2. Add the vanilla essence and then the coffee, a little at a time, to give a spreading consistency.
3. Use at once for decorating or filling.

Almond Icing or Paste

Covers top and sides of one 23 cm/9 in cake

Freeze 2 months (after applying)

	Metric	Imperial	American
Caster (superfine) sugar	175 g	6 oz	¾ cup
Icing (confectioners') sugar	175 g	6 oz	1 cup
Ground almonds	350 g	12 oz	3 cups
Eggs	2	2	2
A few drops of almond essence			
Lemon juice	5 ml	1 tsp	1 tsp
Sherry (optional)	10 ml	2 tsp	2 tsp

1. Sift together the sugars and add the almonds. Mix together. Make a well in the centre and beat in the eggs, one at a time.

2. Add the almond essence, lemon juice and sherry if using, and knead the paste until quite smooth.
3. If not to be used at once, put the almond paste in a polythene bag to prevent it from drying out.

Royal Icing

Covers the top and sides of one 20 cm/8 in cake

Not suitable for freezing

	Metric	Imperial	American
Icing (confectioners') sugar	450 g	1 lb	3⅓ cups
Lemon juice	5 ml	1 tsp	1 tsp
Egg whites	2	2	2
Blue food colouring (optional)			
Glycerine (optional)			

1. Sift the icing sugar. Mix the lemon juice and egg whites in a bowl and gradually add the icing sugar. Beat until the icing is smooth and white. It should coat the back of the spoon and only slowly settle to its own level.
2. A few drops of blue food colouring can be added to prevent the icing developing a yellowish tinge when kept, and glycerine to prevent the icing becoming brittle.
3. Cover the icing at once with a damp cloth and leave to stand for about 15–20 minutes to allow any air bubbles to rise to the surface. Gently tapping the bowl on the table will help these bubbles to rise.
4. This consistency of icing can be run onto a cake as when using glacé icing. For piping, icing sugar must be added so that it is stiff enough to stand in peaks.
5. Icing for decorating the cake can be made at the same time as the cake icing and stored in a bowl covered with a damp cloth.

FILLINGS

Warmed jam and whipped cream are the simplest fillings for cakes, but do not freeze them. Butter icings are sometimes used, often enriched with extra fat. Almond paste is also sometimes used. Most other fillings are custard-based and cannot therefore be frozen. See Freezing Hints, page 255.

Almond and Walnut Filling

Fills 6 small tartlets, one 15–18 cm/6–7 in sandwich (layer) cake or 12 petits fours or biscuits

Freeze 2 months

	Metric	Imperial	American
Ground almonds	45 ml	3 tbls	3 tbls
Vanilla essence	5 ml	1 tsp	1 tsp
Finely chopped walnuts	15 ml	1 tbls	1 tbls
Warmed smooth apricot jam	45 ml	3 tbls	3 tbls

Mix all the ingredients together and use as a filling for biscuits, sandwich (layer) cakes or petits fours.

Chocolate Filling

Fills two 15–18 cm/6–7 in sandwich (layer) cakes or 12 tartlets

Freeze 2 months

	Metric	Imperial	American
Plain or bitter-sweet chocolate or cocoa powder (unsweetened)	25 g	1 oz	1 square/ ¼ cup
Butter or margarine	100 g	4 oz	½ cup
Icing (confectioners') sugar	225 g	8 oz	1²/₃ cups
Vanilla essence			

1. Break up the chocolate and place it in a heatproof bowl over a pan of warm water until melted. Alternatively, dissolve the cocoa in a little hot water.
2. Beat the fat and sugar to a creamy paste, add the chocolate or cocoa and the vanilla, and beat until blended in.

Confectioners' Custard

Makes 350 ml/12 fl oz/1½ cups

Not suitable for freezing

	Metric	Imperial	American
Butter or margarine	25 g	1 oz	2 tbls
Flour	25 g	1 oz	¼ cup
Milk	275 ml	½ pint	1¼ cups
Sugar	50 g	2 oz	¼ cup
Egg	1	1	1
Egg yolk	1	1	1

Pinch of salt
Vanilla essence

1. Make a white sauce with the butter or margarine, flour and milk, and cook, stirring, for about 5 minutes until smooth and glossy.
2. Remove from the heat, add the sugar and beat for a few minutes, then add the eggs, salt and vanilla essence.
3. Beat the custard well and cook without boiling until very thick. Use cold.

Marshmallow Topping or Filling

Covers one 20 cm/8 in cake or two 18 cm/7 in sponge cake layers or tops and fills one cake

Not suitable for freezing

	Metric	Imperial	American
Icing (confectioners') sugar	100 g	4 oz	¾ cup
Water	50 ml	2 fl oz	¼ cup
Glucose	10 ml	2 tsp	2 tsp
Gelatine (unflavored gelatin)	5 ml	1 tsp	1 tsp
Flavouring			

1. Put the sugar, water, glucose and gelatine into a pan and mix well. Bring slowly to boiling point and boil for 1 minute.
2. Pour into a bowl, add the flavouring and allow to cool a little. Beat until very thick and use at once for icing or filling cakes.

Notes:
1. If the filling is not used at once, it will become too stiff, but may be softened again by standing the bowl in hot water.
2. When beginning to stiffen, this icing can also be piped in small rosettes or baby meringue shapes on waxed paper for use as petits fours.

Mincemeat

Freeze 2 months

	Metric	Imperial	American
Seedless raisins	675 g	1½ lb	4 cups
Sultanas (golden raisins)	450 g	1 lb	3 cups
Currants	450 g	1 lb	3 cups
Apples	1 kg	2 lb	2 lb
Chopped (candied) peel	450 g	1 lb	3 cups
Finely chopped suet	450 g	1 lb	2 cups
Brown sugar	800 g	1¾ lb	3¼ cups
Grated rind of 1 lemon			

Grated rind of 1 orange			
Juice of ½ lemon			
Juice of ½ orange			
Ground mixed spice (allspice)	25 g	1 oz	¼ cup
Grated nutmeg	2.5 ml	½ tsp	½ tsp
Brandy, rum or beer	275 ml	½ pt	1¼ cups

1. Chop the raisins and sultanas and mix with the currants. Peel, core and chop the apples; finely chop the candied peel, and add these with all the other ingredients to the fruit, adapting spice quantities to taste. Mix very thoroughly.
2. Pack into clean dry jars and cover with jam papers or squares of polythene, secured with string or elastic bands.
3. Mincemeat should be kept for at least a few weeks before use.

Mocha Filling

Fills two 18 cm/7 in sponge sandwich cake layers or tops and fills one cake

Freeze 2 months

	Metric	Imperial	American
Softened butter or margarine	25 g	1 oz	2 tbls
Cocoa powder (unsweetened)	15 ml	1 tbls	1 tbls
Instant coffee	10 ml	2 tsp	2 tsp
Warm water	10 ml	2 tsp	2 tsp
Icing (confectioners') sugar, sifted	100 g	4 oz	¾ cup

1. Cream together the fat and cocoa powder.
2. Dissolve the instant coffee in the warm water. Add to the creamed fat.
3. Gradually beat in the icing sugar. Beat until smooth.

DESSERT AND CAKE DECORATIONS

Chocolate Curls
Scrape a vegetable peeler along the flat side of a thick bar of plain dark or bittersweet chocolate, breaking it off into curls.

For wider, thicker curls, spread melted plain chocolate on a marble or Formica surface. Scrape the cooled chocolate off into long curls with a sharp knife held almost flat against the chocolate. This is called chocolate caraque.

Moulded Marzipan Shapes
Almond Paste (page 239) or marzipan can be moulded into flower or vegetable shapes. Knead the paste until pliable; it must not be sticky. Tint it with a few drops of food colouring if you wish.

Cut out small ovals for leaves and pinch into shape. For flowers, cut out small circles, and make radiating cuts from the edge almost to the centre for petals. Pinch the ends of the petals into points.

For potatoes, make uneven balls of paste, and dust with cocoa.

For other vegetables, make appropriate small shapes tinted the right colour, e.g. for carrots make small rolls of orange-tinted marzipan tapered at one end and stick a scrap of candied angelica at the broad end as a stalk. For apples, form green paste into small balls, indent one end and stick in a small whole clove as a stalk.

Praline

Makes 225 g/8 oz/½ lb (approx)

	Metric	Imperial	American
Caster (superfine) sugar	100 g	4 oz	½ cup
Vanilla pod (bean)	½	½	½
Water	15 ml	1 tbls	1 tbls
Browned or toasted flaked (slivered) almonds or chopped hazelnuts	100 g	4 oz	1 cup

1. Heat the sugar, vanilla pod and water until the sugar is light golden-brown. Stir in the nuts.
2. Immediately, turn the mixture onto an oiled metal tray or marble slab. Remove the vanilla pod. Leave to harden.
3. Crush the praline in a blender or food processor, finely if for flavouring, more coarsely for decorating or coating cakes, desserts and gâteaux.
4. Store in an airtight jar for use when required.

27
JAMS AND JELLIES

JAMS

A good jam has a distinct colour and flavour of fruit; it should be well set but not gluey or solid, and should keep well.

Quality of Fruit

The fruit should be fresh, dry and, if anything, underripe; overripe fruit does not set properly and may go mouldy in storage. Fruit contains a natural gum-like substance called pectin which sets or 'jells' when boiled with sugar, so one must extract this pectin from the fruit by simmering it before adding the sugar to make jam. This is easiest to do when the fruit is slightly underripe and when acid is present. (Acid also helps to set the jam, brightens its colour, and prevent the sugar crystallising.)

Fruits vary a great deal in the amount and quality of acid and pectin they contain. Many fruits contain enough natural acid and pectin to make jam but in fruits which are short of them, the lack can be made up by mixing two fruits, e.g. blackberries and apples, by adding an acid such as lemon juice or tartaric acid, or by adding commercially-made pectin in liquid or powder form. (To use this with fruits short of pectin, follow the maker's instructions.)

The chart below shows which fruits need 'help' before being made into jam.

When fruit is simmered to extract pectin, water is usually added, except to very soft fruit or when making whole-fruit jam. Add only enough water to prevent the fruit burning; the firmer the fruit, the more it will need. Less water is needed if the fruit is simmered, covered, in the oven.

Sugar

Is is important to add the right amount of sugar and to boil it until the jam will be sweet enough and will neither ferment (because it has too little sugar) nor crystallise (because it has too much). White sugar is normally used; lump sugar or preserving sugar makes the least scum. Fruits poor in pectin should have less sugar added than pectin-rich fruits. The sugar must be dissolved before the jam is brought to the boil to prevent crystals forming, and it will dissolve more easily if warmed before use.

To make a well-set jam of good keeping quality the added sugar should provide 60% of the weight of the completed jam.

EQUIPMENT

Preserving Pan

A heavy, good-quality pan should be used, large enough to let a jam boil fast without overflowing or splashing. It can be made of stainless steel, heavy aluminium or unchipped enamel. A brass or copper pan should not be used because a proportion of the ascorbic acid (Vitamin C) in the fruit is destroyed by these metals. Fruit also reacts with iron or zinc, and the colour and flavour of the preserve is then spoiled. No lid is required.

Jars

Jam jars can be of any size or shape, provided they are reasonably wide-mouthed, and the glass is of even thickness all over. Jars should be clean, dry

Fruits rich in protein	Fruits lacking in pectin	Fruits containing acid for jam making	Fruits lacking in acid
Blackberries	Ripe cherries	Sour apples (some types)	Ripe fruits,
Cranberries	Rhubarb	Early blackberries	especially:—
Currants	Ripe strawberries	Cranberries	Black cherries,
(Red and black)	Vegetable marrows	Currants	Blackberries
Damsons	Fruits grown in	Damsons	(late)
Plums	wet seasons	Gooseberries	Cherries
Loganberries		Loganberries	Strawberries
Raspberries		Raspberries	

(to prevent mould forming) and warm (to prevent the glass cracking) when the jam is poured in. They should stand on wood or newspaper, not on a metal or tiled surface.

GENERAL METHOD FOR MAKING JAMS

1. Prepare the fruit as for any other cooking. Remove stems, leaves and damaged or bruised portions. Remove stones if you wish. If you like the flavour, crack a few apricot or plum stones and cook the white kernels with the jam.
2. Weigh the fruit, and note the weight. Put the fruit in the preserving pan, with water if needed, to prevent burning, e.g. with hard fruit. More will be needed in a wide shallow pan than a deep one, when the fruit is under-ripe or if the quantity is small. Any acid required is added at this stage. Usual quantities per 1.8 kg/4 lb fruit are:

   30 ml/2 tbls lemon juice; or
   2.5 ml/½ tsp citric or tartaric acid: or
   150 ml/¼ pt/⅔ cup redcurrant or gooseberry juice.
3. Simmer the fruit gently until pulpy. Black-currants, damsons, gooseberries or plums need about 30 minutes cooking to break down the fruit and soften the skins. Fruits with added water should be boiled down to about two thirds of the original volume.
4. Test for pectin. Take 5 ml/1 tsp stewed fruit, put it into a small warmed glass and allow to cool. Then add 15 ml/1 tbls methylated spirit and stir. Leave for 1 minute. If there is plenty of pectin, a transparent jelly-like lump will be formed; a moderate pectin content results in 2 or 3 smaller clots; a poor content results in a dribble of small clots. The fruit may need more stewing, or added pectin. Either blend in some fruit or fruit juice rich in pectin, or commercial pectin. Take care not to add too much: it will spoil the flavour of the jam.
5. Add 350–600 g/¾–1¼ lb sugar to the fruit. Fruits rich in pectin will set more sugar than fruits with only a fair pectin content; as a general rule, add 450 g/1 lb sugar to 350 g/¾ lb fruit which is rich in pectin, but use 450 g/1 lb sugar to 450 g/1 lb fruit with only moderate pectin. Cane or beet sugar can be used in the form of preserving sugar, granulated or lump sugar.

   The sugar dissolves more quickly, and cools the fruit less if warmed before use. Stir until it is dissolved, then boil quickly, stirring occasionally to prevent the sugar sticking to the pan bottom, until the jam sets when tested (see right). The time can vary from 5–35 minutes, depending on the type of fruit used.

To Test Jam for Setting

Drop a scant teaspoonful of the jam on a cold plate; if it is ready it will set and wrinkle when you push it with your finger.

Reduce the heat under the jam to prevent it over-boiling while testing.

Finishing the Jam

Take the jam off the heat, and remove any scum quickly, using a perforated spoon dipped in hot water and wiped just before use. Have the jars ready, warmed and dry. Fill the jars with jam to the brim to allow for shrinkage in cooling. Leave whole-fruit jam in the pan until a thin skin forms before you pot it, to prevent the fruit rising in the jars; then stir gently and pot. (This also applies to marmalades.) See page 246.

After filling, wipe off any drips of jam on the neck and rim of the jar, cover with a waxed paper disc which just fits the top of the jam in the jar; place it waxed side down. Take care that there is no space between the paper and jam where mould can collect during storage.

When cold, cover with cellophane or parchment, moistening only the upper surface not touching the jar.

Label with the name of the jam and the date it is made, and store in a cool, dry, dark place.

JAM RECIPES

Cherry Jam

	Metric	Imperial	American
Cherries (see note)	2.5 kg	5½ lb	5½ lb
Juice of 2 large lemons or			
tartaric acid	5 ml	1 tsp	1 tsp
Sugar, warmed	1.6 kg	3½ lb	3½ lb

1. Wash and stone the cherries and put in a preserving pan with the lemon juice or acid.
2. Place over a very low heat until the juice begins to flow, then simmer until the fruit is soft.
3. Test for pectin.
4. Add the warmed sugar, stir until dissolved and boil until setting point is reached.
5. Remove the scum.
6. Allow to cool a little to prevent the fruit rising. Pour into heated jars and cover.

Note: Not all cherries are suitable for jam making; the best kinds are May Duke, Morello and Flemish.

Blackcurrant Jam

	Metric	Imperial	American
Blackcurrants	1.8 kg	4 lb	4 lb
Water	1.7 l	3 pt	7½ cups
Sugar	2.7 kg	6 lb	6 lb

1. Remove stalks, and wash the fruit.
2. Put in a preserving pan with the water, bring to the boil, and simmer until the fruit is pulpy.
3. Test for pectin.
4. Add the sugar, stir until dissolved and boil for about 5 minutes until setting point is reached.
5. Remove scum, pour into warmed jars and cover.

Gooseberry Jam

	Metric	Imperial	American
Gooseberries	1.8 kg	4 lb	4 lb
Water	1 l	1¾ pt	4¼ cups
Sugar, warmed	2.3– 2.7 kg	5–6 lb	5–6 lb

1. Top, tail and wash the gooseberries.
2. Put into a pan with the water and simmer until the fruit is soft.
3. Test for pectin.
4. Add the warmed sugar, stir until dissolved and boil until setting point is reached.
5. Remove the scum, pour into heated jars and cover.

Note: The colour of the finished jam depends upon the type of fruit and its ripeness and also the boiling time after the sugar has been added. The longer the boiling, the deeper the red colour the jam will develop.

Raspberry Jam

	Metric	Imperial	American
Hulled raspberries	1.4 kg	3 lb	3 lb
Sugar, warmed	1.4 kg	3 lb	3 lb

1. Wash the fruit, put in a pan and cook slowly until the juice begins to flow.
2. Test for pectin.
3. Add the warmed sugar, stir until dissolved and bring to the boil.
4. Boil until setting point is reached, remove the scum, pour into heated jars and cover.

Greengage Jam

	Metric	Imperial	American
Greengages	1.4 kg	3 lb	3 lb
Water	150– 275 ml	¼–½ pt	⅔–1¼ cup
Sugar, warmed	1.4 kg	3 lb	3 lb

1. Wash the greengages and cut into halves without removing the stones (pits).
2. Put in a preserving pan with the water and simmer until tender; ripe or juicy fruit will only need a little water and brief cooking, firm varieties will take longer and need more water.
3. Test for pectin.
4. Add the sugar, stir until dissolved and bring to the boil.
5. Remove the stones as they rise to the surface.
6. Boil rapidly until setting point is reached, remove the scum, pour into heated jars and cover.

Note: The stones can be split and the kernels returned to the jam for the rest of the boiling time.

Plum Jam

	Metric	Imperial	American
Plums	1.4 kg	3 lb	3 lb
Water	275 ml	½ pt	1¼ cups
Sugar, warmed	1.4 kg	3 lb	3 lb

Use method given for Greengage Jam (firm varieties).

GENERAL METHOD FOR MAKING WHOLE FRUIT JAMS

Use this method when you want to prevent the fruit pulping. Large fruits such as plums can be cut up before cooking, but the pieces should remain whole when making the jam.

1. Prepare the fruit, weigh it, wash it and drain well.
2. Use equal quantities of fruit and sugar, e.g. 450 g/1 lb fruit to 450 g/1 lb sugar. Put alternate layers of fruit and sugar in a bowl and leave in a cool place for 24 hours.
3. Stir gently, pour into a preserving pan and add lemon juice or tartaric acid if needed. Bring to the boil slowly, stirring carefully to avoid breaking up the fruit.
4. Boil rapidly until the jam sets when tested (page 243). The time can vary from 5–35 minutes. When ready, the fruit will sink in the

syrup and the scum will stop rising. Add a small piece of butter, and stir to dispel the scum.

5. Leave the jam in the preserving pan until fairly cool, when a thin skin begins to form on top. Stir gently, then pot as described on page 243.

WHOLE FRUIT JAM RECIPES

Rhubarb Jam

	Metric	Imperial	American
Rhubarb	2.7 kg	6 lb	6 lb
Preserving sugar	2.7 kg	6 lb	6 lb
Grated rind and juice of 2 lemons			
Bruised fresh ginger root	50 g	2 oz	2 oz

1. Prepare the rhubarb and cut into 5 cm/2 in pieces.
2. Put into a bowl with the sugar and leave for 24 hours.
3. Pour into a pan, add the lemon juice, the ginger and the lemon rind tied in muslin (cheesecloth).
4. Follow general method of making Whole Fruit Jams, removing the muslin bag and its contents before pouring the jam into the jars.

Strawberry Jam

	Metric	Imperial	American
Hulled strawberries	1.8 kg	4 lb	4 lb
Sugar	1.6 kg	3½ lb	3½ lb
Juice of 1 lemon			

1. Follow the general method of making Whole Fruit Jams.

JELLIES

Fruit which will make good jam will also make good jelly. The notes given on jam-making (pages 242–243) also apply to jelly-making. In addition, the jelly must be strained and cleared through a jelly bag.

Jelly bag: You can buy a special jelly bag made of thick flannel, which will make clear jelly. It has cotton tape loops which can be used to hang the bag from a swinging towel rail or the legs of an upturned stool; a bowl is placed under the bag to catch the dripping juice. Several thicknesses of fine butter muslin or cheesecloth draped in a fine sieve can be used instead if you do not have a jelly bag.

GENERAL METHOD FOR MAKING JELLIES

1. Cut up large fruits, but do not peel or stone them. Wash the fruit.
2. Put the fruit in a preserving pan with 150–425 ml/¼–¾ pt (⅔–2 cups) water per 450 g/1 lb fruit, the quantity depending on the hardness of the fruit.
3. Simmer until the fruit is soft and broken. Test for pectin (page 243).
4. Pour into the jelly bag and leave until all the juice has dripped through; this may take several hours or overnight. Do not squeeze the bag or try to press the juice through with a spoon or the jelly will be cloudy.
5. Measure the juice and weigh out 350–450 g/¾–1 lb sugar for each 175 ml/1 pt/2½ cups juice, the quantity depending on how much pectin the juice contains. Warm the sugar.
6. Heat the juice, add the sugar, stir until dissolved and bring to the boil. Boil until setting point is reached. This usually takes from 15–30 minutes or until a temperature of 105°C/220°F is reached. Test by placing a sugar thermometer in the boiling jelly. Dip the thermometer in very hot water just before and after placing it in the jelly; do not let it touch the bottom of the pan. Alternately test as for jam (page 243). (Note that, if over-boiled, jelly darkens and looks like syrup or treacle.)
7. Remove the scum. Pour the jelly into *small* warmed jars, and cover like jam (page 243).

JELLY RECIPES

Redcurrant Jelly

Redcurrants
Sugar, warmed

1. Wash the redcurrants and remove any leaves. You need not remove small stalks.
2. Put the fruit in a pan with 425 ml/¾ pt/2 cups water per 450 g/1 lb fruit. As redcurrants are rich in pectin, even more water can be added to firm fruit. Simmer for about 20 minutes until the fruit is pulpy.
3. Test for pectin.
4. Strain the juice through a jelly bag or muslin (cheesecloth) as described left. Measure the juice, return to the preserving pan and heat.
5. Add 450 g/1 lb sugar per 575 ml/1 pt/2½ cups juice, stir until dissolved, then boil until setting point is reached.
6. Remove the scum, pour into small warmed jars, and cover like jam.

Note: This jelly can be served with lamb, jugged hare, etc.

Apple and Mint Jelly

	Metric	Imperial	American
Green cooking (tart) apples	1.5 kg	3 lb	3 lb
Juice of 2 lemons			
Bunch of fresh mint			
Sugar, warmed			
Chopped mint			

1. Wash the apples and cut into pieces including peel and cores.
2. Put into a preserving pan and cover with water. Add the lemon juice and a few sprigs of mint. Stew until the fruit is soft and broken.
3. Test for pectin.
4. Strain the juice through a jelly bag or muslin (cheesecloth) as described on page 245. Measure the juice.
5. Return the juice to the preserving pan and heat it. Add 450 g/1 lb sugar for each 575 ml/1 pt/2½ cups juice, stir until dissolved, add a little finely chopped mint and boil until setting point is reached.
6. Remove the scum, pour into heated jars and cover.

Note: This jelly can be served with lamb or pork.

GENERAL METHOD FOR MAKING MARMALADE AND JELLY MARMALADE

1. Oranges (sweet or bitter), lemons or grapefruit can be used, separately or mixed. Limes and tangerines are sometimes used, but are generally mixed with other fruit.
2. The peel needs longer cooking than fruit used for jam. More water is therefore used.
3. The main source of pectin is the white pith of the peel. If the pith is not wanted in the finished marmalade, it should be pared from the inside of the peel, cut up roughly, soaked, tied in muslin (cheesecloth) with the pips (seeds) and boiled in the marmalade until just before the sugar is added, to get the pectin out.
4. Cutting up: Wash and dry the fruit, cut in halves and squeeze to remove the juice. Strain the juice into a large bowl, putting the pips on one side. Scrape the pulp from the peel, cut it up finely and add to the juice. Separate the white pith from the peel, cut it up roughly and put it aside with the pips. Shred the peel finely and add to the juice.

Note: A quicker method than hand-cutting for the peel is to use a mincing machine, but the appearance is poor. A marmalade-cutting machine may also be used. (*Jelly marmalade: Mix together the pips, pulp, pith and juice, but keep the shredded peel separate.*)

5. Soaking: Allow 1 l/1½ pt/3½ cups/3 pt water to each 450 g/1 lb fruit. Soak the cut-up pith and pips separately in enough water to cover, and add the remaining water to the juice, pulp and peel. (*Jelly marmalade: Soak the shredded peel separately in enough water to cover and add the rest of the water to the pips, pulp, pith and juice together.*) In both cases, soak the peel overnight or even longer, to assist the softening. Otherwise longer boiling will be necessary.
6. First boiling before adding sugar: Strain the pith and pips and tie them in a muslin (cheesecloth) bag. Add them, and the water in which they were soaked, to the pulp, juice, etc., in a preserving pan and boil for 1½–2 hours until the peel is soft and the original bulk has been reduced to half. (*Jelly marmalade: Strain the shredded peel and tie in a muslin bag. Add it, and the water in which it was soaked, to the pulp, juice, etc., and boil for 1½–2 hours until the original bulk has been reduced to half. Remove the muslin bag containing the shredded peel after 1¼ hours so that the peel will not be overcooked. Rinse the peel in cold water.*)
7. At this stage it is advisable to test for pectin (see page 243) and if a good clot is not obtained, lemon juice, tartaric or citric acid should be added in the following proportions:
   To 900 g/2 lb fruit add the juice of 2 lemons
   or 7.5 g/1½ tsp citric acid,
   or 7.5 g/1½ tsp tartaric acid
   Further boiling will be needed before testing again.
8. Ordinary marmalade: Remove the bag of pith and pips, squeezing out as much liquid as possible. *Jelly marmalade: Strain through a jelly bag (see General Method for Making Jelly, page 245).*
9. Sugar addition: Add the sugar and stir to dissolve. Return to the heat and bring to the boil.
10. Final boiling: Boil until setting point is reached (see page 245). The time will vary between 15 and 35 minutes. Prolonged boiling will darken the colour of the marmalade. (*Jelly marmalade: Add the rinsed peel with the sugar for the final boiling.*)
11. Filling the jars: Remove the scum (see page 243) immediately. Allow marmalade to cool in the pan for about 10 minutes, stirring occasionally. Then pour into jars; the peel should be evenly distributed.
12. Cover and label like jam (see page 243).

Orange Marmalade

	Metric	Imperial	American
Seville oranges	1.5 kg	3 lb	3 lb
Lemons	2	2	2
Water	4 l	7 pt	10 pt
Preserving sugar	3 kg	6 lb	6 lb

1. Wash the fruit, cut in half, then squeeze out and reserve the juice.
2. Chop the peel and tie the pips in a piece of muslin (cheesecloth).
3. Soak the peel for 24 hours in 1.5 l/3 pts of cold water.
4. Place the water, peel, pips and remaining water into a preserving pan and simmer for 1½–2 hours until the peel is soft.
5. Test for pectin (page 243) and then discard the pips.
6. Add the sugar and stir until dissolved.
7. Return to the heat and boil for 20–30 minutes until setting point is reached.
8. Remove the scum, cool slightly, then pot and cover.

Grapefruit Marmalade

	Metric	Imperial	American
Grapefruit	1 kg	2¼ lb	2¼ lb
Lemons	3	3	3
Water	3 l	6 pt	13 cups
Sugar	3 kg	6 lb	6 lb

Follow the method for Orange Marmalade.

Orange Jelly Marmalade

	Metric	Imperial	American
Seville oranges	900 g	2 lb	2 lb
Lemons	2	2	2
Water	3 l	5 pt	13 cups
Sugar	1.5 kg	3 lb	3 lb

1. Wash and scald the fruit. Squeeze the juice from the lemons and reserve. Peel the oranges.
2. Remove the pith from the orange peel but do not discard. Shred the peel finely.
3. Place the peel in a pan with 1 1/1½ pt/4 cups of the water, cover and cook gently for 1½ hours.
4. Coarsely chop the rest of the fruit and place in another pan with the pith, lemon juice and remaining water. Simmer gently for 2 hours.
5. Drain the liquid from the peel and add to the other pan. (Put the shred to one side.)
6. Carry out pectin test.
7. Strain the pulp and liquid through a scalded jelly bag or muslin (cheesecloth) as described on page 245.
8. Place the strained juice in a pan with the sugar and stir until dissolved. Add the peel shreds. Bring to the boil and boil until setting point is reached.
9. Remove any scum and allow to cool until a thin skin forms. Pour into warmed jars, cover and label.

Variations
Lemon jelly marmalade: Use 1 kg/2 lb lemons in place of the oranges.
Grapefruit jelly marmalade: Use 1 kg/2 lb grapefruit, 3 lemons, 3 l/5 pt/13 cups water and 3 kg/6 lb sugar. Make as above.

28
PICKLES AND CHUTNEYS

PICKLES AND CHUTNEYS

Pickles and chutneys are made by steeping vegetables or fruits in salt and water (brine) and/or in vinegar so that they do not go mouldy. Sugar and spices are added for flavour.

Vinegar

Strong bottled vinegar is normally used. White vinegar should be used if you want the colour of the preserves to show (in this case, whole spices should be used for the pickling, not powdered ones which spoil the colour.) Often, the vinegar (brown or white) is spiced before use. A standard, all-purpose recipe for Spiced Vinegar is given right.

Pans and Sieves

Aluminium or stainless steel pans are best, or unchipped enamelled ones. Iron, brass or copper pans should not be used. Sieves (strainers) should be of nylon or stainless steel.

Jars

Any jars can be used provided the glass is the same thickness all over, and the jars can be fitted with vinegar-proof coverings.

Covers

Metal lids should not be used unless enamelled on the underside. The vinegar will eat away metal. Paper covers let the vinegar evaporate, so that a pickle or chutney dries out; a chutney can sink dramatically to half its original depth in a few weeks.
    Use, if possible
1. enamelled lug-topped or screw-on lids (jars with lids which have held commercially-made pickles are ideal);
2. preserving jars with glass lids and screw-bands or spring clip fastenings; or
3. melted paraffin wax and a cloth, wax-coated cover.
    (Synthetic skin coverings are also sold which can be fitted over the pickle jars, and secured.)

To Seal Jars with Paraffin Wax

Paraffin wax is sold in blocks by pharmacists. Chip a chunk off the block with a knife-tip, and melt it very gently in a small saucepan. Make sure that any solid pickles in the jar are covered with liquid, and that there is at least 2 cm/¾ in headspace above the pickle inside the jar. A waxed paper circle cut to fit the neck of the jar and placed on the liquid prevents the wax from touching the vegetable. Pour the melted wax all over the liquid pickle or on top of the waxed disc. Within a moment or two it will harden and seal the jar.
    Pour some water into the saucepan in which you melted the wax. Heat it to the boil, then let it stand until cold; any wax still in the pan will be floating on top, and can be scooped off and stored for later use.
    The wax seal on the pickle can be flipped off when the pickle is needed. Melt it in a little water, and any paper sticking to it will float off. The wax can then be re-used.

Spiced Vinegar

	Metric	Imperial	American
Vinegar	1 l	2 pt	5 cups
Ready-mixed bought pickling spice	20–25 ml	4–5 tsp	4–5 tsp
Onion, halved	1	1	1
Salt (optional)	2.5 ml	½ tsp	½ tsp

1. Pour the vinegar into a saucepan. Tie the spices in a piece of muslin (cheesecloth), and add to the pan with the onion, and the salt if used. Brined vegetables and most fruits do not need salt.
2. Boil the mixture, covered, for 2 minutes. Leave to stand, still covered, for 3 hours. Remove the spice bag and onion.

Note: The vinegar can be used cold or reheated, depending on the type of vegetable or fruit being pickled. Use white vinegar and strain out the spices before use if you want a clear pickle.

Brine

Vegetables (except red cabbage or beetroot) should be steeped in brine before pickling to leach out some of the water in them. If you omit this step, the vinegar will be weakened and will not preserve the vegetables. You can use dry salt to leach the water out of red cabbage or cucumbers.

To make brine: Boil 100 g/4 oz preserving salt in 1 1/2 pt/5 cups water until dissolved. Leave until cold before use.

RECIPES FOR PICKLES AND CHUTNEYS

Pickled Beetroot

Method 1: Slice cold cooked beetroot into 5 mm/¼ in thick rounds. Pack into bottles, and cover with cold spiced vinegar made with salt if you wish. Seal.
Method 2: Dice cold cooked beetroot, pack loosely in bottles or jars and cover well with boiling spiced vinegar. Seal.

Pickled Cauliflower

Break the cauliflower head into small sprigs. Soak in brine for 24 hours, then rinse. Pack into bottles or jars and cover with cold spiced vinegar.

Pickled Onions or Shallots

Soak small even-sized onions or shallots in brine for 12 hours before skinning them. Skin with a stainless steel knife, then soak in fresh brine for 24–36 hours, keeping them below the surface. Drain thoroughly, pack into bottles or jars, and cover with cold spiced vinegar. Keep for 3 months before using.

Pickled Red Cabbage

Remove any discoloured leaves and shred the cabbage. Layer with salt in a large bowl, using 100 g/4 oz/¼ lb salt per 450 g/1 lb cabbage. Leave for 24 hours. Drain thoroughly, rinsing off any surplus salt. Pack loosely in bottles or jars, then cover with cold spiced vinegar. Keep for 1 week before use, but not for longer than 2 months.

Pickled Walnuts

Use green walnuts before any shell forms. Prick each with a needle, and discard any in which you can feel the shell, about 5 mm/¼ in from the end opposite the stalk. Soak walnuts for 7–10 days in a brine made with 225 g/8 oz/½ lb salt and 2.3 l/4 pt/10 cups water, changing the brine twice. Drain, spread on plates and leave for 24 hours or until the walnuts turn black. Pack into jars, and cover with cold spiced vinegar. Keep for at least a month before use.

Note: Walnut juice makes ineradicable stains.

Mixed Pickles

Cauliflower florets, onions, cucumbers, marrow (squash) and French (green) beans make good mixed pickles. Prepare the vegetables, and cut up if required. Layer with salt in a large bowl, using 15 g/½ oz salt per 900 g/2 lb vegetables. Leave for 48 hours, then drain thoroughly. Pack loosely into jars, and cover with cold spiced vinegar.

Note: Use white vinegar and strain out the spices before pouring it over the vegetables if you want a clear pickle.

Apple Chutney

	Metric	Imperial	American
Apples	*2.7 kg*	*6 lb*	*6 lb*
Onions	*900 g*	*2 lb*	*2 lb*
Water	*275 ml*	*½ pt*	*1¼ cups*
Salt	*40 g*	*1½ oz*	*1½ oz*
Ground ginger	*40 g*	*1½ oz*	*1½ oz*
Ground cinnamon	*30 ml*	*6 tsp*	*6 tsp*
Cayenne pepper	*1.5 ml*	*¼ tsp*	*¼ tsp*
Vinegar	*1 l*	*2 pt*	*5 cups*
Sugar	*900 g*	*2 lb*	*2 lb*
Golden (light corn) syrup	*450 g*	*1 lb*	*1 lb*

1. Prepare the apples and onions. Chop them finely, and simmer gently in the water for 10 minutes, in a fairly large pan.
2. Add the salt, ginger, cinnamon, cayenne pepper and 575 ml/1 pt/2½ cups of the vinegar. Cook until the apples and onions are soft.
3. Add the rest of the vinegar, with the sugar and syrup. Cook very gently until the chutney has a smooth consistency with little or no free liquid, and a mellow aroma.
4. Pour into heated jars, and cover at once.

Green Tomato Chutney

	Metric	Imperial	American
Green tomatoes	*1.4 kg*	*3 lb*	*3 lb*
Onions	*225 g*	*8 oz*	*½ lb*
Apples	*225 g*	*8 oz*	*½ lb*
Ready prepared mixed pickling spice	*25 g*	*1 oz*	*1 oz*
Vinegar	*575 ml*	*1 pt*	*2½ cups*
Brown sugar	*100–225 g*	*4–8 oz*	*¼–½ lb*
Salt	*10 ml*	*2 tsp*	*2 tsp*

1. Skin the tomatoes and onions. Peel and core the apples. Chop all three finely.
2. Tie the pickling spice in a piece of muslin (cheesecloth).
3. Put all the ingredients in a preserving pan and boil gently until soft and thick.
4. Remove the spice, and pour the chutney into warmed jars. Cover at once.

29
FREEZING HINTS

THE FREEZING PROCESS

Freezing is a natural way of preserving food, i.e. it alters the food very little. When food is penetrated by intense cold below freezing point, bacteria and enzymes are immobilised until the food is thawed. It does not matter whether the food is raw or cooked, solid or pulped; provided it is a suitable food for freezing, it will be virtually the same when thawed as it was before it was frozen.

As the food freezes, all the liquids in it turn to minute ice crystals. If it freezes slowly, quite large crystals are formed, which may break down the cell tissues around them. If this happens, the food when thawed will be limp and the liquid will drip out. To prevent this happening, foods should be frozen as quickly as possible, using the freezer's fast-freeze mechanism. A few foods which contain a lot of water should not be frozen at all, but most others can be fast-frozen with hardly any change in their texture. If packaged and frozen correctly, and if used within their high-quality storage life (see below), their appearance, flavour and nutritional value are unimpaired.

No freezer works miracles, however. No food will improve in quality by being frozen. It is a waste of freezer space to store products of inferior quality in the hope that they may taste better or be useful after a while.

High Quality Storage Life

Some enzyme activity does go on in frozen foods, and, very slowly, they lose flavour after a time. It is almost impossible to state categorically how long any foodstuff will remain in peak condition in the freezer, since even top-quality produce can vary widely, and much depends on how it has been packaged and frozen. However, experiments have provided average times that most foods will keep well and in prime condition. The recommended high quality storage life of any food is generally stated to be slightly shorter than this. Commercial manufacturers of frozen foods are particularly conservative in their estimates.

Since home-prepared foods and dishes can vary even more than bought foodstuffs, the storage times recommended in this book should only be taken as a rough guide.

Foods not to Freeze

Some foods are unsuitable for freezing because of their high water content or because their constituent elements freeze at different rates and so they 'separate' or go 'grainy' in storage. Here is a list of some types of food *not* to freeze:

Single, double and sour cream; they 'separate'. Whipping and clotted cream freeze well.

Cottage cheese, yoghurt, milk (unless homogenised)

Milk puddings, custards (including custard fillings)

Whole eggs in shell; they crack. Beaten whole eggs can be frozen, or egg whites or yolks alone.

Hard-boiled eggs, even in pies, fillings, sandwiches, etc.

Soft meringue toppings (there is no point in freezing crisp meringues)

Mayonnaise and salad dressings

Royal icing, and icings made without fat; they chip (butter icings freeze perfectly).

Salad vegetables with a high water content, e.g. lettuce, cucumber, radishes, watercress; celery, chicory and cabbage cannot be frozen to eat raw – nor can avocados and tomatoes (see note)

Boiled potatoes (except mashed); potatoes can be frozen if fried as chips, but not in soups or stews, i.e. with liquid.

Whole apples, pears, bananas, and melons to eat raw; apples can be frozen if puréed but the other fruits are not very satisfactory – bananas and pears are normally available year-round anyway.

Stuffed poultry.

Jellies and foods containing a lot of gelatine or covered with aspic jelly.

Sauces thickened with flour unless reheated with great care to prevent separation; Cornflour (cornstarch) separates less easily than flour but tends to taste gluey.

Sauces thickened with potato or potato flour, or with egg and cream.

Soups thickened like sauces

Dishes strongly flavoured with onion, garlic, herbs or spice; they may taste musty when thawed (see notes).

Notes:
1. Do not freeze products such as cabbage which are cheap and easy to buy year-round. It will cost you more to store them than to buy fresh, and they use valuable freezer space. Milk does not freeze well. Cartons of U. H. T. (Longlife) milk which does not need refrigeration make a good standby.
2. Celery and tomatoes can be frozen to eat in cooked dishes.
3. Freeze pasta, rice and other grains, and potatoes, without liquid to prevent them going mushy.
4. Thicken sauces before freezing by reducing them or by adding a vegetable purée. Egg and cream liaison can be added after thawing.
5. Extra onion, garlic, herbs or spices can be added to casseroles when reheating. So can strongly-flavoured toppings, such as anchovies on pizzas.
6. Valuable foods to freeze as standbys (if you use them) are grains and pulses which take a long time to cook, such as chickpeas, haricot (navy) beans, brown rice. Also pancakes (page 168).
7. Remember to mark on packages or your freezer list any additions to be made after thawing.

WHAT TO FREEZE

HOME-GROWN PRODUCE

The four big advantages of freezing home-grown vegetables and fruit are listed below.

1. You can harvest vegetables, especially, while young and tender; shop-bought vegetables tend to be large, old and coarse.
2. You can prepare and freeze your produce straight from the ground or tree, with minimal nutrient loss and in portions to suit your needs.
3. You can freeze all the favourite varieties which you have chosen to grow, besides making good use of glut crops (but beware of freezing them 'for the sake of it' if they will be cheaper to buy and perhaps better; windfall apples, for instance, are seldom economic to freeze).
4. You can process your produce before freezing in varied ways, to suit your needs and be sure of purées, juices and syrups with fresh summer food value year-round.

Whatever you grow, freeze as wide a variety of fruit and vegetables as you can, for instance by supplementing home-grown produce with commercially frozen produce, such as sweetcorn, and with some bought seasonal delicacies such as aubergines (eggplants). For one thing, you will be able to choose from a much wider range of recipes whenever you want to. For another, your family will not get bored; they might if you stacked up half the freezer with, say, beans.

Vegetables

1. Wash all vegetables well in cold water, and prepare them according to kind as for normal cooking: e.g. top and tail or string green beans, remove leaves and roots of root vegetables, break cauliflower into florets. Sort or cut vegetables into pieces of the same size.
2. Blanch all vegetables to arrest the action of natural enzymes which will otherwise spoil the vegetables' colour, crispness and nutritive value. Blanching will also shorten the cooking time of the thawed vegetables. You can blanch either in boiling water, in steam or in a microwave oven. Water blanching removes slightly more vitamins and minerals, but it is quicker, and more suitable than steam blanching for leafy green vegetables because they keep crisper.
   To water-blanch vegetables, bring a big pan containing 3.4–4.5 l/6–8 pt/15–20 cups water to a fast boil. Put only a small quantity, say 450 g/1 lb vegetables, in a wire basket, chip pan or muslin (cheesecloth) bag and immerse completely in the fast-boiling water. Blanch over high heat for the time given in the chart below, beginning when the water returns to the boil. When the process is complete, plunge the vegetables at once into ice-chilled water and leave until you are sure that they are quite cold. Otherwise they will go on cooking in their own heat, and be limp and mushy when thawed. Cooling generally takes about as long as blanching. Drain and dry vegetables thoroughly before packing, preferably on soft kitchen paper. Make sure the chilled water is still chilled, and bring the hot water back to a fast boil before blanching the next batch.
3. Most vegetables are usually packed dry. Pack the cooled vegetables in boxes or bags, in portions you will normally use; bags are cheaper, but more awkward to store. However, if you wish, you can open-freeze some varieties or mixtures of vegetables, then pack them in big bags as a free-flow product (see below). Label the boxes or bags with the name of the vegetable, the quantity packaged, and the 'use-by' date.
4. Fast-freeze the vegetables, then pack for storage. Record the name of the vegetable, the quantity processed and the 'use-by' date on your freezer list (page 256).
5. Most vegetables are best cooked while still frozen; only broccoli and spinach need partly thawing and corn-on-the-cob complete thawing. The cooking time is very short, only about a third to half that needed for raw vegetables. If boiled, very little water should be used; it

should be boiling when the vegetables are put in, and they should then be covered and simmered gently. Preferably, season after cooking.

6. If you prefer, you can steam the vegetables to save losing nutrients in the cooking water; or you can simmer still-frozen vegetables gently in butter, in a covered pan, until separate, then sauté them gently until tender.

WATER BLANCHING TIMES FOR SOME COMMON VEGETABLES

Name	Minutes to Blanch	Special Notes
Artichokes, globe	7	Add 15 ml/1 tbls lemon juice to water.
(Jerusalem artichokes are not blanched)		
Asparagus	2–4, depending on thickness	
Aubergines (eggplants)	4	Cut in 2.5 cm/1 in slices before blanching
Beans, broad (lima)	1½	Use young
Beans, French (green)	3 (whole beans) 2 (cut beans)	
Beans, (runner)	2 (cut beans)	
Beetroot		Use small young beetroot, cook completely and rub off skins
Broccoli	3–5, depending on size	
Brussels sprouts	3–4, depending on size	
Cabbage, green or red	1½	Shred first
Carrots	3	Small whole, or sliced
Cauliflower	3	Florets. Add 15 ml/1 tbls lemon juice to water
Celeriac	8–10	Sliced
Corn on the cob	5–8, depending on size	
Courgettes	3	Cut in 2.5 cm/1 in slices first
Fennel	3	Use small young bulbs
Leeks, cleaned and sliced	1½–3, depending on thickness of slices	
Mushrooms	1½	Slice large mushrooms first: or fry and freeze
Onions, sliced	2	
Onions, small, whole	4	
Parsnips	2	Slice first
Peas	1½	Pod first
Peppers (any colour)	2	Remove seeds first
New potatoes	4	
Spinach	2	
Turnips and Swedes (rutabaga)	3, sliced or diced	

Fruit

Harvest fruits at their peak for freezing; underripe fruits are pale and tasteless; overripe fruits are only fit for purée. Strongly flavoured fruits are a better choice than bland ones such as pears.

Choice of Methods:
Fruit can be prepared and frozen in various ways, depending on their type and your preference. They can be frozen whole or cut up, separately or in a dry pack (unsweetened or sweetened), in syrup or as purée. Currants and gooseberries can be frozen just as they are, but store longer in the freezer with added sugar. Soft fruits such as raspberries are usually packed in dry sugar; other fruits which are less juicy can be packed in dry sugar for dessert use, or in sugar syrup.

Discoloration:
All fruits must be processed very quickly once they are peeled, sliced or puréed, because contact with air makes them darken – especially apples, pears and peaches. For the same reason, they must be used quickly, once thawed, preferably while still slightly freezer-crisp.

Vitamin C helps to prevent darkening and can be added to fruit in 3 ways.

1. Add 5 ml/1 tsp citric acid to each 450 g/1 lb sugar in dry sugar packing.
2. Add the juice of 1 lemon to each 850 ml/1½ pt/4 cups water in sugar syrup.
3. Add 500 mgm ascorbic acid (see note below) to each 575 ml/1 pt/2½ cups water. Dip the fruit in the solution immediately it is cut up, and dry it if to be open-frozen or frozen in dry sugar; or dissolve the ascorbic acid in 5 ml/1 tsp water and add it to 575 ml/1 pt/2½ cups sugar syrup before use.

Note: Ascorbic acid can be bought from a pharmacy in tablets of different strengths or in crystal form. 5 ml/1 tsp crystals = 6 x 500 mgm tablets. Do NOT prepare a solution in a copper or iron container; it produces off-flavours.

Preparation

Pick over fruit, removing stems and damaged fruit. Have packaging materials and dry sugar or syrup at hand, with Vitamin C added. Wash all except soft fruit in iced water to keep it crisp. Dry thoroughly on soft kitchen paper. Remove stones or cut up if required and process at once.

Freezing Method 1: Open-Freezing
Most suitable for small, whole berries. Only wash if essential. Spread on metal or plastic trays and fast-freeze, then pack in bags for storage, and label. You can then shake out as many as you need, at any time, and return the rest to the freezer. Bonus note: Stalks on currants will 'freeze off', saving hours of work.

Freezing Method 2: Unsweetened Dry Packing
Suitable for currants and gooseberries, and for fruit for cooking or jam-making (not apples, pears or peaches). Wash and dry the prepared fruit, using as little water as possible. Open-freeze or pack into cartons. Label.

Freezing Method 3: Dry Sugar Packing
Particularly useful for berries or for sliced fruit. Allow 100–175 g/4–6 oz/½–¾ cup sugar to each 450 g/1 lb fruit, depending on sweetness. Either mix or layer the fruit with the sugar (if layering, in the freezer containers). Use a plastic spoon. Pack in cartons. Label.

Freezing Method 4: Sugar Syrup Packing
Make the syrup the day before you need it, cool and refrigerate it. It is usually made up in one of three strengths:

> light syrup (30%) made with 225 g/8 oz/1 cup sugar to 575 ml/1 pt/2½ cups water
> medium syrup (40%) made with 350 g/12 oz/1½ cups sugar to 575 ml/1 pt/2½ cups water
> heavy syrup (50%) made with 500 g/18 oz/2¼ cups sugar to 575 ml/1 pt/2½ cups water

A medium syrup is the one most often used. Stir the sugar into the water, bring to the boil and simmer just until the sugar is dissolved. Cover the pan and cool.

Slice large fruits and immerse smaller ones whole in the syrup, allowing 275 ml/½ pt/1¼ cups syrup per 450 g/1 lb fruit. If you need more than 575 ml/1 pt/1¼ cups syrup, keep the same proportion of sugar to water when making the extra quantity. Pack the fruit in rigid containers, leaving at least 1 cm/½ in headspace; crumple a piece of cellophane and lay it on top of the fruit to keep it submerged. Cover, seal and label.

Purées and Juices:
Fruit which does not quite come up to standard can be used to make purée or juice. Apples and tomatoes must be cooked first. Fruit purée is an excellent, compact way to store fruit, and has many uses: for fruit fools, sauces, in fillings or fruit puddings instead of jam, as a topping for ice cream, as baby food or in milk shakes. Add sugar to taste – 100 g/4 oz/½ cup sugar to 450 g/1 lb fruit is usual. Purée the prepared fruit in a food processor or blender and sieve the purée if (like raspberries) it has pips in it. Then pack, seal and label as usual.

Citrus fruit juices, in particular, are an excellent standby if you have a juice extractor. Apart from healthful breakfast drinks and milk shakes, fruit juices make delicious fresh-tasting jellies, sorbets, 'creams' and syrup; blackcurrant juice is particularly good. Sweeten the juice to taste, and pack it in cartons or other rigid containers; seal it carefully, making sure that none spills when putting the juice in the freezer. Label as usual.

Fruit for Jam or Marmalade:
If you are really pushed for time, fruit for jam can be frozen, unsweetened, until you are able to make it into jam. Similarly, whole Seville oranges can be frozen and used for making marmalade later in the year.

OTHER PRODUCTS

Meat

Both raw and cooked meat freeze well, but it is usually a waste of freezer space to store low-quality meat with a lot of bone. It is best to freeze raw only top-quality cuts which you really want or which are hard to come by, and to prepare cooked dishes with cheaper cuts and freeze those.

Bulk Buying

Some authorities hold that the housewife should not freeze large raw meat joints at all, because very low temperatures indeed are needed to freeze them safely. This must be borne in mind by anyone who thinks of buying a whole or half carcass, or a bulk pack of assorted joints for freezing. The cost of having a carcass butchered must be considered; and in either case, there is some risk of overloading the freezer by trying to freeze too much meat all at once.

One compromise is to buy a bulk or catering pack of ready-frozen joints or assorted cuts, which are available from large-scale suppliers, and to re-package them without thawing if you estimate that genuine savings can be made. This, however, is doubtful; and you will almost certainly have to accept, in a mixed pack, some items which are only marginally useful to you. The frozen cuts may also be difficult to identify and to package. On the whole, therefore, it is probably wiser to buy and freeze only what you know you will use.

Preparation

Meat is usually the bulkiest as well as the most expensive item in the freezer so it must be prepared to take up as little space as possible. Since some of it can be cooked straight from the freezer, it must also be frozen ready for cooking.

With all types of meat, trim off excess fat and remove the bone(s) if practicable. Fat can be rendered down if worthwhile, and bones can be used for stock, which should be free of fat.

Packaging

Any projecting bone ends must first be wrapped in foil to prevent them piercing the wrappings. All meat must then be wrapped tightly against the surface of the meat because any air inside the wrappings may make the fat turn rancid. Besides this tight wrapping, it should be over-wrapped with strong paper or cloth.

It is also important to package meat in quantities likely to be used at one time because this cannot be done when the meat is frozen, and to cook more first-class meat than you need is usually wasteful.

a. *Joints*: Trim fat, and tie in shape if required. Wrap any projecting bone ends in foil or cloth. Double-wrap, first in clingfilm, then cloth or foil. The thinner the wrapping, the faster the meat will freeze.
b. *Small cuts, such as steaks or chops*: Wrap each separately in clingfilm or foil, then pack in a large polythene bag.

c. *Offal*: Blanch brains or sweetbreads before freezing. Soft offal, and liver which may drip when thawing, are best packaged in rigid polythene containers.
d. *Meat for casseroles and stews*: Prepare for cooking, and cube or slice. Pack in useful quantities, in containers or bags.

To thaw

All meat can be cooked from frozen but cuts are more successful than joints, and most joints tend to cook more evenly if wholly or partly thawed. As a general guide, allow almost double the time to cook frozen steaks and chops, but the normal cooking time for diced meats and minced (ground) beef. When cooking joints, it is advisable to thaw first because of the length of cooking time needed.

Poultry and Game

Hang, draw and pluck if required. Prepare for cooking. Freeze whole, halved or jointed. Double-wrap like meat, wrapping drumsticks carefully, and sealing securely, as poultry is susceptible to freezer 'burn'. Poultry and game must be completely thawed before cooking.

Fish

a. *Whole round and flat fish*: Scale if required, clean and remove fins and eyes or whole heads. Wash and dry well.
   The fish are then best glazed. To do this, freeze the fish unwrapped, then dip them in ice-cold water and return to the freezer. Repeat this three or four times until a 3 mm/⅛ in film of ice covers the fish. Place the fish on a rigid plastic tray to prevent cracking the glaze, then wrap and store as usual.
b. *Fish fillets and steaks*: Prepare the fish, ready to cook. Pack together as many pieces as you will probably use, separating them with pieces of freezer-wrap. Pack in freezer-wrap or foil.
c. *Shellfish*: Only attempt to freeze shellfish within 12 hours of their being caught. Prawns and shrimps are the best to freeze, since they take up least room per serving, and have many uses, as garnishes, in sauces, etc. Freeze them uncooked for choice, with or without shells. Wash in weak brine, drain, dry, open-freeze and pack in bags.
   Crab and lobster must be cooked before freezing and cooled thoroughly. Remove the meat from the shells for freezing. Oil the shells and store separately to use for serving if you wish.

Dairy Foods

Milk, single (light) cream, yoghurt and cottage cheese should not be frozen at home and certain other dairy foods such as butter and Cheddar cheese which are always available are not worth freezing. A rough-and-ready guide to whether other dairy foods can be frozen is that the higher the butterfat content, the more likely the food is to freeze well.

a. *Eggs:* Although they fluctuate in price, eggs are seldom worth freezing, although a single small egg may be useful to save for glazing pastry or biscuit; mix the white and yolk gently with a small pinch of salt, and freeze in an ice cube container. Egg yolks left after making meringues and egg whites after making egg custard, are well worth freezing. Beat lightly, and freeze in sealed cartons.

b. *Fats:* Pure chicken fat or good home-made dripping may be worth freezing in cartons for special uses. Clarified butter, which is expensive to make, can also be frozen if you wish, although it keeps well in the refrigerator.

c. *Cheeses:* Hard cheese frozen in a block tends to go grainy in storage, and can only be used for cooking. Cheddar, grated before freezing, is an excellent cooking standby and it is worth while to grate and freeze pieces which have hardened 'on the shelf'. Other cheeses worth freezing are ones with a high butterfat content which are worth keeping as a rare treat; only beware of any which are very strongly flavoured, as in spite of careful packaging, they may cross-flavour other foods. Most rich, soft cheeses freeze well.

d. *Ice Cream:* Home-made ice cream, whether churned, beaten or simply frozen in a refrigerator tray, is a delicious, light, rich dessert; sorbets are also deservedly popular. Any of them can normally be frozen in a rigid polythene container or carton, although a fancy iced pudding may be frozen in a jelly mould for turning out; some moulds are sold with lids.

Bought ice cream has a shorter 'life' than home-made ice cream especially if bought in bulk and served from the large container; it will only keep in peak condition for about 1 month. It is certainly cheaper to buy in quantity, but should be re-packaged into smaller containers, so that most of it stays undisturbed in the freezer until wanted.

Breads, Cakes, Biscuits and Pastry

Unbaked doughs and completed baked goods are satisfying foods to freeze: partly because sweet dishes are always popular, and anybody feels pride in being able to produce home-made bread or baked goods whenever required; and partly because both home-made and bought goods stale so quickly that half the results of your work or purchases may be lost without the freezer to preserve them.

Baked goods freeze perfectly, and so do most unbaked doughs. Unbaked yeast doughs, however, have only a very short high-quality storage life, and so bread, rolls, muffins, etc., are best baked before freezing, and frozen as soon as they have cooled. If frozen in foil, a loaf need only be transferred to the oven on a baking sheet to thaw; even after several weeks' storage, it will have a fresh-baked texture and flavour.

Like breads, baked cakes freeze better than unbaked doughs and it is worth keeping one or two in hand even though they are bulky compared with a dough. A Swiss (jelly) roll is useful since it is an easy shape to store, and can be decorated when thawed to serve as either a dessert or a cake. Soft sandwich (layer) cakes should be packed with greaseproof (waxed) paper between the layers, and should then be open-frozen to harden them before wrapping for storage. Do not freeze fruit cakes or gingerbreads; store them in airtight tins.

Baked cakes are best frozen without decoration, as they can then be close-wrapped at once. If it is more convenient to decorate large or small cakes before freezing, use a butter icing (and filling for sandwich cakes) and open-freeze so as not to damage the icing on top. Wrap when hard, and unwrap *before* thawing.

Biscuit doughs thaw quickly, and are more compact to store unbaked. Chill and cut biscuit doughs (refrigerator cookies, page 225), are designed to be baked 'from frozen' and most drop cookie doughs only need partial thawing.

Both unbaked pastry dough and baked pastry freeze perfectly, and both are useful to keep in stock. Bought puff pastry is a worthwhile standby, as few people have the time, energy, or indeed the skill, to make it well. One or two flan cases, a few vol-au-vent cases and perhaps cornets are also useful to buy from a Freezer Food Centre and keep in stock.

Leftovers

The chief things to be sure of concerning leftovers is that they really are worth freezing. It is very easy to scrape half a bowlful of soup or sauce into a carton, put it in the freezer – and realise a week or so later either that it has 'separated' or that there is not enough of it to be useful. Obviously there are some leftovers which are worth packaging, sealing and labelling, but many are not worth the nuisance of refurbishing them.

Ready-Prepared Foods

The types of commercially-prepared foods available today, from basic products to complete prepared meals, are legion and ever-changing. Full directions for storage, thawing and cooking are given on the packets. The only problem is what to choose.

The best way to decide on the most useful products for your particular circumstances is to pay a visit to a large Freezer Food Centre, which will have a wider selection than most supermarkets, and note down the products which will be most useful to you. Then, when re-stocking your freezer, as you must do periodically, you can arrange to stock up with commercially-frozen goods from your list. One of the great merits of a freezer is that you need not do this very often. It is, in a way, a shop at home.

As for home-prepared products, the high quality storage times of all the dishes which you can prepare from this book are given in the recipes; in almost all cases, these times are for the completed cooked products. This section therefore, only describes how to package and freeze them.

PACKAGING AND LABELLING

Any packaging and sealing materials for storing food in the freezer must be:

a. moisture-and vapour-proof, to prevent the food losing moisture;
b. odour-resistant;
c. thin, to let the food freeze as fast as possible;
d. either rigid or very flexible, so that food can be wrapped closely, without air-spaces between the food and covering which can cause oxydisation;
e. if rigid, a convenient shape and size for stacking, or for holding particular types of food, e.g. pies and puddings;
f. crack-resistant;
g. able to be sealed completely.

The commonest types of packaging which meet all these requirements are:

a. Polythene bags available in a wide range of sizes which can be sealed with plastic-covered wire twist ties;
b. flexible polythene sheet, which can be used for close wrapping and sealed with stick-on freezer tape, or can be used for interleaving between layers;
c. plastic cartons, boxes and tubs with airtight lids;
d. aluminium foil sheet on a roll in varying sizes and thicknesses; one of the most versatile packaging materials to use; seal with double folds;
e. aluminium foil cartons, pie dishes, pudding basins, plates, tartlet cases and trays. Some containers have lids; cover others with foil sheet;
f. polystyrene trays and platters (can be used for *thawing* in a microwave oven, though not for cooking);
g. waxed cartons and tubs with airtight lids (not always satisfactory as they hold odours, and may stain).

Choosing Packaging

Most foods can be packaged in various ways. Use whatever suits your convenience and the space in your freezer. Remember that, except for open-frozen, 'free-flow' packs, packages should ideally hold only as much of the food as you want to use at one time. As a general rule, unevenly shaped solid products such as meat, poultry and whole fish, are best in flexible wrapping such as freezer wrap or foil; remember that they will need double-wrapping, say with cloth, or in a plastic bag for easy labelling. Cakes can be flexibly wrapped too, after open freezing to harden them. Obviously, prepared pies and puddings need to be packaged in appropriately shaped containers. Beyond that, the choice is yours.

Packing

There are three important points to note about packing any food for the freezer.

1. All the air must be excluded from the package to prevent oxidisation and deterioration. Squeeze out the air from soft packages or by smoothing foil over a joint or bird. Tap a carton on the table top to 'pack down' the contents. Use a pump, which can be bought quite cheaply, to suck the air out of bags before closing with a twist-tie.
2. Liquids expand when they freeze, so leave a headspace of at least 1 cm/½ in above the contents of wide-topped packs, and 2.5 cm/1 in above the food in narrow-topped packs.
3. Whatever packaging you use, make sure you can label the pack with a tie-on or stick-on label. Special sticky labels for low temperature use can be bought.

Another point about packing is that you need not always store the food in the container in which you freeze it. For instance, liquids such as concentrated stock frozen in ice cube trays can be turned out into a bag when hard, and stored in the bag so that the ice cube tray can be returned to its proper use. Food frozen in a rigid plastic container lined with doubled foil, can be turned out and stored in the foil alone, leaving the container free for re-use. This use of containers as moulds is a useful economy measure.

Labelling

Both labelling and recording what you have in the freezer are essential. It is almost impossible to remember the contents even for a short time. If possible, keep different sections of the freezer for long-term storage items and for quick turnover items, but do not rely on memory even for the latter. Label each package with the name of the food, quantity and 'use-by' date. Record these details in a notebook or on a chart, and include any details of processing to be done when thawing. This is not only vital to ensure that you produce beautifully-prepared food from your freezer; it will also be a big help in deciding what foods to buy when you re-stock, and how much of each.

30
MICROWAVE COOKING

A microwave oven is an accessory to your conventional cooker.

Microwaves are electromagnetic, high frequency radio waves produced by a magnetron. These waves bounce off the metal interior of the oven into the food, passing straight through paper, china and most pottery or plastics and glass on the way. They cause the water molecules within the food to vibrate millions of times per second. The friction caused by the vibrating molecules creates heat to cook the food.

Utensils

Microwaves ignore some materials such as glass, china and plastic. These are excellent materials to use for containers since they let the waves reach and bombard the food.

By contrast, microwaves bounce off metals, so do not reach food to cook it. Metals also cause arcing which damages the magnetron. No metal container or utensil of any kind, such as a conventional oven or meat thermometer, should therefore be used in a microwave oven. Nor should any container or utensil trimmed with metal or painted with a metallic paint or glaze be used. You may use small amounts of aluminium foil safely if the food being cooked is a much greater mass than the amount of foil being used. These small pieces of foil may be used to cover tips of joints of meat or poultry, or thin parts of fish. The foil will act to slow the cooking of the thinner parts since the metal will reflect the microwaves away and prevent overcooking. The foil should be as smooth as possible and securely anchored to these foods because it must not come into contact with the walls of the oven. (Wooden cocktail picks are ideal.)

Do not use the following in a microwave oven: Mugs or cups with glued on handles because the glue will absorb the microwaves and separation will occur;
Lead crystal or very delicate stemware;
Dishes that are cracked or crazed may not be able to withstand the heat conducted from the food;
Some rigid plastics which absorb a certain amount of microwave energy, so that food heats less efficiently because the container is absorbing the microwaves;
Flimsy or waxed containers such as yoghurt containers. These are unsatisfactory because the heat of the food may melt them;

Metal baking sheets or trays;
Opened cans;
Conventional meat thermometers;
Foil-lined bakeware or fruit juice containers;
Dishes with gold or silver trim.
(For further details on the use of metal in microwave ovens, see page 258)

Suitable Utensils

Special utensils may not be needed. For instance, when reheating a pre-cooked meal, service platters and vegetable dishes may well be suitable. Attractive ranges of freezer-to-oven-to-table ceramic and ovenproof glass containers are now available in various shapes, all carefully designed for microwave use. Besides these, a wide range of other utensils in various materials are available for selected uses.

Type of Utensil	Uses
Ovenproof glass	Cooking, defrosting, reheating
Boil-in-the-bag pouches	Cooking, defrosting, reheating
Roasting bags (but check they are secured with non-metal ties)	Cooking meat and poultry
China and porcelain	Cooking meat and poultry
Wood or straw utensils, e.g. small baskets	Quick heating of bread rolls
(check there are no metal staples)	
Freezer bags, freezer wrap	Defrosting
Clingfilm (preferably plasticizer-free)	Covering during cooking
Paper towels	Short cooking operations of very moist foods

The shape of the container in which the food is cooked in a microwave oven affects its quality and cooking time. In a round dish the waves can get at all sides of the food and the heat may only reach the centre slowly. In a ring mould, the slow-to-cook centre does not exist and waves can get to the food from the centre as well as the outside. In a square or rectangular dish waves get to the food in the corners from both sides and overcooking may occur. It is therefore important to stir foods in square or rectangular dishes more frequently.

It is not always possible to use an ideally-shaped dish, but careful arrangement of the food and frequent stirring will compensate in many cases.

When choosing dishes to use in the microwave oven, remember that dishes with lugs or long handles must be positioned carefully when using a revolving turntable so that they don't hit the oven walls as they swing round.

The size of food and its shape

a. A large cake will take longer to cook than a smaller one of the same shape and type. A thick food item, such as a sponge cake 7 cm/3 in deep will take longer than a thin sheet of sponge mixture for a Swiss (jelly) roll. An unevenly-shaped item, such as a leg of lamb which is smaller at one end than the other, can present problems. This is resolved by wrapping a small piece of smooth foil around the thin end before placing the joint in a roasting bag. Choose small food items, such as bread rolls, potatoes or tomatoes, of equal size to cook in the microwave.

b. If you only put one item in the oven, it gets the 'full blast' of all the microwave energy in the oven. If you put two items in, the energy is divided between them, so each gets less and they take longer to heat through. Add about 50% extra time for each item, e.g. if one food item takes 2 minutes to heat, 2 items will take 3 minutes, 3 items will take 4½ minutes, and so on.

c. Density – compact solid foods take longer to cook than light porous ones, e.g. bread will cook more quickly than chops.

d. Sloppy foods (i.e. with a high moisture content) take relatively longer to heat compared with fatty, sugary foods which heat very quickly.

e. Chilled foods take longer to heat than those at room temperature.

Microwave Power Levels

Every microwave oven has a magnetron which emits the microwaves. The amount of microwave energy fed into a particular oven may be 500, 600, 650 or 700 watts, depending on the type of oven. It is important to know the wattage of the oven you are using because it affects the cooking times. A 700 watt oven cooks food more quickly than a 600 watt one, so cooking time in recipes designed for a 600 watt oven must be reduced in one of a higher wattage.

COOKING TECHNIQUES

While commonsense applies just as much to using a microwave oven as to any other cookery, the way microwave energy heats food requires the use of a few special techniques.

a. *Standing Time* This applies to all foods cooked in a microwave oven. Correctly timed food is taken out of the oven before it has completely finished cooking right through. This is because the microwave energy is absorbed by the outer part of the food and the heat generated takes time to reach the centre. A few minutes' standing time completes the process.

b. *Arranging* Arrange all food items for the microwave oven with the thickest part towards the outside of the dish. Arrange small food items of equal size, such as stuffed tomatoes or small cakes, in a circle, leaving the middle of the dish or plate empty. Some food items need re-arranging part-way through cooking to make sure they cook evenly and completely.

c. *Turning* Many foods cook more evenly if they are turned over part-way through cooking.

d. *Stirring* Foods such as sauces and custards should be stirred once or twice during cooking or heating.

e. *Breaking up or separating* As in conventional cooking, wet foods frozen in a solid mass should be broken up with a fork once or twice during thawing, to speed the process. Stir frozen liquids part-way through thawing, scooping thawed liquid into the centre.

f. *Pricking* It is important to prick with a knife-point foods with skins, such as apples or potatoes for baking, to prevent them bursting. Also prick or slit any plastic bag or similar covering for the same reason.

g. *Covering* Covering foods speeds up heating. Cover with pierced clingfilm any food which must be kept moist, such as stews, plated meals or vegetables. Cover liquids such as soups to prevent condensation. Do NOT cover foods which you want dryish. Take a cake out of the oven while the top is still just moist and let it complete cooking while standing.

h. *Shielding* In spite of the strictures about using metal in the microwave oven, small strips of aluminium foil can be used on items such as chicken drumsticks or the breast of a turkey, to prevent overcooking. Use very thin strips of foil, and make sure they do not touch any part of the oven itself. This technique may be helpful when preparing a plated meal of items which differ in thickness.

Cooking Hints

1. Never salt the surface of food before microwave cooking as it will cause dehydration.
2. Add a little stock to sliced meat before reheating to keep it moist.
3. Use wooden cocktail picks or skewers for enclosing stuffings or trussing poultry.

4. Reheat soup in individual bowls to save washing up.
5. Always undercook if you are not sure how long food should cook for.
6. Underheat rolls when reheating; they will go on heating after removal from the microwave.
7. Never grease and flour a container; grease it only, or line with clingfilm. Use unsalted (sweet) butter for greasing.
8. Take dishes out of the microwave oven carefully in case they have become hot. Don't take off a covering inside the oven in case steam billows out.

Foods which Cannot Be Microwave Cooked

These include:
Yorkshire Pudding
Meringues
Soufflés
Cream buns, éclairs and choux
Puff pastry
Flaky pastry
Roast potatoes
Any deep-fried foods
Battered foods
Pancakes
Crisp pastry

Care and Maintenance of the Microwave Oven

The microwave oven needs minimal care. Wipe off any splashes in the oven as soon as possible. Wipe the inside of the oven with a damp cloth immediately after use. Wipe and polish with a dry cloth the exterior and see-through door panel. Check periodically that the door seal and hinges are in good condition.

Handy Hints

1. Brown shredded coconut or nuts for cake decoration by using Full power for 2–3 minutes, depending on quantity. Breadcrumbs for coating foods may be dried in the same way.
2. Melt chocolate for cake toppings by placing it in a bowl and heating it in the oven on full. Allow about 2 minutes per 100 g/4 oz/4 squares, stirring after 1 minute.
3. Soften cream cheese or butter for spreading on Defrost. The timing depends on the quantity.
4. To refresh stale dry fruit, place it in a bowl, sprinkle with water and heat on Full for about 45 seconds.
5. Hard lumps of brown sugar can be softened by placing the sugar in a dish, topping it with a slice of apple and heating on Full for 30–60 seconds.

HANDY RECIPES

Scrambled Eggs with Herbs

Serves 2

Power level Full power (500-w/600-w/650-w ovens)

Not suitable for freezing

	Metric	Imperial	American
Eggs	4	4	4
Dried mixed herbs (or herb of your choice)	5 ml	1 tsp	1 tsp
Milk	30 ml	2 tbls	2 tbls
Butter	15 g	½ oz	1 tbls
Salt and pepper			
Slices of buttered toast	2	2	2

1. Beat together the ingredients, except the toast, in a 1.1 1/2 pt/5 cup microwave-proof measuring jug.
2. Heat in the oven for 1½ minutes (any oven).
3. Stir with a fork to break up the egg.
4. Return to the oven for 1/1/½ minute.
5. Stir, and spoon onto buttered toast to serve.

Salmon Cutlets

Serves 2

Power level Full power (500-w/600-w/650-w ovens)

Not suitable for freezing

	Metric	Imperial	American
Butter or margarine	50 g	2 oz	¼ cup
Celery, finely diced	50 g	2 oz	2 oz
Dried dill	2.5 ml	½ tsp	½ tsp
Salt	5 ml	1 tsp	1 tsp
Pepper			
Dry white wine and water mixed	150 ml	¼ pt	⅔ cup
Salmon cutlets, about 225 g/8 oz each	2	2	2

1. Put the butter, celery, dill, seasonings, wine and water into a dish and cook for 1 minute.
2. Wash and dry the cutlets and add to the mixture.
3. Cover with clingfilm and cook for about 7/6/5½ minutes.
4. Stand for 5 minutes before serving.

Tomato-Cheese Soup

Serves 4

Power level Full power (500-w/600-w/650-w ovens)

Freeze 2 months

	Metric	Imperial	American
Unsalted (sweet) butter	*15 g*	*½ oz*	*1 tbls*
Bacon rashers (slices), chopped	*2*	*2*	*2*
Small onion, chopped	*1*	*1*	*1*
Tomatoes, sliced	*450 g*	*1 lb*	*1 lb*
Caster (superfine) sugar	*5 ml*	*1 tsp*	*1 tsp*
Salt	*2.5 ml*	*½ tsp*	*½ tsp*
Pinch of paprika			
Pinch of grated nutmeg			
Celery tops with leaves	*3–4*	*3–4*	*3–4*
Instant potato granules	*15 ml*	*1 tbls*	*1 tbls*
Water	*150 ml*	*¼ pt*	*⅔ cup*
Milk	*150 ml*	*¼ pt*	*⅔ cup*
Grated cheese	*30 ml*	*2 tbls*	*2 tbls*

1. In a 2.3 l/4 pt/10 cup casserole, melt the fat for 1 minute (any oven).
2. Add the bacon and onion, coat with fat and cook for 5/4½/4 minutes.
3. Add the tomatoes, sugar, salt, paprika, nutmeg, celery tops and instant potato granules. Mix well. Add the water, cover and return to the oven. Cook for 15/11/10 minutes.
4. Remove the celery. Purée the soup in a blender or food processor. Add the milk and cheese and pour back into the casserole. Cover and cook for 6/4/4 minutes. Stand for 5 minutes, then serve hot.

Crown Roast of Lamb

Serves 4

Power level Full power (500-w/600-w/650-w ovens)

Freeze 2 months

	Metric	Imperial	American
Crown roast of lamb, prepared by your butcher	*1.1 kg*	*2¼ lb*	*2¼ lb*
Red or yellow pepper for garnish	*½*	*½*	*½*
Stuffing			
Butter	*25 g*	*1 oz*	*2 tbls*
Lamb's kidney, skinned, cored and chopped	*½*	*½*	*½*
Chopped mushrooms	*50 g*	*2 oz*	*½ cup*
Dried mixed herbs	*5 ml*	*1 tsp*	*1 tsp*
Fresh white breadcrumbs	*100 g*	*4 oz*	*2 cups*
Grated lemon rind	*5 mlk*	*1 tsp*	*1 tsp*
Egg, beaten	*1*	*1*	

1. For the stuffing, place the butter in a bowl and place in the oven for 1 minute to melt. Add the kidney and mushrooms and cook for a further 2 minutes.
2. Add the remaining stuffing ingredients and mix well.
3. Place the meat in a suitable container and spoon the stuffing into the central cavity.
4. Cook, uncovered, for 28/26/25 minutes.
5. Remove from the oven and garnish with pieces of pepper. Wrap tightly in foil, shiny side in and allow to stand for 25 minutes before serving.

Brandied Baked Apples

Serves 4

Power level Full power (500-w/600-w/650-w ovens)

Freeze 1 month (without topping)

	Metric	Imperial	American
Cooking (tart) apples, cored	*4*	*4*	*4*
Demerara (light brown) sugar	*60 ml*	*4 tbls*	*4 tbls*
Ground cinnamon	*5 ml*	*1 tsp*	*1 tsp*
Butter	*25 g*	*1 oz*	*2 tbls*
Brandy	*90 ml*	*6 tbls*	*6 tbls*
Water	*30 ml*	*2 tbls*	*2 tbls*
Brandy Butter (page 188) or whipped cream			

1. Prick the apples well all over with a knife-point. Put them in a shallow baking dish.
2. Mix together the sugar and cinnamon and spoon into the apples. Top each with a quarter of the butter. Put 30 ml/2 tbls brandy and 30 ml/2 tbls water into the dish. Cover with pierced clingfilm.
3. Cook in the oven for 7–9/6–6½/6–6½ minutes.
4. Remove the apples to serving plates. Spoon some of the syrup over each. Top with Brandy Butter or cream.
5. Warm the remaining brandy and pour a little over each apple. Ignite and serve flaming.

INDEX